Southeast Asia in the Age of Commerce
1450–1680

Southeast Asia in the Age of Commerce 1450–1680

Volume Two
Expansion and Crisis

Anthony Reid

Yale University Press
New Haven and London

Published with assistance from the Louis Stern Memorial Fund.

Designed by James J. Johnson.
Set in Trump Mediaeval Roman types by Keystone Typesetting, Inc., Orwigsburg,
Pennsylvania.
Printed in the United States of America by Edwards Brothers, Inc., Ann Arbor,
Michigan.

Library of Congress Cataloging-in-Publication Data

Reid, Anthony, 1939–
Southeast Asia in the age of commerce, 1450–1680 / Anthony Reid.
2 v. : ill. : 24 cm.
Bibliography: v. 1, p. 237–266.
Includes index.
Contents: v. 1. The lands below the winds — v. 2. Expansion and crisis.
ISBN 0-300-04750-9 (v. 1: pbk.)
    0-300-05412-2 (v. 11: cloth)
    978-0-300-06516-9 (v. 11: pbk.)
1. Asia, Southeastern—History. I. Title.
DS526.4.R46 1988   87-20749
959—dc 19

A catalogue record for this book is available from the British Library.

10 9 8 7 6 5

for
Helen

Contents

Illustrations

FIGURES

Preface

The rationale for this study was published five years ago with its first volume. Here I need only apologize that the second half should be so delayed.

This volume can be read on its own as an explanation of what the age of commerce as a period meant for Southeast Asia. Together with the first volume, *The Lands below the Winds* (1988), however, it aims to present a "total history" in which wars, royal dynasties, and foreign traders have no more priority than the diet, health, and amusements of ordinary people.

Volume 1 described the structures of material and social life in the region; volume 2 delineates the period of momentous change that transformed it. But the continuities and the changes cannot be separated neatly. The structures of life changed constantly, but slowly and in the short term often imperceptibly. On the other hand, the characteristic ways in which Southeast Asians related to one another and to their environment survived and modified even the dramatic events that destroyed cities and displaced peoples.

The reader will quickly find that the "age of commerce" is defined differently in different places in this book. In chapter 1, I discuss the economic data, which point to a beginning around 1400 and a peak in 1570–1630. The crises that ended the period are considered in chapter 5, with the conclusion that 1629 could be taken as a symbolic turning point, though the characteristic features of the period remained pronounced until mid-century, and the 1680s can be considered its death throes.

In spite of all this, the dates 1450–1680 appear on the cover of this book and reflect its content. Even if 1400 were the most acceptable point to locate the beginning of a sustained period of commercial expansion, the data for the fifteenth century are simply inadequate for the type of history I have sought to write. If nothing else, I hope that these inconsistencies will underline the obvious—that periods are modes of dealing with specific questions and must change with the questions.

Like other large regions of the world, Southeast Asia is immensely varied. Though this book charts a rhythm in the history of the whole area, not all peoples and places experienced it to the same degree. Maritime commerce, silver coinage, new weaponry, urban ways of life, and the associated changes in values and political systems naturally touched the cities more than the countryside, islands and riverine estuaries more than mountain fastnesses, major arteries of trade more than rice-growing plains. Histories focused on a single kingdom or culture tend to discern different rhythms, particularly on the frontiers of the region—northern Vietnam and Burma. The unevenness of coverage becomes overt in chapter 3: the changes wrought through Islam and Christianity had no exact parallel in Buddhism. Nevertheless, there was a coherence to the region as a whole, more clearly evident the larger the unit considered. The rhythm of international commerce affected the inhabitants of Southeast Asia unequally, but none known to history were untouched by it. The evidence from this period gives no support to the picture of autarchic, unchanging, subsistence communities once popular in the literature.

In order to enable Southeast Asia to take its place in the comparative study of the early modern world, I believed it important to attempt to convert the measures used in specific places and periods into a system that can be generally understood. I have therefore sought to give weights and measures a metric equivalent, and currencies a value in terms of weight of silver (see the Glossary for the values used in these conversions). To avoid any illusion of precision, however, I have rounded the resulting calculation out to an approximate figure. Original estimates in the sources are in most cases already approximations, while the precise values of all measures in relation to each other and currencies in relation to silver varied considerably through both place and time. These estimates naturally give only a rough indication of orders of magnitude, and of long-term rises and falls.

In general I have used place names current at the time, though in modern spelling. Siam and Cochin-China were the terms used by foreigners for two kingdoms on the Mainland, and are more appropriate than reading backward a modern national term such as Thailand or (Central) Vietnam. For the peoples of Southeast Asia, in contrast, I have used modern terms, including Indonesian, Filipino, Thai, and (for the broader linguistic group) Tai. To indicate one of the major geographical and cultural cleavages within Southeast Asia I have used the capitalized terms Mainland (for the area now occupied by Burma, Thailand, Laos, Cambodia, and Vietnam) and Archipelago (for what is today Malaysia, as well as Indonesia and the Philippines).

In referring to sources, I continue to cite in the text only the original author and the date of first publication or, where more appropriate, the date of writing. All other bibliographic information, including the location of manuscript sources in English and Dutch archives, are found in the References. I acknowledge again here the great debt I bear to all those who have edited, transcribed, and translated the sources I have used. The magnitude of this debt can be appreciated only by perusing that list of references.

My personal and institutional debts have grown still longer since the first volume. The Australian National University continues to support my research generously—indeed, there are few other places in the world such a book could have been written. Nevertheless, it would have been produced still more slowly without the precious months free of other obligations provided by the following institutions: Ecole des Hautes Etudes en Sciences Sociales, Paris, 1987; All Souls College, Oxford, 1987; Washington University and the Rockefeller Foundation, 1989; the School of Oriental and African Studies, London, 1990; and, again, the Rockefeller Foundation, at the Villa Serbelloni, 1991.

For help with materials, with ideas, and with critical comment, I wish to express my gratitude to Peter Boomgaard, John Bowen, Jennifer Brewster, Harold Brookfield, Henri Chambert-Loir, Chen Xi-yu, Bruce Cruikshank, Dhiravat na Pombejra, Tony Diller, Dan Doeppers, Laura Dooley (of Yale University Press), Humphrey Fisher, Cornell Fleischer, Mary Grow, Ito Takeshi, Ishii Yoneo, Charles Keyes, Ann Kumar, Ruurdje Laarhoven, Li Tana, Denys Lombard, Pierre-Yves Manguin, David Marr, Mo Yi-mei, Maung Maung Nyo, Richard O'Connor, Norman Owen, Peuipanh Ngaosyvathn, Craig Reynolds, M. C. Ricklefs, Michael Summerfield, and Christopher Wake. Patricia Herbert, Annabel Gallop, and Henry Ginsburg at the British Library, and Doris Nicholson at the Bodleian, were most helpful in providing manuscript material. Closer to home, Ian Heyward and Nigel Duffy drew the maps, and David Bulbeck, Julie Gordon, Dorothy McIntosh, Kris Rodgers, Jude Shanahan, Tan Lay-cheng, and Evelyn Winburn provided invaluable assistance in a variety of ways.

I

The Age of Commerce, 1400–1650

Commerce has always been vital to Southeast Asia. Uniquely accessible to seaborne traffic and commanding the maritime routes between China (the largest international market through most recorded history) and the population centres of India, the Middle East, and Europe, the lands below the winds naturally responded to every quickening of international maritime trade. Their products of clove, nutmeg, sandalwood, sappanwood, camphor, and lacquer found their way to world markets even in Roman and Han times. Why, then, single out the fifteenth to seventeenth centuries as peculiarly dominated by commerce?

First, the sustained boom of the "long sixteenth century," which affected not only Europe and the eastern Mediterranean but also China, Japan, and perhaps India, was one in which Southeast Asia played a particularly critical role. The most important items (excluding gold and silver) of that long-distance trade which Fernand Braudel (1979 II: 408) insists was essential to the creation of merchant capitalism—pepper, cloves, and nutmeg—originated in Southeast Asia. Second, during this period Southeast Asian merchants, rulers, cities, and states had a central part in the trade that flowed from and through their region. The hubs of commerce in the lands below the winds were such Asian cities as Pegu, Ayutthaya, Pnompenh, Hoi An (Faifo), Melaka, Patani, Brunei, Pasai, Aceh, Banten, Japara, Gresik, and Makassar. Until these cities gradually lost their crucial role in the long-

distance trade to such European beachheads as Portuguese Melaka
(from 1511), Spanish Manila (1571), and especially Dutch Batavia
(1619), they were the leading regional centres of economic life, political power, and cultural creativity.

The evolution of modern Southeast Asian society is explained
here through the experiences of this critical period. In this chapter, I
put the case for an age of commerce in its economic dimension, the
only one that can be measured and compared with other parts of the
world. Subsequent chapters detail the transformations in urbanism,
commercial organization, religious systems and values, and state
structures against the background of rapid economic change. In Braudel's terms, if volume 1 dealt with the deep-seated structures of history, this volume moves from the underlying conjunctures towards the
political and military events that create the surface excitement. The
final chapter explores the crisis which overcame Southeast Asia in the
mid-seventeenth century and examines some of its longer-term effects.

Spices and Pepper

> The Malay merchants say that God made Timor for sandalwood and
> Banda for mace and Maluku for cloves, and that this merchandise is
> not known anywhere in the world except in these places.
> —Pires 1515: 204

In the total picture of Southeast Asian trade, the spices that lured
merchants from the other side of the world were very minor items.
Bulk foods, such as rice, salt, and pickled or dried fish, and palm wine,
textiles, and metalware all filled more space in the ships that criss-
crossed the calm waters of the Sunda shelf. The spices were important
because the biggest profits were made on them and because the traders
who came in search of them introduced many other trade items to
ports and production areas. Hence they played a disproportionate role
in the growth of commercial centres. As an index of trade cycles the
spices have other advantages. Not only is information relatively abundant on the quantities and prices of spices because they aroused such
interest in Europe, but clove, nutmeg, and mace were available only in
eastern Indonesia, so that the quantities reaching Europe had all
passed along the whole length of the trading route from Maluku to the
Mediterranean; finally, spices, unlike many Southeast Asian forest
products, could be cultivated for export on a large scale in response to
changing demand.

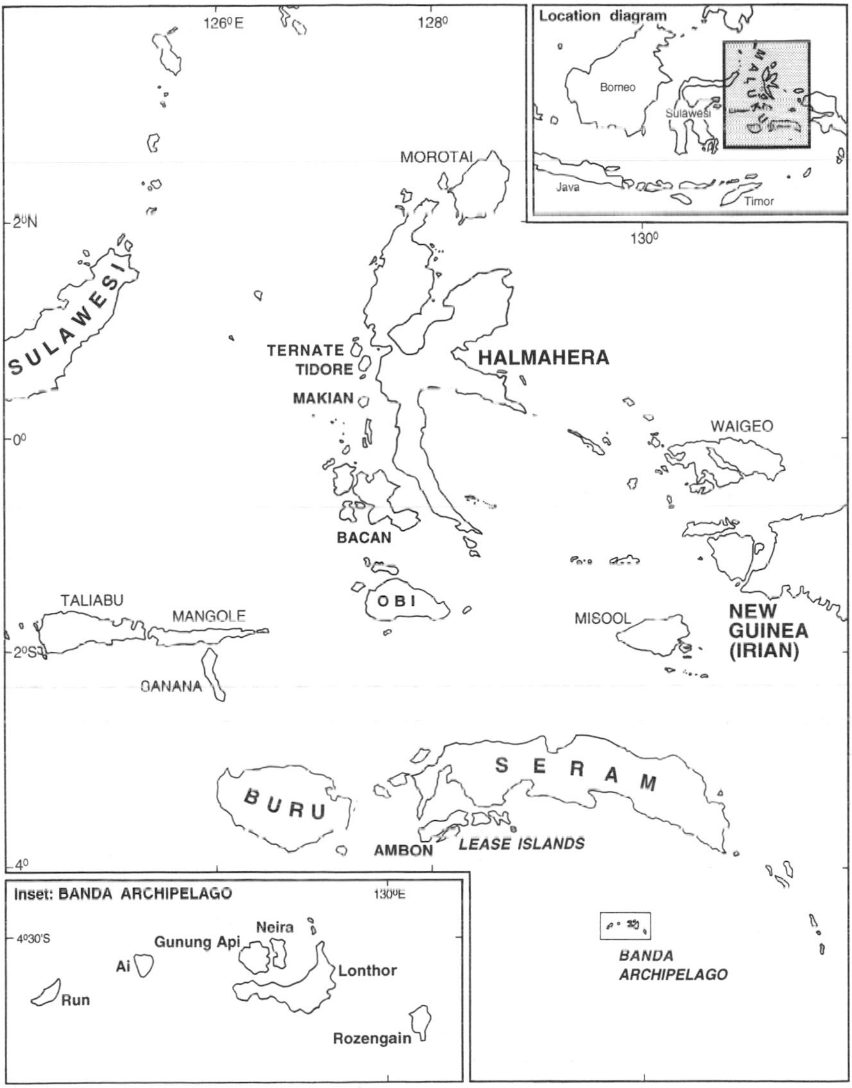

Map with labels:

126°E · 128°

Location diagram
Borneo
Sulawesi
Java · Timor
130°

MOROTAI

2°N

SULAWESI

TERNATE
TIDORE
MAKIAN

HALMAHERA

WAIGEO

0°

BACAN

TALIABU
MANGOLE
OBI
MISOOL
NEW
GUINEA
(IRIAN)

2°S

OANANA

SERAM

BURU

AMBON LEASE ISLANDS

4°

Inset: BANDA ARCHIPELAGO   130°E

4°30'S
Neira
Gunung Api
Ai
Lonthor
Run
Rozengain

BANDA
ARCHIPELAGO

Map 1 Maluku

The clove "nail" as traded is the dried flowerbud of the tropical evergreen *Szygium aromaticum* or *Caryophullus aromaticus*. These trees, one of which can produce up to 34 kg of cloves in a good harvest, grew only in Maluku (the Moluccas) until the monopoly was broken in 1770. At the time of the earliest direct reports, soon after 1500, cloves were cultivated only on the small islands of Ternate, Tidore, Makian, and Motir off the west coast of Halmahera and had just begun to be worked on the somewhat larger island of Bacan (Pires 1515: 214–19; Pigafetta 1524: 79). During the sixteenth century the industry spread further south to Ambon and Seram, and in the seventeenth these southern islands became the major centres of production (map 1).

Nutmeg is the seed, and mace the outer covering of the seed, of the tree *Myristica fragrans,* which until the eighteenth century grew only in the cluster of tiny islands collectively known as Banda, to the south of Seram (see figs. 1a, 1b).

Cloves and occasionally nutmeg and mace were mentioned in commercial records of Cairo and Alexandria as early as the tenth century (Goitein 1967: 253, 357; Ashtor 1969: 139–40; Goitein 1973: 224–26, 257), but they remained extremely rare and expensive in Europe until the late fourteenth century. The Chinese also knew of clove and nutmeg as early as the Tang dynasty but used them sparingly before the fifteenth century.

From the Chinese geographer Wang Ta-yuan (1349, cited Rockhill 1915: 259–60) we know that Chinese vessels regularly visited Maluku in the 1340s for small amounts of clove: "This tree covers the hills, though no very large number produce at the same time." By contrast, the more extensive Chinese reportage at the time of the the massive fleets sent out under the admiral Zheng He (Cheng Ho) in the early fifteenth century is silent about Maluku, indicating that the Chinese visits had been a relatively short-lived fourteenth-century phenomenon. This is precisely what the people of Ternate and Tidore told the Portuguese: their ancestors had first learned the value of the cloves from Chinese whose vessels, coming from the north, had been the first to frequent the islands. Eventually Javanese and Malays followed suit, travelling from the south, and the Chinese stopped coming (Galvão 1544: 79–81; Barros 1563 III, i: 577–79). Although the Ternatan language has its own word for cloves, Malay (and Javanese, Makassarese, and Tagalog) uses a Chinese term for nail, *cengkeh.*[1] Malay-speakers were using this word by 1500 (Pigafetta 1524: 72, 83; Edwards and Blagden 1931: 725), a detail that helps to confirm a shift, sometime around 1400, from direct Chinese buying of cloves in Maluku to a Chinese demand mediated through Malay and Javanese traders. Given the large contribution to Indonesian commerce of Chinese migrants and defectors from the Zheng He expeditions, it would not be surprising if these Malays and Javanese were themselves partly descended from Chinese (Reid 1992: 181–98).

Malukan spice exports to China and Europe leapt suddenly

---

1. *Zhi jia* in Mandarin, but *zhen ga* in the Minnan dialect of Canton and Xiamen.

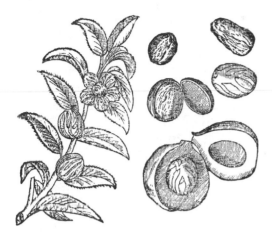

Fig. 1a The nutmeg plant

Fig. 1b Bandanese bringing nutmeg for sale to Dutch factors, 1599, as represented by engravers in Holland

around 1400 and grew slowly through the fifteenth century—though this probably disguises a mid-century slump and a boom in the last decades (see below). This pattern should be set against what evidence we have from Maluku. Although Tomé Pires (1515: 219) did not visit the islands, he was informed that up to about the year 1500, clove trees had been wild and disregarded in the interior of Bacan Island but had rapidly become cultivated and developed there "in the same way that wild plums become cultivated plums and wild olives become culti- vated olives." His figures for the "normal" annual production of the different islands appear impossibly high.[2] Like other production esti- mates, Pires' were probably exaggerated by the natural pattern of a bumper harvest every four years (Galvão 1544: 137; van den Broecke 1634 I: 68; Knaap 1987: 229), the irregularities produced by warfare on the spice routes, and the tendency of rival rulers to exaggerate the share of the crop they could deliver. Yet trade estimates by Portuguese in Melaka (Araujo 1510: 29–30) also suggest that clove exports rose to an exceptionally high level just before Portuguese disruption, which in eastern Indonesian did not occur until 1512. By then Maluku was probably capable of supplying all the world's needs for clove and nut- meg, so that it was warfare and rapacity along the trade routes that caused the major variations.

Antonio Pigafetta (1524: 79) did visit one of the oldest clove- producing islands, Tidore, where he learned that until Muslims began coming to Ternate and Tidore, which he estimated to be about 1470, the Moluccans "did not care for the cloves." In reality we know that Javanese, including some Muslims, must have been sailing to Maluku for cloves since at least the mid-fourteenth century, when Maluku and Ambon were claimed as dependencies of Majapahit (Nagara-kerta- gama 1365: 17; Pires 1515: 174) and names of some quasi-Islamic kings are recorded in the Ternate chronicles (de Clercq 1890: 148–49). Pigafetta was probably right, however, to the extent that continuous Javanese-Islamic influence, to which the Ternatans attributed their coinage, writing, religion, music, laws, "and all the other good things they have" (Galvão 1544: 105), appears to have begun only in the second half of the fifteenth century (ibid.: 83–85; Pires 1515: 213; de Clercq 1890: 148–49). Although we are less well informed about Banda, this archipelago appears to have been systematically visited by Muslim Javanese traders even more recently than the clove islands.

---

2. These add up to 1000 tonnes each of clove and nutmeg and 180 tonnes of mace (Pires 1515: 206, 213, 217). Such figures may have been obtained by adding together the maximum harvests of each island, which in fact were very irregular. Pires' estimate of 6000 bahar of clove production appears nevertheless to have become conventional, repeated by Rebello in 1570 and by Reyer Cornelisz (on Portuguese evidence) in 1599. Some more realistic estimates were those of Pigafetta (1521) and Coen (1614), amount- ing to 460 tonnes a year, while VOC estimates for the Ambon area, where production had shifted, were in the range of 200–300 tonnes in the period 1620–50 (Meilink- Roelofsz 1969: 352–53; Knaap 1987: 13, 20, 233–34).

Ludovico de Varthema (1510: 244), who claimed to have visited the islands in 1505 but was probably relying on old, second-hand information, described the Bandanese as primitive pagans "like beasts," who simply collected nutmegs when required from wild trees in the forests. Pires (1515: 206–07) and Barbosa (1518 II: 197) reported that the few thousand people of Banda were a mix of Muslims along the coast and animists inland. Pires added that conversion to Islam had begun only in the 1480s and that the cloth brought by the Javanese and Malay traders was still "a great novelty to them," so that they regarded the traders with supernatural reverence. Despite the evidence of the European figures (fig. 3, below) that the initial take-off in spice exports occurred in the 1390s, this local information implies a vigorous growth from about 1470, coincident with the flowering of the port of Melaka and no doubt serving the Asian market far more than the European.

Though only a fraction of the price of the Malukan spices, pepper is crucial to the economic picture because it was exported in ten times the quantity. In the sixteenth and seventeenth centuries it ranked as the most important export of Southeast Asia. It was, moreover, a cash crop grown explicitly for the market, which cultivators had to decide to plant and tend carefully for three years before the first harvest, diverting time and capital from other crops. The involvement of hundreds of thousands of Southeast Asians in cultivating and marketing pepper in response to world demand was one of the most overt economic consequences of the trade boom.

Pepper was, however, produced elsewhere. Round or black pepper (*Piper nigrum*), the great article of trade, was native to Kerala, the Malabar coast of southwest India, which was still known as the "pepper country" to medieval European and Arab travellers (fig. 2). In the twelfth century, Chinese sources begin to refer to pepper as a product of Java, though a note added to the travel account of Chau Ju-kua (1250: 223) warns, "Some say that most of the pepper comes from the country of Malabar . . . and that the produce bought by the foreign traders in Java comes from Malabar" (cf. Wheatley 1959: 100–01). Pepper was not mentioned among the products of Sri Vijaya, nor as growing in Sumatra at the time of the visits of Marco Polo (1292) or Ibn Battuta (1355). Since it was reported in northern Sumatra by Chinese observers of the early 1400s (Ma Huan 1433: 118; Rockhill 1915: 155–56), it was probably introduced there from India or Java shortly before. Pepper flourished so well in Sumatra that the earliest Portuguese accounts estimated that Pasai alone already produced half as much (1400–1800 tonnes) as did Malabar. Pires thought that the neighbour-

Fig. 2 The pepper plant, as represented by Marsden, 1783

ing Sumatran port of Pidië had once produced even more than this, though in his day it yielded only about 500 tonnes (Pires 1515: 82, 140, 144). Pires' figures for Southeast Asian pepper production totalled nearly 2500 tonnes, against 3600 for Malabar. Up to about 1530 most of this pepper either remained below the winds or was taken north to supply the vast Chinese market.

During the sixteenth century, pepper production spread both in India and through Indonesia in response to growing demand. From Malabar the pepper vines spread northward into Kannara; from northern Sumatra they spread down the west coast of that island, into its Minangkabau heartland, and across to the Malayan Peninsula (map 2).

Map 2 The extension of pepper growing

Whereas around 1500 India supplied virtually all of Europe and the Middle East, sixty years later the Portuguese were buying much of their pepper below the winds, while the revived Red Sea route drew its supplies largely from Sumatra. In the seventeenth century the intense competition among Dutch, English, Chinese, and Portuguese buyers was centred in Southeast Asia. Production in India was 50 percent more expensive and lost its geographical advantage for the European market with the pioneering of the route around the Cape of Good Hope. India itself imported pepper from Indonesia in the second half of the seventeenth century (Glamann 1958: 81, 85; Arasaratnam 1986: 107). Even though the English East India Company was less strongly placed than the Dutch in the Indonesian area, it drew four-fifths of its pepper from the islands in the 1660s and 1670s (Glamann 1958: 84; Chaudhuri 1978: 527–29). One must conclude that virtually the whole of the increase in the international market was filled by Southeast Asian production, which must therefore have increased two- to threefold in the century after 1520.

Estimates in the seventeenth century are more numerous and more soundly based than those of Pires. Around 1600, Sumatra, the Malayan Peninsula and west Java together produced more than 4500 tonnes, of which Banten alone was responsible for 2000 in an average year. The growth areas in the years 1610–70 were in Sumatra, some centres on the Malayan Peninsula (Kedah, Patani, Songkhla, Pahang), and Banjarmasin in southern Borneo. Total production would have had to be more than 6000 tonnes by 1630 and more than 8000 tonnes by the peak in 1670, without allowing for small centres of little interest to Europeans (Reid 1990: 17–19). By the 1650s the Dutch and English were buying very little Indian pepper, so abundant had the cheaper Indonesian product become (Glamann 1958: 81, 84).

A Trade Take-off around 1400

> We have learned that to master the blue oceans people must engage in commerce and trade, even if their countries are barren. . . . All the lands within the seas are united in one body, and all living things are being nurtured in love; life has never been so affluent in preceding generations as it is today.
> —Sultan Mansur of Melaka to King of Ryukyu, 1 September 1468; in Kobata and Matsuda 1969: 111

There had been booms in demand for Southeast Asian produce before, particularly as a result of times of prosperity or tolerance of trade in China. Tang Dynasty trade must have done much to stimulate the rise of Sri Vijaya in the eighth and ninth centuries; the trading activity of the Sung, complementing the effect of the Crusades on increasing the European demand for eastern luxuries, similarly encouraged the prosperity of Majapahit in the thirteenth century. There was, however, a distinct lull in the seaborne trade for almost a century before 1370, as Christian-Muslim hostility in the Levant and the "Mongol peace" in Central Asia redirected trade away from the sea lanes and towards such arduous overland caravans as the "silk route" from China to the Black Sea (map 3). The great plague of 1346–48 and

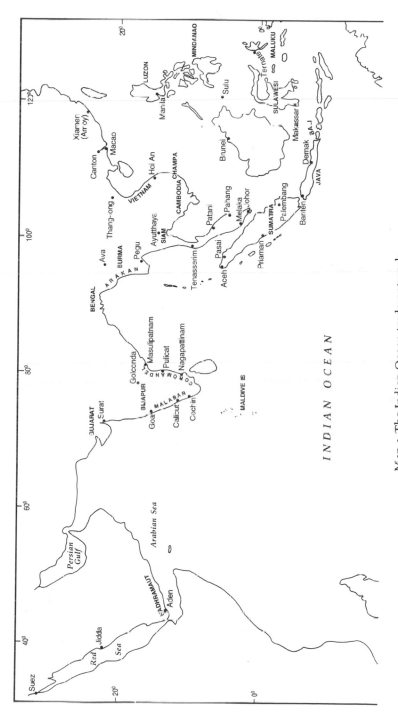

Map 3 The Indian Ocean trade network

the resulting population decline reduced the demand for exotic goods in the northern hemisphere. The relative decline in trade is reflected in the paucity of Chinese porcelain remains for this period in Southeast Asia, especially by contrast with the great abundance after 1400.

Before the seventeenth century China was undoubtedly the most important market for Southeast Asian goods. Marco Polo (1298: 209) had claimed that for every Italian galley in Alexandria a hundred spice-laden ships docked at the Chinese port of "Zaiton" (Quanzhou). Although India was almost equally important as a trading partner for Southeast Asia, it appears that the dramatic changes in Chinese imperial policy with regard to the Nanyang trade were responsible for the most striking discontinuities in Southeast Asia's external trade.

Ming China began two centuries of expansion in wealth and population at the end of the fourteenth century. The effect of this on the Southeast Asia trade was not automatic because of repeated prohibitions, not uniformly effective, on overseas trade by Ming rulers. There seems no doubt, however, that an enormous boost in the demand for Southeast Asian products was given by the six state trading expeditions of the Ming emperor Yongle (1402–24) and the contemporary Chinese expansion into Vietnam and Burma. If one moment must be singled out for the beginning of Southeast Asia's "age of commerce," the first state trading mission under the eunuch admiral Zheng He, in 1405, is the best candidate.

The expeditions undoubtedly stimulated Southeast Asian production of crops for the China market. T'ien Ju-kang (1981) has shown that the leading products of the Nanyang (South China Sea) trade— pepper and sappanwood—were shipped to China in such quantities that for the first time they became items of mass consumption there in the fifteenth century and so abounded in government warehouses that they were used as part-payment to hundreds of thousands of Chinese officials and soldiers. These missions were probably responsible for the introduction of Indian pepper plants to northern Sumatra, as well as the rapid growth in Southeast Asian pepper production for the China market that followed. They may have had an influence on the rise in Malukan spice exports around 1400. Such trading cities as Ayutthaya, Melaka, Pasai, Brunei, Gresik, and Demak all owed their early prosperity in part to being used as bases for Chinese activity in the early fifteenth century. Abrupt changes in Ming policy left a number of crucial communities of Chinese (often Muslim) traders in the burgeoning entrepôts of the region.

The short-lived Chinese military adventure in Vietnam (1406–

27), and the more enduring expansion into the northern Shan states, greatly expanded the production of silver, gold, and minerals from the mines in these areas. It has been calculated that Chinese production of silver expanded as a result of these conquests to a peak of 36 tonnes a year in the early fifteenth century, which contrasts with barely 4 tonnes a century later (Deyell 1983: 222–24; Moloughney and Xia 1989: 56–57). Though it was not visited by the Chinese fleets, Burma also felt the quickening of maritime trade. The new port of Ye (south of Martaban) opened in 1438, and the reign of Shinsawbu in Pegu (1453–72) inaugurated a period when merchants from afar "arrived in great numbers, unusual wearing apparel became abundant, and the people had fine clothes and prospered exceedingly," as a Mon chronicle put it (Lieberman 1984: 22).

The Chinese pattern of increasing population, prices, and demand for exotic goods was curiously replicated in a Europe recovering from the horrors of the Black Death. In 1345 Venice had concluded a commercial treaty with the Mamluke rulers of Egypt, though for some time the annual galley fleets to Alexandria were inhibited by continued papal opposition to trading with the Saracen enemy. In the late fourteenth century the Mamlukes consolidated their control of the caravan routes to Beirut and Damascus as well as Alexandria. This progress towards peaceful conditions for the caravans taking Asian goods to the Mediterranean from the Red Sea and Persian Gulf ports coincided with a collapse of the Central Asian overland routes. The last two decades of the fourteenth century, therefore, witnessed a boom in Venice and the beginning of the heyday of the *karimi*, the spice merchants of Cairo, who amassed enormous fortunes handling the exotic produce of India and Southeast Asia (Lapidus 1967: 23–24, 121–26; Ashtor 1976: 325–28).

Although it was a minor part of the market for Southeast Asian produce at this time, Europe provides the best figures. Systematic data on the quantities of Malukan spice imported to Europe begin as early as the period 1390–1404, when Italian commercial agents reported the cargoes of eastern produce being shipped annually from the Mamluke ports of Alexandria and Beirut to Venice, Genoa, and Barcelona. Although the records are too patchy to be useful for most of the fifteenth century, a relatively consistent series can be assembled from 1496, which covers the effect of Portugal's entry into the trade.

What emerges when these data are averaged and weighted for missing reports is a rapid rise in the the 1390s to a level of about 30 tonnes of cloves and 10 tonnes of nutmeg over the years 1399–1405,

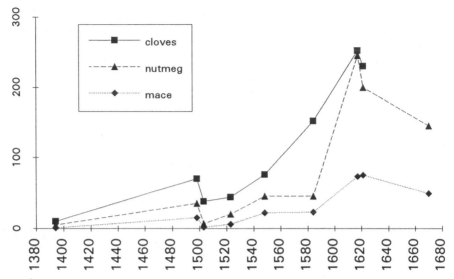

Fig. 3 Estimated spice exports to Europe

and a slow increase (no doubt with drastic fluctuations we can no longer trace) in the fifteenth century until at its end the levels were about 75 tonnes of cloves, 37 of nutmeg, and 17 of mace (Ashtor 1979; Wake 1979; Reid 1990; see fig. 3).

This flourishing trade was drastically disrupted from 1499 by the entry of Portuguese ships into the Indian Ocean, where the Portuguese sank or plundered every Muslim spice ship they could. No Malukan spices at all reached the Italian ports through the Middle East in most years between 1502 and 1520. To be fair, there were other short-term disruptions, including Venice's conflicts with the Ottomans in 1499 and with Egypt in 1505–08, and the instability of the Mamluke regime before the Ottoman conquest of Egypt in 1517 (Lane 1933: 13–14; Magalhães-Godinho 1969: 701–02, 713–28). It was primarily the losses suffered at Portuguese hands by the established Muslim shippers and ports in the Indian Ocean, however, which kept shipments of Southeast Asian goods to Europe (and presumably India) very low for the first three decades of the sixteenth century. The Portuguese themselves brought to Europe less than a quarter of the amounts the Muslim fleets had done until they captured the great Southeast Asian emporium of Melaka in 1511. From 1513 to the 1530s the Portuguese fared better, dominating the European market by bringing in more than 30 tonnes of cloves and 10 of nutmeg in an average year, while the Middle Eastern route still brought minor and uneven amounts. European pepper imports followed a similar pattern of expansion followed by disruption around 1500, but only after 1530 did Southeast Asia contribute much to them (Magalhães-Godinho 1969: 701–18; Wake 1979; Reid 1990: 26–27).

The Southeast Asian age of commerce, therefore, must be sharply distinguished from the "Vasco da Gama epoch" that Panikkar (1953) proposed from 1498. On the contrary, the growth in demand for Southeast Asian produce appears to have begun relatively suddenly around 1400, whether we look at data from the Mediterranean or the Chinese markets, while the great disruption of 1500–1530 is very clear.

The pattern of trade between these points is harder to judge. It appears that, despite Chinese bans on private trade, shipping across the South China Sea continued to grow in the fifteenth century. This was possible first because Ming official enforcement of the ban was weak between 1457 and the 1520s, so that merchant junks sailed annually in this period from South Fujian to the Nanyang (Wills 1974: 7; Mills 1979: 70). Second, the system of official tribute voyages was at its peak in the fifteenth century, called forth by the expansive initiatives of the first three Ming emperors.

After the Ming capital moved in 1421 from Nanjing to Beijing to combat the Mongol threat from the north more effectively, China's southern policy was purely passive. Southeast Asians, including many traders of Chinese descent now based there, kept the system going for primarily commercial purposes. Java was at first the most ardent state in stretching tribute to its limits for commercial purposes, and the Chinese court wrote explicitly in 1443 and 1453 to require the Javanese king to send tribute less often (*Ming Shi Lu*: 366, 387). Siam and Melaka, however, were more persistent in continuing with tribute missions in the second half of the century, despite mounting Chinese apathy or irritation, and this helped them to replace Java as the primary entrepôts for Southeast Asian trade with China (table 1). Melaka missions continued to be exceptional by their high level, with Sultan Muzaffar's children being sent in 1456 and twelve senior officials traveling to China in 1463 (Wade 1991: 79). After the Portuguese conquest of Melaka in 1511, only Siam and Champa continued to send tribute missions by sea, and then no more than once every reign period (*Ming Shi Lu*, also Fairbank and Teng 1941: 123–29; Wang 1970: 74; Suebsang 1971: 106–20; Reid 1992: 191–94).

A third means of circumventing the Chinese ban was developed by the island kingdom of Ryukyu, following its unification by King Sho Hashi in 1429. This enterprising ruler took advantage of the suspension of state trading in 1433 and the Ming ban on private trade to encourage merchants of Fujian to settle near his capital at Okinawa

Table 1. Frequency of tribute missions to China

from:	Java	Pasai	Siam	Champa	Cambodia	Pahang	Melaka	Brunei	Philippines
1400–09	8	3	11	5	4		3[a]	3[a]	2[a]
1410–19	6	7	6	9	3	3	8[a]	4[a]	2[a]
1420–29	16	5	10	9			5[a]	2	5[a]
1430–39	5	3	4	10			3		
1440–49	7		3	9			2		
1450–59	3		2	3			3		
1460–69	3	1	1	4			2		
1470–79			4	3			1		
1480–89		3	3	3					
1490–99	2		3	3					
1500–10			1	2			2		

Note: [a]Ruler led one mission in the decade
Sources: Ming Shi Lu; also Wang 1970: 74 and Wade 1991

and to conduct trade under his auspices. He and his successors maintained access to China and Japan by regularly sending deferential but highly lucrative tribute missions to both courts. Ryukyu therefore became a crucial link between Southeast and Northeast Asia when direct trade was most inhibited. The records of this trade preserved in the Ryukyuan Rekidai hoan show that in the thirteen years 1430–42 at least seventeen Ryukyu trade missions were sent to Ayutthaya, eight to Palembang, and six to Java. Intensive trade activity is also attested by surviving documents from 1463–81, when Melaka, Ayutthaya, and Pasai (north Sumatra) were the principal trading partners, and 1508–54, when Ayutthaya, Patani, west Java, and Melaka (until its conquest by the Portuguese in 1511) were the ports most frequented. The pattern was one of decline in the sixteenth century, however, and Ryukyu ceased to be a factor in Southeast Asian trade by the 1550s (Sakamaki 1964; Sakai 1968; Kobata and Matsuda 1969).

The Boom Years, 1570–1630

In the most rapid period of expansion of tropical Asian exports, Europe and Japan joined China and India as the major external catalysts for growth. For Japan these years were the "great transformation," which Hayami (1986: 5) has labelled "the decisive turning-point heralding the start of Japan's 'modernity.'" Unification, urbanization, the creation of distribution and marketing networks, and the commercialization of attitudes were all a part of this Japanese leap, but it also

Fig. 4 Detail of a Japanese silk scroll of about 1630, depicting the arrival in Hoi An (Faifo) of the red-seal ship of the Chaya family in Kyoto. The ship is being towed by three Vietnamese galleys towards the river of Hoi An. Umbrellas near the river mouth denote a market area, behind which lies the Japanese street with its shops and houses. Across the river is the Chinese quarter, shown as three long houses.

Table 2. Japanese red-seal ships clearing for Southeast Asia

	Tongking	Cochin-China[a]	Champa	Cambodia	Siam	Patani	Philippines[b]	Total[c]
1604–05	5	9	2	10	4	5	9	45
1606–10	2	9	3	10	18		13	59
1611–15	3	26		4	14	2	13	62
1616–20	9	22		3	2		8	45
1621–25	6	7	1	4	8		9	35
1626–30	3	5		4	8		2	22
1630–35	9	9		9	2		2	31
Total	37	87	6	44	56	7	56	299

Notes: [a]Includes Annam (1604–11), Cochin-China (from 1609), and Hue and Kachian (1 each in 1604)
[b]All identified as "Luzon" (Manila) except 1 each in 1605 and 1606 to the Visayas
[c]Includes some single sailings to minor ports—Brunei (1605, 1606), Melaka (1607), Maluku (1616), and Datan (which Iwao locates between Cambodia and Siam—1606, 1607)
Sources: Iwao 1976: 300–01; Innes 1980: 58

involved a brief period of intensive trade with Southeast Asia. From about 1580 Japanese ships began to frequent southern harbours, carrying the silver that was being brought out of Japanese mines in unprecedented quantities. During the thirteen years (1604–16) for which the Tokugawa government carefully recorded its issuing of licences (shu-in) to these ships, 173 Japanese vessels sailed to Southeast Asia (fig. 4). For the period 1604–35 Iwao has traced at least 299 vessels (table 2). On average, each vessel carried to Southeast Asian ports cargoes (chiefly silver) worth nearly 2 tonnes of silver, so that annual imports from Japan from an average of ten ships a year would have been valued at about 20 tonnes of silver. This activity stopped abruptly in 1635 when Iemetsu prohibited any Japanese from travelling abroad on pain of death (Iwao 1976: 300–01; Innes 1980: 51–66).

The same period was one of exceptional commercial expansion in China, fuelled in part by these silver supplies from Japan, as well as from America. In 1567 the emperor Muzong responded to repeated appeals from Fujian by lifting for the first time the Ming ban on Chinese private trade to the south. Fifty junks per year were licensed to trade at first, but this figure grew to 88 by 1589 and to 117 by 1597. Although there are no adequate records thereafter and the system had broken down by the 1620s, there was an estimate of 190 junks in 1613 and an official report of "several hundred" junks around 1616. Customs revenue in Zhangzhou almost tripled between 1576 and 1594 (Zhang 1617: 131–33; Blussé and Zhuang 1991: 146).

Roughly half the Chinese junks in 1589 were licensed for the "eastern seas"—the Philippines and Borneo. Of the half licensed for the "western seas," the principal destinations were west Java (8), Cochin-China (8), southern Sumatra (7), Siam (4), Cambodia (3), and Champa (3). It seems certain that many vessels also managed to travel without licences, particularly to the nearer Vietnamese ports (Innes 1980: 52–53). In China this was a period of prosperity, urban expansion, population increase, and commercialization, based to some extent on the unaccustomed freedom of international trade and the importation of Japanese and American silver.

Because Chinese bans against trading with Japanese "pirates" continued, Southeast Asian ports became the necessary entrepôts where Japanese exchanged their silver for Chinese silk and Southeast Asian sugar, spices, and deerskin. The greatest beneficiaries of this exchange were Manila and Hoi An (Faifo), the strategically placed port developed after 1600 by the Nguyen rulers of the southern Vietnamese kingdom Europeans called Cochin-China. Sixteen Chinese vessels a year were licensed for Manila in the 1590s, and a similar number probably sailed to Hoi An in following decades (Chen 1974: 12–16; Innes 1980: 53). Political troubles and economic crisis in China began to affect this booming trade in the 1620s, however, and from 1640 to 1680 the Chinese arm of Southeast Asian trade was in an undoubted slump (see chapter 5).

Of all the markets for Southeast Asian produce, Europe expanded its demand most rapidly in the late sixteenth and early seventeenth centuries, taking an ever larger share of Malukan spices and Southeast Asian pepper. The "spice orgy" that progressively took hold of European tables (Braudel 1979 I: 221), the increasingly efficient transport systems around the Cape of Good Hope, and in the seventeenth century the Dutch monopoly and the impoverishment of Asia relative to Europe all played their part in this changing balance. Before the boom of the fifteenth century, less than a tenth of Malukan exports can have found their way to Europe. By the 1490s Europe's share may have expanded to about a fourth (Magalhães-Godinho 1969: 591–92), though this share must have dropped as a result of the initial Portuguese disruption of trade in the Indian Ocean. Thomaz (1981: 100–01) calculated that the Portuguese never exported more than an eighth of total Malukan clove production to Europe, but if the revived traffic by the Muslim route in the second half of the sixteenth century is added, the European share would once more have been at least a fourth.

In the mid-seventeenth century, Dutch estimates were that Europe took one-third to half the world supply of Malukan spice (Knaap

1987: 234, 245–46). In fact, however, Dutch manipulation of the market was altering the balance even more. Francisco Pelsaert had already pointed out in 1627 that older Indian merchants in Agra said three times as much cloves had reached India before the Dutch East India Company (VOC) assumed the major role in distribution (Glamann 1958: 103). Over the period 1641–60, when the VOC still faced some competition from English, Portuguese, and Indian traders, it sold on average 31 tonnes a year in Surat and about 25 tonnes on the Coromandel Coast. Thereafter Indian consumption declined more rapidly than European. Surat took 23 tonnes a year in the 1660s and Coromandel only about 5 tonnes, as Dutch prices were fixed at two to three times the earlier levels (from table in Glamann 1958: 301–02; Raychaudhuri 1962: 193–94).

The rise in Southeast Asian pepper exports in the boom period was even sharper. Not only did Indonesian growers fill the expanding demand from their established market in China; they also took over India's role as principal supplier to the rapidly growing European market. During the period of disruption, 1500–1530, the Mediterranean ports had had to look to Lisbon for supplies of Asian produce (Braudel 1966 I: 543–34). Gradually, however, the Muslim trade route revived. The novel elements of European naval warfare introduced by the Portuguese soon lost their surprise value. The Ottoman conquest of Egypt (1517) and subsequently of the Red Sea coast of Arabia (1538) provided the backing of a great power for Muslim shipping in the Indian Ocean. Portuguese factors responded to the requirements of profitable trade by licensing or even financing their erstwhile Muslim rivals. Finally, the growing of pepper and cloves spread to new areas the Portuguese could not control as they did the Malabar coast (for pepper) and Ternate (for cloves).

In 1536 the Portuguese conceded that "an immense swarm" of small boats laden with pepper had eluded their patrols and left Calicut for the Red Sea. Portuguese commanders continued to complain of their inability to stop this trade without greater resources. In the mid-1540s they achieved temporary success, and their shipments of pepper then reached a record 1500 tonnes a year—more than Europe had imported in the fifteenth century (Magalhães-Godinho 1969: 773–74). Perhaps as a result of this an alternative Islamic route to the Red Sea was established that avoided Portuguese strongholds on the Indian coast by going directly across the Indian Ocean by way of the Maldives from Aceh, which was assuming the role of the principal commercial and military rival of the Portuguese in Southeast Asia. By the 1560s there are a number of convincing estimates that between 1250 and

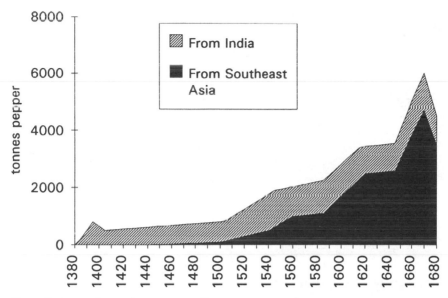

Fig. 5 Estimated pepper exports to Europe

2000 tonnes of pepper each year were passing through Egypt on the revived Muslim route (Lane 1940; Braudel 1966: 545–51; Boxer 1969: 418–19; Subrahmanyam 1990: 130–33). Portuguese shipments, predominantly from India, did not decline until some disastrous setbacks in the 1590s. It is therefore probable that most of the pepper travelling to Egypt came not from India but from new pepper fields in Sumatra (see fig. 5).

Further east, Muslim Javanese and Malay traders defied Portuguese attempts to establish a monopoly of Malukan spices and shipped much of their clove and nutmeg westward on the same route via Aceh to Egypt. Portuguese influence in Maluku declined after 1550, and in 1575 they lost their principal east Indonesian stronghold in Ternate. Thereafter "the inhabitants of Maluku refused to give cloves to the Portuguese, and sold them to the Javanese, who in turn sold them at [Portuguese] Melaka" (Fernandez 1579: 226). Yet even buying cloves on the open market the Portuguese managed to send record shipments of more than 100 tonnes home in the 1580s. The customs revenue of Portuguese Melaka reached a peak in the 1580s, double what it had been in the 1540s (Thomaz 1979: 116). Total spice shipments reaching Europe by both Portuguese and Muslim routes in the second half of the sixteenth century were probably two or three times the recorded Portuguese tonnages alone, and about double the previous peak of the 1490s.

In the last three decades of the sixteenth century the output of silver from Spanish mines in Mexico and Peru increased markedly, and much of it was carried to Asia by the Portuguese and by the Spanish "Manila galleon" from Acapulco. The trade of Spanish Manila grew rapidly to a peak value of more than 600,000 pesos a year in 1616–20 and remained at levels higher than 500,000 until 1645, when the trade fell away drastically to less than half that amount (Chaunu 1960: 78–82, 245; see table 7, below). The annual Jesuit letter from Manila reported in 1627 that "from the time the Philippines was conquered it has never been as prosperous and opulent as it is today" (cited de la Costa 1967: 347).

The Dutch and English joined the competition for pepper and spices from 1596, leading to high prices and an enormous expansion in production. Whereas only 5–8 spice vessels a year were reaching Europe by Portuguese and Islamic-Venetian routes combined in the last two decades of the sixteenth century, an average of 13.3 European vessels returned from Asia each year in the 1620s (Steensgaard 1973: 170–71). This marked the definitive victory of the sea route around the Cape of Good Hope. A few shiploads of pepper from Aceh were still reaching the Red Sea in 1616, but these dried up completely over the next decade as even the markets of the Turkish empire had to obtain their pepper from western European shippers (Steensgaard 1973: 171–72). Total quantities shipped to the West continued to increase rapidly, peaking at about 6000 tonnes a year in the 1670s—twice what they had been forty years earlier. It is harder to estimate quantities taken to China at different periods, but they appear to have varied between peaks of up to 2000 tonnes at the beginning and end of the seventeenth century and very small amounts during the collapse of the Ming dynasty in the 1640s. Smaller quantities went to consumers in eastern India and mainland Southeast Asia.

Shipments of Malukan spices to Europe appear to have peaked around 1620 (see fig. 3, above), when competition for spices was intense between European shippers, and the VOC was not yet able to manipulate the market through a monopoly. European annual purchases then reached about 300 tonnes of cloves, 200 tonnes of nutmeg, and 80 tonnes of mace. Because annual production of cloves in Maluku had not risen much above 400 tonnes, divided equally between the old north Maluku suppliers and the new Ambonese area (Knaap 1987: 20, 231), Europe must temporarily have dominated world consumption. The VOC established its monopoly over the nutmeg and mace of Banda in 1621, and immediately sought to reduce supplies reaching Europe to about half those peak levels, with prices correspondingly high (Glamann 1958: 98–101; Steensgaard 1973: 155 57). Not until about 1650 could it do the same for the much more widespread Malukan supplies of clove. The VOC's destruction of clove trees outside its own areas of direct control in southern Ambon and the Lease Islands then reduced total production to about 180 tonnes throughout the 1650s and 1660s. The selling price in Europe was doubled to 7.5 guilders per *pond*, and in India tripled to 5 guilders (Knaap 1987: 234–35).

As a result of heavy Dutch pressure on their Ambonese subjects, the output grew again from the 1670s to a peak of about 500 tonnes in the 1690s. The VOC was obliged to reduce prices to 3.75 guilders in Europe in 1677, but this desperate measure came too late to prevent a permanent reduction of European clove consumption. A cheaper alternative, Brazilian "clove-wood," had become popular during the period of high prices (Glamann 1958: 97–101; Knaap 1987: 245–46). In the last decades of the century, therefore, the VOC was faced with an oversupply of cloves and a reduction in profits from what had been its most lucrative Asian operation.

Pepper grew too widely in monsoon Asia for the VOC to obtain a monopoly or manipulate the market. Rather, oversupply caused a drop in prices and eventual reduction in Asian purchases. Prices in Europe were at their highest in 1616–41, and at their lowest during the last quarter of the century (Glamann 1958: 77–83). Indian textiles became a more profitable bulk item with which to fill ships for the homeward European voyage and had replaced pepper in first place for the English Company by mid-century, and for the Dutch by 1680 (see chapter 5).

The broad pattern of growth in Southeast Asian trade seems equally clear whether we look at its western or its eastern branches. There was a sudden take-off around 1400, with intermittent growth through the remainder of the fifteenth century, probably strongest at its end. A sharp downturn occurred in 1500 but was made good by 1530. There was growth thereafter, accelerating around 1570 and reaching its peak in the period 1600–1630. The mid-seventeenth century was a time of triumph for the VOC but one of crisis for Southeast Asia.

The pattern of exchange in this age of commerce was for Southeast Asia to import cloth from India, silver from the Americas and Japan and copper cash, silk, ceramics and other manufactures from China, in exchange for its exports of pepper, spices, aromatic woods, resins, lacquer, tortoiseshell, pearls, deerskin, and the sugar exported by Vietnam and Cambodia. The producers of spices and other export items were by no means the major beneficiaries of the boom in demand for their products. Profits of more than 100 percent were common at each stage of the routes by which goods passed around the world. Tomé Pires (1515: 213–14) noted that merchandise bought in Melaka for 500 reis would be sufficient to buy a bahar of cloves in Maluku, which on return to Melaka would sell for between 9 and 12 cruzados—a seven-to-tenfold increase. Many would have shared in this profit: the captain and crews of the ships on the different sectors Melaka-Java and Java-Maluku, the capitalists who may have advanced money for the voyages, the rulers and port officials of Melaka, Ternate, one or more Javanese ports, and probably a port in Bali or Sumbawa, and dealers in the foodstuffs and cloth which the vessels would collect in Java, Bali, or Sumbawa to furnish the Malukan trade. A similar process occurred as the spices moved westward or northward and the cloth moved eastward, growing more valuable at each stage of the voyage. The multiplier effect of the boom in long-distance trade was felt throughout the trading ports of Southeast Asia, and often far into the interior where commercial goods were gathered for export. Only in the mid-seventeenth century when the VOC completed its monopoly over the spices of Maluku did this extraordinary lifeline cease to benefit a variety of Asian traders and trade centres.

Imports of Silver and Gold

At the peak of high pepper prices in the 1640s, Southeast Asia was exporting about 6500 tonnes of pepper at an average price of 9 reals per pikul, representing an average export in local price terms of about a million reals or 25 tonnes of silver a year. In the same period Maluku was exporting nearly 400 tonnes of cloves at peak prices (100 reals per bahar of 300 kg), worth about 150,000 reals or 4 tonnes of silver at Maluku prices, or nearly double that in the major markets of Southeast Asia. Siam in the 1630s was exporting 2000 tonnes of sappanwood, mainly to China and Japan, and Siam and Cambodia were exporting about 300,000 deerskins to Japan (Ishii 1988: 6). The ten Japanese "red seal" ships that visited Southeast Asian ports each year in the period 1604–29 brought about 20 tonnes of silver and took back a corresponding value of Chinese silks and Southeast Asian skins, raw silk, sappanwood, sugar, benzoin, cotton, and spices. Chinese ships visiting Southeast Asia were about ten times as numerous as the Japanese, though their cargoes may have been somewhat less valuable. In very rough terms, the overall trade of Southeast Asia at its peak, including the entrepôt trade between Chinese and Japanese, Chinese and Dutch, and so on, might be estimated as follows: exports to India, the Middle East, and Europe, in exchange for Indian cloth, metals, and specie, were worth the equivalent of about 120 tonnes of silver, while exports to China and Japan, in exchange for manufactures, metals, and specie, were worth about 100 tonnes of silver.

Although both Japanese and Europeans did have to pay for much of their Asian imports with specie, most of the return to Southeast Asians for the above exports was of course in the form of trade goods. Nevertheless, the available figures for the inflow of specie—relatively detailed though never complete—are the most useful indicator to establish more clearly when the trade boom in Southeast Asia reached its peak and began to tail off.

Medieval European moralists frequently lamented the eastward "drain" of precious metal, which reached very high levels at the end of the fifteenth century to meet the first peak in pepper and spice flows to the west. Magalhães-Godinho (1969: 316–17, 334) calculated that Europe was paying 400,000 cruzados a year, equivalent to more than 10 tonnes of silver, for eastern luxuries in the late fifteenth century. This price suffered a "sensational" drop to less than 80,000 cruzados (equivalent to about 2 tonnes of silver) in the early 1500s, as the smaller amounts of pepper and spice were obtained as much by plunder as purchase. The recovery of the Levantine trade, still largely paid for in gold, and greater Portuguese access to silver supplies, caused a rapid climb in the export of precious metal in the second half of the century. In particular, the enormous increase in output of silver from Spanish America after 1570 proved irresistible as a means to fund the *carreira da India*. The union of the Spanish and Portuguese crowns in 1580 removed another barrier, and in the 1580s, according to two independent estimates, the Portuguese were shipping to Goa each year about a million cruzados (30 tonnes of silver) (ibid.: 329–30). In total, Magalhães-Godinho (1969: 335) estimates that Europe was sending 72 tonnes of silver equivalent to the east at the end of the sixteenth century, through both Portuguese and Levantine routes.

In the seventeenth century the Portuguese, Dutch, English, and Spanish all carried substantial amounts of specie, primarily American silver, to the east. Almost in step with the improvement in extraction techniques that dramatically increased the flow of silver from Potosí in Peru (contemporary Bolivia) was a similar improvement in Japanese extraction through use of mercury. For eastern Asia this Japanese supply was the more important. The extraordinary factor is that it peaked at almost the same period as the American, but much more sharply.

Some figures more reliable for their trend than for their absolute

levels are set out in table 3. The European data represent official shipments, substantially undervaluing the total flow, especially in the case
of the Portuguese. The Japanese figures, by contrast, are rough approximations based on extrapolation from fragmentary data. Nevertheless,
these are the most useful indicators of just when the Asian trade boom
reached its peak and began to decline. The Manila galleon did not for
more than a century bring such large quantities across the Pacific as it
had in 1610–30. Japanese silver exports never again reached the scale of
the extraordinary years between 1610 and 1640. In 1668 further silver
export was banned, though a trickle did continue through Korea. The
English and Dutch reached flatter peaks in the 1620s. Both north European countries again surpassed these amounts before the end of the
century, but by then a much smaller percentage of their purchases was
in Southeast Asia.

Most Japanese (and Manila galleon) silver was absorbed by China,
where it helped fuel the commercialization and urban expansion of
the late Ming. A large proportion of it went there indirectly through
the markets of Hoi An, Manila, Patani, Ayutthaya, and Cambodia,
however, and certainly added to the commercial expansion of those
and other cities. Portuguese, Dutch, and English silver was destined
primarily for India, where it purchased the cloth that was essential for
doing business in Southeast Asia. Even so increasing amounts of silver
did find their way to all the markets of the East, and Dutch, English,
and French pepper-buyers in Indonesia were frequently asked to make
their payments in silver reals. These Spanish coins became the effective international currency of Southeast Asia during the first half of
the seventeenth century. Although it is not possible to isolate the
percentage of the influx of silver that ended up in Southeast Asia, this
influx certainly reached its peak in the 1620s and served in Southeast
Asia, as in Europe and China, to expand cities, to stimulate demand for
goods, and to increase the commercialization of society. The progressive diminution of this influx after 1630 contributed to the mid-
seventeenth-century crisis in Southeast Asia.

Cloth Imports from India

Cloth was consistently the largest item of nonessential Southeast
Asian expenditure, and in good times the major exports of the region
paid primarily for imports of brightly coloured and finely woven Indian cloth. If the level of such cloth imports could be measured over a
substantial period, this would provide the best single index of commercial prosperity.

Table 3. Supplies of silver and gold in eastern Asia
(decennial annual averages in metric tonnes of silver equivalent)

	Portuguese[a]	VOC[b]	English[c]	Manila galleon[d]	Japanese exports[e]
1581–90	8.6			4.0	30
1591–1600	?			2.7	40
1601–10	5.9	5.7	1.3	12.0	80
1611–20	4.7	10.9	4.7	19.4	110
1621–30	4.4	12.7	7.7	23.1	130
1631–40		8.7	5.5	18.4	130
1641–50		9.5	?	10.1	70
1651–60		8.6	?	9.0	50
1661–70		11.8	9.9	8.0	40

Notes: [a]Calculated from Magalhães-Godinho 1969: 330–31
[b]Calculated from Bruijn, Gaastra, and Schoffer 1987: 187, 224
[c]Calculated from Chaudhuri 1965: 115 and Chaudhuri 1978: 512
[d]Calculated from TePaske 1983: 444–45, adding private to public remittances; the figures for 1581–90 and 1661–70 are estimates because only public remittances are known
[e]These are rounded estimates based on Glamann 1958: 58; Iwao 1976; Innes 1980: 634–42; Yamamura and Kamiki 1983; Tashiro 1987; and Moloughny and Xia 1989

The first useful statistics on the subject are those of Tomé Pires (1515: 269–72). He estimated that at the peak of Melaka's dominance of the Straits of Melaka trade, just before the Portuguese conquest, five vessels a year brought cloth from Gujarat to the city, of which one carried a cargo worth 70–80,000 cruzados, and the others 15–30,000 cruzados each. Three or four Malabar ships a year each brought 12–15,000 cruzados worth of cloth, while one or two ships from Pulicat were valued at 80–90,000 cruzados. Averaging these estimates produces totals of 165,000 cruzados from Gujarat and 174,750 cruzados from South India. From Bengal, Pires (1515: 92) claimed first that once "and sometimes twice" each year a junk worth 80–90,000 cruzados in cloth arrived in Melaka, and a little later that "four or five ships and junks" sailed each year for Melaka and Pasai. Presuming these latter to be smaller vessels playing a small part in the cloth import trade, let us assume an import from Bengal of just 120,000 cruzados of cloth. This gives a total value of Melaka's cloth imports from India of 460,000 cruzados, equivalent to almost 20 tonnes of silver.

Undoubtedly some of Southeast Asia's imports of Indian cloth went directly to Pegu, Tenasserim, Pasai, and elsewhere without passing through Melaka, though these must have been partly offset by the Indian cloth re-exported outside the region (notably to China and

Ryukyu) from Melaka. Net Southeast Asian imports may therefore have been in the region of 24 tonnes equivalent of silver. Assuming that Pires was referring to their value in Melaka, the purchase price in India would have been closer to 12 tonnes of silver.

By the end of the sixteenth century these large import levels had expanded even further. The English trailblazer James Lancaster seized a single Portuguese ship in 1602 carrying a cargo valued at 300,000 cruzados, mostly in cloth, from Coromandel to Melaka (Lancaster 1602: 107). In the harbour of Aceh, which had taken over part of Melaka's role as the terminus for Indian Muslim shipping, there were sixteen to eighteen Indian vessels in 1602 (ibid.: 90). Half of these were probably from Gujarat, which sent eight large "junks" there in 1608 (Verhoeff 1611: 242). This Gujarat shipping to Southeast Asia appears therefore to have roughly doubled in the course of the sixteenth century. The Gujaratis could not for long compete with the northern Europeans in supplying the European market (through the Middle East) with Southeast Asian pepper and spices, and came less often after 1620. In the 1630s and 1640s they were sending only about three cargoes of cloth a year to Aceh (Clark 1643: 282; Vlaming van Outshoorn 1644: 547; Mundy 1667 II: 329, 338). The Dutch blockade of Aceh in 1656–59, and the subsequent prising away of the west Sumatran pepper-coast from Acehnese control, reduced the number of Indian ships bringing cloth to Aceh to five or six—of which one or two might be Gujarati (Dampier 1699: 101; Coolhaas 1968: 93, 324, 476; Das Gupta 1982: 431; Arasaratnam 1986: 126).

Bengal and Coromandel shipping was less vulnerable to European competition and continued to expand for much of the seventeenth century. The figures collected by Prakash (1979: 51–53) suggest that the number of Bengali vessels bringing cloth to Southeast Asia probably peaked in the middle decades of the century, when there were about six ships on the Aceh run and often more sailing to Tenasserim to serve Siam. In the 1680s about eight ships still served Southeast Asia as a whole, but this fell to only one or two a year in the last years of the century.

The exports of Coromandel to Southeast Asia appear to have grown dramatically in the sixteenth century and up to the 1620s. From then until the 1640s they may have been static as VOC exports rose, Portuguese and Danish fell, English peaked in the 1630s before again falling, and exports in Asian vessels declined slowly (table 4). The Dutch estimated in 1675 that the whole Coromandel coast had exports worth 10–12 million guilders, equivalent to 100–120 tonnes of

Table 4. Coromandel ship departures to Southeast Asia

	from Masulipatnam to			from Nagapattinam to		
	Aceh	*Pegu*	*Total*	*Aooh*	*Melaka*	*Total*
1624	2	4	13	2	5	10
1625	3	2	10	2	3	11
1626a	2	4	11			
1627	2	2	6			
1628	2	2	9			
1629	2	2	7	0	1	6
1630	1	3	6			
1632	1		3	1	2	6
1633 34	1	1	7			
1639				3	3	8
1645				2	1	6
1649a				2	0	6
1650				3		5

Note: a = arrivals
Source: Subrahmanyam 1990: 203, 208, 214, 334

silver (Arasaratnam 1986: 96). The majority of this was cloth, for which Southeast Asia was the primary market until 1650, after which a rapidly increasing percentage of it was dispatched to Europe.

VOC monitoring of shipping in the two principal Coromandel ports of the period makes it possible to show the trend of non-VOC ship movements between these two ports and Southeast Asia (see table 4). Of the Nagapattinam departures (or in 1649, arrivals), one each year was to Manila in 1624–25 and to Makassar in 1645–50. Otherwise these vessels all departed to the eastern side of the Bay of Bengal—Aceh, Melaka, Johor, Kedah, Bangeri, Junk-ceylon (Phuket), Mergui, and Pegu. The shipping of Nagapattinam was largely Indo-Portuguese, while that from Masulipatnam was owned either by Southeast Asian rulers (Aceh, Siam, Arakan) or by the Persians of Golconda.

Only for the VOC do we have reliable figures over time for the export of Indian cloth to Southeast Asia. Under Jan Pieterszoon Coen's energetic guidance (governor-general, 1619–29) the Company rapidly saw the advantages of using Indian cloth to sell against Southeast Asian produce. It grew from being a minor player to becoming the dominant factor in the trade in the course of the seventeenth century. VOC purchases of cloth in Coromandel grew rapidly from the equivalent of 3 tonnes silver in 1619 to 5 in 1621, 7 in 1623, and 8 in 1640

Table 5. Value of VOC exports from Coromandel to Batavia, in five-year annual averages

	Exports (thousand guilders)	metric tonnes silver equivalent
1646–50	1,443	14.8
1651–55	1,447	14.9
1656–60	1,171	12.0
1661–65	1,356	13.2
1666–70	2,038	19.8
1671–75	1,494	14.5
1676–80	1,298	12.6
1683–85	2,880	27.7
1687–89	791	7.6

Source: Calculated from Raychaudhuri 1962: 140–43

(Coen 1619A: 583; Colenbrander 1921: 94, 296; Subrahmanyam 1990: 174). Dutch exports from Coromandel to Batavia (chiefly but not entirely cloth) leapt dramatically in the 1640s as a result of a bigger injection of capital, the elimination of Portuguese Melaka as a rival (1641), and the opening of new Bengal factories classified under Coromandel. Dutch purchases were high in 1644–55 and slumped during the following decade, which included the South Indian famine of 1660–61. They reached their peak in the years 1664–69, averaging over 2 million guilders or 20 tonnes of silver a year, at a time when all other exporters were in eclipse.

Thereafter it was all downhill for the VOC's Southeast Asian cloth trade, despite a desperate attempt in 1683–85 to beat the opposition by attempting to buy up all available cloth. This policy backfired, the cloth was unsalable at the higher price the Company now had to ask, and local cloth production in the Archipelago soared. In the last fifteen years of the century the Dutch bought very little cloth, and particularly little for the shrinking Southeast Asian market. This allowed a modest revival for non-Company traders based at Madras and other Coromandel ports, but nothing to counteract the steady decline in Southeast Asian imports (Raychaudhuri 1962: 139–43, 162; Arasaratnam 1986: 134; Laarhoven 1988).

Around 1620, two-thirds of VOC cloth purchases in India were destined to be sold in Southeast Asia (Coen 1619A: 583); this proportion dropped to a little over one-third in 1652–53 and to about 15 percent by the end of the century (information from Ruurdje Laarhoven; also Arasaratnam 1986: 134). After adding the smaller amounts of cloth the Dutch purchased in Gujarat and Bengal for the Southeast Asian market, it appears that the VOC alone was bringing a value of Indian cloth into Southeast Asia equivalent to about 5 tonnes of silver around 1620, and 8–10 tonnes in the period 1640–85, after which the amount fell rapidly.

Except for its brief attempt at monopoly in 1683–85, the Company never took more than a third of Coromandel textile exports. Before 1640 it took a much smaller fraction of the total Indian export trade to Southeast Asia. The Gujaratis brought large quantities to Aceh until 1615, and substantial quantities until the 1690s. The English exported about 0.6 tonnes of silver in Coromandel cloth to Southeast Asia in the 1620s, more than double that in the late 1630s, but slumped again after 1641 (Subrahmanyam 1990: 175–77); the Portuguese and English together were bringing more than 100,000 reals (2.5 tonnes silver) of cloth to Makassar alone in the 1630s (Coulson and Ivy 1636: 293–94); and even after abandoning eastern Indonesia to the Dutch, the English sent one shipload of cloth from south India to Banten every year in the 1660s and 1670s, with an average value of 10,000 pounds, or a tonne of silver (*English Factories* 1668–69: 280; 1670–77: 3, 30, 120–21, 141, 157, 264). The Danes were a further modest factor in 1620–40, at their peak shipping about half a tonne of silver in cloth to Southeast Asia from Coromandel (Subrahmanyam 1990: 181–88). Whereas the northern Indian traders progressively dropped out of the Southeast Asian contest in the last half of the seventeenth century, Coromandel shipowners continued to carry most of their cloth exports, profiting from the more localized nature of the trade, up until at least the 1680s (Arasaratnam 1986: 119–25).

It is probable, therefore, that the peak period for Southeast Asian imports of Indian cloth was in 1620–55, at a value of about 40 tonnes of silver equivalent per year, about fourfold what it had been in 1510. This would represent about 1.5 million pieces of cloth a year (the VOC alone brought a million pieces to Batavia in 1652, of which 314,000 for the Indonesian market—Laarhoven 1988). If an average piece was about fourteen square metres, as has been calculated, this would be enough for about six million sarongs a year for a total Southeast Asian population of little over twenty million.

By the 1680s, when the VOC dominated the supply, the total inflow must have dropped to only half that level, and it dropped further by the end of the century. The collapse of the Southeast Asian market for Indian textiles is discussed in chapter 5.

Cash Cropping

> [The eastern islands] are fertile in peculiar fruits and merchandise,
> such as spices and other drugs that are found nowhere else; . . . So this
> one product wherewith they abound must furnish them with every-
> thing else; this is why all kinds of food are very dear, save their own
> product, which is cheap, and why these people are constrained to keep
> up continual intercourse with one another, the one supplying what the
> other wants.
>
> —Pyrard 1619 II: 169

Southeast Asia, taken as a whole, has always been an exporter of
raw materials and an importer of manufactures. Its own manufactures
were significant items of local trade, but (with the exception of Vietnamese silk) they were not needed in China or India, the two populous
manufacturing centres on its borders. It was the products of tropical
agriculture and horticulture—pepper, cloves, nutmeg, sugar and benzoin—that received the greatest stimulus from the trade boom, followed by such forest products as deerskin, sandalwood, sappanwood,
camphor, and lac.

The competitive dynamic of the cash-cropping industry is evident
from the constant shifts in production centres. When warfare, trade
disruption, soil exhaustion, or an increase in demand created difficulties for one production area, others were quick to meet the opportunity. Clove trees may well have grown wild in many of the islands of
Maluku, but it was Ternate and Tidore that reaped the benefit of first
bringing them into regular cultivation. By 1500 production had spread
to the three small neighbouring islands. A century later the output of
these centres was greatly reduced and most cloves were coming from
Ternatan-ruled areas in western Seram and northern Ambon. New
production centres developed in the following decades in the small
islands of Ambelau and Manipa, where Makassar traders could more
easily buy the cloves without detection from the Dutch. And in the
second half of the seventeenth century, the VOC enforced a new concentration of clove-growing in Ambon and the other small islands it
controlled off the southwest coast of Seram (Knaap 1987). In each
centre in turn, almost the whole working population was involved in
clove production, at least during the busy harvesting season.

Round pepper (*Piper nigrum*) had more spectacular travels—from
southern India to the tip of northern Sumatra around 1400, the Malayan peninsula by 1500, the western coast of Sumatra by about 1550,
the inland Minangkabau districts of Sumatra, western Java, and southern Sumatra by 1600, and southern Borneo by 1630. It spread in lightly

populated areas of shifting cultivation, where pepper could be planted without necessarily foregoing staple food crops. Eighteenth-century production estimates show that a family pepper farm (*kebun*) of about a thousand vines would produce on average about 200 kg of pepper a year, after allowing for the three initial unproductive years of each vine and all the vagaries of subsequent harvests (Kathirithamby-Wells 1977: 61, 70; Marsden 1783: 132; de Rovere van Breugel 1787: 342). The roughly 8500 tonnes of pepper that Southeast Asia produced during the mid-seventeenth-century peak, therefore, must have required the participation of more than 40,000 families, or 200,000 people. About 6 percent of the entire population of Sumatra, the Malayan Peninsula, and Borneo earned their living from growing this one crop for the international market.

Cane sugar also had a spectacular expansion in the seventeenth century, after Chinese refining methods were introduced to Cochin-China (the Quang Nam area), Siam (on the hillsides surrounding the central rice plain), Cambodia, and Java (around Batavia and Pekalongan) to make it acceptable as a bulk export to China and especially Japan. Japan, which had to import virtually all its sugar in the seventeenth century, established an annual import quota of 2100 tonnes after 1685, which probably reflected the average levels in the period 1640–1700 (Innes 1980: 504–08). Much of this was imported from Taiwan or south China, but the chaos in China from the 1640s meant that ever larger proportions had to come from Southeast Asia—probably a third to a half by the 1680s. In 1636 the Dutch already hoped to buy 250–300 tonnes of sugar in Cochin-China, though they obtained much less (Innes 1980: 507), and in the 1680s a single Chinese vessel regularly brought 100–200 tonnes from Siam to Nagasaki (Ishii 1971: 170). Siam and Java sugar was also taken to Europe by the Dutch in the 1630s. In 1649 the amount of Java-grown sugar sent to Europe rose to 100 tonnes (Glamann 1958: 152–56).

Benzoin (or benjamin), the resin of the *Styrax benzoin* tree, used for incense, was readily cultivated in quite large plantations alongside hill rice in northern Sumatra, Laos, and northern Cambodia (Marsden 1783: 154). Cambodia exported 270 tonnes of it a year in the 1630s, which probably included the 18 tonnes reported in Laos a few years later (Wusthoff 1642: 202; Coolhaas 1960: 592). It was used all over Asia as an incense—Persia alone imported about 60 tonnes a year in the 1630s (van Hall and van der Koppel 1946–50 III: 659). Tobacco, introduced by the Spanish to Luzon only in 1575, was an important export crop in Mindanao a century later (Dampier 1697: 228).

How were these frontiers of new cash-cropping organized? Almost invariably there were intermediaries between the cultivators and the international traders—village "big men" or port-rulers who extended credit to tide farmers over the initial years of planting and in return took a large part in marketing the crop. The ruler who controlled the port and external market expected a substantial percentage as duty, but often also tried to control the trade. In Ambon around 1600 the *orangkaya* elite organized both the sale of cloves to Javanese, Malay, and later European traders and the distribution of cloth imports to the growers. The raja of Hitu and his leading ministers shared a levy of 10 percent of the cloves thus sold. Farmers could approach foreign buyers directly only in great secrecy (Gijsels 1621: 22–23; Knaap 1987: 232). The ruler of Ternate also took a levy of 10 percent on all cloves produced in his domains, plus a further 10 percent on the value of all clove exports (van Neck 1604: 199–200). The orangkaya oligarchy of Banda monopolized the sale of all its nutmeg but also controlled the land and labour that produced it (Villiers 1981: 728–29).

In eighteenth-century Banten (more tightly controlled than its independent predecessor before 1682) the growers reportedly received from their chiefs, to whom they were often indebted, only half a real per bahar (180 kg) of pepper produced. The chiefs and the intermediate traders made the biggest profits, since the pepper was delivered to the sultan at a fixed price of 7 reals per bahar—though one Sumatran trader claimed he usually bought for 6 reals and sold to the sultan for 12. The sultan in turn sold to the VOC under a monopoly agreement, at a price between 12 and 20 reals (La-uddin 1788: 5; de Rovere van Breugel 1787: 342–43).

Detailed accounts of the financing of pepper cultivation in Sumatra are not available before the nineteenth century, but the central element in the system was then so widespread that it must long have been associated with pepper-growing. This was the entrepreneur who controlled two scarce factors—capital and access to the market—and through them the third and vital element—labour. He advanced enough money, tools, and rice to maintain a pioneer cultivator (often a seasonal immigrant) through the first season of opening up the forest, planting the pepper, and growing the subsidiary food crops necessary for survival. In consequence, the growers were bonded to him and obliged to sell their pepper to him, even though the land they had opened up remained effectively theirs. The entrepreneur became in time a small raja of a new pepper-district, playing the essential royal role of controlling trade and other relations with the outside world. Even if the original advance was repaid, the obligation to sell through this entrepreneurial figure remained. And he in turn owed some of his

success to his relationship with a higher authority—the sultan of
Aceh, Banten, or Jambi—to whom about 10 percent of export proceeds
would go either as tribute or through obligatory sale at specified prices
(Anderson 1826. 61, 260–61; Veth 1877: 242–43; Gould 1956: 100–04;
Siegel 1969: 17–21).

Land was abundant and labour scarce; control of labour was the
key to opening up new production areas. In many places we hear of
cash-cropping by "slaves" of the merchant-aristocrats of the city—on
the hill gardens (*dusun*) of the Melaka elite before 1511 (Pires 1515:
260); along the coast of Banten a century later (Lodewycksz 1598: 129);
and in Aceh in the seventeenth century (Dampier 1699: 91). In Maluku
the orangkaya used their abundant "slaves" to harvest cloves from
trees they had hired from the farmers who had planted them, since it
was only at harvest time that intensive labour was needed. Convention gave half the product to the owner of the trees; half to the harves-
ter (Reael 1618: 88; Gijsels 1621: 22). Some of these cash-croppers may
have been purchased or captured slaves; others would have been long-
term dependents or cultivators indebted for their starting capital. The
labour mobility needed to open up virgin forest to cash-cropping was
based on a system of flexible bondage.

Pepper cultivation was also developed in a particularly sparsely
populated region of seventeenth-century Banjarmasin (southern Borneo) that had no previous tradition of pepper or even of intensive rice
cultivation. Many of the original pepper cultivators there may have
been imported slaves, since one of Makassar's major exports to the
region was "male and female slaves fitted for labour in the pepper-
gardens" (Speelman 1670A: 112). Whatever the original character of
the bonds that tied the cultivator to his lord, however, his central
obligation in the long term was the same—to deliver his valuable crop
exclusively to this patron at the marketing centre.

Conditions at these cash-cropping frontiers were often harsh,
with high mortality, few women, and a poor cultural life. Young men
appear to have hoped to make money there quickly, repay their debts,
and return to family life in a more settled area, but as an Aceh poet
remarked, "If you are in luck you will return; if not you will die in the
rantau [the agricultural frontier]" (*Hikayat Ranto:* 10–11). Some fortunes were made, but many were ruined when prices dropped or when
Dutch blockades prevented the exportation of pepper. Cash-cropping
clearly brought rapid social change by settling new areas, creating new
elites and sometimes destroying old ones, and challenging the more
stable status relations of the rice-growing plains.

Cash-croppers in the seventeenth century, as in the twentieth, generally began to plant when prices were high but learned to cope with fluctuating prices by maintaining some land under food crops to which they could resort when the market was low. When prices stayed low, or when the cash economy turned sour for political reasons, growers either opted out or were forced out by their rulers (see chapter 5 for the movement away from cash-cropping).

The Heyday of the Southeast Asian Junk

> *[The Javanese] are all men very experienced in the art of navigation, to the point that they claim to be the most ancient of all, although many others give this honour to the Chinese, and affirm that this art was handed on from them to the Javanese. But it is certain that they formerly navigated to the Cape of Good Hope, and were in communication with the east coast of the Island of S. Laurenzo [Madagascar], where there are many brown and Javanized natives who say they are descended from them.*
>
> *—Couto 1645 IV, iii: 169*

A distinct type of vessel sometimes called Southeast Asian, sometimes Austronesian or Malayo-Polynesian, sometimes simply *prahu*, has been well delineated in the nautical literature. Its most abiding features are a keel, a hull built by joining planks to the keel and then to each other by means of wooden dowels, without use of iron nails or a frame, similarly pointed stem and stern, two oarlike quarter rudders, and a rectangular latteen-rigged sail. This is a very practical small freight vessel, the dowelled planks providing a much tighter fit than planks nailed onto a frame, and it continues to be built in many parts of Indonesia (Horridge 1981: 8–70). Thousands of such vessels carried cargoes of anything from 4 to 40 tonnes across the seas of Southeast Asia in the age of commerce, as for centuries before and since. They appear in the literature of that period with such names as *prahu*, *balok*, and *pangajawa* (fig. 6b).

It was not this vessel, however, that dominated the major trading routes of the fifteenth and sixteenth centuries. Much larger vessels with two or three masts but many of the same "Southeast Asian" features (dowelled hulls, double rudders, keels) carried most of the longer-distance tonnage for their Southeast Asian owners (fig. 6a). These are unanimously described in the literature by words equivalent to the English "junk." In spite of its quintessentially Chinese ring in modern ears, the word came into European languages through its Malay and Javanese form, *jong*, while Chinese texts of the period also believed it was the Malay word for ship (Edwards and Blagden 1931:

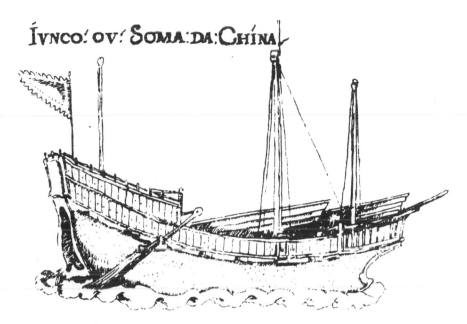

IVNCO: OV: SOMA:DA:CHINA

Fig. 6a A Southeast Asian junk, drawn in Melaka by Godinho de Eredia. Note the double rudder.

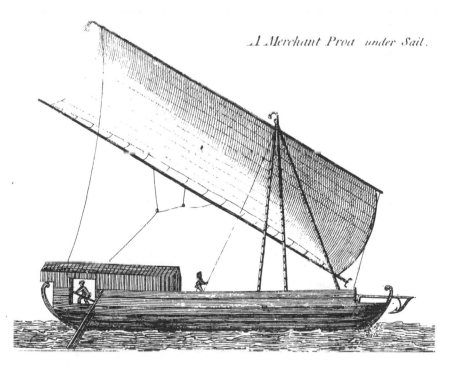

A Merchant Proa under Sail.

Fig. 6b A Malay trading prahu

734). Although both the word[3] and some of the technology probably entered Java as a result of the Mongol expedition, the junk was in the sixteenth century at least as much Southeast Asian as Chinese (Manguin 1985: 24; Reid 1992: 178–84).

The earliest European description of a junk is that of Ludovico di Varthema (1510: 239), who explained that in Pidië (north Sumatra) as well as in Tenasserim around 1504 they made "great ships which they call *giunchi*, which carry three masts, and have a prow before and behind, with two rudders." During the ensuing half-century numerous Europeans extolled the size and strength of these ships, and the marvellous workmanship that could construct them without nails, using only the simplest tools—adze, drill, and chisel in particular (Empoli 1514: 48, 131; Pires 1515: 194–95; Pigafetta 1524: 59; Manguin 1980: 267–68; Scott 1982: 530). The largest junk seen was an enormous troop-carrier of about 1000 tonnes, with several hulls superimposed for extra strength, built for the Javanese attack on Melaka in 1513— "beside it the *Anunciada* did not look like a ship at all" (cited Cortesão 1944: 152n).

Excavations in recent decades of the wrecks of junks from sites in the Gulf of Thailand, the Riau Archipelago, the southern coast of China, and the western coast of Korea have supplemented the information of these contemporary writers. The ships excavated were all involved in trade to or in Southeast Asian waters between the thirteenth and seventeenth centuries and revealed a common basic pattern. All had keels (not the flat bottoms of north China vessels), most had the planks joined by dowels in the "Southeast Asian" manner, but despite the insistence to the contrary of contemporary observers, all also employed iron nails and clamps to supplement the dowels that joined the planks. This new evidence has led Manguin (1984, 1985) to identify the junks of the period as the product of a hybrid "South China Sea" development, eclectically incorporating elements of Chinese and Southeast Asian traditions. In support of this theory is a Javanese epic poem which asserts that a type of junk "such as was made in the land of the Tartars" was first copied in Java in the 1290s, when there was an unprecedented Chinese military intervention in eastern Java by a force of twenty thousand soldiers and a thousand Chinese vessels (*Kidung Sunda:* 77; Manguin 1984: 201).

This theory neatly meshes with other evidence about Chinese economic activity in fifteenth-century Nanyang. The accession of the

3. The term appears likely to have been borrowed from the Fuzhou dialect term for ship, *song* (cf. Mandarin *chuan*).

Ming dynasty in 1368 and its ban on private overseas trade left Chinese communities marooned in the south. Their numbers and status were augmented by those who failed to return from the massive Zheng He expeditions of 1405–35. These communities built the trading fleets of such cities as Gresik and Demak (both in Java), Palembang, Melaka, Patani, and Ayutthaya, organized their tributary trade to China, and established trading networks throughout the region. They naturally had their ships built in Southeast Asia, where wood was better and cheaper, skilled craftsmen were available, and there was no danger of detection by Chinese authorities. A large proportion of South China Sea junks must have been built by Southeast Asian carpenters for owners who were Chinese either by birth or by ancestry. Hybrid features were therefore to be expected, even if what featured more prominently in European accounts were such exotic Southeast Asian features as a nailless hull and twin rudders.

Javanese shipping particularly flourished in the fifteenth century. The first Portuguese chroniclers described the Javanese around 1500 as dominating the trade in Indonesian waters, including Melaka in the west and Maluku in the east. The Melaka Maritime Code was drawn up at that time by a group of Melaka shipowners, most of whom were of Javanese origin. Their Melaka-based vessels regularly made the voyage to China, where Pires (1515: 122–23) reported they were obliged to anchor offshore because the Chinese were rightly afraid that "one of these people's junks would rout twenty Chinese junks." Yet Pires also insisted that Java's trade had been much greater a century earlier—"for they affirm that it navigated to Aden and that its chief trade was in Benua Keling (south India), Bengal and Pasai, that it had the whole of the trade at that time" (Pires 1515: 174). The likeliest explanation for this flowering is a creative melding of Chinese and Javanese marine technology in the wake of the Zheng He expeditions. In each of the "seasons" of 1406, 1408, 1410, 1414, 1418, and 1432, fleets of a hundred or more Chinese vessels spent long periods refitting in the ports of east Java.

Portuguese ships grew larger in the course of the sixteenth century. The great freight-carrying *nao* of the *carreira da India* were about 400 tonnes' burden at the beginning of the century and nearer 1000 tonnes at its end (Pyrard 1619 II: 180–82; Boxer 1969A: 209–11). Asian ships grew smaller. Manguin (1980: 268) places the average junk of the early sixteenth century as around 400–500 tonnes. Even if these were in reality the top of the range, their counterparts at the end of the century were less than half as big. Dutch accounts make clear that only the biggest Javanese junks, those taking rice from Java to cities in

Fig. 7a Vessels of the Java coast, as represented by the first Dutch expedition. *Clockwise from top:* a Javanese trading prahu, a Chinese junk, a local fishing boat, and a Javanese junk.

Sumatra and the Malayan Peninsula, exceeded 200 tonnes. As late as 1620 the King of Mataram still had at least one rice junk of 400 tonnes ("Verhaal" 1622: 540). In general, Southeast Asian ships had become smaller but more numerous, so that one Dutch traveller reckoned "a thousand or more" vessels of 20–200 tonnes in the Surabaya area alone (ibid.: 532). Not having seen the largest rice-carrying junks, Lodewycksz reported that "the East Indian islands are very rich in ships, but all little vessels, so that the largest junk I have seen would not carry more than forty tonnes" (1598: 132–33; see fig. 7a). By the mid-seventeenth century indigenous craft were no longer referred to as junks at all. The biggest belonged to the rulers, in the form of war galleys or freight ships built to European or Chinese design by the kings of Banten, Arakan, and Ayutthaya. The word *junk* was becoming reserved for Chinese-owned vessels of 200–800 tonnes, even if these retained many Southeast Asian features until two centuries later (Manguin 1984: 202–04; Blussé 1986: 106; see fig. 7b).

The disappearance of the large but unwieldy Southeast Asian junk is not difficult to understand given Portuguese accounts of the havoc the Europeans wrought among them. The very large ships maximized the profit on peaceful trading voyages, but they lacked both the speed

Fig. 7b A Chinese junk, represented on Velarde's 1734 map of the Philippines

to flee and the manoeuvrability and firepower to fight against European vessels. Even before he reached and conquered Melaka in 1511, Alfonso de Albuquerque had seized several richly laden junks and confiscated their cargo. Thirty-five of the largest Javanese junks, each of about 500 tonnes, were reportedly employed in the attack launched by Patih Yunus of Japara against Portuguese Melaka in 1513, but virtually all were burned or sunk in a naval battle with the Portuguese (Empoli 1514: 148–49). After the defeat of Patih Yunus' fleet, Pires claimed: "They do not have any junks, because most of the Javanese junks came from Pegu, where the Javanese—and other people who bought in Melaka—used to send for them to be made; . . . And because . . . the Governor of India burned and defeated all the enemy junks, they were all left without any" (1515: 195). Of course this was an exaggeration. Even though the teak of Burma and Siam was recognized as the best shipbuilding material and the Pegu craftsmen as particularly skilled, Javanese continued to build their own vessels with the teak of the Rembang area and timbers from Borneo. The risks of sending large and valuable cargoes in the unwieldy junks, however, was becoming too great. Their vulnerability was proved again in 1618, when the Dutch seized or burned the largest rice junks of Mataram, one of them more than 200 tonnes (Coen 1619: 419). In the seventeenth century only the Europeans and Chinese felt secure enough (and, increasingly, had the necessary capital) to equip very large freight-carrying ships. Rulers below the winds did not encourage their subjects to build large armed vessels. Their own efforts went primarily into galleys for purely military purposes (Manguin 1993; and see chapter 4, below).

It should be stressed that the limits on the size of ship built by the simple Southeast Asian methods were not technological. In Indonesia today small-scale traditional builders are again building wooden vessels of more than 500 tonnes by these methods. Whenever rulers wanted very large craft built this was still done—in 1629 the Acehnese built a grandiose galley about a hundred metres long. Boatbuilding skills were widespread, but large junks or galleys were built in specialist villages whose men were full-time builders. The shipyards of Martaban, the Pegu port best placed for large stands of Burmese teak, supplied many of the biggest junks for the merchants of Melaka and indirectly for those of Java, Sumatra, Luzon, and even south China who bought the Pegu vessels in Melaka (Pires 1515: 145, 195; Bouchon 1979: 139). Each year "about twenty of the largest vessels" could be built in these shipyards (du Jarric 1614: 845). Nevertheless Melaka itself was an important shipbuilding centre under the sultans, and after conquering it Albuquerque (1557: 168) took away "sixty Javanese carpenters of the dockyard, very handy workmen" to serve the Portuguese in India. Mergui and Tenasserim on the west coast of the Malayan Peninsula were also renowned for their shipbuilding and fine timber. The Spanish in the central Philippines found that on two small islets off the well-forested island of Panay lived about four hundred skilled shipbuilders, who "set out every year and scatter themselves all over the islands to build ships" (Loarca 1582: 78–79). In the 1590s the largest junks of Banten were being built in Borneo, but Lasem on the Javanese north coast had become an important shipbuilding centre thanks to its proximity to the best teak forest on the island (Lode-wycksz 1598: 132–33). Lasem must have built much of the large fleet of nearby Japara.

Navigation

> When you want to glance at the horizon
> Don't forget the sharp edge of the reef
> Grasp the rudder, don't lose your concentration
> So that you correctly reach the harbour
> —Hamzah Fansuri, Poems: 112

The close interaction between Chinese and Southeast Asian ship-ping makes it virtually certain that the Chinese compass was known to at least some navigators below the winds. Alcina (1668 III: 54–55) insisted that Filipino sailors knew of the compass from ancient times, long before the Spaniards. He very reasonably adduced in evidence that there was an indigenous word for it in Indonesian and Filipino languages—some variant of the Malay *pedoman*, probably derived from the Javanese word for needle (*dom*). Malays had a fine sense of direction, with their own terms for the eight points of the compass probably developed in the Malacca Strait area, since south was *selatan* (from *selat*, [Singapore] straits) and northwest was the same as the word for (Indian) Ocean, *laut*. Ludovico di Varthema (1510: 247) claimed that the captain of the ship on which he travelled from Borneo to Java "carried a compass with the magnet after our manner, and had a chart which was all marked with lines."

Yet early Dutch reports insisted that Malays and Javanese were ignorant of the compass unless they had recently learned of it from the Portuguese (Lodewycksz 1598: 131). The first consignment of Dutch compasses taken out for sale to Indonesian navigators had to be brought back unsold (Meilink-Roelofsz 1962: 104–05), which has usu-ally been taken as evidence that the islanders knew nothing of them. It seems more likely, however, that existing needs were adequately met by the Chinese compass. "Even though the ones they use are of Chi-nese make and very different from ours in the directions or winds, they are nevertheless sufficient," remarked Alcina (1668 III: 55).

Southeast Asian (and Chinese) pilots did follow the coast wher-ever possible, and relied on an extensive knowledge of winds and currents to guide them. The Malay Maritime Code described their task: "To speak of the pilot, he must pay attention to navigation at sea and onshore, to the winds, the waves, the currents, the depth or

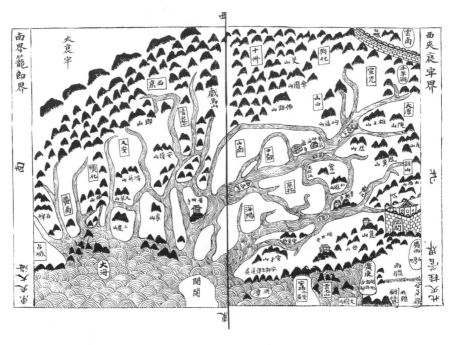

Fig. 8 A Vietnamese map of Vietnam, thought to date from the late seventeenth century (though traditionally dated 1490), showing the capital Thang-long at right, the Chinese border at top right, and the names of provinces in boxes

shallowness of the sea, the moon and stars, the [time of] year and the monsoon, the inlets, headlands and stretches of coast, the submerged reefs, . . . coral and sandbanks; the dunes, mountains and hills" (*Undang-undang Laut:* 38). Alcina believed that Filipino pilots excelled Spanish, Dutch or Chinese in their ability to make use of such features. On these grounds, it appears likely that only the longest distance navigators who lost sight of land for substantial periods felt the need for a compass, and these would have had it from the Chinese.

Very few Southeast Asian maps and charts from before the nineteenth century have survived. The major exceptions are some Vietnamese maps in the Chinese tradition, and one Siamese map which may also have had some Chinese influence (figs. 8, 9). It has generally been assumed that Southeast Asian navigation in the age of commerce was not fundamentally reliant on charts. Yet Pires (1515: 211) reported that his information on the route to Maluku was obtained in Melaka from local Muslims and "their charts, which I have seen many times," and which were more reliable for navigation than for the written information on them. It is still more surprising that Albuquerque should have obtained in Melaka in 1511:

A large map of a Javanese pilot, containing the Cape of Good Hope, Portugal, and the Land of Brazil, the Red Sea and the Sea of Persia, the Clove Islands, the navigations of the Chinese and the Ryukyuans, with their rhumbs and direct routes followed by the ships, and the hinterland, and how the kingdoms border on each other. It seems to me, sire, that this was the best thing I have ever seen. . . . It has the names in Javanese writing, but I had with me a Javanese who could read and write (Albuquerque to King Manuel 1 April 1512, translated Cortesão 1944: lxxviii)

This astonishing map, tragically lost in the wreck of the *Flor de la Mar*, demonstrates the exciting openness of that brief moment in Southeast Asian history. One Javanese pilot, heir to some of the graphic skills in which Java has never been lacking and curious to learn from his contacts with Chinese, Indian, and Arab counterparts in such cosmopolitan ports as Melaka, may have seized on the arrival of the Portuguese to add to his map what could be gleaned from them. Alternately, since Malay and Javanese pilots were expected to be literate in Arabic and to lead the crew in prayer, there may have been an Arab or Indian Muslim intermediary who conveyed the knowledge of the Portuguese discoveries.

Such curiosity about the world was certainly not unique. European travellers were regularly interrogated about their homelands, and their knowledge of astronomy and geography was eagerly seized upon. At the courts of seventeenth-century Ayutthaya and Makassar there was particular enthusiasm to understand and copy European charts, and it was probably the Makassar copies which inspired the tradition of Bugis navigational charts (Le Roux 1935: 699–701; Reid 1981: 21–22). Thomas Forrest (1792: 82) was struck at how interested Bugis *nakhoda* (shipowners) of his day were in sea charts. "I have given many to certain Noquedas . . . for which they were very grateful, and often wrote names of places in their language." Unfortunately, the earliest Bugis maps extant appear to be of the late eighteenth and early nineteenth centuries (fig. 10), but these almost certainly had seventeenth-century antecedents.

The evidence is insufficient to determine how far map-making was really Southeast Asian in the age of commerce, as opposed to the use of maps brought in by foreign pilots. If there was a distinctive tradition in Java, it died with the rapid decline of Javanese seafaring at the beginning of the seventeenth century.

Fig. 9. An eighteenth-century Siamese map of the Malayan Peninsula, upside down from a modern perspective. The lack of first-hand Thai experience of seafaring is indicated not only by the European ship that decorates the map but also by its Chinese features and the uncertainty about areas outside the Siamese realm. The islands to the south of the peninsula are labelled "muang Pahang" (which should be on the mainland), and beyond it "Yache," presumably meant to represent Aceh, to which the routes of trade and diplomacy from the Siamese ports of Mergui and Tenasserim(?) are shown.

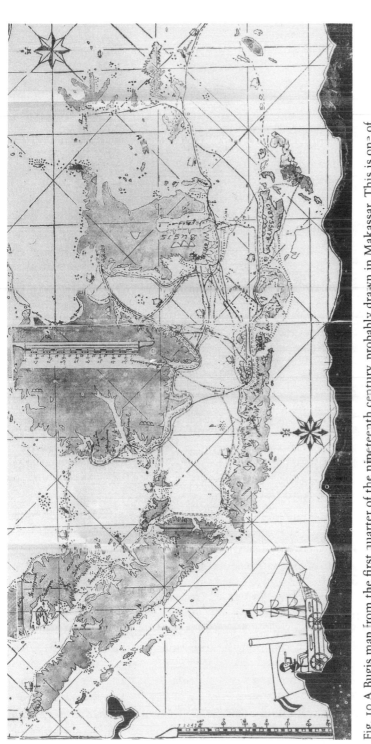

Fig. 10 A Bugis map from the first quarter of the nineteenth century, probably drawn in Makassar. This is one of several almost identical Bugis maps of the period, although the others have place-names in Bugis script and lack the trade routes. These routes indicate freight costs to different destinations, and they conform so closely to the Amanna Gappa specifications that they may have been inserted from it by a later hand. The coastlines in all extant Bugis maps are clearly derived from European maps of at least a century earlier and suggest a continuous map-making tradition going back to seventeenth-century Makassar.

Shipboard Organization

The organization of the crew and cargo on board the Southeast Asian junk is revealed in three major sources. First, there are foreign descriptions, of which the most important is Tomé Pires' account of Melaka shipping around 1511. Second, there is the *Undang-undang Laut*, a Malay code of maritime laws devised by prominent nakhoda of Melaka-based junks during the last decade of the Melaka sultanate. Though the extant texts are all of much later date, the latter-day prologue insists that the laws must be upheld even when they conflict with Islamic law because they reflect "the customs of the ancients since the time when the Sultanate of Melaka was still strong" (*Undang-undang Laut*: 30). The Melaka Malay model was influential also in the Bugis maritime codes, which survive in various texts attributed to the third head of the Bugis in Makassar after the Dutch conquest (Amanna Gappa 1676).

Third, the accounts have happily been preserved of a few of the first commercial voyages the Portuguese sent from Melaka after conquering that great port. For these voyages to Pegu, Pasai, and Coromandel, the Portuguese relied almost entirely on the commercial expertise of their leading Asian collaborator, the wealthy Hindu merchant they called the Kling Nina Chetu—probably a Telugu of the money-lending chettiar caste. He equipped his ships for these voyages as usual with a local Javanese and Mon crew, and the only Portuguese contributions were half the capital, two Portuguese passengers, and the innovation of keeping a record of the voyage for royal account books.

These sources make clear that discipline on the large Southeast Asian junks was as tough as on contemporary European ships and bore little resemblance to the familylike atmosphere of the modern Indonesian prahu. Negligence by one of the sailors, or even the pilot, was to be punished by a number of lashes specified in the Maritime Code. Just as in contemporary Indian and Chinese practice the supreme authority on board was not a sailor but the shipowner or his representative, called in either case the nakhoda. His authority was explicitly compared to that of the raja on land, and the other officers with authority over the crew—the helmsmen, boatswains (*jurubatu*, in charge of anchor and leadline), and deck officers (*tukang*)—were likened to royal officials carrying out the king's commands. Resistance to the authority of the nakhoda could be punished by death, and to the commands of these officers by three, four, or seven lashes, administered by the jurubatu (*Undang-undang Laut*: 32, 36–37). The pilot (*malim*, a term also used for an Islamic teacher), on whom the safety of all depended, was outside this authority structure and compared in the code with the learned imam responsible for avoiding spiritual, as well as physical, hazards on the journey (ibid.: 38). The midshipmen served and protected the nakhoda at sea and on land, and ensured that the junk was always ready to repel attack (ibid.: 43).

Southeast Asian junks, like Chinese ones, had larger crews than European ships of similar tonnage. The two junks equipped by Nina Chetu in 1512, probably of about 200 tonnes' burden, each had more than eighty crew members, consisting in each case of a Malay or Javanese nakhoda, a Pegu (Mon) pilot and his assistant, a master (*tukang agung*) and two to four assistants (*tukang tengah*), six boatswains, four helmsmen, three to six men to look after the boats, four men to supervise the sails, and four midshipmen. The remaining men, forty-five in one case and sixty-five in the other, were described either as *awak perahu* (sailors) or in terms of specific function, and most appear to have been slaves (Thomaz 1966: 194–95; Bouchon 1979: 135). The Maritime Code and Pires (1515: 212) confirm that slaves were an important element in every crew.

In sharp contrast with European, Arab, Indian, or Chinese practice of the period, women were frequent passengers on Southeast Asian trading junks. Surprised to see that the first Dutch expedition had travelled so far without a single woman aboard, the Javanese of Banten quickly brought several women out to the Dutch ships (Lodewycksz 1598: 133; cf. Empoli 1514: 131). Because of the way Southeast Asian and Chinese junks were built, with numerous tiny cabins both in the hold and on the deck, there was more privacy than on European ships. More, but not enough. Eyeing the stern of the ship where the nakhoda's cabin was located was regarded as an offence against his status, "for if the nakhoda brought his wife or his concubine that would be a serious matter" (*Undang-undang Laut:* 49). Whereas European ships imposed horrendous punishments for sodomy on shipboard, adultery and fornication drew the heaviest penalties on Malay and Javanese vessels. From the different categories of wife or concubine provided for in the *Undang-undang Laut* (32–34), it is clear that even ordinary sailors sometimes took their women on voyages, while both free and slave women also travelled as passengers — perhaps as traders.

In the remuneration of their crews, as in their structure, Southeast Asian junks resembled Chinese ones. Whereas Indian crewmembers received specified salaries (with shares in the hold provided only for the nakhoda, pilot and clerk; Abu'l-Fazl 1596: 291), Southeast Asian and Chinese sailors were primarily traders whose reward lay in their chance to transport goods. The careful accounting of Nina Chetu's two junks did reveal an allowance in rice or money for each category of crew, but this appears only to have been rations—particularly in the case of the slaves. The more substantial allowance for the freemen was that of space in the ship for their trade goods—one *petak* (partition) each for the leading officers and a half a petak for the sailors not categorized as slaves (Thomaz 1966: 194–95; Bouchon 1979: 136).

The division of cargo space into petaks was also central to the way merchants organized their trade. The Maritime Code, confirming the evidence of Tomé Pires and other European observers, makes clear that merchants routinely hired one or more petaks in a ship belonging to another merchant on a basis agreed beforehand. It has an important section on this called *hukum kiwi*, the law of the travelling merchant. This outlines (unfortunately with some ambiguity) four different types of financial relation between the kiwi and the nakhoda, the nakhoda representing the interest of the shipowner (*Undang-undang Laut:* 39). The Malay word *kiwi* is a Chinese loan-word characteristic of the age of commerce that subsequently fell out of use. It was probably borrowed from the Amoy dialect term *kheh-ui* (*kewi* in pinyin), literally passenger-space (Douglas 1873: 125).[4] The Maritime Code uses it for those merchants travelling with the ship and having a share in its cargo. They were totally under the authority of the nakhoda in terms of shipboard discipline, but they had to be consulted when cargo was jettisoned, and their representative (*maula kiwi*, or *mulkiwi*) was regularly consulted on matters that would affect the commercial outcome of the voyage. After reaching port, the nakhoda was entitled to sell first the merchandise for which he was responsible; four days later the kiwis might begin to sell their merchandise, and two days after that the sailors could sell theirs. Kiwis were prohibited from offering better prices than the nakhoda or from purchasing slaves without his knowledge (ibid.: 44).

At least three different commercial arrangements can be discerned from Malay and European sources. The most common was probably that described by Pires (1515: 283–84), whereby the merchant or his agent travelled with the ship, traded his own goods, and bore full risk of shipwreck, paying as rent for his petak a percentage of

---

4. Chen Xiyu of Xiamen University kindly pointed this derivation out to me. The term also occurs in European sources, such as the *Dagh-Register* (1624–29: 130), which gives *quewijs* as the (plural?) term for forty merchants on a 450-tonne Chinese ship. The Kiwi category appears to have disappeared in the Bugis code, where the "passenger-crew" (*sawi manumpang*) had no rights to a petak in the hold but only to carry cargo on deck (Amanna Gappa 1676: 49).

the value of the goods with which he set out: "The owner fits out his junk with everything that is necessary. If you want a petak, or two, you set two or three men to look after it and manage it, and note what you take; and when you come back to Melaka you pay twenty percent on what you put in the junk in Melaka." The Bugis code specifies rates for this service depending on distance. For the shortest sectors within eastern Indonesia the standard charge was 2.5 reals for 100 reals worth of cargo, while for the longest voyages from Sulawesi to Aceh or Cambodia it was 7 reals (Amanna Gappa 1676: 44–46).

Another alternative in the Malay Maritime Code, a type of *commenda* (entrusting) whereby the merchant stayed behind but entrusted goods or capital for the nakhoda to trade with, was also described by Pires (1515: 284) in Melaka: "If I am a merchant in Melaka and give you, the owner of the junk, a hundred cruzados of merchandise at the price then ruling in Melaka, assuming the risk myself, on the return [from Java] they give me a hundred and forty and nothing else, and the payment is made, according to the Melaka ordinance, forty-four days after the arrival of the junk in port." Exactly the same type of commenda was favoured in Banten a century later, where "the merchants who are rich usually stay at home, and . . . they give a sum of money to those who are travelling, on a speculation . . . of which they make an obligation, and if the voyage is speedily concluded the creditor is then paid, according to the contract . . . whereas if the ship is lost, the creditor loses all his money" (Lodewycksz 1598: 120). By trading such merchandise along with his own, the nakhoda could often expect to double its value, but the return to the capitalist and risk-bearer was 40 percent for the Melaka-Java round trip and 50 percent for more profitable journeys to Pegu, Siam, or even Sunda (west Java), where risks and profits were greater because the principal merchandise was slaves.

The first and third types of contract between kiwi and nakhoda in the Maritime Code are less clear but probably cover a fixed charge for renting (literally buying, *membeli petak*) either one petak in the first case or up to eight in the third.

To understand the scale of business conducted by the typical Southeast Asian merchant it would be very helpful to know the size or weight equivalent of a petak. Some of the transverse divisions were no doubt permanent bulkheads. Northern Chinese ships, and some of the "hybrid" wrecks that have been found, were constructed around twelve watertight bulkheads onto which the hull was nailed (Needham 1971: 420). Even though Southeast Asian builders did not usually use such bulkheads as a structural principle, they appear to have

inserted them in their junks. The petaks would then have been variable subdivisions of these permanent watertight bulkheads. The petaks of a Makassarese junk trading to Melaka in 1603, seven of which
were held by four Portuguese passengers, were described as "private
boarded-off places several hands broad" (van Warwijck 1604: 34). Their
number was very likely adjusted for the number of kiwis making a
voyage, as Stavorinus (1798 II: 287) reported of a Chinese junk encountered in Makassar. The allotments of half or full petaks to crew members as provided in the Nina Chetu junks (and implied in the Maritime
Code) would then refer to relative shares, not absolute space entitlements.

Where specific weight entitlements are mentioned in the *Undang-undang Laut* (39, 45) these are surprisingly large. The allowance
of sailors in a standard junk is given as one *koyan*, while one of the
options for kiwis is to take two or three koyan in the (nakhoda's) cargo.
A koyan is roughly 3.5 cubic metres, over 2 tonnes in weight of rice, so
such an allowance of cargo for each sailor would mean that they were
trading on a substantial scale and filling up to a quarter of the ship
with their goods.[5] However, on Chinese junks in the eighteenth century officers and men received much less—900 kg and 420 kg, respectively (Blussé 1986: 110). The Malay koyan allotment, therefore, can
probably best be understood as the entire space for the seaman to sleep
and eat (perhaps with a wife) as well as store trade goods—which is the
impression given by Ibn Battuta (1354: 235–36) and Empoli (1514:
131). The kiwis undoubtedly did fill their petaks with large amounts
of cargo. On one Chinese junk examined in detail by Dutch officials in
1713, sixteen travelling merchants shared 220 tonnes of pepper, eight
of them having 3 tonnes each and the other eight an average of 24
tonnes each. The largest trader carried almost a third of the cargo, 66
tonnes (Blussé 1986: 110).

Van Leur's (1934: 133) image of "a small scale, peddling trade," in
which each merchant had only "a few pieces of silk, a few bags of
pepper," grossly underestimated the sophistication and variety of
Asian trade and the larger quantities of such everyday staples as rice,
vegetables, palm wine, pepper, and sugar it carried. He was right,
however, to emphasize the large numbers of traders who moved about
the waterways below the winds, accompanying their merchandise,
guarding it night and day, and selling it themselves or through their

---

5. Meilink-Roelofsz (1962: 47) drew the opposite conclusion, that the crew's share
was "quite small," by reading Dulaurier's translation of the Code (Dulaurier 1845: 421)
as an allowance of one koyan for the whole crew. This would be a less plausible way to
read the Nina Chetu data, which appear to allow half a petak for each seaman.

womenfolk in a distant marketplace that might be like a second home to them. The movement of people, along with the movement of goods and of ideas, was the leitmotiv of the age of commerce.

Inland Transportation—River and Road

They affirm, and it seems reasonable, that they can go overland from Pegu and Siam to take the pepper and sandalwood to China—on the hinterland side of China—because the people of Pegu and Siam trade with [upper] Burma in lancharas and prahus up the rivers there are in the said kingdoms.

—*Pires 1515: 111*

Inland trade is relatively sparsely documented, but there can be no doubt that it, too, received a great stimulus from the boom in seaborne trade during the age of commerce. Most of the Southeast Asian products in international demand had to be transported from forests or plantations remote from the great emporia where they were shipped. In exchange for these products the cotton cloths of India were carried up rivers and along caravan paths to create a demand even in the upper reaches of the Irrawaddy and the Mekong, while Chinese traders, predominantly Yunnan Muslims, brought their metalware and silks down the same rivers to markets in Southeast Asia (Fitch 1591: 307; Garnier 1870: 277; Forbes 1988). Similarly, the local trade in foodstuffs required that rice, salt, fish, sugar, and other goods be carried from lowlands to highlands and from hinterlands to cities.

One remarkable indication of how deeply Indian cloths had penetrated the interior was the report of two Dutch factors who in 1642 made the arduous journey to Vientiane, the capital of Laos—600 kilometres from the coast. They carefully specified the twenty types of Indian cloth in demand in the Vientiane market. Among the traders they met was a Malay who had frequently made the further journey six days' walk into the mountains behind Vientiane. In that provincial centre, the Dutchmen were told, they could corner all the local gold, benzoin, and gum lac if they returned carrying "fine coloured cloths and white cottons" (Wusthoff 1642: 198 201, Wusthoff 1669: 50).

Carrying goods in the interior was far more difficult than at sea. A calculation made for thirteenth-century Europe is relevant here, that transport costs were twenty times greater by land than by sea (T'ien 1982: 38). Even if the Irrawaddy, the Mekong, and many smaller rivers were navigable for hundreds of kilometres, they could not offer the freedom from political interference of the high seas. Tolls were exacted at numerous points along the roads and waterways, robbery was an even greater danger than at sea, and warfare or political rivalry could make the natural arteries of commerce unusable. King Surinyavongsa of Laos might complain to a Siamese envoy with feigned outrage: "What manner of policy is it not to allow merchants that freedom of trade which was considered normal in the whole world" (Wusthoff 1642: 185); but he knew that the relative predictability with which Laotian trade flowed out through Ayutthaya in the early part of his reign was an exception to the usual pattern among the quarrelling Tai states. Orderly trade along well-maintained roads and across adequate bridges was only to be expected within the domain of a strong ruler. Waterways, too, were often interrupted by tolls and frontiers, though the greatest navigable stretches in themselves facilitated the political unification needed to keep them open.

The navigable section of the Chao Phraya (Menam) River from Phitsanulok to the sea was always the central communications artery for Ayutthaya, as the Red River was for the northern Vietnamese state. In each case the capital marked the point in the river at which ocean-going ships gave way to the long canoes of river travel. The great navigable Y-shape formed by the Tonle Sap River and the 560 kilometres of the Mekong below the Khone Falls formed the natural arteries of Cambodia, whose capital during the age of commerce was always at or near Pnompenh, the major junction of the rivers where ocean-going ships were received. The river states of eastern Sumatra—Palembang, Jambi, Indragiri, and Siak—similarly built their capitals near the transshipment point between ocean-going and river craft. Even in Java, whose waterways have not been navigable in modern times because of deforestation, the Brantas and Solo rivers were the major arteries of trade until the eighteenth century. Long, shallow vessels with eight oars as well as sails took rice and cotton down to the port cities of Gresik, Sedayu, and Surabaya in the high-water season (December–January), bringing back salt and trade goods to the Surakarta area on the Solo River and to Kediri on the Brantas (Schrieke 1942: 112–17; Nagtegaal 1988: 44). The numbers were large. In 1709 a single prince of Mataram was able to send seventy vessels downriver to Gresik to trade (Knaap and Nagtegaal 1991: 130).

The extraordinary navigable length of the Irrawaddy—1400 kilometres from Bhamo to the sea—was too great for any but the strongest of rulers to hold together. The quickening of commerce from the fifteenth century brought unprecedented prosperity to the Mon ports of Bassein, Pegu, Syriam, and Martaban, where the products of Burma and many Tai states were transshipped. From Pegu and Syriam, river vessels of a unique type sailed with the southwest monsoon for the two months it took to reach the Burman heartland centered around Ava (modern Mandalay). The return trip could be done in two or three weeks. These vessels had a large spread of sail, a shallow, rounded bottom, and sides equipped for poling (Ferrars 1900: 133–37; Hall 1927: 31, 57; Hall 1939: 141–42; see fig. 11a). Control of both the flourishing ocean ports and the higher navigable reaches of the Irrawaddy was achieved only exceptionally, notably by mighty King Bayinnaung (1551–81). In the mid-seventeenth century Burmese trade had so deteriorated that foreigners could sail their own ships up the Irrawaddy, but they had to remove their guns and traverse river customs posts where passes were shown.

The Irrawaddy was exceptional in its accessibility to sailing craft. The Mekong, even greater in its length and volume of water, was not sailed significantly above the river junction at Pnompenh. There communication was by long dug-outs poled or paddled in both directions and twenty-metre-long bamboo rafts that carried produce downriver in the wet season, when the numerous rapids were least hazardous. The falls at Khone were an impassable barrier, and therefore a natural frontier between Cambodia and Laos. Here the river trader had to "get out of the boats, and destroy part of them, and travel by carts for three miles; while the mariners struggle for ten days to get the remaining boats through the rapids" (Marini 1663: 446; fig. 11b). The whole route upstream to Vientiane took three months (da Cruz 1569: 78).

After the Jesuit Giovanni-Maria Leria had suffered this arduous route upriver to the Laotian capital in 1642 he proposed to King Surinyavongsa that some dams be built to facilitate river commerce. Eager as the king was to expand the trade and diplomatic contacts of his landlocked kingdom, he valued his security more. "He said that this would give the key of his kingdom to his enemies, and that by this means the door, which was always closed to them in these precipices, would be open to them whenever they pleased" (Marini 1663: 447).

The most substantial stretch of easily navigable river above these falls was the 500 kilometres between modern Savannakhet and Vientiane, and this formed the communications artery for a Lao state and identity to emerge during the age of commerce. Even thus remote from the ocean ports the effect of the commercial boom was tangible. In the 1640s several boats a day came down the river to unload cargo, often carrying merchants from upper Burma or China who had made their journey partly in carts, partly by river (Wusthoff 1642: 203, 218–19). When Siam was disturbed by warfare or blockade, as in the 1550s and again in the 1630s, substantial numbers of Lao merchants used the Mekong route to the sea via Cambodia (da Cruz 1569: 77). Given tolerable conditions of peace, however, the shorter caravan route to

Fig. 11a An Irrawaddy *laung-zat* under full sail, pictured in the late nineteenth century

Fig. 11b A passage of the lowest rapids on the Mekong, during the French expedition of 1866–67

Ayutthaya was preferred. In the 1640s only ten to twelve carts each year made the transit of the Khone falls (Wusthoff 1642: 210), whereas Thai, Lao, and Muslim traders brought forty thousand pieces of Indian cloth each year over the Siamese land route, taking back even greater quantities of deerskins, lacquer, benzoin, musk, and other forest produce. From the southern end of the navigable stretch of the Mekong, at the then-Lao city of Lakon (present-day Nakhon Phanom), another caravan route led ten days' walk through the mountains to the Vietnamese coast at Ky Anh (Wusthoff 1642: 35; Pallu 1668: 34–35; Marini 1669: 260–61, 536). The "golden age" of King Surinyavongsa (1637–94) in Laos, as of many explicitly maritime states, was made possible by the expanding trade demands of the age of commerce.

By road there were essentially three alternatives for transporting goods—men, pack-animals, and carts. The quickest way, and in some hilly areas the only way, was on men's backs. Crawfurd (1820 III: 146) reckoned that there were 5000 professional "itinerant porters" constantly traversing the pathways of Java around 1800. A hardy Shan porter could carry 36 kg about 24 kilometres a day. More frequented long-distance caravan routes used bullocks, ponies, or mules to carry bigger loads more slowly but more cheaply—about 60 kg for a mule and 60–100 kg for a bullock. Slowest of all, but most convenient for the major caravan routes where protection was necessary, were two-wheeled carts pulled by bullocks or buffaloes, carrying between 240 and 360 kg (Wusthoff 1642: 196; Aymonier 1885: 257; Ferrars 1900: 146). These carts were excruciating for passengers, as they lacked springs or boxes and rested the body of the cart directly on a wooden axle fixed to a solid disk of wood for the wheel. French missionaries to Siam and Indo-China usually crossed the Malayan Peninsula from Tenasserim in such carts, and they dreaded this section:

We almost always had to walk on foot, the carts with which we were provided being designed rather to torment travellers than to relieve them. They seemed to be more like coffins than carriages, for these machines at their widest point were no more than three feet, and a little less at the narrowest; we had to fit ourselves into these, and they rested on an axle which passed through two large wheels, which being often thrown off balance by the unevenness of the roads, the cart was no longer pulled by the movement of the wheel, but |dragged| along the edge of the hub. (Bourges 1666: 134; cf. Missions Etrangères 1680A: 165)

Although the usual two-wheeled cart was pulled by two bullocks or buffaloes, there were larger ones pulled by six or eight animals (de Haen 1623, cited Schrieke 1942: 118; Symes 1827 I: 287).

All long-distance caravan routes traversed areas of forest where tigers might prey upon the draft animals, and bandits were a constant danger (see fig. 12). A Jesuit crossing the Peninsula from Tenasserim in 1606 saw one of his travelling companions ripped to pieces by a tiger (du Jarric 1608–14 III: 888). Further south, another missionary believed it impossible to go by foot more than half a league from Junkceylon (Phuket) without life and property being endangered by bandits (Missions Etrangères 1674: 71). Consequently, traders travelled in convoy for protection, whatever their means of transport. The average caravan on the Vientiane-Ayutthaya route was from sixty to a hundred carts (Wusthoff 1642: 196), and the mule-trains from Yunnan seldom had fewer than one hundred pack animals.

The caravans moved in the cool of the morning. In the afternoon the animals were allowed to graze, and then at night they were herded inside a ring formed by the carts in which the travellers slept.

To defend ourselves we built each evening a fortress composed of our carts in a circle, or a triangle; the cattle which towed them and our baggage in the middle. Often we had to fortify our camp with some hedges of thorns; we were not spared the sound of . . . boars, rhinoceros and especially the cruel tigers prowling around. . . . We had our arquebus fired off and made fires all night to keep them away; each person was obliged to stand guard by turn; nevertheless we slept easily at the bottom of our portable tombs. (Bourges 1666: 135–36; cf. Navarrete 1676 II: 383; Marini 1663: 536–37)

Those who had no cart to sleep in built a little palm-leaf tent to protect themselves from the rain, and "you felt the water flowing beneath your back" (Noguettes 1685: 42).

Only roads of great strategic importance to the stronger states were permanently maintained, repaired after each monsoonal downpour, and provided with bridges, way-stations, and security. Descriptions are fullest for the lifeline between the Javanese capital at Mataram and the sea at Japara or Semarang, frequently travelled by Dutch envoys between 1622 and 1648. This was a four-day journey very close to the modern Semarang-Surakarta-Yogyakarta route, with recognized stops where guests of the court were provided with hospitality. During that exceptional half-century, when the Javanese capital had withdrawn far inland but continued to draw much of its wealth from the control of coastal ports, this artery was of enormous strategic value. No expense was spared by Sultan Agung to keep it open to his troops. He built magnificent teak bridges, such as that over the Kali Ketanggi River, a hundred metres long, supported on thick teak beams and topped with teak planks 25–30 centimetres square. The road across this bridge was "capable of carrying a marching army with a thousand elephants and heavy guns" (van Goens 1656: 207; cf. van Milaan 1942).

Such roads to the royal capital had also existed in pre-Muslim Java (Pires 1515: 191), and they were maintained in periods of relatively

Fig. 12 Bandits holding up a Siamese cartman, from a Thonburi temple mural of the nineteenth century

strong government in Burma and Cambodia (Mouhot 1864: 193–95; Garnier 1870: 183). Although they enormously facilitated trade by ox-cart, this was in no sense their purpose. Military calculations were always more important, and roads were maintained or neglected purely in relation to which armies were more likely to make use of them. Stone bridges constructed in northern Vietnam under Chinese rule were destroyed when independence was achieved in 1428 to block another Chinese invasion (Richard 1778 I: 45). The major international overland routes were deliberately neglected by rulers for similar reasons. On such routes traders were usually left to their own devices except when they were levied for frontier tolls. "A caravan route is very easy to create; it requires only three conditions: an initial delineation—simple cutting down of trees when the forest is too dense, and that case is fairly rare [in eastern Siam and Laos]; water at each stage of between twelve and twenty kilometers . . . ; finally, and above everything else, security" (Aymonier 1885: 74).

The routes crossing the Malayan Peninsula between the Bay of Bengal and the Gulf of Thailand were crucial for the long-distance trade. These were slower and more painful than the sea route in most seasons, but nevertheless preferred by those who needed to avoid whoever dominated the Straits of Malacca—notably Indian Muslim traders after the Portuguese capture of Melaka in 1511, but also French missionaries who had to avoid both the Portuguese and the Dutch. The Siamese-controlled route from Mergui and Tenasserim was the most frequented during the age of commerce, but there was also constant traffic between Trang and Nakhon Sithammarat, yet further south between Kedah and Patani, and in the north from the Burmese ports of Martaban, Ye, and Tavoy into the Chao Phraya valley. From Yunnan a variety of caravan routes led over the mountains to northern

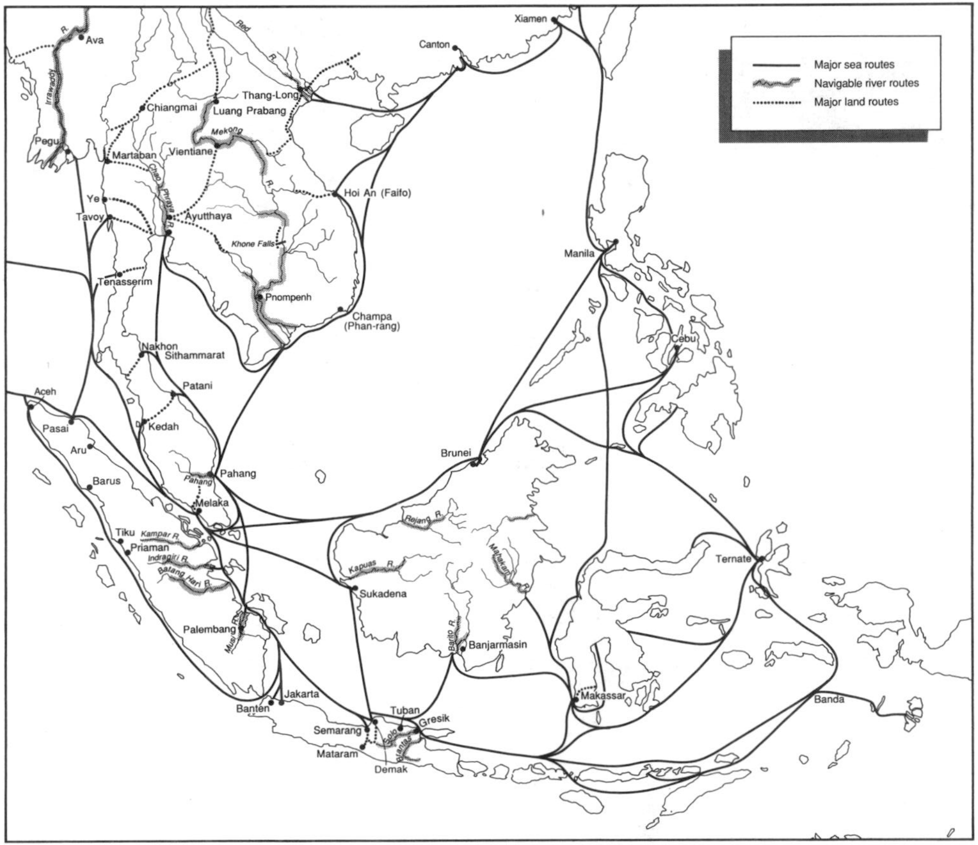

Map 4 Major sea, river, and land routes

Major sea routes
Navigable river routes
Major land routes

Vietnam, the northern Tai centres of Luang Prabang, Vientiane, Nan, Phayao, and Chiengmai, and the northern tributaries of the Irrawaddy. An important caravan route from Bengal and northern Arakan met the Irrawaddy at Sinbyugyun (Symes 1827 I: 303). Laos was dependent on the long haul from Vientiane to Ayutthaya and the shorter but hillier paths from the Mekong valley into Vietnam (map 4).

A man could walk swiftly along these routes. In peacetime a message could be taken overland between the Cambodian and Siamese capitals (more than 600 kilometres) in fifteen days (Missions Etrangères 1674: 139). For the caravans of carts, however, progress was slow and painful. The heavily laden carts on the 600-kilometre route from Vientiane to Ayutthaya "must move in a half-circle around the foot of all the hills, and since they go in great caravans of 60 to 100 carts, if one of them breaks down the whole train is held up; also in the hot sun the buffaloes pull very badly, as well as other obstacles; so that five months is needed for the journey; on the return since they have less heavy loads they do it in three months" (Wusthoff 1642: 196). With bullocks alone the journey took only a month, but since food had to be taken for the animals as well as the people, not much freight could be carried that way.[6] Even the journey of less than 100 kilometres across the Peninsula could take from two weeks to three months, so difficult were the roads in times of flood (Floris 1614: 67; Methold 1619, cited Anderson 1890: 40; Bourges 1666: 126–40; Navarrete 1676 II: 383).

The size of these caravans makes clear that some overland traders, like maritime ones, dealt in large quantities of produce. One Muslim trader had to hire sixty carts to carry to Ayutthaya the benzoin, lacquer, and other goods he had acquired during two years' trading in Vientiane—15–20 tonnes of precious forest products (Wusthoff 1642: 18). As with the junk trade, some large merchants stayed home and consigned their goods to the chief of the caravan, whose role was analogous to that of the nakhoda at sea. For the Vientiane-Ayutthaya run they charged the equivalent of 37 guilders (15 reals) per cartload, "and often more" (ibid.: 196).

The difficulties of such trade were such that water routes were taken wherever possible. If Southeast Asia was highly favoured by nature for maritime trade, the opposite was true by land, where thick forests, abundant rainfall, and turbulent rivers made roads extremely difficult to maintain. It was the sea trade which created the age of commerce; the caravan trade flourished as a consequence.

6. In the nineteenth century this route was broken at the great market of Khorat, with carts doing the flat Vientiane-Khorat sector in fifteen days, and pack-oxen the hilly and forested sector from Khorat to the Chao Phraya valley in a further fifteen (Aymonier 1885: 257, 271).

2

The City and Its Commerce

Everywhere, markets among the houses, like an immense fresco,
No end of busy quarters, where purple jostles vermilion . . . .
Indeed it is
A rich, wonderful, royal city.
　　　　　　　　　　　　—Nguyen Gian Thanh 1508, on Thang-long

The age of commerce was a period of sustained urban growth. The fifteenth century marked a decisive shift in power to trade-based cities at the expense of older capitals that had owed more to tribute in labour and agricultural produce. Ayutthaya, enjoying extensive trade and diplomatic relations through its control of the Chao Phraya River, destroyed the ancient capital of Angkor in 1432, and the city of temples was abandoned. When a Cambodian capital was re-established it was based no longer around the elaborate old irrigation works but at a major entrepôt for Chinese and Japanese trade at the junction of the Tonle Sap and Mekong rivers near modern Pnompenh.

In Burma and Java the "long sixteenth century" marked the only period before the twentieth century when coastal ports played the dominant political and cultural role. The Mon port-city of Pegu flourished throughout the fifteenth century, attracting traders and embellishing itself with Buddhist monuments, while the interior of the country was in chaos. In 1539 an expansionist Burmese dynasty seized control of the city from the Mons and used its wealth to unite the whole Irrawaddy valley. Between 1555 and 1599 Pegu was the wealthy capital of an empire embracing all the Burmans and Mons (as well as many of the Tai). In Java the battle between the Muslim cities of the north coast and the Hindu kingdom of Majapahit was a long one, with the Hindu capital retreating progressively eastwards. Trade wealth and military technology gave the upper hand throughout the sixteenth century to such coastal cities as Demak, Japara, Tuban, Gresik, and Surabaya.

There is only one exception to this pattern whereby the trade boom gave the initiative to a new type of cosmopolitan, commercial city. In Vietnam the fifteenth century was a brilliant period of national liberation and consolidation under the Le dynasty, which expanded and embellished the capital at Thang-long (modern Hanoi). The ideological basis for reorganizing the state, however, was a Confucianism that distrusted commerce and emphasized agriculture as the only sound basis for the state. Le Thanh Tong (1460–97), greatest of the Le kings, used the slogan "Concentrate all our forces on agriculture, expand our potential" (cited Nguyen 1987: 87), and the Confucian saying "Emphasize agriculture, commerce is peripheral" (*Trong nong mat thu'o'ng*) became popular. Although Vietnamese ceramic exports appear to have peaked in the late fourteenth century, they declined by the end of the following century as Vietnam presented a face by turns hostile or disinterested towards the rising current of external trade. Foreign merchants were frequently turned away and always subject to scrutiny of every item on board. The best items were seized by rapacious mandarins in the name of the king. When the English protested about such treatment in 1672, they were told that "the King was King of Tongking before we came and would be after we were gone, and that his country had no need of any foreign thing" (cited Farrington 1992).

(Northern) Vietnam could succeed in this path because it was already a populous and largely self-sufficient country more remote than other Southeast Asian states from the main routes of international commerce. Its military successes at the expense of the maritime kingdom of Champa, notably in 1471, however, gave Vietnamese access to a coastline that had played a central role in Asian trade for a millennium or more. Hardly had the new Vietnamese colonists established themselves in the Thuan Hoa and Quang Nam areas than fighting broke out between south and north, and by 1600 the breach had become irrevocable. Dynastic and personal factors played a part in this (see chapter 4), but it is impossible to ignore the very different attitude of the southern kingdom to trade. It was recorded of Nguyen Hoang, the eventual founder of a new southern dynasty, when he was first sent as governor of the wealthy southern provinces in 1558, that "he ruled with geniality, seaborne merchants favoured him. . . . Seaborne merchants from foreign kingdoms all came to buy and sell, a trading city was established" (cited Taylor 1993: 49). This city was Hoi An (Faifo to Europeans), where Japanese and Chinese flocked to trade with each other and the Vietnamese—the window to the world for the Nguyen kingdom known to Westerners as Cochin-China. Nguyen Hoang himself supported the trade by writing to some of the Japanese merchants who conducted it, though he was enough of a Confucian to protest that his domain was "a land of poetry, history, good manners, and justice, not a land crowded with traders and merchandise" (Fujiwara Seika: 348).

Port-Cities and the Trade Network

> Melaka is a city that was made for merchandise, fitter than any other in the world; the end of monsoons and the beginning of others. Melaka is surrounded and lies in the middle, and the trade and commerce between the different nations for a thousand leagues on every hand must come to Melaka.
>
> —Pires 1515: 286

Musim—the Malay term means seasonality itself, any annually repeating phenomenon, of which the seasonal winds that determined the rains were but the most important. Europeans adopted it as *monsoon* to describe the extraordinary regularity they discovered in the winds of tropical Asia. From April to August the monsoon winds blow dependably northwards towards the Asian land mass; from December to March they blow equally dependably southward, from the land masses into the Indian Ocean and South China Sea. It was this predictability that determined the pattern of Asian maritime trade. Shipowners sought to minimize the risky period at sea by making long journeys at times of good following winds and to return within the year on the opposite monsoon. For this reason ships were not well equipped for manoeuvring and tacking close to the wind.

Chinese, Japanese, and Ryukyuan ships sailing south to the Nanyang always used the northern monsoon in January or February and returned home when the wind was from the south in June, July, or August. South Indian ships found the southwest monsoon of the Indian Ocean between April and August the most dependable way to sail eastwards. They could return with the same monsoon after a short stay, but most stayed to trade "below the winds" until at least December, avoiding the cyclone-prone change of monsoons in October and returning with the northeast monsoon (Arasaratnam 1986: 34–37). Gujarati vessels had a longer, more difficult voyage to Southeast Asia. The southwest monsoon was the best for sailing to Sumatra or Malaya, but ships had either to leave home in March before these winds closed the Indian ports or to wait until August or September when they opened again. Gujaratis were usually away for at least a year, making sure that they were in a Southeast Asian market for the arrival of the Chinese ships in January or February.

This seasonality of voyaging ensured that entrepôts arose in Southeast Asia where traders could await the change of monsoon or the arrival of trading partners. Although individual traders, with their goods, might be away for several years, changing ship for each of the sectors between Cairo and Canton, Asian ships in the age of commerce did not make such long voyages. Their owners were eager to see them back in the home port on the following monsoon. During the months their crews and passengers were in the ports of Southeast Asia they populated whole quarters of the city, enlivened its markets, and took part in its ritual occasions.

The major entrepôts below the winds were necessarily located at the intersection of these monsoonal trading sectors, in the sheltered waters of the Andaman Sea, the Gulf of Thailand, and the Java Sea, but especially the Straits of Malacca. Funan (with its great port of Oc Eo in the Mekong Delta), Champa, and Sri Vijaya successively played this role in the first thousand years for which there are inscriptions and Chinese records. The latter two were Austronesian in language and therefore prepared the way for the dominance of Malay as trade language of the age of commerce. In the fifteenth century Pasai (northern Sumatra) and Melaka became the key entrepôts, and the relative security they brought to the Straits reduced the need for the difficult portage across the Malayan Peninsula. The Portuguese conquest of Melaka in 1511, and Portugal's subsequent attempts to control passage of the Straits, drove trade to alternative routes, by caravan across the Peninsula or down the west coast of Sumatra to the Sunda Straits. This shift gave birth to new entrepôts or stimulated old ones at Aceh, Tenasserim, Ayutthaya, Patani, Pahang, Johor, and Banten. Manila, Makassar, Brunei, Cambodia, Champa, and the seventeenth-century Nguyen port of Hoi An were too far east for Indian ships but became major entrepôts for trade between Chinese, Japanese, Southeast Asian, and European shippers. After a very pluralistic century and a half, Dutch Batavia began by about 1650 to assume as dominant a role in the inter-Asian trade as Melaka's had been in 1500.

If the location of these ports was determined largely by the needs of foreign traders, they quickly developed their own parallel home-based shipping. The trade voyages of the Malay epic hero Hang Tuah from Melaka to South India and South China were not invention; the Portuguese also noted that such longer voyages were equipped each year in Melaka—"Melaka sends junks out, and others come in" (Pires 1515: 285; cf. ibid.: 93; Thomaz 1986: 13). When he was in Calicut (Malabar, South India) in about 1504, Ludovico di Varthema (1510: 151) encountered among the diverse merchants there "some from Pegu . . . and a great quantity from Sumatra [Pasai]". In the second half of the sixteenth century, merchants based in Aceh were sending their pepper-laden vessels all the way to the Red Sea, and as late as 1620 the sultan had a very large ship built to continue this trade (Coen 1621: 607; Boxer 1969: 418–24). Indian-style ships "belonging to Malays" in Aceh were reported as returning from voyages to southern India in the 1630s (Compostel 1636: f.1198). In the middle of the century the kings of Aceh, Ayutthaya, Banten, and Makassar sent their ships as far as Manila, Japan, and south India.

Tribute missions to China provided a training-ground for Southeast Asian seamen on the run to Canton. No doubt locally domiciled Chinese were always involved in these missions, since a knowledge of the language and procedures of China was essential. Some envoys were simply sent on returning Chinese ships, but the commercial advantages of these voyages persuaded most states to send their own ships to Canton with local trade goods and a mixed crew. That growing numbers of non-Chinese did reach not only Canton but Beijing is attested by Chinese attention to Southeast Asian languages in the official translation office (Ssu-i-kuan) at the capital, where a special Thai section was created in 1579 (Ishii 1989: 3).

The seasonal flow of ships across each sector of the Asian trade routes therefore included ships based at both ends of the sector. Of Melaka it was estimated that of the hundred ocean-going junks in port at the peak season, at least thirty belonged to the ruler and merchants of that city, the others being based in India, China, Pegu, Java, and elsewhere (Araujo 1510: 22). That all major Southeast Asian ports were active players in the international trade, however, does not mean that all major nations or ethnicities were. Such ethnic labels as Malay, Minangkabau, Javanese, Cham, Luzon, Pegu, and Chinese were most commonly applied to the Southeast Asian trading class, as discussed below. Here it is important to understand that the Southeast Asian trading city was a pluralistic meeting-point of peoples from all over maritime Asia.

The Dutch described the mix of merchants who greeted them in Banten in 1596 as follows:

The Persians, who are called Khorasans in Java, are those who usually earn their living in [precious] stones and medicines.... The Arabs and Pegus are the ones who mostly conduct their trade by sea, carrying and bringing merchandise from one city to another, and buying up much Chinese merchandise, which they exchange against other wares from the surrounding islands, and also pepper, against the time when the Chinese return to buy. The Malays and Klings [South Indians] are merchants who invest money at interest and in voyages and bottomry. The Gujaratis, since they are poor, are usually used as sailors, and are those who take money in bottomry, on which they often make one, two, and three times profit. (Lodewycksz 1598: 120–21)

If the long-distance trade from China, India, and the Malukan spiceries brought these multitudes together, it in turn evoked an even busier local trade in supplying the port-cities with foodstuffs, building materials, and local trade items. Most shipping movements were by small Southeast Asian craft bringing rice, vegetables, dried fish, livestock, palm wine, sugar, and salt to feed the urban areas and cash-cropping centres, moving local metalware, ceramics, and cloth from producers to consumers, collecting export items, and redistributing imports. Those who serviced the extensive maritime network within the calm seas of Southeast Asia were overwhelmingly locally domiciled. They formed the sinews that linked the cities to their watery hinterlands and carried ideas and people as well as cargoes back and forth.

Urban Dimensions

When the first modern censuses were taken around 1900, the colonized countries of Southeast Asia were among the least urban in the world.[1] It is often assumed that the rapid urban growth since independence is a new development in a "traditionally" rural region. The evidence is growing, however, that colonialism itself was the major reason so few Southeast Asians lived in cities in the century before 1940. Peter Boomgaard (1989: 111) has pointed out that in Java, where the colonial impact was heaviest, the proportion of people living in towns of more than twenty thousand inhabitants declined during the nineteenth century, from about 7 percent in 1815 to 3 percent in 1890.

1. In 1960, after extensive flight to the cities during the turbulent 1940s, Southeast Asia was still calculated as only 17.6 percent urban as against 21.5 percent for Asia as a whole and 60 percent for developed countries (U.N. Centre for Human Settlements 1987: 53).

The reason was that European colonial cities were compact islands that dominated the commerce of the region without encouraging (or sometimes even allowing) Asians to migrate towards them to share in their wealth. When major commercial centres remained under Asian control they attracted large numbers of aristocratic and court retainers, foreign commercial minorities, religious students, peddlers, craftworkers, and labourers. The areas that escaped colonialism longest demonstrate the point. Bangkok had 10 percent of Thailand's total population at the 1909 census and probably not much less throughout the nineteenth century, despite its then modest commerce (from Skinner 1957: 68–87). The Burmese capital (at Amerapura, but embracing Sagaing across the river) had 10 percent of the Burmese population at the 1783 enumeration, and 13 percent in 1802 (Koenig 1990: 59). Colonial cities were far smaller than the Asian centres whose economic functions they usurped. Dutch Batavia did not pass the old Javanese capitals of Yogyakarta and Surakarta in population until the nineteenth century, and Rangoon was only fractionally larger than the old Burmese capital (then at Mandalay) in the census of 1891, long after the British centre had assumed commercial and political dominance of the country. Mandalay, then 170,000, declined under the British to 135,000 in 1931.

Until the seventeenth century, Asian cities were in general bigger than European ones, with both Beijing and Edo (Tokyo) having a million inhabitants around 1600. Skinner (1977: 28–30) has shown for China, Smith (1988: 17–18) for Japan, and Habib (1982: 167–71) and Bayly (1983: 112–13) for India that there was a marked decline in the dominance of the larger population centres between the seventeenth and nineteenth centuries. In Southeast Asia, which suffered earlier and more directly from European commercial hegemony, it would not be surprising to find that cities were bigger in 1600 than in 1850.

There are no reliable pre-modern enumerations of urban population except for the European enclaves. Estimates were frequently made by visitors, based either on their rough count of houses or on the claims of local authorities about the fighting men who could be levied from the city and its suburbs. In addition we can often trace the physical dimensions occupied by cities at their peak, which gives a useful control on the reliability of the estimates.

Table 6. Estimates of sixteenth-century city populations

		Estimate	Equivalent population[a]
Ayutthaya	1540s	400,000 houses (Pinto 1578: 420)	2,600,000
	1545	10,050 houses burned (Luang Prasoet: 10)	>100,000
Pegu	1540s	400,000 houses (Pinto 1578: 362)	2,600,000
	1596	150,000 "men"[b] (du Jarric 1608 I: 624)	600,000
Melaka	1510	10,000 houses (Araujo 1510: 21)	65,000
		4000 fighting men (ibid.: 21)	16,000
		30,000 houses (Castanheda)[c]	195,000
		10 times Pasai (Pires 1515: 144)	200,000
		100,000 people (Albuquerque 1557: 84)	100,000
		20,000 fighting men (ibid.: 99)	80,000
		200,000 at maximum season (Correia: 284)[c]	<200,000
		190,000 (Sejarah Melayu 1612: 181; 1831: 247)	190,000
		90,000 in city alone (Sejarah Melayu 1612: 180)	90,000
Pasai	1512	20,000 inhabitants (Pires 1515: 143)	20,000
	1518	3000 guards (Barros 1563 III, v: 522–23)	>12,000
Brunei	1521	25,000 houses (Pigafetta 1524: 58)	162,000
		20,000 houses (Maximilian 1522: 301)	130,000
	1579	4–5000 captured (de Sande 1579: 126)	>18,000
	1580s	8000 tribute-payers (Dasmarinas 1590B)	32,000
Demak	1512	8–10,000 houses (Pires 1515: 184)	58,500
		30,000 fighting men (ibid.: 185)	120,000
Gresik	1512	6–7000 "men" (ibid.: 194)	>25,000

Notes:
[a]In tables 6 and 7 this final column is derived by using a factor of 6.5 to convert houses and a factor of 4 to convert fighting men. A census of Dutch Melaka in 1679 gave a population of 4884 living in "150 brick and 583 atap [thatch] houses," that is, 6.7 per house, as well as 219 servants of the Dutch Company at 4.6 per house (van Goens 1679: 281). Asian cities would probably have had a higher ration of people per "house," since there were large aristocratic compounds, as well as the royal citadel itself, which contained many people.
[b]This remarkable figure purports to be the men defending the city during a siege, and therefore may not be intended to reflect the normal population
[c]I owe these references to Thomaz 1993: 71n

Of the sixteenth-century population estimates given in table 6, only Pinto's are entirely unbelievable. He ought to be understood as saying that Ayutthaya and Pegu were very large cities. Elsewhere Pinto (1578: 218) provided a list of eighteen great Asian capitals all dwarfed by Beijing. Eight were Southeast Asian: Demak and Pasuruan in Java; Pegu, Ava, and Martaban in Burma; "Uzangué" in Vietnam; and Ayutthaya and Luang Prabang. Doubt has also been cast on the Magellan expedition's estimate for the size of Brunei. We may accept that before its sack by the Spanish in 1579 it was bigger than for three centuries thereafter, as the then centre of the trade of Borneo and the Philippines, but its physical dimensions do not appear to justify a population greater than fifty thousand. For Melaka, in contrast, there are too many corroborating estimates to be dismissed, and its commerce, rice imports, and physical dimensions all confirm them. The Malay written tradition is that there was unbroken habitation all the way along the coast from north of Melaka to the Muar River—about 45 kilometres (*Sejarah Melayu* 1612: 181; 1831: 247).

Although there are no sixteenth-century estimates for the Vietnamese capital of Thang-long (Hanoi), physical evidence as well as tradition point to the city's slow decline from a peak in the late fifteenth century. Since it was still very large in the seventeenth century, it would have been the largest Southeast Asian city of the sixteenth century, with well over 100,000 inhabitants. Ayutthaya (before its devastation by the Burmese in 1567) and Pegu would also have been in the 100,000 class, as would Melaka in the relatively short period (roughly 1470–1511) during which it was the dominant Southeast Asian entrepôt. Demak, then the major port-city of Java, may have had 60–80,000 inhabitants at this time, but Brunei, Gresik, and Pasai were probably nearer half that. For such inland cities as Ava, Luang Prabang, Vientiane, and Chiengmai it is difficult to make an estimate in this period.

The commercial peak of the period 1570–1630 undoubtedly brought a substantial increase in urbanization, with some established cities growing and new ones appearing (table 7). A useful check on the extremely variable estimates available for the seventeenth century is provided by the physical dimensions of these cities, where they can be deduced from contemporary description combined with modern archaeology (table 8). In most cases there was a well-defined royal citadel, the walls of which can be traced in modern times, surrounded by a less clear-cut area of suburbs, where the foreign commercial communities were located, along with people drifting in from the countryside, and often the compounds of leading nobles. In Siam and Burma the

Table 7. Estimates of seventeenth-century city populations

		Estimate	Equivalent population
Thang-long	1640	"as much as one million" (Rhodes 1651: 26)	1,000,000
	1688	20,000 houses (Dampier 1699: 36)	130,000
Kim-long	1674	150,000 (de Courtelin, in Nguyen 1970: 120)	150,000
Hue	1749	60,000 (Poivre 1750: 97)	60,000
Pnompenh	1606	20,000 houses (Jaque, in Groslier 1958: 152)	130,000
Sithor	1600	"more than 50,000" (San Antonio 1604: 95)	>50,000
Ayutthaya	1617	"as big as London" (Anderson 1890: 69)	200,000
	1681	10,000 children per annum die (Noguettes 1685: 71)	>200,000
	1686	200,000 (Tachard 1688: 190)	200,000
	1687	60,000 fighting men (Gervaise 1688: 47)	240,000
		16,000 foreigners (La Loubère 1691: 112)	>30,000
Ava	1688	"as big as Rheims" (Goüye 1692: 73)	30,000
Syriam	1688	"as big as Metz" (ibid.: 73)	25,000
Prome	1688	"as big as Syriam" (ibid.: 73)	25,000
Pagan	1688	"as big as Dijon" (ibid.: 73)	30,000
Patani	1602	4–5000 men in procession (van Neck 1604: 226)	20,000
	1690	10–20,000 people (Tosen 1690 in Ishii forthcoming)	15,000
Pahang	1618	11,000 carried off by Aceh (van den Broecke 1634 I: 177)	>12,000
Johor	1604	4000 fighting men (Mandelslo 1662: 108)	16,000

Table 7. (*continued*)

Brunei	1608	2–3000 houses on water (van Noort 1601: 202)	16,200
Aceh	1602	7–800 houses burned (Lancaster 1603: 133)	>10,000
	1621	40,000 fighting men (Beaulieu 1666: 106)	160,000
	1688	7–8000 houses (Dampier 1699: 90)	>48,700
Pagarruyung	1684	8000 men at court alone (Dias 1684: 355)	32,000
Banten	1672	"more than 100,000" (Missions Etrangères 1680: 90)	>100,000
	1673	55,000 fighting men (VOC, in Guillot 1989: 150)	220,000
	1674	200,000 fighting men (Cortemünde 1675: 122)	800,000
	1684	700,000 (Fryke 1692: 80)	700,000
	1696	"31,848 men of Surasowan" (Pigeaud 1968: 64)	125,000
Jakarta	1596	3000 houses (Lodewycksz 1598: 163)	20,000
	1606	4000 fighting men (Matelief 1608: 53)	16,000
	1618	6–7000 fighting men (van den Broecke 1634 I: 187)	26,000
Mataram	1624	200,000 fighting men (de Haen 1623: 35)	800,000
Semarang	1654	100,000 (van Goens 1656: 205)	100,000
Japara	1654	100,000 (van Goens 1656: 268)	100,000
Tuban	1600	32–33,500 fighting men ("Tweede Boeck" 1601: 184)	130,000
Surabaya	1625	50–60,000 (VOC, in Meilink-Roelofsz 1962: 270)	>50,000
Makassar	1614	1260 houses burned (EIC, G/10/1: 5)	>20,000
	1615	16,000 fighting men (EIC, G/10/1: 9)	64,000
	1636	60,000 died from plague (EIC, G/10/1: 73)	>100,000
	1660	160,000 fighting men (Gervaise 1701: 60)	640,000

walled city probably accounted for half or more of the city's population, whereas in the Archipelago there was often no wall except around the royal citadel (*kraton* or *kota*). Vietnam and Laos had both an inner royal citadel and an outer wall embracing virtually the whole populated area.

Deriving population estimates from the area settled is hazardous because of the irregular nature of settlement. Often houses adjacent to the foreshore, port area, market, and major religious buildings were tightly packed, while elsewhere the population was spread in almost-contiguous villages rather than in a well-defined urban area. The more congested localities may have had on the order of three thousand houses (or about twenty thousand people) per square kilometre, whereas the total urban areas would have had no more than half this density.[2]

When this evidence of approximate size is combined with contemporary estimates of population, the conclusion becomes firmer that the largest cities were Thang-long, Ayutthaya, and Mataram, amounting in the mid-seventeenth century to about 150,000–200,000 people (as Pegu may have done before its destruction in 1599). Aceh, Makassar, Banten, and the Cochin-China capital of Kim-long probably formed the next tier of cities at their peak in mid-century, with close to 100,000 people. The other cities of the Javanese north coast fluctuated rapidly in fortune in the course of the century, but Tuban and Surabaya for a time probably reached 50,000. Mrauk-u (the Arakan capital), Patani, Vientiane, and Pnompenh would also have been in the category between 20,000 and 50,000, and probably nearer the larger figure. The return of the Burmese capital to Ava in 1634 caused this city to grow steadily, and it may have reached 50,000 by 1700. These were probably the thirteen biggest indigenous cities.

The European enclaves had extensive commerce and a core of solid stone buildings, but they were never the biggest cities. Batavia grew to about 30,000 both inside and outside the walls in 1630 and a peak of 130,000 in 1670 (Hageman 1859: 364; Blussé 1986: 84–85). Manila was about 40,000 at the peak of its prosperity in 1630 (Phelan 1959: 178). Melaka had some 12,000 citizens when it was the Por-

2. Jourdain (1617: 293) acquired a foreshore block "forty fathoms square" in Makassar with twenty houses on it, which would work out to 267 m² per house, or 3750 houses per km². In contrast, modern censuses (relating to administrative categories, not built-up areas) give urban densities of 5000–10,000 per km². According to the Census of Netherlands India of 1930, the most "Indonesian" cities, Yogyakarta and Surakarta, had densities of about 6300 houses per km².

Table 8. Approximate size of seventeenth-century urban areas

	Citadel or walled area (km²)	Approximate urban area (km²)	Source
Thang-long	0.4	5.6 × 4 = 22	Hanoi 1977: 40–46 and maps
Vientiane	0.3	4 × 0.8 = 3.2	Lajonquière 1901: 100–01
Chiengmai	3.8	5	Wijeyewardene 1985: 86; 1986: 6
Ayutthaya	3.6 × 2 = 7.2	15	Sternstein 1965
Pegu, 16th c.	5.8[a]	15	Symes 1827 I: 214; Frederici 1581: 244–45
Mrauk-u	0.4	7	Collis 1943: 174–75
Patani	0.1	5 × 0.4 = 2[b]	Welch and McNeill 1989: 38; Bougas 1988: 15–16
Aceh	0.2	12	ENI 1893–1905 II: 321
Banten	1.0	5	Scott 1606: 169; Guillot 1989
Mataram	0.4	7.5 × 5.5 = 41[c]	van Goens 1656: 66, 212–15; Nurhadi and Armeini 1978: 17
Makassar	0.8 + 0.8 + 0.2[d]	10 × 0.6 = 6	Reid 1983: 140–50; Bulbeck 1992: 351–72

Notes: [a]This is my estimate of Bayinnaung's new citadel, which was the royal centre in 1566–99, while the older walled city of Pegu was given over to commerce and had extensive suburbs

[b]Welch and McNeill identified an area of dense potsherd remains only 90 ha in extent, but their description of the site, like that of Bougas, shows a larger area spread along 5 km of coast. I have opted for the larger estimate, assuming that smaller pockets within this area were intensively occupied over a longer period but that the whole beach-ridge area was occupied during the half-century after 1590, when the city flourished—when the Hikayat Patani (113) noted that a cat could walk along the roofs of houses without coming down for a distance of about 2.5 km, and when van Neck (1604: 222) thought it extended along the coast for half a German mile.

[c]Van Goens' map of Mataram shows an unusually spread-out city, following the successive moves of the kraton (citadel) from Kuta Gede to Kerta to Plered

[d]Makassar was a complex city and state, with three fortified royal centres: Gowa, Tallo', and Sombaopu

tuguese headquarters before 1641 (Mandelslo 1662: 106) but had only 5000 under the Dutch thereafter.

To total the population of these cities is even more hazardous than estimating their size, since they peaked at different periods, sometimes at the expense of one another. Even a conservative addition, however, would give a total of more than a million people in cities of more than 30,000 population around the middle of the seventeenth century. About 5 percent of the total Southeast Asian population would therefore have inhabited large cities, a proportion larger than contemporary northern Europe (de Vries 1976: 154), though probably not as great as Mughal India or China (Habib 1982: 169; Skinner 1977: 28).

The smaller cities and regional centres are still harder to quantify. Given the estimates we have and what we know of the economic and political functions of cities for which there are no estimates, one can say little more than that the following cities would probably have exceeded 10,000 (map 5): Prome, Pagan, Toungoo, Syriam (near Rangoon), Tavoy, and Martaban in Burma;[3] Tenasserim, Chiengmai, Lopburi, and Nakhon Sithammarat (Ligor) in Siam; Luang Prabang in northern Laos; the Cambodian royal capital at Lovek; the Cochin-China port of Hoi An; Johor and Pahang (until sacked by Aceh in 1618) in the Malayan Peninsula; Palembang, Jambi, and the Minangkabau capital at Pagarruyung in Sumatra; Banjarmasin and Brunei in Borneo; Japara, Semarang, and Balambangan in Java; the Balinese capital at Gelgel; and the Magindanao capital of Sinoay (said to have had 36,500 men on call in 1690; Laarhoven 1989: 112).

If the percentage of city dwellers was relatively high for the whole region, it was spectacularly so for the most highly commercialized areas surrounding the Straits of Malacca. In the entire Malayan Peninsula it is difficult to envisage a population much above half a million, since it was no greater than that in the early nineteenth century (Reid 1987). This means that Melaka alone, a trade emporium with no agricultural hinterland, must have had at least 20 percent of the Peninsula's population around 1500, and Patani, Pahang, Johor, and Portuguese Melaka together a similar proportion in 1600. Kedah, which became a significant minor port in the early eighteenth century, was

3. Seventeenth-century Burma had four categories of town above village level, of which the smallest was reckoned to send between 100 and 1000 men to war, and to dominate an area of 10-km radius. All the cities listed here fell into the biggest category, the provincial capitals, reckoned each to dominate an area of 100 *taing* (c.320 km) radius (Than Tun 1983: 72–73).

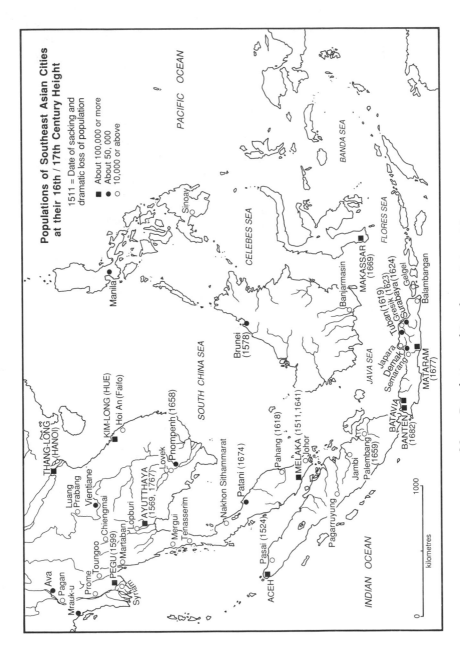

Map 5 Populations of Southeast Asian cities

then reckoned to have a population of 7000–8000 in the city against only 20,000 in the whole country (Taillandier 1711: 409). The cities of Aceh, Banten, and Brunei at their respective peaks probably also embraced at least a fifth of the population under their control.

A relatively high degree of urbanization for the time was made possible by the bounty of Southeast Asia's environment on three grounds. First (a factor shared with all of monsoon Asia), it was easier with modest technology to provide a large marketable surplus of rice than of wheat and meat. Second, all the urban centres except Mataram (like Ava and Thang-long at the centre of a rich rice-growing area) were easily accessible by water, a far more efficient means of provisioning than the cart tracks of the great land masses. And third, trade played a relatively large role within the overall economy of most parts of the region. The port-cities were not parasites having to exact a surplus from a reluctant hinterland; they drew the greater part of their wealth from trade and paid for their food on the open market.

According to early seventeenth-century estimates, Patani was dependent on seaborne imports for more than half its rice needs, and Banten for three quarters (Scott 1606: 136; Terpstra 1938: 163). Melaka before the Portuguese conquest was even more dependent. It was served by about forty-five rice ships each year from Burma, thirty from Siam, and fifty to sixty from Java, as well as many from Coromandel (Araujo 1510: 28; Empoli 1514: 155; Pires 1515: 98, 107). Although the size of such ships varied greatly, an average of 50 tonnes per vessel is probably a minimum estimate, giving about 7000 tonnes a year of rice imports from the more long-distance suppliers alone. This would have been enough to feed more than 50,000 city-dwellers. Aceh in the 1680s, after its prime, could still have ten ships in the harbour laden with rice from India, and individual retailers of imported rice in the market could make as much as 80 pounds sterling a day (equivalent to a sale of 3500 kg rice; Dampier 1699: 94).

The Structure of the Southeast Asian City

> *Sunan Gunung Jati instructed his son to build a city on the coast, and indicated where the palace* [dalem], *the market, and the central square* [alun-alun] *each had to be.*
> —Sadjarah Banten, *summarized by Djajadiningrat 1913: 34*

As a creation of the age of commerce, Banten embodied the contradictions of the period. Built against the sea to take advantage of shipping, it grew rapidly as a cosmopolitan metropolis in which all

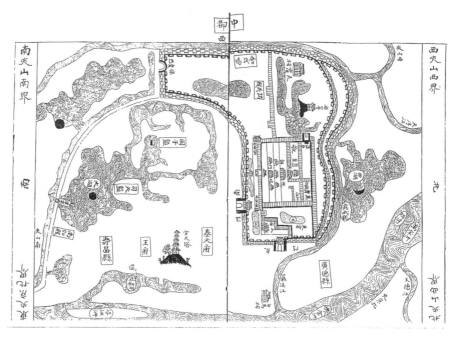

Fig. 13a A Vietnamese plan of Thang-long (Hanoi) traditionally dated 1490, though perhaps later. North is at right, the Red River at bottom, and the royal "forbidden city" is shown inside the citadel. The larger populated area was protected by outer earthern walls and canals.

traders were welcome and the uncontrolled agglomeration of compounds, ditches, lanes, and markets defied all order. Nevertheless, it was heir to an Indic tradition in which the grandeur and layout of the central buildings reflected the cosmic pretensions of its monarch. Braudel (1967: 384–95) has suggested a dichotomy between the chessboard cities of East and South Asia and the congested disorder found in medieval Europe and in Islamic cities "from Gibraltar to the Sunda Islands." This contradiction penetrated the whole of Southeast Asia. It was not simply that Mainland cities were more ordered than Archipelago ones or inland imperial capitals more ordered than flourishing ports. All cities had some degree of cosmic order at their core, which always risked being completely overwhelmed by the chaotic influx of people attracted at times of prosperity.

In Buddhist kingdoms where the concept of city as a distinct walled space was relatively developed, this central, planned area might occupy the whole walled city, several square kilometres in extent. In the Archipelago only the royal citadel and adjacent public buildings

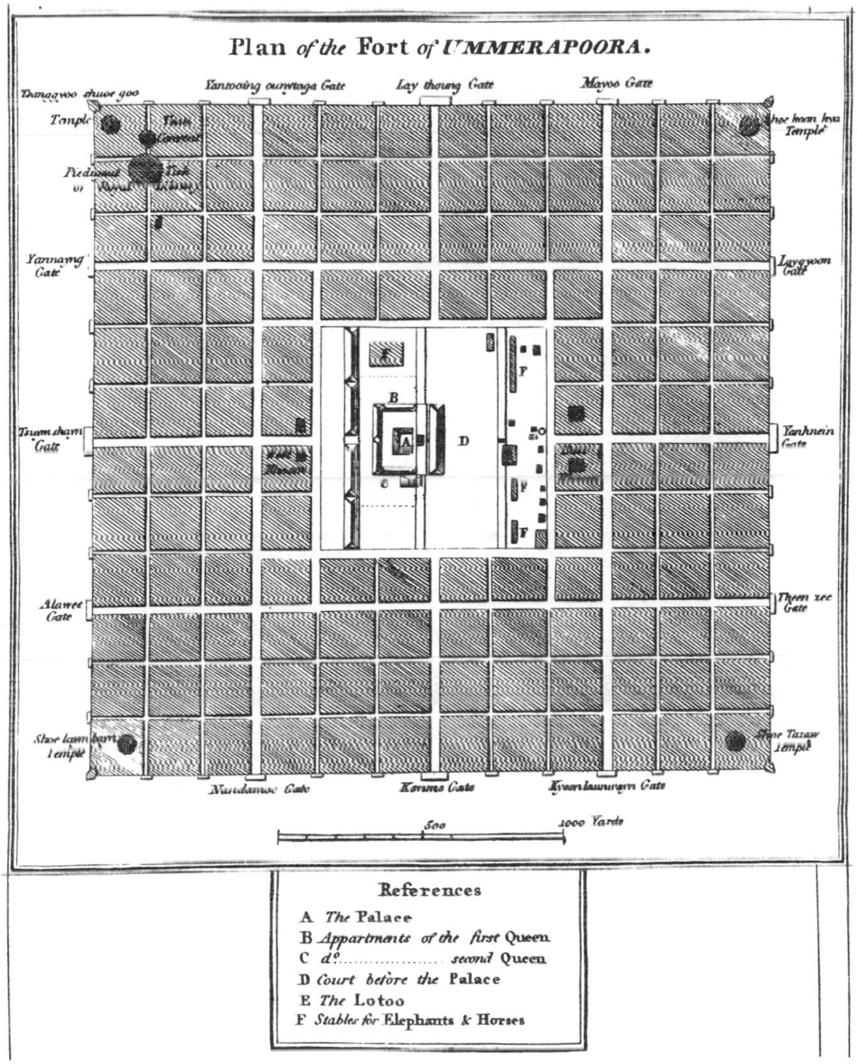

Fig. 13b The citadel of Amerapura, the Burmese capital, in 1795. It bore a similar regular pattern to the capital built by Bayinnaung at Pegu, but on a 4 x 4 rather than a 6 x 6 pattern.

were truly planned, while outside settlements clustered irregularly around markets, waterways, and the compounds of powerful patrons. Vietnam had the same capital in the Hanoi area for almost a millennium, and its population was much too great for the original cosmic plan (fig. 13a) on which it had been built: "This town is of a frightful

extent, and without a surrounding wall. . . . Everywhere one encounters so many people, that although the streets are very broad, one
nevertheless has a great deal of difficulty passing in several places"
(Missions Etrangères 1674: 176).

Burmese kings were much given to demonstrating their power by
building a new city on cosmic lines, and the most powerful of Burma's
kings, Bayinnaung, built the most impressive city. As Burmese chronicles recorded it: "Before the end of the year 928 [1566] he had completed it even to the gates and the turrets on the walls. There were
twenty gates and one thousand and nine turrets, and he made ten main
streets and many lesser streets, and a moat also he caused to be digged
around the city, in breadth twenty fathoms and twenty cubits deep. To
the twenty gates which he built he gave the names of towns and
villages" ("History of Syriam" 1915: 6). Of the ten streets mentioned,
five ran north-south between the five gates on the northern wall and
the five on the southern. Five more streets similarly ran east-west.
Hence, the city was divided into a six-by-six grid of thirty-six blocks,
save that what would have been the four central blocks were occupied
by the palace, which thus became the fulcrum of the city with all the
central avenues leading to it. That left thirty-two city blocks outside
the palace, which were clearly intended to represent the thirty-two
provinces into which Bayinnaung divided Pegu (ibid.: 7), so that both
the city and the country reflected the Buddhist heaven in which Indra
at the centre was surrounded by thirty-two other gods (Guillon 1989:
115).

European visitors to this new city were astonished at its grandeur.
Cesare Frederici was there soon after its completion, and his description concurs with the Burmese:

In the new city is the palace of the king, and his abiding place with all his
barons and nobles, and other gentlemen. . . . It is a great city, very plain and
flat, and four square, walled round about and with ditches that compass
the walls about with water, in which ditches are many crocodiles; it hath
no drawbridges, yet it hath twenty gates, five for every square on the walls;
there are many places made for sentinels to watch, made of wood, and
covered or gilt with golde; the streets thereof are the fairest that I have
seen, they are as straight as a line from one gate to the other, and standing
at the one gate you may discover to the other, and they are as broad as ten
or twelve men may ride a breast in them. . . . these streets . . . are planted at
the doors of the houses, with nut trees of India, which make a very
commodious shadow; the houses be made of wood and covered with a
kind of tiles in form of cups. . . . the king's palace is in the middle of the
city, made in form of a walled castle, with ditches full of water round about

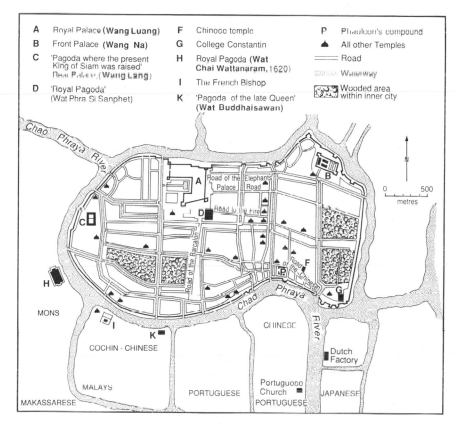

A	Royal Palace (**Wang Luang**)	F	Chinese temple		P	Phaulcon's compound
B	Front Palace (**Wang Na**)	G	College Constantin		▲	All other Temples
C	'Pagoda where the present King of Siam was raised' Rear Palace, (**Wang Lang**)	H	Royal Pagoda (**Wat Chai Wattanaram**, 1620)			══ Road
		I	The French Bishop			░░░ Waterway
D	'Royal Pagoda' (Wat Phra Si Sanphet)	K	'Pagoda of the late Queen' (**Wat Buddhaisawan**)			▓▓ Wooded area within inner city

Map 6 Ayutthaya in 1687

it, the lodgings within are made of wood all over gilded, with fine pinnacles, and very costly work, covered with plates of gold. (Frederici 1581: 245)

The other Burmese capitals—Ava, Amerapura, and Mandalay—were all built with similar purposeful regularity, the palace located at the centre of a vast walled and moated square citadel intersected by straight streets from gate to gate (O'Connor 1907; fig. 13b). Northern Tai cities were closest in type to this regular Burmese pattern. Chiengmai, reportedly built in four months for King Mangrai in 1292 following various appropriate auguries, was also designed according to cosmic principles as a walled and moated square enclosure with rectangular streets (*Chronique de Xieng Mai*: 56–61; Wijeyewardene 1986: 8). If Ayutthaya had similar origins, however, it quickly outgrew

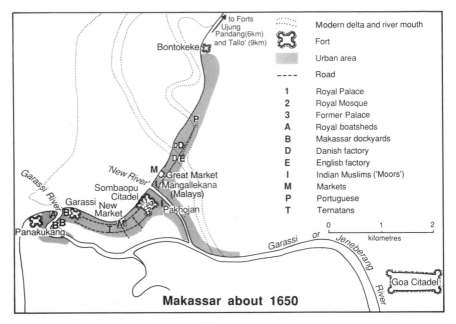

Map 7 Makassar, c. 1650

them. The irregular shape of the Siamese capital was determined by its
waterways (map 6), and though within the great partly walled island in
the Chao Phraya River were a few "large, straight and regular" streets,
most communication was by "small narrow lanes, ditches and creeks
most confusedly placed" (Schouten 1636: 124).

If these Buddhist citadels embraced most of the city proper, those
of Vietnam and the Archipelago were purely for the king, his numerous women, and the direct servants of the court. In Pahang only
the "nobles" lived within the wooden palisades of the citadel; "they
keep the ordinary folk outside in the suburbs" (Matelief 1608: 122).
The dualism at the heart of Makassar gave rise to three major citadels,
of which the most important, Sombaopu, contained only the dwell-
ings of the royal family and their retainers (map 7). A cosmic align-
ment of walls, streets, and buildings was difficult to perceive in the
complexity of these maritime entrepôts. Only at the royal heart of the
city was there a definite pattern, whereby the royal palace opened
northward onto an open field, on the west side of which was the great
mosque, and on the east or north a market. This was the pattern of
Banten (map 8) and of most later Javanese cities, where the royal
square (*paseban* or *alun-alun*) was the scene of feasts, displays, and

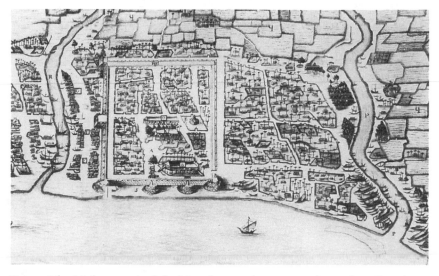

Fig. 14 The Makassar citadel of Sombaopu about 1638, drawn by a Dutch artist. The channel to the left (north) of the citadel was artificially dug, with Portuguese *(F)* and Gujarati *(G)* quarters beside it. To the right (south) is the outlet of the Jeneberang River, with the royal war galleys *(H)* lined up along its banks. Inside the citadel, *B* marks the sultan's palace, elevated on wooden pillars, *C* the former palace, *D* the royal warehouses, and *E* the royal mosque.

tournaments patronized by the court. The same layout was replicated in Aceh and Patani, though not in Makassar (fig. 14).

Most citadels comprised a series of courtyards progressively more difficult of access, with the innermost court reserved exclusively for the king and his women. In Aceh there were seven doors to pass through before reaching the inner area (Warwijck 1604: 15), and no palace had fewer than three. The outer courtyards contained buildings for the royal elephants, guardrooms, artillery magazines, and reception areas. The outer court of Aceh was large enough to hold public elephant-fights (Ito 1984: 23). The royal apartments of the inner palace were of wood, usually of a single story but raised on great wooden pillars. These, the ornate roofs, and the elaborate carving of the palace walls were the features that impressed European visitors, who tended to find the wooden inner palace a let-down after the forbidding outer walls of stone (Warwijck 1604: 15; Marini 1666: 117; Baron 1685: 3; Tavernier 1692 II: 532).

The ruler usually had a place of prayer within the palace, but the principal mosque or temple was adjacent to the palace, to permit all

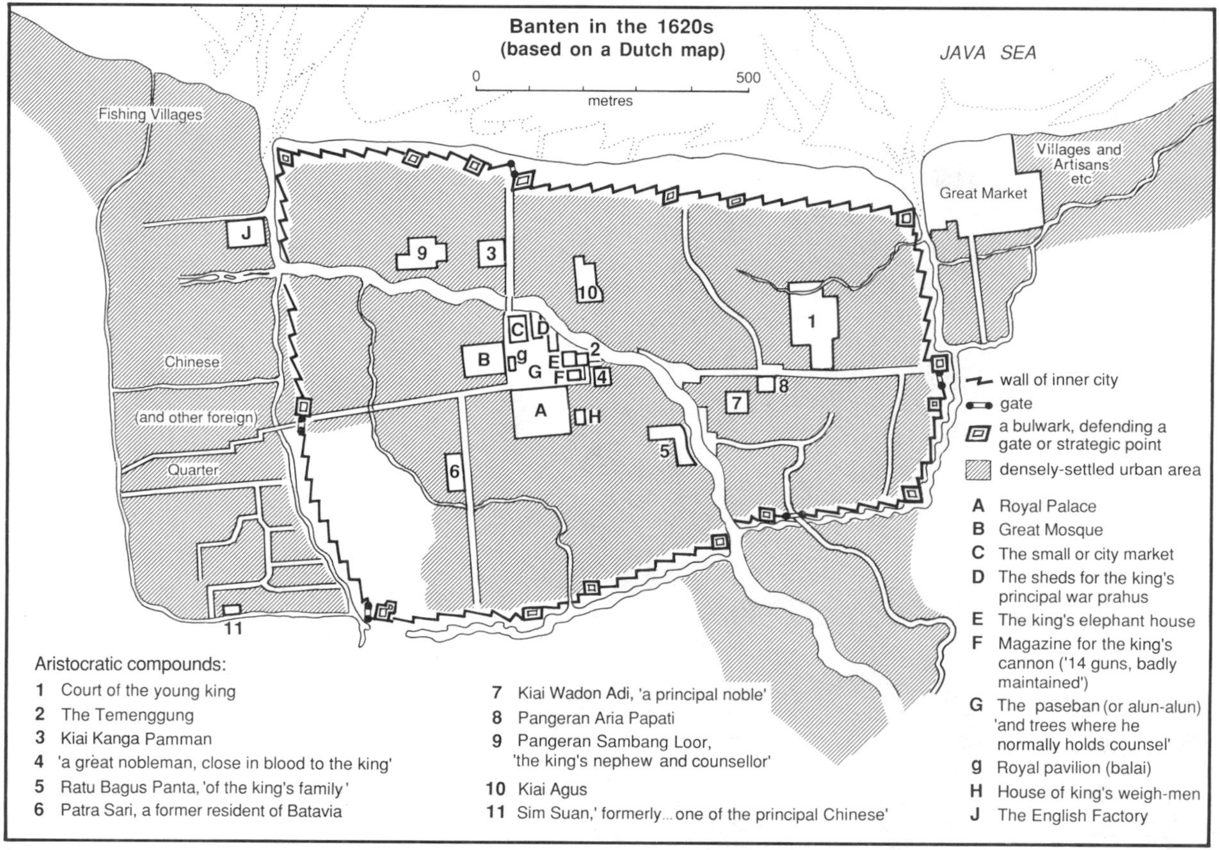

Banten in the 1620s
(based on a Dutch map)

JAVA SEA

Great Market

Villages and Artisans etc

metres

0   500

Fishing Villages

Chinese

(and other foreign)

Quarter

⌐ wall of inner city

● gate

▣ a bulwark, defending a gate or strategic point

▨ densely-settled urban area

A Royal Palace
B Great Mosque
C The small or city market
D The sheds for the king's principal war prahus
E The king's elephant house
F Magazine for the king's cannon ('14 guns, badly maintained')
G The paseban (or alun-alun) 'and trees where he normally holds counsel'
g Royal pavilion (balai)
H House of king's weigh-men
J The English Factory

Aristocratic compounds:

1 Court of the young king
2 The Temenggung
3 Kiai Kanga Pamman
4 'a great nobleman, close in blood to the king'
5 Ratu Bagus Panta, 'of the king's family'
6 Patra Sari, a former resident of Batavia
7 Kiai Wadon Adi, 'a principal noble'
8 Pangeran Aria Papati
9 Pangeran Sambang Loor, 'the king's nephew and counsellor'
10 Kiai Agus
11 Sim Suan, 'formerly... one of the principal Chinese'

Map 8 Banten in the 1620s

the populace access. Muslim cities typically had only one great mosque, facing the square, its multi-tiered roof usually the highest landmark in the city. Although Aceh was said by some to have "a great number of mosques" (Dampier 1699: 90), these were all modest structures, often connected with religious schools and institutions. By contrast Theravada capitals appeared to be a forest of gilded spires, with a stupa or temple on virtually every corner. Ayutthaya was reputed to have some 300–500 temples, and Vientiane 62, while the remains of 85 have been found in Chiengmai (Schouten 1636: 125; Gervaise 1688: 47; Lunet de Jonquière 1901: 102; Wijeyewardene 1985: 91). The desire to earn merit by building, restoring, or decorating religious edifices kept multiplying the number of temples, even if just one or two played a dominant role as the focus of public religious ceremonies and festivities. In Muslim countries it was the graves of saints and powerful figures that parallelled the diversity of Buddhist places of worship, attracting like them a particular clientèle of devotees.

All major cities lay either against the sea (Melaka, Banten, Jakarta-Batavia, Gresik, Makassar, Ternate, Manila) or a large navigable river. The core walled area was also intersected by or adjacent to a smaller river that provided water for washing and cooking, as well as access for small boats. The bridge over it on the land artery leading to the central royal complex was often a bottleneck. In Melaka it was lined with small shops and became an extension of the market as well as a thoroughfare. Beyond this, bridges were few and rudimentary. Ayutthaya had the greatest need for bridges over its many canals: "Those which are laid over the great canal are of stone, with ballisters of the same, but as there are no wagons, nor carts in this place, they are narrow; in the middle they are high and eighty paces long; but the bridges over the by canals are . . . for the greatest part of wood" (Kaempfer 1727: 44; cf. Gervaise 1688: 47).

The most convenient means of transportation was water, and roads were not greatly developed. The Burmese, Thai, and Vietnamese capitals each had a few paved avenues. In Thang-long, parts of the main thoroughfares were left unpaved for the passage of animals (Richard 1778 I. 29). In the Archipelago, and wherever cities grew at the command of commerce rather than a king, the roads were of sand and earth: "They have in the city [Banten] only three proper streets, all three leading to the paseban before the court. One runs from the paseban to the sea, the second to the land-gate, and the third to the mountain-gate. The city is not paved, but all sandy; . . . the city is also very boggy, and foul and stinking, because the inhabitants wash very often in public, men as well as women, which stirs up the ground and makes the water turbid and muddy" (Lodewycksz 1598: 106). Even without paving there were some impressive avenues, like the one Navarrete traversed on the way to the Makassar citadel of Sombaopu (probably from the north; see map 7, above), "through a row of palm-trees, the finest and beautifullest in the World. The sun's rays could not pierce it, and it was above a League long. . . . How it would be valued among us" (Navarrete 1676 I: 115; cf. Gervaise 1688: 47, on Ayutthaya).

Successful cities attracted wealthy foreign traders as well as dependent vassals. Both were to some extent incorporated into the dominant elite of the city and created the pluralism that made commerce possible. When this pluralism was able to flourish at the expense of centralist royal ambitions, it was reflected in the architecture of the city. Aristocratic residences were dispersed in different quarters, each having jurisdiction over the adjacent area. Each powerful vassal lived in a defended compound that replicated the royal palace on a smaller scale. In Banten the pattern was clear from Dutch maps (see map 8, above) and accounts:

The city is divided into many sections, and over each section a nobleman is placed to protect it in time of war, fire, or whatever, and each has his own jurisdiction and enclosure differing from the others. . . .
Each nobleman has ten or twelve men watching in his house throughout the night. When you enter their houses, you first encounter a square area they call *paseban*, where they give audience to those who seek it, and there the above-mentioned guard is placed. . . . In a corner of this square they also have their own mosque, where they perform their mid-day prayer, and beside it a well, where they wash. Going further in, one comes to a door with a narrow passage, which is strengthened with many stores and shops, in which many of their slaves live for their protection, so that they cannot be attacked by their enemies at night; for they neither trust anyone, nor are faithful to them. (Lodewycksz 1598: 107–08)

This pattern of fortified urban compounds in which great men surrounded themselves with wives, children, slaves, and dependents, usually living in separate houses, was repeated in other cities of Java and Bali (fig. 15), in Makassar and Aceh, and in Siam (Pires 1515: 190; Lintgens 1597: 98–99; van den Broecke 1634 I: 185, 206; La Loubère 1691: 30). The term *kampung*, used for any village or settlement in modern Malay, meant in the age of commerce the compound of a wealthy individual, usually in the city. In Melaka there were extensive legal provisions for the sale and lease of kampungs and their bestowal on a vassal by the king (*Undang-undang Melaka*: 106–09).

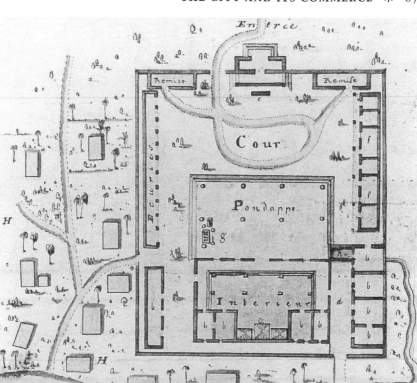

Fig. 15 The compound of a Javanese noble in Surakarta. The rooms of retainers surround the central dwelling and reception area—men at the front and women at the back.

Basic to the notion of a Southeast Asian "city" was this agglomeration of aristocratic compounds, each surrounded by clusters of houses of those more or less dependent on them. Except in Burmese and northern Tai cities, there was little concept of a specific urban space defined by defensive walls and contrasted in character from the surrounding countryside. In the Archipelago cities were seen by Europeans to be "no more than an aggregate of villages" (Crawfurd 1820 I: 168), and indigenous languages did not usually distinguish between the city and the state. Both were described by the Malay term *negeri* (cf. Thai *nakhon*), derived from the Sanskrit word for city but passing into modern Indonesian and Malay as the term for state. When Ma Huan (1433: 86–87) visited Java, none of the trading cities was walled (at least in the Chinese sense). Large Malay cities like Melaka, Aceh, Johor, and Brunei had no city walls at all, except when bamboo stockades were erected for temporary defence. A chronicler of Aceh, aware of how odd that city's defencelessness seemed to Arab and Indian visitors, claimed that "this city is not fortified like other cities because of the very large number of war elephants" able to protect it (*Hikayat Aceh:* 166).

City walls spread in the sixteenth and seventeenth centuries with the rapid growth of cities and the need to defend them against European naval attack. Ayutthaya built its wall in 1550, and by 1600 the Javanese cities of Banten, Japara, Tuban, Pati, and Surabaya all had them. In 1634 the people of Makassar constructed a wall about 10 kilometres long to protect the city from Dutch attack by sea (though there was no landward boundary of the city at all), and a similar sea-wall was the main defence of the Balinese capital Gelgel (Reid 1983A: 142; Lintgens 1597: 101–02). These walls might protect, or partly protect, the core area central to royal interests, but most urban growth occurred outside them. Since foreigners were usually forbidden to dwell within the walls, the constant influx of migratory traders and new immigrants all added to the village-like settlements outside them.

In contrast to European or Chinese cities, even the walled areas seemed green and sparsely settled. In Pahang the stockaded citadel was "full of coconut and other trees, so that it gives the appearance rather of a suburb of courtyards and gardens than a populated city" (Matelief 1608: 122). In Ayutthaya only the area adjacent to the port was densely settled, covering about a sixth of the walled area (La Loubère 1691: 6; see map 6, above). Outside the royal citadel or walled area the truly urban congestion around the markets shaded imperceptibly into adjacent villages, with no difference in building style.

Visitors to such urban villages knew that they were in a quite different type of city from those they had known above the winds: "The city of Achien [Aceh], if it may be so called, is very spacious, built in a wood, so that we could not see a house till we were upon it. Neither could we go into any place, but we found houses and great concourse of people; so that I think the town spreadeth over the whole land" (Davis 1602: 147). As the first landfall for travellers from the west, Aceh's particular greenness was always a surprise.

Imagine a forest of coconut trees, bamboos, pineapples and bananas, through the midst of which passes a quite beautiful river all covered with boats; put in this forest an incredible number of houses made of canes, reeds and bark, and arrange them in such a way that they sometimes form streets, sometimes separate quarters: divide these various quarters by meadows and woods: spread throughout this forest as many people as you see in your towns, when they are well populated; you will form a pretty accurate idea of Achen, and you will agree that a city of this new style can give pleasure to passing strangers. (Premare 1699: 344–45)

This was not simply a case of migrants from the countryside continuing an earlier way of life. Indigenous quarters of such cities as Melaka, Jakarta, and Makassar retained their trees, chickens, and single-story elevated houses for centuries. Climate was undoubtedly one factor. The treeless, congested quarters that Chinese and later Europeans built in brick or stone were stuffy, unhealthy, and exposed to both sun and flood. Eventually these alien urban models became pestilential and were abandoned to the poorest inhabitants. The importance to the household economy of coconut and fruit trees, betel vines, and herbs was another reason for this cultural preference. Trees, not houses or land itself, were the principal item of immovable private property discussed in the law codes (*Undang-undang Melaka*: 106–09). When the English acquired a block of land for their factory in Makassar in 1613, the sultan required them to recompense the previous occupants only for their coconut trees. The houses were simply carried to a new site by the owners (Jourdain 1617: 293).

Cultural preference was not the only explanation, however. The inhabitants of Naples or Canton would probably also have enjoyed trees had the option been open to them. The other factor was that the city wall, where it existed, never constrained urban growth. The fundamental strategy was not to defend the city as an entity, if indeed that entity could be imagined. The king defended himself and his immediate circle in his citadel as much against overmighty subjects as against foreign powers or savages. For the population at large, and for the ruler when faced with a stronger enemy, the strategy was to gather their valuables and flee to the surrounding forest. Enemy attack was usually designed to capture people, not property or territory. If the people could escape, the enemy could do little but burn houses, cut down trees, and pillage the immovable treasures of the royal and aristocratic compounds.

The Spanish found in the Philippines that when attacked the Filipinos "readily abandon their houses and towns for other places, or precipitately disperse among the mountains and uplands" (Legazpi 1569: 60). Even in the great city of Melaka, when resistance against the Portuguese attack proved fruitless, the king and his court withdrew inland, "being of the opinion that Afonso Dalboquerque simply meant to rob the city and then leave it and sail away with the spoil" (Albuquerque 1557: 129). Because of the lightness of building materials, whole cities could be rebuilt in a few days, if necessary, in a safer location. An English party spent two days in 1634 looking for the once-flourishing port of Indragiri (Sumatra), until they discovered that the whole town had moved three days' journey upstream in response to an Acehnese attack (Reid 1980: 244–45).

In spite of the trees and the abundance of space, the influx of new people to established quarters close to markets created areas where the wooden houses were contiguous. In Patani, "A cat could walk from Payung Hujung to Kuala Aru without descending to the ground" (*Hikayat Patani*: 113). Here the danger of fire was intense. Eight hundred houses were reportedly burned in Aceh in 1602, 1260 in Makassar in 1614, and 10,0000 in Ayutthaya in 1545. Most of Manila was burned in 1583 and most of Patani in a slave revolt of 1613. Particularly in the more pluralistic cities where fire was sometimes intentionally used against rivals, this became the principal nightmare of merchants with substantial stores to protect. After seeing the eastern section of Banten near the great market burned five times in three months, an English factor penned this lament:

Oh this word fire! Had it been spoken near me, either in English, Mallayes, Javans or Chyna, although I had been sound asleep, yet I should have leaped out of my bed; the which I have done sometimes when our men in their watch have but whispered one to another of fire. . . . Such was the fear we lived in, and not without cause; for many times, when I have watched until twelve oclock at night, I have been raised up after three times before morning by alarms of fire. And I protest before God I would not sleep so many nights in fear again for the best ship's lading of pepper that ever came from thence. (Scott 1606: 97–99)

On this ground, at least, Scott would have been happier in the more regulated Burmese capital, where citizens could only cook in pits of prescribed depth between prescribed hours, and where fire wardens checked the houses five times a day to see that there was no un-authorized flame (Than Tun 1983: 84–85).

Markets

"I will add one mas *and one* kupang."
"Impossible, I would lose."
"I can give no more."
"Well, Bismillah, go and look elsewhere, to see if you can get it cheaper; you will not find it anywhere at a cheaper price; I can give it to you at as good a price as anybody in the city; but I must have a little profit. I don't sit at my stall here to lose, I have to live from this;

you know that things are expensive, and one thing follows from an-
other. If you don't want to give me five mas, I can do nothing for you;
you are too miserly."
—*Part of a Malay conversation appropriate to the Aceh market, in*
Houtman 1603: 65–66

In spite of the extraordinary growth in commercial activity between 1400 and 1600, the market remained the central organizing
principle of trade. Markets grew in size and complexity, and the biggest transactions (notably of Europeans) increasingly took place by
personal negotiation outside them, but the direct exchange of goods
and money through competitive bargaining remained the way it was
done.

Two distinct principles appeared to be at work. In the large Archipelago cities most international transactions took place in a single
vast market, and no city had more than three markets of interest to
foreigners (as opposed, of course, to fruit and vegetable markets in
every locality). These were essentially free markets in which anyone
could take up a stall on paying a regular fee to the authorities. In Aceh
the cost according to the *Adat Aceh* was prescribed as one small gold
coin (*mas*) per stall per month (Lombard 1967: 46; cf. Chou Ta-kuan
1297: 27). This appears also to have been the pattern in early Tai cities
like Sukhothai.

In Thang-long and Ayutthaya, by contrast, royal control was
much more marked. It took the form of allocating to certain quarters
the monopoly of the sale of particular products. "Every different commodity sold in this city [Thang-long], is appointed to a particular
street, and these streets again allotted to one, two or more villages, the
inhabitants whereof are only privileged to keep shops in them" (Baron
1685: 3). The specialist goods sold or produced gave their name to the
quarters (*phuong*), some of which survive in modern Hanoi. In Ayutthaya there were also numerous markets selling specific products,
which had reached as many as ninety in the eighteenth century. Many
were in or near the courtyard of a busy temple. The reason for this
difference appears to be the tendency of the Vietnamese crown, and
increasingly also the Siamese, to monopolize a large number of trade
and craft items regarded essentially as tribute belonging to the king,
each farmed out to be managed by a particular court official under
whose authority lay the market for it (O'Connor 1983: 52–53; Le
1971: 222–23).

Even in the Archipelago not all commerce was limited to the great
market. Pires reported that in Melaka women sold "in every street,"

paying a fee for this privilege to the orangkaya responsible for the area (Pires 1515: 274). Martin (1604: 53) observed a large number of fruit and vegetable markets held each morning in Aceh, whereas Dampier (1699: 92) noted that the female money-changers of Aceh were positioned not only in the market but on street corners. Besides these local women there was a quite different group entitled to do business outside the market. Some large-scale foreign merchants, particularly Chinese, west Asians, and Europeans, were allowed to sell their goods from their residences in foreign quarters outside the city centre. In many cities, during the season the Chinese ships were in port, the Chinese quarter came to resemble a fair, and townspeople went there to buy tools and small manufactures, to eat and to drink (Guillot 1989: 142–43; Lodewycksz 1598: 113; Borri 1633: I; Dampier 1699: 94–95). Such privileges to do business outside the market had undoubtedly to be paid for in some way, but the larger foreign merchants were in a position to negotiate for such rights.

Nevertheless, it was in the great markets that prices were fixed by a process of bargaining. Frederick de Houtman (1603: 44–48, 60–71, 86–94) gives vivid examples of haggling that went on to fix the price of all goods and services, as prices fluctuated with the arrival and departure of ships. In explaining why the Malukans had lost interest in growing cloves after the Dutch arrival, Laurens Reael (1618: 89) pointed among other things to the Dutch refusal to bargain, "for, they say, there it is a custom among merchants to haggle, whereas they must accept the cloth from us at a fixed price and in a half-forced manner." Southeast Asians would have sympathized with (and some indeed may have read) the exemplary Persian story of a merchant who quarrelled all day about the amount a tradesman owed him, and then when he received it gave it all to the tradesman's apprentice. He explained, "I am a merchant and it is the rule of commerce during buying, selling and negotiation that if one should be beguiled out of a single dirham it is as though one were tricked out of half one's life. On the other hand, when the time comes for generosity, if one were to be guilty of ungenerous conduct, it were as much as to assert one's origins to be unclean" (Qabus Nama 1082: 159). For the European companies, however, this process of bargaining often seemed laborious and unnecessary.

The fullest accounts are of the great market of Banten, outside the eastern city wall hard by the sea (see map 8, above). About 1600 this appeared to combine wholesale with retail functions, foreign with domestic, men with women, and everyday foodstuffs with long-distance trade items. "You find there each morning merchants of every nation, such as Portuguese, Arabs, Turks, Chinese, Klings, Pegus, Malays, Bengalis, Gujaratis, Malabaris, Abbyssinians and from every quarter of the Indies to drive their trade" (Lodewycksz 1598: 110). Local women sold pepper, as well as foodstuffs, to foreign buyers, while each group of foreign merchants had a place to sell their goods. This was at once the everyday market for foodstuffs—rice, vegetables, fruits, sugar, fish, and meat—and the venue for selling livestock, cloth, pepper, clove and nutmeg, arms, tools, and other metalwork (fig. 16). The market was regulated by the Syahbandar, who held a regular court to resolve commercial disputes (Lodewycksz 1598: 110–13; Coen 1623: 774; Missions Etrangères 1680: 93).

The domestic markets of rural Southeast Asia were almost entirely an affair of women. Local men would appear in the market to browse, to flirt, to gossip and socialize, but they were not usually concerned with buying and selling except at the highest level. The exception was the traffic in a few items always produced by men and strongly associated with men, of which metal weapons and tools were the most important (Reid 1988: 162–65). In the cities, however, there was always an abundance of foreign men selling in the market. "There are [in Aceh] a large number of stalls belonging to merchants dressed like Turks, who come from Asia Minor, Nagapattinam, Gujarat, Cape Cormorin, Calicut, the Island of Ceylon, Siam, Bengal, and various other places, remaining six months or so in the place to sell their merchandise, which comprise very fine cotton cloths . . . silks . . . cotton thread, porcelain vessels of various sorts, and many drugs, spices and precious stones" (Martin 1604: 54). Such male traders from above the winds, as well as the east Asians, were of course accustomed to marketing at home. In addition, the Southeast Asian seamen and petty traders who travelled with a small stock of goods had little choice but to sell their wares themselves in the market on arrival, unless they stayed long enough to acquire a temporary wife to do it for them. Hence at Banten, for example, there were separate cloth markets where the sellers were men (foreigners selling Indian or Chinese cloth) and where they were women (locals selling local cloth).

Coinage and Commercialization—The Triumph of Silver

The increase of production for the world market would not have been possible without a great increase in the money supply. Some transactions certainly took place through direct barter of the major trade items—cloth for pepper or cloves, for example. But the hundreds of thousands of large and small producers and handlers who contrib-

Fig. 16 A Dutch engraving based on contemporary descriptions of the Banten great market. The artist clearly had no first-hand experience of a Southeast Asian market, but he schematically indicated much of the range of merchandise, including, *from right: A.* melons, cucumbers, and coconuts; *B.* sugar and honey; *C.* beans; *D.* bamboo; *E.* krisses, swords, spears, and small cannon; *F.* male cloth-sellers; *G.* female cloth-sellers; *H.* spices and drugs; *at rear, I.* Bengalis and Cujaratis selling ironwork and utensils; *K.* Chinese booths; *L.* meat; *M.* fish; *N.* fruit; *O.* vegetables; *P.* pepper; *Q.* onions; *R.* rice; *T.* jewellers; and *X.* chickens.

uted to the flow of goods could not all be paid in this way. The age of commerce produced a constant demand for usable coinage. Apart from Indian cloth, specie in the form of silver, copper, and lead was the most important trade item flowing into the region. That it was frequently in short supply despite this influx is evidence both of the rapid commercialization of Southeast Asian life and of the inadequacy of an indigenous supply of currency to meet it.

Before the fifteenth century Mainland Southeast Asia appears to have generated no coinage to facilitate commerce. Silver coins were produced between the fifth and tenth centuries but were of such strictly local distribution that they were probably intended rather for paying fines and taxes (Wicks 1983: 67–68). The classic empires of Pagan and Angkor produced no coins at all. The minting of trade coins in the fifteenth century was an innovation driven by the needs of commerce, the desire of rulers to tax it, and the model of Islamic states. Arakan introduced a silver coin of Bengali Muslim type soon after 1430, Siam moved towards standardization of its silver weights not long after, while Pegu and Tenasserim introduced silver and lead coinages in the 1530s (ibid.: 68–69, 116–20).

In the Archipelago there was a longer exposure to foreign merchants and their coins, while indigenous coins, particularly of gold, were also more widely minted. Varthema (1510: 239) claims to have seen in Pidië (north Sumatra) about five hundred money changers, made necessary by the diversity of merchants frequenting the port. Some kingdoms in Java, Sumatra, and Luzon produced coins between the ninth and thirteenth centuries but then gave way to imported Chinese copper cash (Wicks 1983: 244–56). Before the age of commerce gold and silver were evaluated primarily by weighing—predominantly gold in the Archipelago and silver in the Mainland. Gold was a measure of value, but was equally important as a means of saving and as a mark of status for kings and for the Buddha. We know less about the base coinage of early periods, though cowrie shells and strips of cloth were certainly among them. Cowries continued to be used in Siam, and cloth in eastern Indonesia and Mindanao, as late as the eighteenth century.

Chinese copper cash, and local coins modelled on them, were the basic lubricant for the increasing commercialization of the region after 1400. The word *cash* is of Sanskrit origin,[4] but the Portuguese applied it (as *caixa*) particularly to the exported Chinese copper coin-

---

4. The word is probably related to the Acehnese *keu'eh*, by which cash continued to be locally known (Kreemer 1922 II: 53–54).

age, and later Europeans followed suit. The peoples around the Java Sea usually referred to them by the Javanese word *picis*. These small round coins had a square hole in the centre to facilitate stringing them in groups of a thousand (though six hundred or some other figure were often conventionally substituted). These coins were used in Chinese-governed Vietnam during the Tang dynasty and have been found in archaeological sites in the Straits region dating from the tenth century (Crawfurd 1856: 286).

In Java, inscriptions cease to mention Javanese weights or coins after about 1300, referring only to picis—the Chinese copper cash (Wicks 1983: 246–52). Particularly interesting is the Kediri copper-plate, tentatively dated about 1350, which quotes the testimony of the owner of some contested land: "It is property given as security by my great-great-grandfather for one and a half measure of silver, at the time that this land of Java did not possess the means of the *picis*" (Pigeaud 1960–63 III: 154). This suggests that the Mongol invasion of eastern Java, which brought about twenty thousand Chinese troops to the area in 1293, was the initial impetus for the new coinage, as of many other changes in Java (Wicks 1986: 59–63; Reid 1992: 181–84). Chinese copper coins appear to have spread to the Philippines at about the same period, but their career as the major base coinage of Southeast Asia can be clearly documented only from the fifteenth century.

In Vietnam the Le dynasty, having rid itself of the short-lived Ming occupation, began around 1430 a consistent minting of its own copper coins of similar type to the Chinese cash. The mining of copper in the northern hills was intensified, and by mid-century officials were being paid in this coinage as well as in land. The indigenous supply was never sufficient, however, and in the seventeenth century two forms of copper cash were in circulation—a larger coin imported from China or Japan and a smaller Vietnamese one circulating primarily near the capital (Whitmore 1983: 365–69; Le 1971: 223; Rhodes 1651: 59). The southern Nguyen rulers required a similar supply of copper cash but lacked a copper supply of their own. The importation of copper and copper coins from China, Japan, or northern Vietnam was thus one of the major preoccupations of the regime.

It was probably the great Ming fleets under Zheng He that made Chinese cash familiar to such other Archipelago ports as Melaka and Pasai in the early fifteenth century. Tin was far more readily available than copper in the Malacca Straits area, however, and states there began to replicate the coins in that metal. In 1414, when Sultan Megat Iskandar Shah visited the Chinese capital to obtain imperial approval of his succession, he also received permission to mint his own "small pewter money which he called *cash*," according to the Portuguese (Albuquerque 1557: 77; cf. Pires 1515: 243; Wang 1968: 104–05). Surviving examples of Melaka tin coins carry the titles of rulers as far back as Muzaffar Shah (1446–59). At the same time, the kingdoms of north Sumatra issued large numbers of a small but thick tin coin bearing the names of their rulers (Wicks 1983: 273; Ma Huan 1433: 120; Dakers 1939; Pires 1515: 144; Varthema 1510: 231).

The first European descriptions of Brunei, Sumbawa, Maluku, and Champa, as well as Java, show that Chinese copper cash was the basic coinage in all these places (Pires 1515: 114, 170, 181, 203, 206–07; Pigafetta 1524: 59–60; Galvão 1544: 138–39). Not all was necessarily brought from China. Because the level of direct Chinese contacts was lower around 1500 than in the Yongle period, it is likely that in Java and elsewhere the "Chinese" cash had often to be replicated locally to maintain supply. Pigafetta (1524: 60) in fact reported that the Chinese coins he encountered in Brunei were "the money made by the Muslims in those regions." At any event, Chinese copper cash or local copper or tin coins modelled on them already provided the primary base-level coinage in Southeast Asia by 1500. When the Portuguese attempted in 1537 to have their allies in Maluku accept a Portuguese coin of purer copper than the Chinese coin, they were told that this would be acceptable provided the Portuguese, too, put a hole in their coins for ease of stringing (Galvão 1544: 270–73).

Only in Siam, Arakan, the Burmese port of Martaban, and Kedah was the cowrie still current for small transactions by 1500. Although the better-maintained tributary relations of Siam with China might have been expected to make the import of cash easier, instead cowries were imported from the Maldives, Borneo, Maluku, and the Philippines (Pires 1515: 100; Gervaise 1701: 120). In most of Burma and Arakan the common coin was *gansa*, an amalgam of base metals, preferably copper and tin but often lead, which was measured by weight. "It is not the money of the king, but every man may stamp it that will, because it has his just partition or value" (Frederici 1581: 254; cf. Pires 1515: 99, 96–97).

The lifting of the imperial ban on Chinese trade to the south in 1567 appears to have resulted in a massive influx of Chinese copper cash. The first Dutch fleet to reach Java, in 1596, learned that these coins "had by their multitude filled the islands" in this period, alarming Chinese officials, who saw the outflow of coinage as a drain of an increasingly scarce resource. In consequence, a new coin of cheap lead alloy had begun to be produced about 1590 in Guangdong and Fujian for circulation predominantly in the Nanyang (Blussé 1986: 36–38;

Lodewycksz 1598: 122–23). This was the type much complained of by Europeans: "It is of such base metal that it is wholly consumed by itself in the space of three or four years" (van Neck 1599: 87; cf. Lodewycksz 1598: 122). By 1596 these inferior picis were circulating far into the interior of Java. Chinese middlemen carried the coins into the hills above Banten to buy pepper from the growers there at a quarter of what it was worth in the Banten market (Blussé 1986: 40).

A shortage of picis in the Banten market was often mentioned over the succeeding three decades. Coen claimed that the value of picis against silver had increased nearly fourfold between 1613 and 1618 because of scarcity (from 30,000 to 8000 per real), while in Jambi the value continued to increase, to 6900 per real in 1636 (Blussé 1986: 41–42; Andaya 1993: 105).[5] The great influx of silver in pursuit of the pepper of these ports would have produced this result even had the supply of picis remained stable.

These lead-alloy coins were of such low quality as to be replicated with ease. A shortage of lead was the main obstacle to local production until the English and Dutch discovered this to be one of the few items from Europe for which there was a market. The English in Banten increased their orders for lead from 20 tonnes in 1608 to 50–60 tonnes in 1615 and 100–150 tonnes in 1636. Some of this went into the manufacture of bullets in time of war, but most was for coinage, to supply Banjarmasin and Palembang as well as Banten (*LREIC* I: 21–22; III: 277–78; Willoughby 1636: 153). The Dutch were more cautious in selling lead lest it be used for military purposes by their ubiquitous enemies. Only in 1633, when they began making it available to Chinese in Batavia, did they discover that there was already a major manufacturing industry of "Chinese" picis in Java—specifically in Banten, Cirebon, and Japara. They took advantage of it by providing lead on a monopoly basis to the leading Chinese in the Dutch settlements. This experiment was abandoned in 1640 when the English undercut the VOC monopoly, supplying cheaper lead to rival picis manufacturers in Banten, Japara, Jambi, Palembang, Makassar, and Martapura (Borneo). The VOC shifted to copper coins as its basic means to penetrate the Southeast Asian economy. Nevertheless, Blussé (1986: 46–48) has shown that the period of Dutch-promoted cash was critical in establishing Batavia as an attractive port for Indonesian shippers eager to get hold of picis and Chinese wares.

---

5. Blussé (1986: 40–42) argues that the problem was purely seasonal, with a repeated scarcity before the Chinese junks arrived with their ballast of lead coins, but there is strong evidence that at least some of this appreciation was long-term.

Southeast Asian states continued to mint lead or lead-tin cash, though the rapid deterioration of these coins has left few—and these often difficult to identify—in modern collections. Coins of very pure lead, decorated with the ducklike *hamsa,* have been found in Pegu, including some hundreds in the city walls built in the 1560s. This suggests that the height of Pegu's prosperity may have demanded some rationalization of the base currency in the sixteenth century, though it is not mentioned by contemporary visitors (Robinson 1986: 25–27, 34; Wicks 1983: 94–95). Larger tin and lead coins were issued by Tenasserim or Tavoy in the seventeenth century and appear to have circulated as far as Kedah and Perak (Robinson 1986: 67–70; Gervaise 1701: 120). Surviving examples of lead-tin coins (and in Banten also brass) show that at least Aceh, Banten, Cirebon, Brunei, and probably Johor were issuing base coins inscribed with the ruler's name or title in the sixteenth and seventeenth centuries (Beaulieu 1666: 58; Dampier 1699: 92; Davidson 1977: 48; Netscher and van der Chijs 1864: 149–53; Wicks 1983: 273–76, 319–23, 408–28). According to a Spanish source (Dasmariñas 1590: 13), Brunei had found its original silver coinage excessively popular with foreign traders, who took it away, so that a ruler in the second half of the sixteenth century decided instead to cast one "of the size of half a real and of tin or lead which they call pitis."

The period of the VOC attempt at monopoly provides some measure of the demand for picis at that time. In 1637 the Company provided 133 tonnes of lead, and in 1638, 153 tonnes, to its picis manufacturer (Blussé 1986: 47). Given that the English provided a similar amount and that the Chinese were still bringing in their cash, while the VOC itself had hoped to acquire a larger share of the market amounting to up to 240 tonnes, we may estimate that about 350 tonnes were required each year to provide picis for the Indonesian Archipelago at that time. If the average weight of a lead-tin picis was about 2 grams (surviving examples vary widely, with many less than a gram but others of 5 grams—Wicks 1983: 275–76, 279, 410–13; Museum Nasional 1980: 267; 1984–85: 507–08), then about 170 million coins were introduced each year. Since they deteriorated within five years, we may very roughly calculate that more than 800 million of these coins were probably in circulation in the Indonesian Archipelago. For a population of some ten million this amounted to little in terms of value but enough coins to familiarize society with monetary transactions.

VOC records also indicate the scale of coinage supplies in the Nguyen kingdom of Cochin-China in the same period. In the five years

1633–37, the VOC imported 105,834 strings, each comprising 960 Japanese copper coins, to serve as the base currency of Cochin-China (van Aelst 1987). This Dutch import alone thus represented an import of 20 million coins a year. Chinese and Japanese traders also imported large amounts. In 1635, when further Japanese overseas trade was banned, the main Japanese supplier turned over his stock of 200 tonnes of copper coins for Cochin-China to the Dutch (Klein 1986: 161). Total annual importation can therefore hardly have been less than 40 million coins. Copper cash had a longer life than the low-grade lead picis but was also more likely to be melted down to create utensils. Yet it is difficult to see how the total number of coins in circulation in Cochin-China can have been less than 200 million, which for a population of about just two million would imply a rate of monetization slightly higher than the Indonesian Archipelago's.

For coinage of higher value, gold was the natural preference, as much a mark of wealth, status, security, and beauty as a facilitator of commerce. Although a gold coin or medallion was known in ancient Java, the minting of gold coins of consistent value under the ruler's name was introduced to Southeast Asia with Islam. The oldest such coins are those of Pasai, the first important Muslim state below the winds. Gold coins are extant from eight of Pasai's known rulers, from Sultan Muhammad (1297–1326) to Abdallah Malik az-Zahir (1501–13) (Alfian 1979: 15–27; Wicks 1983: 263–68). The Islamic inspiration for this consistent coinage is clear not only from the Arabic titles the coins carry but also from the Arabic term *dirham* (Acehnese *deureuham*) by which they were locally known. Its Makassar equivalent was known as the *dinara'*, from Arabic *dinar*. The Malay term *mas* (also the standard word for gold in general) was, however, the international term for all such indigenous gold coins. This small coin between 10 and 14 millimetres in diameter continued to be minted by north Sumatran rulers for at least four centuries, at a remarkably consistent 17 karat purity and 0.6 gram weight (fig. 17a).

In the seventeenth century the Aceh mas was part of a consistent system of values, in which 1 *tahil* (in weight of silver) equalled 16 mas, and 1 mas equalled 4 *kupang*, which equalled 1600 cash (Lombard 1967: 106–07; *LREIC* III: 314). Because the relative values of cash, gold, and silver changed, notably with the influx of new silver, these relations were difficult to maintain in practice. There seems to have been a shortage of cash in Aceh as in Banten, for whereas 2100 cash were exchanged for a mas in 1602 (Martin 1604: 55–56; Lancaster 1603: 136), only 600 to 1000 equalled a mas in the 1630s (Mundy, quoted Lombard 1967: 107n), after which some of the original balance

17a   17b

Fig. 17a Seventeenth-century coinage of Aceh, Makassar, and Cambodia, sketched by Tavernier. *From top:* 1 and 2, gold mas of Aceh; 3 and 4, tin coin of Aceh; 5 and 6 gold mas of Makassar; 7 and 8, silver coins of Cambodia; 9 and 10, Chinese copper cash used in Cambodia.

Fig. 17b Coinage of Siam, sketched by Tavernier. *From top:* 1 and 2, a standard weight of gold; 3, 4, 5, and 6, silver baht or tikal; 7 and 8, Chinese copper cash used in Siam.

was restored. Against silver the Aceh mas also tended to increase, for it was worth one-sixth of a Spanish real in 1602 and one-fifth in 1613 as well as 9 English pence at the beginning of the century and 15 pence for Dampier in 1688 (Lancaster 1603: 136; *LREIC* III: 314n).

Although Aceh's kupang appears to have been only a unit of account, other states minted both mas and kupang of gold, with the mas four times the value of the kupang. Both Johor and Kedah produced such coins of octagonal shape in the late seventeenth century. Johor's mas was four times as heavy as Aceh's but was regularly adulterated with alloy (Hamilton 1727 II: 172; Wicks 1983: 307–18; Taillandier 1711: 411). Gold coins of round Acehnese type have also been found at Patani, with a bull on one side and "malik al-adil" on the other, but they cannot be attributed with certainty to a specific ruler or place (Wicks 1983: 360–68).

Better documented is the gold coinage created by Makassar as part of its deliberate effort to become the great entrepôt of the eastern Archipelago. As the chronicles point out, it was the architect of Makassar's greatness, Karaeng Matoaya of Tallo', chancellor from 1593 to 1637, who was "the first to make the [gold] coin called *dinara'* and the coin of tin" (*Sejarah Kerajaan Tallo'*: 18). Though similar in appearance to Acehnese coinage, this Makassar gold coin was four times larger, at 2.4 grams. A gold kupang one quarter the size was issued at least by 1657 (Macassar Factory 1658; Bassett 1958: 26–27; Netscher and van der Chijs 1864: 185).

Other rulers in the Malay world may well have produced a gold mas that is no longer traceable. This certainly became the measure of value most firmly embedded in Malay thinking from Melaka onwards. Fines for offences in the Malay law codes were expressed in terms of mas, even though this meant different things in different states in relation to the effective silver currency. Even in Siam and Cochin-China, foreigners referred to the unit of account representing a sixteenth of a tahil as a mas (Thai *salung,* Vietnamese *tiên*) (Smith 1974: 317; Chen 1974: 24).

Cambodia's royal chronicles assert that a usurper king named Kan, of common (perhaps merchant) origins, built a new capital at Sralap in 1516 that was much frequented by Khmers and foreigners. "The king gave the order to mint coins, the *slin* of silver and the *slin* of gold, carrying the image of a naga, for business" (*Chroniques Cambodge* 1988: 21). Although this king came to a bad end with his head on a pole ten years later, it is known that around 1600 Cambodia was minting its own gold and silver coins decorated with "a cock, a serpent or a heart" (probably a hamsa, naga, and lotus—San Antonio 1604: 9). The largest coin, close to a real in value, was called a *maiz,* which may suggest Malayo-Muslim influence, or simply that the Spanish learned about Cambodia through the filter of the Malay language. In the 1630s it was a resident Chinese trader who had the contract for minting Cambodian coins, for he sought silver for the purpose from the Dutch (Gaelen 1636: 74, 112).

These attempts at monetary reform through gold coinage must be seen against the background of the unprecedented influx of silver into the region after 1570. The simultaneous effect of new mercury extraction methods on silver mining in Spanish America and Japan produced at least a fourfold increase in the flow of silver into eastern Asia, as sketched above (table 3). Even if China and India ultimately consumed much of this silver influx, the bulk of it passed through Southeast Asia and much stayed there. Tongking was in no sense a transshipment point, yet VOC shipments of Japanese silver there averaged 2.5 tonnes a year in the period 1640–54, and the silver imports of this least commercial of Southeast Asian states totalled about 10 tonnes a year (Klein 1988: 166–69; Baron 1685: 7).

It has been calculated that the supply of silver rupees in circulation in India expanded threefold between 1591 and 1639 (Habib 1982A: 363–65). The order of increase could have been no less in Southeast Asia, where competitive buying for Asian produce was most intense. There is no doubt that silver came to represent the overwhelming bulk of the money supply in the cities of the region. Its relative abundance is the best explanation for its declining value against both cash and gold. Southeast Asian states could have been expected to seize the opportunity of adopting and enforcing their own silver currencies as a means to control their internal economies, as Mughal India and many countries of Europe did.

Although the Pangeran of Banten asked the Dutch in 1618 for help in minting a small silver coin, and Kedah produced a few silver coins on the dies meant for gold ones (Netscher and van der Chijs 1864: 149–51; Wicks 1983: 387), the only serious attempts at a silver coinage were in the Buddhist countries. These states were less committed to gold, having long used silver as a measure of value. The first true silver coins known to have been issued under the name of rulers below the winds were those of Arakan. Its Buddhist rulers copied the style of Bengali coins in the fifteenth and sixteenth centuries, complete with Arabic titles. Only from the 1530s did these coins include an Arakanese wording, by which time it is certain they were minted locally and not in Bengal. By the seventeenth century Arakan's mints were recasting in the local coinage all imported silver and foreign coin, making Arakan truly exceptional in its resistance to the mighty real (Wicks 1983: 74–91). The Tais, however, had an older tradition of silver weights of standard size.

Tai-speakers knew two principal types of silver weights. A kidney-shaped lump, or bullet coin, was characteristic of Ayutthaya (fig. 17b), and a horseshoe-shaped bar, or bracelet coin, of Chiengmai and the north (fig. 18). Popular tradition attributed the invention of the bullet coin (like much else) to King Ram Kamheng of Sukhothai (1275–1317) and of the bracelet coin to his contemporary, King Mangrai of Chiengmai (1259–1317), but since the markings on these weights are not attributable to specific kings, it is impossible to know the true antiquity of the system. Le May (1932: 19–22, 44–45) has hypothesized that the bracelet type is the more ancient and was adapted by northern Tai from the crescent-shaped Pyu coins mentioned in Chinese sources of the Tang dynasty. The bracelet coin was convenient for carrying overland on strings, but either because travel by water made lumps more appropriate or in order to replicate the existing cowrie shell money in silver, the bullet-shaped coins gradually evolved in Sukhothai or early Ayutthaya.

It is not clear when these weights became a standard coinage, though one possibility is during the reign of King Chairaja (1534–36), whom an early chronicle claims "removed from his land the fraudulent practice of small or false weights and measures" (van Vliet 1640: 71).[6] It is at least safe to conclude that sometime during the sixteenth century the weight and shape of the Siamese bullet of silver became standardized. By 1614 this silver tikal (Thai *baht*) represented "the Kings coyne of Syam" to the English (Best 1614: 53). Throughout the seventeenth century it consistently weighed about 14.6 grams (Wicks 1983: 169–70) and maintained its international value at about three-fifths of a real, or 30 English pence. Its kidney shape was obtained by casting it into an elliptical mould, then cutting the flat side so that it could be bent in at both ends. It was then stamped on each side with an animal, shell, lotus, or wheel device (Le May 1932: 63–65).

In spite of the silver resources in the north of Burma, Pegu had no currency in the sixteenth century, merely weights of the cumbrous gansa. Pires (1515: 100) adds the interesting information that silver was also used in the Pegu market "in rounds marked with the mark of Siam, as it all comes from there." By the early decades of the seventeenth century Burma had effectively adopted the Thai system of silver by weight, with brokers authorized to ensure its consistency. *Tikal* was the word used by foreigners for the standard weight of silver in both countries but the indigenous words were *baht* and *kyat*, terms still used for the units of currency in Thailand and Burma, respectively. In Burma it was one-hundredth of a *viss*, equivalent to about 24 grams.

This coinage did not exclude other currencies, such as the all-

6. Le May (1932) speculated that King Ramat'ibodi (1491–1529) may have originated this standard coinage; Le May counted fifteen types of markings on the extant lumps of standard tikal weight and deduced that the fifteen most recent rulers of Ayutthaya issued them. There is, however, no evidence that the stamps represent distinct reigns rather than the official broker or silversmith who guaranteed the weight.

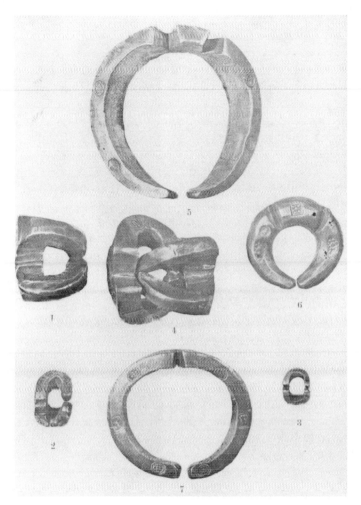

Fig. 18 Northern Tai "bracelet" type of silver weights. In modern times it was believed that these should be used in pairs, representing male and female.

powerful real, but it was an effective response to the silver revolution. The question is why other states did not adopt a silver standard. One answer is that gold was more abundant in the Archipelago than in the rest of Asia and cheaper in relation to silver than in India, China, or Japan. Before 1620 the ratio was about 1:7 in Southeast Asia and 1:10 in India; by the second half of the century it had risen to 1:12 in Southeast Asia and 1:15 in India (*SP* 16252–29: 371; *LREIC* III: 156; La Loubère 1691: 72; Habib 1982A: 367). Profits of nearly 100 percent were said to be made by bringing Japanese silver into Pegu in exchange for gold in the 1620s (Robinson and Shaw 1980: 23–24), and Sumatra and the Philippines continued to export gold throughout the century. Moreover, the traditional reverence for gold as a symbol of power and prestige made it seem the appropriate material to bear the king's name.

Most important, Southeast Asia was more politically fragmented than India or China, and the equation between international and domestic markets was very different. The Sephardic Jewish trader Francesco del Bocchier (1518: 198) explained that Malay Melaka had had no gold or silver coinage because "the merchants there understand merchandise, and deal in weight of gold," but a more profound reason was that the interests of international merchants tended in such cities to prevail over those of the state. By the seventeenth century no local coin could compete with the Spanish real as an international currency. It quickly became the currency and unit of account for the international transactions that dominated the business of the large city markets. The demand of Chinese and Indian traders for Japanese and American silver to take back to their own countries would have imposed a great strain on any indigenous mint. The rulers who issued coins were engaging in what proved to be a losing battle to maintain an internal realm where they had economic sovereignty distinct from the international market by which they lived.

The larger gold coin issued by Makassar and Johor, four times the weight of the Acehnese mas which would otherwise have seemed to be the model, appears to have been an attempt to replicate in gold the silver real which foreign merchants were bringing in. In the 1630s and 1640s the Makassar mas held remarkably consistent in the market at about four-fifths of a silver real, and one suspects that some internal revenues were collected at par. Sultan Hasanuddin began to experience economic difficulties, and in 1655 he attempted to force an artificial parity between a new weaker mas and the old one. The market prevailed, however: people preferred to deal in reals or uncoined gold, and the unpopular new coin had to be withdrawn three years later (Macassar Factory 1658: 148; Bassett 1958: 27).

Sultan Iskandar Muda (1607–36), the strongest of Aceh's kings and the one who directly faced the peak of the silver influx, was almost pathological in his commitment to gold. His letters all showed that he took tremendous pride in his possession of gold ornaments, vessels, umbrellas, and even a golden tomb prepared in advance. Muslim traders were required to pay their 10 percent import duties to the king in gold (Beaulieu 1660: 110). The French admiral Augustin de Beaulieu, who descended on Aceh with nothing but silver reals, was given a difficult time by this king, who not only refused to deal in silver but evidently was able to prevent his subjects from doing so. "He told me that . . . silver . . . was no use to him, and that he made no more fuss of it than of earth: that if I had brought gold, he would have given his pepper at the price current in the town" (cited Lombard 1967: 107). The king's determination to maintain a gold standard in the face of the influx of silver, however, got him into difficulties. Around 1620 he had followed the Makassar example, issuing a new mas nominally worth four times the old, and thus probably intended as a rival and replacement for the real. But it was of a poorer alloy, and thus not acceptable in the market even at its face value of four old mas, let alone for a real. "Even though the king had the hands and feet cut off those who refused it, still the merchants wanted first to see what payment one would give them" (Beaulieu 1666: 65; also Lombard 1967: 108–09). Iskandar Muda's attempt to control the market in this way was a failure. Under his successors his large mas disappeared, the older small one was retained primarily for ceremonial and judicial purposes, and the market functioned on the basis of reals and gold by weight.

One way or another silver had become irresistible as the effective international currency of Southeast Asia by about 1630, whether in reals, as in most of the island world, or in weight. In spite of the status the royal gold coins had, the rulers themselves came to expect taxes and fines to be paid in silver. The triumph of silver undoubtedly furthered the integration of Southeast Asia into a world economy. By exchanging silver for deteriorating base coinage of copper or lead, Vietnamese and Javanese may not have served themselves well, as Europeans were quick to point out (van Neck 1599: 87; Baron 1685: 7). A more fundamental problem was that foreigners controlled the supply of money and through it had direct access to the growers of cash crops. Blussé (1986) has called foreign coin a "trojan horse" for Southeast Asian states. It was certainly a key weapon in the critical struggles of the seventeenth century for economic control of the region.

Financial Organization

The manner of trading generally in the port [Aceh] is so far different from other places, that unless experience had confirmed it, it were incredible. The buyers of goods in quantity are only such as belong to the custom house, excepting some four Dagons who dared not to be seen to bargain for any quantities, until the others have refused them. They pay not ready money for any, and he that will reimburse himself with monie must sell to shopkeepers, who buy only by the corge [twenty pieces cloth] or half-corge, so they can sell the same day in the Bazar. . . . These merchants will not willingly house any goods, only such as they may without detriment bury in the ground, as Tin, Brimstone, etc. . . . If you sell you must oblige them by bill to pay at so many months, which few, or none, fail to perform or pay interest after the time expires, if those vessels are retarded beyond expectations, for the Queen and principal Orang kayas *are very severe in executing justice in that point.—Clark, letter from Aceh 17 December 1643, IOL E/3/18: f.282–83*

In the eyes of European and Chinese visitors, from Chau Ju-kua (1250: 160) in the thirteenth century to colonial officials and entrepreneurs in the early twentieth, capital was always scarce in Southeast Asia. There appeared to be a dearth of large merchants with a stock of goods ready for sale, or of money for purchase. "These people buy only from hand to mouth of Indian cloth, which when they have retailed they come again and buy, and not a merchant will deal for 100 tahil together in money" (Letter from Aceh 12 February 1619, IOC E/3/6: f.213). Whether it was for cash crops like pepper or for manufactures like Vietnamese pots, traders found they had to deal on a very small scale or else "trust" by advancing capital against future delivery.

Nevertheless the concepts of credit, interest, and obligation were deeply ingrained throughout Southeast Asia. Although many financial terms were borrowed in the age of commerce from Tamil, Arabic, Chinese, or Dutch, the common terms for interest on capital have older indigenous roots based on the metaphor of the flower (Malay *bunga*; Thai *dòk*) of a plant or tree. In modern Thai, *dòk-bia*, the flowering of the cowries, still expresses interest but appears to go back as far as fourteenth-century Sukhothai, as does *ku*, to borrow at interest. Moreover, the foreign merchants who advanced money against future production or on local shipping ventures were less concerned about defaulting than they would have been at home. "Their laws for debt are so strict that the creditor may take his debtour, his wives, children and slaves, and all that he hath, and sell them for his debt" (Scott 1606: 173). It was in fact fundamental to Southeast Asian social structure that debt implied obligation, and particularly the obligation to labour. In the cities and the hills, the powerful states and the tribal societies, a defaulting debtor became bonded to his creditor, obliged to serve him until the principal was repaid (Reid 1988: 129–36; 1983: 8–12). The object of creditors within this system was not so much to increase their capital by earning interest as to increase their status and power by acquiring dependents.

The increase in commercial opportunity and the circulation of money during the age of commerce naturally brought great changes to this pattern, but it did not destroy it. In spite of the influx of silver and

of copper cash, complaints remained about the acute shortage of capital. Evidently it was not money that was lacking but the system to
make it available for investment. In Maluku it was said that the
income from clove sales was simply buried: "They treasure these
[copper cash] up, and also jewels, objects of gold, Javanese gongs, fine
silk and cotton fabrics. . . . They keep them stored in earthen vessels
and hidden in the mountains, buried under the ground so that no one
may know of it except two or three slaves who carry it there during the
night" (Galvão 1544: 140–41). An English factor later pleaded that
Indian cloth rather than silver reals be sent to the islands since coins
were of little use to Indonesians, "saving a little for ornaments, being
buried in the ground from posterity to posterity" (*SP 1625–29:* 371).[7]

The political context made it dangerous for the small man to
show his wealth unless he had sufficient dependents to defend and
legitimate it. Capital therefore had first to be deployed into obtaining
people—through buying slaves, lending to those in need, marital and
military alliances, and feasting. Those in a position to lend in the spirit
of the professional moneylender or banker, for profit rather than patronage, were rulers and other powerful figures on the one hand and
foreigners on the other.

Carlo Cipolla has argued that "the true economic revolution" of
early modern Europe was a dramatic drop in interest rates (cited Jones
1981: 41). The global supremacy of Amsterdam in the seventeenth
century was measured by an abundant supply of capital at the world's
lowest interest rates—between 2.5 and 5 percent a year (Israel 1989:
78). Most European cities, however, were no better served than the
best-regulated Asian ones. Those of northern India, for example, had
interest rates between 6 and 12 percent in the first half of the seventeenth century (Habib 1963: 401–04). By this index of the advance
towards capitalism, Southeast Asian cities were well behind. Apart
from a special case in Iskandar Muda's Aceh, interest rates were 2
percent a month at best, and could be three times that. This was
comparable with southern India, and with most of Europe a century
earlier, but it still left a critical gap to the leading financial centres.

The minimum rates just quoted are not the whole story. Even in
Surat, where Irfan Habib has shown rates to be modest, the English

7. A similar apparent "disappearance" of money was also noted in Indonesia in the
nineteenth century during times of exceptionally high prices for cash crops—for example, pepper in west Aceh and sugar in easternmost Java. Elson (1984: 166) cites a village
in Pasuruan in the prosperous 1850s when 4000 guilders was found in copper coins in
forty-three Javanese houses that had burned down, whereas the houses and their furni-
ture were together reckoned to be worth only 1047 guilders.

initially complained that they could not borrow for less than 3 percent a month. Only when they became trusted did they enjoy the lowest rates. Most of the early modern world, like much of the rural third world in modern times, lived in conditions where lending was highly speculative, legal controls were ineffective, and repayment was uncertain. The lowest rates were for customers trusted to repay, usually led by governments. In Southeast Asia in the seventeenth century these included the European companies, important and wealthy rulers, the very biggest merchants, and members of one's own caste or kinship group. Outside these privileged circles extraordinarily high rates could be charged. The earliest Tagalog-Spanish dictionary gave three words for a loan at interest, depending whether the interest was 20 percent a month, 100 percent a year, or 150 percent a year (Scott 1982: 534). One English factor with a desperate need for funds to cover his purchases in Aceh had to borrow at 400 percent a year in 1643 (IOL O.C. E/3/18: 285). In the same city sixteen years earlier it was alleged that the English chief factor was cheating the company by lending its money to Chinese at 6 percent a month (*SP 1625–29:* 414).

Against this background, what is significant is that a more consistent money market was developing for favoured clients in the major Southeast Asian cities. A rate of 2 percent a month occurs often enough in Siam, Banten, Jambi, and Patani to suggest a system was at work in the mid-seventeenth century (Coolhaas III: 322, 399; Smith 1974: 266–67; Schrieke 1942: 386–87). In Patani in 1617 the queen lent to large traders at 2 percent a month, but through a complex arrangement of differential rates for longer loans that worked out at 20 percent a year (*LREIC* II: 80–81, 87).

Islam had a marked effect on commercial procedures. The sections of the Malay law code dealing with commerce are borrowed largely from Islamic law, and words for concepts such as bankruptcy (*muflis*) were taken into Malay from Arabic. The code did not explicitly regulate interest, since *riba*, the Arabic term for usury, was forbidden by Islam. Instead it prescribed an agreed sharing of profits (*laba*):[8] "The one who supplies the capital says to his agent, 'Take this gold or silver money and use it for business. The profit [*laba*] from the transaction to me and to you must be fixed beforehand.' If the capital is wholly or partly lost [the agent] does not have to compensate for the business or the loss of capital, if it was not the result of negligence" (*Undang-undang Melaka:* 146). We have seen that Portuguese ac-

---

8. *Laba,* significantly, is not Arabic but an old Austronesian word, though it is translated as *interest* in the sixteenth-century Buenaventura Tagalog dictionary.

counts confirm that capital was advanced this way on trading voyages, with returns as large as 50 percent. This system was perceived as different from a personal loan, in that the creditor bore the risk of failure and the borrower did not run the risk of enslavement that would otherwise be his lot.

Islamic disapproval of riba does not seem to have had any more effect on the money market in Southeast Asia than it did in Mughal India (Habib 1963: 413–19)—at least merchants did not complain of it. Two attempts were made to put it into law. The Makassar ruler in 1631 forbade "that a debt should earn interest" (*Lontara' Bilang Gowa:* 91), though Europeans did not mention this as an obstacle. Under Sultan Iskandar Muda in Aceh, Beaulieu (1660: 100–01) asserted that "great usury is forbidden." He claimed that interest did not exceed 1 percent a month, whereas in Banten (Aceh's rival) one had to pay 5 percent. Beaulieu was unusually close to the sultan, and he includes this remark after a section on Islamic marriage laws, so his information probably came from the sultan or a *kadi* (Islamic judge), and not the merchant community. Iskandar Muda was unusual in his heavy-handed control of the domestic economy and may well have made such a ruling, perhaps to benefit his own borrowing. That may explain why in the free market of Aceh the exceptionally high rates of interest to which the English referred (above) prevailed.

It is clear from this pattern that Southeast Asia was far from creating such corporate institutions as the banks and stock exchanges that blossomed in European cities in the seventeenth century. Nevertheless, the pattern that had obtained a century or two earlier in Europe, in which the major providers of credit were Jewish money-lenders and such religious institutions as the Italian *monti di pietà*, did have some parallels below the winds. Throughout the ports of the Indian Ocean, Hindu commercial castes—Gujarati sharafs and South Indian chettiars—played the critical role of a tightly organized international minority living by the movement of money. They were in Melaka, Pasai, and Pegu when the Portuguese arrived at the beginning of the sixteenth century, and subsequently spread to other ports.

The key corporate institution that the chettiar community developed in the direction of a bank was the temple fund, guaranteed by a powerful religious sanction, to which all were obliged to contribute and from which all could borrow (Evers 1988: 204). Although by definition the majority communities could not replicate this proto-bank, it is significant that they were aware of it, as an important passage in the most popular of Malay epics demonstrates. The Malay hero visits a temple in south India: "Whenever a *nakhoda* [supercargo] or a merchant lacked capital, he came to the head of the temple and borrowed the gold of the idol; a *bahar* or two *bahar* even were given by the head who looked after this idol. If that merchant wanted to default on the gold of the idol, wherever he went he would be destroyed. If he was true to the idol, his goods would be safe wherever he went. If he borrowed twenty *kati* [of gold], one *kati* had to be offered to the idol" (*Hikayat Hang Tuah:* 362).[9]

These mercantile Hindu castes were in the first instance money changers, but they also operated as bankers and brokers for merchants. They had a developed system of salable letters of credit (*hundi*) that could be issued in one city and cashed in another, not only in India but extending to ports frequented by Indians below the winds—Melaka, Pegu, Banten, or Aceh (Habib 1963: 401; Tavernier 1692 II: 18, 25). Two of the richest merchants of Melaka at the Portuguese conquest, Naina Suradewana and Naina Chatu, were South Indian Hindus, probably chettiars who had risen beyond their original money-lending functions. In describing Melaka merchants, Barbosa refers specifically to "*chettijs* of Coromandel, who are very corpulent with big bellies, they go bare above the waist" (1518 II: 177). Castanheda (1552 II: 458) correctly identified them with Pulicat, then the dominant Coromandel port and outlet for Vijayanagar. He described them as the richest and most extensive traders in the world. They funded voyages to Maluku, Java, Sumatra, Pegu, and China, generally using Malay, Javanese, and Mon (Pegu) crews (Thomaz 1988: 37). Suradewana was described as "the head of all the merchants in the city" by the *Sejarah Melayu* (1612: 185), capable of trying to bribe the Bendahara with a bahar of gold to influence a commercial dispute with his rival.[10] He cooperated with the Javanese ruler of Gresik to dominate Melaka's trade with Java and Maluku, sending out about eight junks a year. Along with the other wealthy chettiar merchants in Pegu and Pasai, Naina Tirivanga and Naina Kunapan, respectively, these were early allies of the anti-Muslim Portuguese, and they contributed capital and expertise to the first Portuguese commercial ventures in the Bay of Bengal (Bouchon 1979: 141; Alves 1989).

Far more numerous as commercial brokers, however, were Muslim Gujaratis, no doubt better able to operate in the increasingly Islamic atmosphere of such ports as Aceh and Banten. The first Florentine merchant to visit Melaka acknowledged that the Gujaratis there

9. My attention was drawn to this passage by Denys Lombard (1988: 18).

10. I am assuming here, with Thomaz, that the Naina Suradewana of the *Sejarah Melayu* was the same as the Nina Curya Deva of the Portuguese.

were "astute and clever merchants, as good as us in all business matters; their cargo ledgers with their lists of bales taken and discharged
are all in perfection" (Florentine Letter 1513: 375–77). Another Florentine merchant with the Portuguese in India was probably referring to
these Gujaratis when he said that "the people here surpass us in everything. And there are Moorish merchants worth 400,000 to 500,000
ducats. And they can do better calculations by memory than we can do
by the pen" (cited Subrahmanyam 1990: 7). Though European merchants were fierce rivals of the Gujaratis, they nevertheless had to
employ them in unfamiliar Muslim ports to avoid being cheated. The
Acehnese were particularly fussy about coin, and a foreigner could
easily be caught with unacceptable damaged pieces. "But if the Broker
takes any bad money, 'tis to his own loss. These sort of brokers are
commonly Guzurats, and 'tis very necessary for a Merchant that
comes hither, especially if he is a stranger, to have one of them, for fear
of taking bad or light money" (Dampier 1699: 94–95; cf. *LREIC* I: 270–
71; IV: 94). It is not surprising that the Malay words for capital (*modal*),
and for a foreign trader (*baniaga*) derive from Indian languages.

By no means all the brokers working with money were Indians,
though some local brokers also had Indian blood. Burma had a semi-
official category of brokers whom foreigners trading in the market
were required to use. Their Indian origins are suggested by the term
tarega by which they were known (from Telugu *taraga*—Yule and
Burnell 1903: 901), but they appear to have been ethnic Mon by the
sixteenth century when we hear about them: "There are in Pegu eight
brokers, whom they call Tareghe, which are bound to sell your goods at
the price which they be worth, and you give them for their labour two
in the hundred: and they be bound to make your debt good, because
you sell your marchandises upon their word. If the broker pay you not
at his day, you may take him home, and keep him in your house" (Fitch
1591: 304). This unique system appears to have been imposed by
Burmese kings to ensure that the royal monopolies on various export
items were respected. Nevertheless, the role of the tarega was appreciated by many foreigners (though less so the companies) because of the
familiar problem of coping with an unknown currency—in this case,
the cumbrous ganza (Hall 1928: 91).

It is also clear that the careful Indian habits of recording commercial contracts in writing were replicated by Javanese, Malays, and
Mons, at least by the seventeenth century. Lodewycksz (1598: 120)
explained how contracts between merchants in Banten and the seago-
ing traders to whom their capital was entrusted were written in Javanese on palm leaves or Chinese paper. Portuguese traders based in

Gresik at the end of the sixteenth century, like those at Melaka at its beginning, were essentially relying on the existing Asian system of contracts to guarantee their investments. When a Dutch visitor asked the Portuguese "how they could understand the statements which were written in Malay," the answer was that they couldn't but that they had several different Javanese read it to ensure its accuracy (Heemskerck 1600: 451).

Southeast Asians were certainly among the urban traders who accumulated substantial capital and invested in trading voyages. Their number and the amount of capital they were willing to deploy in such ventures rose rapidly in the age of commerce, but less rapidly than would have been expected from export earnings. The reasons are not to be found in the inadequacy of commercial techniques or currency. Foreigners from above the winds, even when they had much less of either, like the private Portuguese,[11] found they could make good money by taking these commercial roles. There were other constraints on the development of an indigenous merchant class.

Orangkaya—The Mercantile Elite

> I sing in this song of a merchant great
> And of his wealth. His goods and treasures were
> Beyond all count, his happiness without alloy.
> In Indrapura town there was
> No equal to his fortune. He possessed
> A thousand slaves, both old and young, who came
> From Java and other lands. His rank
> Was higher than Punggawa's. Wives he had
> In goodly numbers.
>
> —*Sya'ir Bidasari: 7*

Words having to do with merchants in Southeast Asian languages are commonly foreign in origin: Malay *saudagar* from Persian, *baniaga* from Sanskrit (already used in Javanese inscriptions of the eleventh century—Hall 1985: 18); Malay *ceti*, Burmese *setthi*, and Thai *sethi* ultimately from Sanskrit through Pali and South Indian languages; Vietnamese *thuong mai* from Chinese. Other terms, like the Malay *orang dagang* and its analogues throughout the Austronesian languages, can mean either trader or foreigner, the visitor from outside being almost inevitably a travelling merchant. One word that seems wholly indigenous is *orangkaya*. In modern Malay and Indonesian this

---

11. Pires compared the attitude of his countrymen, in a hurry to be home, with that of Southeast Asians: "We do our trade like Portuguese who are not accustomed to it . . . and thus we make our way quickly" (1515: 220).

simply means rich man (as does *sethi* in modern Thai and Burmese). In many states of the Archipelago it was (and in Brunei still is) an aristocratic title. *Kaya* is an Austronesian word with deep roots, however, and its older meaning in Javanese and Tagalog, as well as Malay, pertains more to power than to wealth.

The central point is that in Southeast Asian languages wealth and power were not sharply distinguished. Wealth could be obtained only through power, in the sense of inner strength and an intimate relationship with the spiritual world (Acciaioli 1989; Milner 1982). Yet, because wealth was expressed primarily in terms of followers, a wealthy man had to be powerful and therefore potentially threatening to the ruler. For foreigners, and for women, the equation between wealth and power was less certain, and so both categories were given more leeway to accumulate wealth by jealous rulers. Even for them, however, the problem arose.

The term *orangkaya* expressed this ambivalence for the Malay world. As a category of people, it might be translated "wealthy aristocrats" or "merchant elite." As a title, it was borne by the senior officials of the court but might also be bestowed on a foreign merchant whom the ruler wished to co-opt into his service and constrain through the etiquette of his court. The Englishman Thomas Best received the title *Orangkaya putih* (white, or clear-hearted, lord) by Sultan Iskandar Muda of Aceh, whom he had gratified by handing over a Portuguese barque he had captured (Best 1614: 56, 1613: 256). The term also expresses the commercial origin of many ruling families, including those of Jambi, Banda, and Ambon. Where there was a strong pattern of monarchy, however, the orangkaya as a collectivity were seen rather in terms of actual or potential opposition to it. They were the trade-enriched aristocracy of the capital (fig. 19a).

It is useful for analytical purposes to distinguish three types of orangkaya, even if the boundaries between them were frequently crossed. First, there were the foreign merchants, attracted to the port by its trading opportunities but able to leave again; second, the foreign or foreign-descended, partly assimilated merchant-officials, mediating between the court and traders; and third, the indigenous aristocracy drawn into trade by their position or wealth.

The composition of the first category changed over time, with independent traders and financiers tending to give way in the seventeenth century to local representatives of foreign states. Around 1500 the largest merchants in Melaka were Hindu Tamils (including the extremely wealthy chettiars discussed above), and Gujarati, Javanese, and Tagalog ("Luzon") Muslims. Little is known about individual

Gujaratis, most of whom departed in outrage at the Portuguese conquest. The leading Tagalog merchants were "Curederaja" (Kuriadiraja?), who sent a junk to China every year, and "Aregemute Raja," made head of Melaka's remaining Muslims by the Portuguese, who sent ships in 1513 to China, Siam, Borneo, Sunda, and Palembang (Thomaz 1979: 114–16). The Javanese dominated the rice trade from Java and were noted especially for their wealth in manpower. Most of the artisans and labourers of Melaka were Javanese, some thousands of "slaves" being under the protection of their most influential countryman, "Utimutiraja" (Utamadiraja?).

During the sixteenth century, Chinese, "Turkish," private Portuguese, and Spanish traders joined this international commercial elite, while the Hindu and Tagalog merchants assimilated or ceased to be significant. State representatives also began to be important: not only the servants of the Portuguese Estado da India but also figures like Khoja Zeinal, "a very wealthy man" who represented the Sultan of Brunei in Pahang for three or four years in the 1540s, according to Pinto (1578: 61), before killing the Pahang ruler, who had taken liberties with his wife. Drake (1580: 70) visited Ternate at the height of its success as a Muslim and anti-Portuguese power, and found there four "Romanes" (Rumi) dressed like Turks, two Turks, and an Italian all acting as permanent agents for the buying of cloves. Around 1600 the merchants of Aceh included people from "China, Bengala, Pegu, Coromandel, Guserate, Arabia and Rumos [Turkey]" (Davis 1600: 151), while those of Banten included all of those as well as Portuguese, Spaniards, and Malays.

One of the larger Banten merchants with whom the early Dutch and English voyagers dealt was Cheti Maluku, or Sancho, presumably born in Maluku of a Spanish father, who maintained one of the opulent compounds of Banten, sent junks to Gresik and Maluku, and was able to supply the Dutch with 200 tonnes of pepper at once (Lodewycksz 1598: 88, 104–5; *True Report* 1599: 33; Meilink-Roelofsz 1962: 241). Another was a "Turkish" merchant (perhaps from Cairo), Kojah Rayoan, who had been to Venice and spoke Italian. He helped the Dutch in Banten and again in Banda, where he was said to be greatly respected ("Tweede Boeck" 1601: 68, 77; van Leur 1934: 162; fig. 19b). Chinese were more numerous, but few yet stood out as exceptionally wealthy. The favorite of the English, called by them "Kewee," was "a man of the best credit in the town," and important enough to have loans outstanding to the English in 1615 of 2000 reals and 390 tonnes of pepper (*LREIC* III: 274–75). The Dutch equivalent, "Sim Suan," also had large debts to them, but he had his own junk in Banten and a house big

Fig. 19a An orangkaya of Aceh, drawn from life about 1640

Fig. 19b Dutch impression of social classes of Banda, about 1600: *A*. a Turkish merchant, with scales; *B*. a Banda orangkaya, his arms carried by a slave; and *C*. a wealthy woman of Banda, followed by her slave

enough to store some of the Dutch merchandise (Meilink-Roelofsz 1962: 250–51).

By the middle of the seventeenth century, when Dutch monopoly pressure had contributed to an atmosphere much more difficult for independent Asian merchants, the biggest of them tended to be north Indian Muslims, often protected by their links with the leading Indian princes. The Mughal conquest of Gujarat made Surat the major port of the empire, and the Surat-based merchants formerly referred to as Gujaratis were now seen as Mughal subjects or "Moors." At Aceh in 1642 one of the largest private merchants was an employee of a son of the Emperor Shah Jahan—a Nakhoda named Marsaly, "who had a very beautiful flower garden" at his house in Banda Aceh. Had he not been so powerfully protected, however, he would have had a hand chopped off according to the strict laws of Aceh, since he injured several people in a drunken tantrum in the market (Sourij 1642: f582v–583v). In Banten there were some extremely wealthy and respected "Moors," including one who rewarded a German surgeon with a sum equivalent to 300 reals for setting his son's badly broken leg (Fryke 1692: 132–33; see fig. 20). The Nabob of Golconda sent his representatives (often Persians) with trading voyages to Aceh, Burma, Banten, and Makassar. In Siam, Indian and Persian Muslims reached a peak of influence in the 1670s. The French ambassador was impressed by the magnificence of one of their houses, which he was allotted in 1685 after their disgrace (Aubin 1980: 124).

More details are available on the commerce of the two largest private merchants of Makassar in the middle of the century—the Portuguese Francisco Vieira de Figueredo (1624–67) and the Indian Muslim Howsenena Khoja, alias Mapule or (to the English) "Mopley" (d.1675). Vieira skilfully mixed diplomacy and trade in the manner of the period, representing as ambassador at different times the Portuguese and Spanish viceroys, the kings of Makassar and Cambodia, and the Nabob of Golconda, Mir Jumla. During his eventful life he made and lost several fortunes, always by combining his own investment in a trading voyage with that of the ruling circle of Makassar or some other state. This provided him the protection he needed against having his cargo confiscated by the Dutch or some other enemy (Boxer 1967).

Mopley may also have come to Makassar initially as an agent of Mir Jumla, but by the late 1650s he was the principal trading partner of the English there, taking their Indian cloth and supplying them cloves and tortoiseshell (IOL G/10/1: 141, 146–48, 177–78). He also owned a junk that made a lucrative annual voyage from Makassar to Manila,

Fig. 20 Leading figures of Banten as sketched by the Danish merchant Corte-munde in 1673. *From left:* a "Moorish" or Indian Muslim merchant, a Javanese noble, and a Chinese merchant.

registered in the king's name to meet Spanish requirements. The Dutch estimated that its cargo was worth up to 100,000 reals (2.5 tonnes of silver), chiefly in Indian cloth, and that "the Malays paid to put their cargo on it, so that the whole city of Makassar was interested in it, some more, others less, for the profits were enticing, recently being able to exceed 50 to 60%, sometimes more" (Speelman 1670A: 107). As the Dutch noose tightened around Makassar in the mid-1660s, Mopley skilfully shifted his loyalties and would have made a Manila voyage on the Dutch account had he not died in 1675 (Coolhaas 1968: 755; Gaastra 1982: 307).

All of these foreign merchants enjoyed close relations with the ruler and played a careful political game, or they would not have stayed in business. Some are scarcely to be differentiated from the second category, that of merchant-officials mediating explicitly between the court and the market-place. The classic role of this type was that of *syahbandar* (from Persian for master of the port), an office to which a leading foreign merchant was typically appointed by Malay rulers to ensure that protocol was observed and port dues were paid by the foreign merchants arriving by sea. During the peak of Melaka's prosperity there were four syahbandars, one to represent the Gujarati merchants, another for all others coming from the west (from India, but also from Pegu and Pasai), a third for Malay-speakers coming from the east (including Java, Maluku, south Sumatra, Borneo, and the Philippines), and a fourth for the east Asians (China and Ryukyu).

This Melaka model was influential elsewhere. Although most other ports needed only one or two syahbandars, Cambodia in the early seventeenth century had five—two for the Chinese and one each for Portuguese, Japanese, and Malay-speakers (Gaelen 1636: 63). Around 1512 a Hindu chettiar was syahbandar in Pasai (Barros 1563 III, i: 272); a century later a south Indian held the post in Banten, Chinese Muslim converts in Jambi, Japara, and Jaratan and a Gujarati at Hitu in Ambon (Jourdain 1617: 253; Scott 1606: 174; Meilink-Roelofsz 1962: 240, 283, 286, 289).

The office of syahbandar was a strategic one, well-placed for lucrative partnerships with the ruler on the one hand and foreigners in need of official blessing on the other. The Malay annals celebrate the wealth of one South Indian syahbandar, Raja Mendaliar, as "extremely rich, at that time he had no equal in the city of Melaka" (*Sejarah Melayu* 1612: 183). The Indian syahbandar of Banten was said by the Dutch to have arrived in the city with "nothing to live on, so that he undertook vile things to earn his living," but eventually rose to great wealth (Lodewycksz 1598: 75).

Higher offices, including the governance of ports that were not capitals, frequently also went to enterprising traders. A Gujarati ruled Japara for Mataram at the beginning of the seventeenth century, while Indian Muslims and even an Englishman governed Tenasserim for Siam. In Siam itself the two offices dealing with foreign trade—the Kalahom and the Mahatthai—were dominated first by foreign Muslims and then by Europeans in the reigns of Prasat Thong and Narai (Wyatt 1982: 108–09). In Patani, a Malay of Chinese origin, the Datu Sirinara, had the greatest influence over the sultanate's commercial affairs (Warwijck 1604: 43). The exceptionally rapid growth of the region's cities gave almost unlimited opportunities to wealthy and enterprising foreigners who threw in their lot with the ruling class and effectively assimilated to it. Many rulers themselves could trace their origins not many generations back to merchants of foreign origin—notably to the Chinese who developed such port states as Palembang, Demak, and Gresik in the early fifteenth century. The brief kingdom of the Portuguese adventurer Felipe de Brito at the Burmese port of Syriam, in 1600–14, could be seen as one more case of a bold outsider riding the commercial boom to power in an unusually open period.

Foreign-born merchants continued to rise to the highest levels even in established states. The greatest of Melaka's sultans, Mansur (1459–77), for example, continued the close relations of his forebears with China and Java, resulting both in royal marriages and in an influx of influential Chinese and Javanese (*Sejarah Melayu* 1612: 104–10, 117–19). He also appointed "a heathen Kling," probably another chettiar financier, to organize his finances. Having become a Muslim, this Indian became the progenitor, according to the Portuguese, of the great Bendahara dynasty, which provided Melaka's subsequent chancellors (Pires 1515: 249). The commercial orientation of the family continued in office, and the grandson of this Hindu was the hero of the *Sejarah Melayu*, Bendahara Sri Maharaja. He was not only a great administrator responsible for Melaka's prosperity, "extremely just and humane, very adept in the handling of foreign traders"; he was also enormously wealthy, with so much gold that he let his children play with it: "Bendahara Sri Maharaja was always speculating for profit, and never came to grief" (*Sejarah Melayu* 1612: 159–60, 184).

Sultan Mansur also promoted one of his slaves, a non-Muslim from Palembang, who became so powerful that he gave rise to another great Melaka dynasty, that of the Laksamana (Pires 1515: 249). Although Malay states like Melaka were the most effective melting-pots in which outsiders could rise rapidly, similar phenomena occurred in all the trade-based states. Even in Siam, David Wyatt (1986) has shown that the four most powerful official families from about 1610 to the fall of Ayutthaya all derived from able foreigners brought into commercial branches of government in the seventeenth century—from Persian, Brahman, Chinese, and Mon origins, respectively.

The lofty grandeur of the indigenous aristocracy might give the impression of a class so conscious of its position that it would be impossible for outsiders to enter. In Aceh and Johor the gentry distinguished themselves from the common people by growing the nails of thumb and little finger to extraordinary lengths, "showing that they had never worked with their hands" (Martin 1604: 40; cf. Nieuhoff 1682: 181)—though the fact that Makassarese notables were said to cut their nails assiduously "because they imagine that the devil hides there when they are long" (Gervaise 1701: 155) shows that the new Islamic moralism vigorously contested this idea. The Thai, Malay, Javanese, and Makassarese elite astonished Westerners with their retinue of retainers, their exalted sense of dignity, and their refusal to do physical work. "With them it is all pomp, vanity and bombast" (du Jarric 1608: 630). "In Makassar the nobility are prouder than anywhere else on earth" (Gervaise 1701: 87; cf. Barros 1563 II, ii: 24; Scott 1606: 170–71).

Paradoxically, however, this extreme emphasis on status coincided with a high degree of mobility across status lines. Precisely because there were no hard caste divisions, and because so many aristocrats had commercial origins, status had to be constantly displayed. Numerous descriptions of the way the social hierarchy worked in Makassar and Aceh suggest that those on the bottom strove precisely so that they could purchase a slave and thereby acquire gentry status, no longer demeaning themselves with physical work (Gervaise 1701: 71–72; Reid 1983: 166–67). Foreigners, too (perhaps especially), crossed the barrier. The Chinese in Banten were willing to do any kind of work to make money, but when they "turned Javanese" by adopting Islam, cutting their hair and changing their dress, they were "every whit as proud and as loftie as the Javans" (Scott 1606: 174).

Although Southeast Asian royal chroniclers were at pains to show the lofty descent of powerful rulers, this reflected ideology, not sociology, and for the most part the ideology of a later period when surviving chronicles were written. The Portuguese, who wrote much closer in time to the origins of ruling lineages in Java, show that many rulers were known at the time to be of humble or commercial origins. Chinese ancestry was not then something the Javanese elite attempted to hide (Barros 1563 II, ix: 352; Reid 1992: 196–97). Tomé Pires provides examples of meteoric rises in Java, as well as Melaka, in his own day, even though he confirms that Javanese hauteur was second to none. One was the ruler of Japara, Patih Yunus,

the knight of whom the Javanese speak, because they say that he is a great warrior in Java and very prudent. . . . His grandfather was a working man in the islands of Lawe [west Borneo] and he went to Melaka with very little nobility and less wealth; and he married in Melaka and had the son who was father to Pate Onuz. And in Melaka he went on making money and traded in Java, and about forty or forty-five years ago he cunningly killed the patih of Japara, which was weak and nothing much. . . . Afterwards, and through his cunning, it became such that he peopled it. . . . He was such a daring man that he took the island of Bangka under his jurisdiction, and that of Tanjungpura, and Lawe [west Borneo] and other islands (Pires 1515: 187).

The need to display such marks of status as a numerous following was already a feature of Southeast Asia in the age of commerce, but it was then designed to triumph over or conceal origins that were frequently humble. The Southeast Asian aristocracy did not become an exclusive caste until the colonial era, when high birth was the only card it had left to play.

Nor is it easy to draw a line between a passive native aristocracy and a commercially active cosmopolitan orangkaya element. Undoubtedly there were courts, and more of them as the seventeenth century proceeded, where commerce was regarded as unworthy of their attention except as a source of gifts and levies. Northern Vietnamese rulers, reflecting their Confucian ideology, often gave this impression, as did the Burmese kings of Ava. They were thereby also more immune to commercial new blood at court. By contrast, some ruling groups that inherited aristocratic traditions of warfare and agriculture were drawn into trade by the opportunities and pressures of the period. The Makassar and Banten aristocracies moved this way in the first half of the seventeenth century, taking ever more active roles in commercial investment, shipbuilding, and even voyaging. The Dutch account of Tuban, before that great city was destroyed by Sultan Agung in 1619, makes clear that it was the local Javanese aristocracy who sent their junks to Banda, Ternate, and the Philippines, the same group who engaged in weekly tournaments (senenan) and who never went out without a dozen retainers ("Tweede Boeck" 1601: 36–37). One of the great merchants of the emporium of Patani, whose ship was seized by the Dutch off Melaka, was Raja Kelantan, ruler of the adjacent dependent state (Warwijck 1604: 82; Jansz 1616: 217).

In assessing the function of the orangkaya, the great dynamism of the period must be kept in mind. Foreign merchants frequently joined the local aristocracy; indigenous local dynasties were attracted to the port-capital or forced there by a jealous king, and there became involved in commerce; alliances between wealth and power were constantly being made. As commerce lost its appeal in the second half of the seventeenth century, orangkaya who had their roots in trade often became aristocrats with rights in land and people (see chapter 5). In these changes, the balance between the ruler and the orangkaya as a group was always critical. Periods of rapid commercial expansion often coincided with oligarchic rule by orangkaya of partly foreign origin, but such groups were anathema to the kind of powerful, centralizing ruler who could protect them in a hostile world. Contradictory forces were evoked by the conditions of the period, and no satisfactory resolution of their conflict could be found. This issue will be considered more fully in chapter 4.

Commercial Minorities and Ethnicity

The importance of foreign merchants in all Southeast Asian ports should not be taken to mean an absence of "a native middle group carrying on trade on its own account," as Meilink-Roelofsz (1962: 9), among others, has argued. The bulk of Southeast Asian trade, as we have seen, was carried by Southeast Asian vessels with Southeast Asian capital. A large proportion of the population gained its livelihood in commerce as shippers, sailors, and handlers of cash-crops and foreign cloth. The orangkaya can be considered a powerful class with a strong base in trade and interests that conflicted with those of the king. If they did not constitute a "true bourgeoisie" independent of the ruling group, then the mercantile leaders of many contemporary European countries would also have to be denied that title (Indian and Japanese commercial groups had a better claim to autonomy). The first requirement is to analyse what groups were engaged in the higher levels of commerce and what their place in society was.

"Foreign-ness" was a definite advantage in commerce, especially when it involved international connections. The foreigner not only was excluded from agriculture and administration but was also seen by rulers as an asset rather than a threat. In a politically pluralistic region (more like Europe or south India than the empires of Delhi and Beijing) there were, however, degrees of foreign-ness. Some foreign traders, sharing religion and language, could cross the boundary into the local aristocracy very quickly, while all could do so within a generation if willing to accept the dominant religion and culture. In this social mobility Southeast Asia parted company from India and Japan, where caste or class barriers made it virtually impossible for a trader to enter the ruling group. Precisely because commercial success stories were able to move into power, it is more difficult to demarcate a strong middle or "bourgeois" group.

Nevertheless, there were some Southeast Asian groups wholly committed to commerce, owning their own capital and generating a commercial ethos distinct from that of the ruling group. The first of these was constituted by women. They not only dominated the market; many of them became traders and financiers on a large scale (Reid 1988: 163–66). It is not easy to locate statements of a distinct female trading ideology, but there is no doubt that women were free from many of the concerns with status and power that inhibited the development of a commercial ethos among men.

The second group that merits attention were travelling merchants, the *kiwi*, and their leaders, the nakhodas. Ranking just below the office-holding syahbandars, these were in a sense foreigners everywhere; even in the port they considered home they probably resided in an ethnic enclave, where their main contact with the authorities was the syahbandar of their group. This category of trader was defined by function and ethnicity rather than by class in the European sense. There was little to prevent a successful nakhoda becoming a syahbandar or eventually a ruler, as Pires' Patih Yunus shows. As sea-going traders, however, they shared a distinctive ethos.

The nearest we have to a charter of the rights and functions of this group is the Malay Code of Maritime Law, the *Undang-undang Laut*. This code accords a strong position to the nakhoda, who has powers of life and death on shipboard, as well as preeminence in all commercial matters, including the right to sell his merchandise first after arrival in port, before the merchants travelling with him can lower the prevailing prices. This power is hardly surprising, since according to internal evidence the code was drawn up by five nakhodas in Melaka in the first decade of the sixteenth century. From their names it appears that at least three were of Javanese origin. These five then discussed it with all the nakhodas. When the code was agreed at this level, they took it to the Bendahara, who in turn went with the five nakhodas to Sultan Mahmud. The sultan promulgated the code with the words: "Whatever you determine at sea will determine things at sea; the law of the land will determine things on land. For you nakhodas are like kings in your respective junks" (*Undang-undang Laut*: 45–46). The nakhoda is a familiar figure in the Malay literature of this period. The first real Malay autobiography was written by one of them, though in the eighteenth century and at European urging (La-uddin 1788). Necessarily literate and well-informed, the nakhoda was always welcome in a city, as he brought not only goods but news from around the region. The more substantial nakhodas were welcome at royal courts for this reason (Houtman 1603: 14–32). The excellence of Dutch information on Southeast Asia owed much to their reports.

This ethos was associated with some ethnic groups more than others. There is little evidence of ethnic Burmans, Thais, Khmers, Vietnamese, or Balinese trading by sea outside their regions. Rhodes (1651: 56) pointed to three inhibitions for the northern Vietnamese: lack of navigational technique, lack of sea-going ships, and the prohibition of their king, who feared to lose potential tax-payers. Although Ayutthaya was the major power of the Gulf of Thailand it had no sea-going ships of its own until the reign of Prasat Thong (1629–56) (fig. 21). This was still a problem when it attacked Patani in 1634, prompting the patronizing observation in the Patani chronicle that "the Siamese did not yet know how to sail the sea, so no matter how far they would have to go they would go overland" (*Hikayat Patani*:

182). The royal fleet that was developed later was manned predominately by Chinese, Muslims, and Europeans, "the Siamese only being good in their river" (Choisy 1687: 244).

If individuals from these Mainland states or the highland peoples traded overseas, they presumably assimilated into one of the groups noted for commerce—Malays and Chinese preeminently, but until around 1600 also Chams, Mons (from Pegu), "Luzons" (from Manila and Brunei), Javanese, and Bandanese. Most of these latter groups who remained active traders probably assimilated as Malays when their homelands were conquered by forces unsympathetic to their commerce—Champa by the Vietnamese, Pegu by the Burmans, Manila by the Spaniards, the Javanese coast (pasisir) by Mataram. In the seventeenth century Makassarese and Bugis began to emerge as a distinct group of maritime traders. The Portuguese came to constitute another commercial minority, and commercially oriented Asian Christians tended to assimilate under that label. All these groups spoke Malay, as a second if not a first language. When in port they resided in the urban enclave of their own group if it was strong enough to have one, and if not, in that of some other group they could identify with. Ethnicity was probably as much a consequence of entrepreneurial minority status as its cause.

The pluralism that was a marked feature of the sixteenth century was in sharp decline in the seventeenth, for reasons examined more fully in chapters 4 and 5. European monopoly buying and other pressures encouraged rulers to take more and more trade into their own hands and helped to centralize those commercially oriented states that remained independent. The commercial minorities native to the region were gradually reduced to Malays and Chinese, and the Chinese became less native, less inclined to assimilate, in the seventeenth century.

The Malay diaspora requires special attention as the principal Southeast Asian commercial minority with some contractual autonomy. At the height of Melaka's prosperity, its Malay-speaking "native" elite was known to be of diverse origins, with Javanese or Sino-Javanese perhaps the biggest element (Barbosa 1518 II: 176). The diaspora began with the Portuguese conquest of Melaka, which drove out most of the resident Muslim merchants. Whatever their ethnic origins, the Melaka diaspora was henceforth seen as *Melayu* or Malay par excellence. For the Malay-speakers of Brunei and Maluku, "Malay style" (*cara Melayu*) meant the ways of Melaka (Pigafetta 1524: 88). These merchants made their bases first in Pahang, Patani, Johor, and Aceh and later in new entrepôts at Banten, Makassar, Ayutthaya, and Cam-

Fig. 21 Foreign traders at sea, as represented in a Thai manuscript of 1776, depicting the incident in the *Mahayana-jataka* when the boddhisatva, Prince Mahachanaka, is miraculously saved from a shipwreck by clinging to the mast. Shown in the ship are a Chinese and a European, while a Muslim Indian is escaping in a boat.

bodia. The Malay community of Banten was noted in 1596 as one of the wealthiest, which like the south Indians "loaned money at interest and for voyages and bottomry" (Lodewycksz 1598: 121). In Cambodia the Malays became strong enough in the 1640s for the king to throw in his lot with them and with Islam (see below).

In eastern Indonesia, Chinese were few and Malays were accorded special status as the only substantial commercial minority. The Makassar royal chronicle records a social contract entered into by King Tunipalangga (1548–66) whereby the Makassarese agreed not to enter the Malay settlement, effectively promising the Malays their own internal jurisdiction. Their representative then was Nakhoda Bonang, but the Makassar court named one of its leading figures as syahbandar to look after them and other traders. New clerical positions —one for a Malay translator and another for a writer for the financial administration of trade—were also created (*Sejarah Goa*: 26–28; Cense 1978: 422).

The chronicle of Bima (Sumbawa) records the signing of a similar contract when the first Muslim ruler of Bima sought to reward the Malays for their role in spreading Islam. Offered land for growing rice, they declined, saying they were "sailors and traders, not peasants," and asked instead for exemption from import and export duties. They were also guaranteed the rights to their settlement at the capital (Syamsuddin 1982: 296–97).

Like any commercial minority, the strength of the Malays lay largely in their international connections and mobility. There were Malay-speaking Muslim communities in every commercial centre in Southeast Asia, but the clearest picture of them emerges in Makassar. The group that originally obtained concessions there in the sixteenth century was said to come from Johor, Patani, Pahang, Minangkabau, and Champa (*Sejarah Goa*: 28; cf. Paiva 1544: 295). It was greatly extended in numbers and wealth from about 1620, when Makassar became the base for all those seeking to avoid Dutch attempts at monopoly on cloves and nutmeg. In the 1620s there were thousands of Malay traders in the city, and six hundred Malay merchants were said to be involved in the fleet that set out for Maluku to gather spices in 1624 (*Dagh-Register* 1624–29: 78, 125). About this time some dissident members of the Patani royal family arrived to add status to the community, and one of them, the Patani queen's uncle, Datu Maharajalela, was later acknowledged by the court as the community's leader. Although the majority Makassarese continued to use their own language for literary purposes, Makassar became an important centre for

Malay literature largely through the activity of this commercial minority (Skinner 1963: 25–27).

The Malays fought vigorously for Makassar against the Dutch, and when the city fell in 1669 they were dispersed. A British factor noted that the Portuguese and Malays, "the two pillars of this trade," would probably leave Makassar for Siam (cited Bassett 1958: 30). A smaller Malay community eventually returned to accept Dutch protection and remained one of the leading commercial elements of the colonial city. The Indian Muslims who had been led by the great merchant "Mopley" eventually assimilated into this community (Cense 1978: 424–26). In Dutch Batavia there was also an important Malay minority, whose first leader was another Patani man, Entji Amat, who "made a fortune as a ship chandler" and served the VOC as writer, translator, diplomat, and protocol officer (de Haan 1922 I: 483).

Urbanism and Capitalism

In evaluating the changes to the economic order in Southeast Asia during the age of commerce, we can begin with those features which Southeast Asia shared with other leading players in the global commercial expansion. The entire period 1400–1630 was one of rapid monetization and commercialization of the economy, with the most rapid expansion in the period 1570–1630. A large proportion of the population, by any contemporary standard, was drawn into production and marketing for the world economy and came to rely on long-distance imports for such everyday items of consumption as cloth, ceramics, utensils, and coinage. Trade occupied a relatively high share (again by international standards) of Southeast Asian national income and made possible a degree of urbanization probably higher than was achieved again before the twentieth century. Within these cities were communities that devoted themselves wholly to trade and commerce, and such institutions as bottomry, profit-sharing, and lending for interest were well established.

In a number of crucial areas, however, China, India, and Japan were more economically advanced than Southeast Asia, even though their techniques were known to many urban Southeast Asians. These included embryonic banks, whose function in Southeast Asia was still conducted on a personal basis by goldsmiths and money-lenders. With more confidence we can endorse Meilink-Roelofsz's view, against van Leur, that leading European cities had developed impersonal institutions to share and safeguard capital that were totally absent in Southeast Asia. The stock exchanges, banks, and chartered companies of Amsterdam, Antwerp, London, and Paris made possible the mobilization for productive purposes of the savings not only of princes and mercantile minorities but also of a wide stratum of the city dwellers and the rural elite.

Behind this question of capitalist techniques lies a more profound political issue: the security of person and property, as Meilink-Roelofsz put it, "against the whim of an arbitrary sovereign" (1962: 8). This is not something that can be measured by any yardstick, but it was the most critical difference between Southeast Asia and Europe in this period. The first visitors to Europe were astonished most of all by the development of personal and property rights there. The first Bantenese taken to Holland, who turned out to be a slave of Chinese origin, reported back to the Banten court "that every man there was his own master, and that there was not one slave or captive in the whole land" (*True Report* 1599: 36–37). The aristocrats who made up the Banten embassy to London in 1682 were for their part "astonished to understand, how our laws gave us propriety in our estates, and so thinking we were all kings, for they could not be made to comprehend, how subjects could possess any thing but at the pleasure of their prince" (Evelyn 1955: 286). In practice, power was diffused and fragmented in various ways, but the systems of law and ideology placed few constraints upon it.

This question in turn leads us back to the city. Property rights were able to develop in late medieval Europe partly because European feudalism created a space for the autonomous city. To a degree, Confucian east Asia also developed autonomous walled cities with their own acknowledged rights and requirements, and in the case of Tokugawa Japan these were vital to the accumulation of capital and a mercantile way of life. In Southeast Asia, by contrast, the city and the state were seen as virtually coterminous. Every city had a ruler or governor, and the hierarchy of these rulers was the same as the hierarchy of the cities. Women, and certain ethnic minorities, might establish an autonomous value-system more favourable to commerce, but it was very difficult for the city as a unit to do so.

The city, however, embraced a market as well as a palace, and the values of one were not the values of the other. At moments when commercial growth was particularly rapid it is possible to see the market making substantial gains against the palace. Johns' argument that the sixteenth-century *Hikayat Bayan Budiman*, with its story of a merchant going away on business and leaving a parrot to preserve his wife's chastity, may be a product of an emergent individualist and mercantile ethos in Melaka has not been accepted without challenge (Johns 1979: 212; cf. Day 1983: 148–49). Lombard (1990 II: 155–62) has recently mounted a stronger case for a sense of individual responsibility in the work of Hamzah Fansuri and Bukhari of Johor around 1600, which is difficult to find in earlier or later work. Repeatedly Hamzah likens his readers to merchant travellers (*anak dagang*) embarked on the ocean in search of knowledge, and urges them to "know yourself" (*kenali dirimu*) (*Poems:* 72, 80, 112, 116; *Sharabu'l Ashiqin:* 305, 308–09). Many other writings of the period reflect a mobile community of traders aware of their individual worth, position, and moral responsibility. The Melaka law code, the Malay Maritime Code, Entji Amin's poem of the Makassar war, and the Javanese "code of Muslim ethics" are well-known examples. The last of these emphasizes hard work, asceticism, and alms-giving, and seems to expect that people would find Muslim converts more stingy than they had been as pagans (Drewes 1978: 28–37). To show how much ethnic stereotypes change over time, it is sufficient to quote a VOC official (of all people) complaining that "a Javanese would sell his own father for a little business" (Heemskerck 1600: 451).

In addition to the forces of the market, there was also the force of the urban mob, a periodic factor in the largest cities. In Patani, a "slave revolt" by the Javanese in 1613 razed most of the city and drove the elite from their homes (Floris 1615: 94–95). In Aceh during the mid-seventeenth century the city population was in the streets on a number of occasions, playing a role at each contested succession. The populace would have killed the unpopular orthodox ulama Raniri had he not fled the city at the end of 1643 (Ito 1978). Ethnic and religious quarrels were often fought out in the streets. These new elements were certainly urban, and capable of posing a challenge to arbitrary kingship, but they had difficulty institutionalizing their power. A fuller consideration of the conflicts between absolutism and pluralism must be postponed to chapter 4.

3

A Religious Revolution

Listen, you [merchant] traveller
Don't be obsessed with what is forbidden . . .
You are forever recounting your money
Forever restringing it for fear of losing it
Running hither and thither like a kijang *[small deer]*
So that your [divine] Lover is dazed
Give up this world
Don't be a stranger to your real self
                                    —*Hamzah Fansuri*, Poems: 94–96

More than half the population of Southeast Asia adopted Islam or Christianity in some sense during the age of commerce. Other changes of that period may have proved temporary, but the formal acceptance of these two "religions of the book" was of great permanent importance. The conformity of individuals and states to ideal models of Muslim or Christian behaviour was of course a quite different thing. Indeed, the rapid movement in this direction was slowed or reversed with the ending of this era, although written traditions ensured that later generations would be repeatedly challenged to conform to their more rigorous demands.

Islam (both Sunni and Shi'a), Catholic and Nestorian Christianity, Confucianism, Judaism, and various Hindu and Buddhist cults had all been represented in Southeast Asia since the first millennium by traders and travellers. Hindu and Buddhist ideas were readily absorbed by court circles, on whom they made no demands for exclusivity or orthodoxy. Muslims and Christians, like Jews and adherents of Chinese religion, were initially in what has been called in Africa the "quarantine" stage, tolerated as a commercial minority but with little expectation that they should either convert or be converted by the host population (Fisher 1973: 31). In the late thirteenth and fourteenth centuries Islam established more substantial commercial communities in the ports of north Sumatra, east Java, Champa, and the east coast of Malaya. That the quarantine description fits the first important Muslim state below the winds, at Pasai in North Sumatra from 1297, is indicated by one claim that all its inhabitants knew Arabic (*Sejarah Melayu* 1612: 76).

The major successes of Islam below the winds occurred between 1400 and 1650 (map 9). In the fifteenth century Melaka became both Muslim and the greatest port of the region, encouraging the extension of the faith throughout the coastal regions of the Malay Peninsula and eastern Sumatra. New Muslim port-states grew up along the spice route to north Java and Maluku, as well as another trading route to Brunei and Manila. On the Portuguese arrival in 1509, Islam was still a minority coastal phenomenon around these Muslim trade centres. "The heathen are three parts and more out of four," reported Tomé Pires (1515: 213) of northern Maluku, while a century later a Dutch resident was convinced that there were no more than three hundred practising Muslims in Ambon (Gijsels 1621: 26). The initial Portuguese onslaught on Melaka and on Muslim shipping made no converts to Christianity but did consolidate political power in the hands of Muslim dynasties able and willing to resist the new threat. Aceh and Banten were established as anti-Portuguese Muslim centres in the 1520s, while the remnant of the great Hindu-Javanese kingdom of Majapahit fell to Muslim arms in about 1527.

The most intense period of both Islamization and Christianization coincided with the high tide of the age of commerce, the silver boom of 1570–1630. Following the Spanish capture of Muslim Manila in 1571, virtually the whole lowland population of Luzon accepted Christianity by 1620 and of the Visayas by 1650—a rapidity of conversion that has been hailed as unprecedented in Christian missionary history (Schumacher 1984: 252). The Counter-reformation and the Jesuit missionary impetus brought Christian evangelism (not simply Iberian arms) to eastern Indonesia and Vietnam.

For Islam this was the period of direct commercial, religious, and military contact with Mecca and the Ottoman caliphate, sharpening the spirit of confrontation with unbelief as aggressively represented by

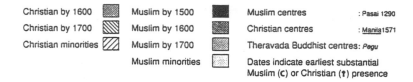

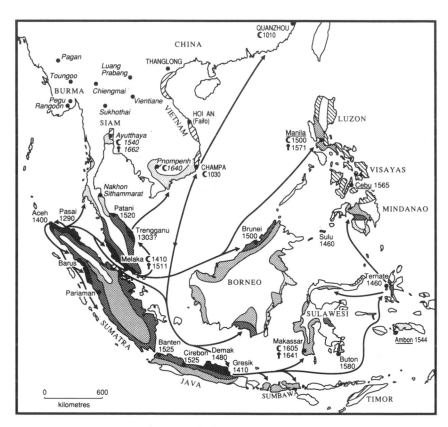

Map 9 The spread of Islam and Christianity

the Portuguese. Christian-Muslim rivalry redefined states as members of an international brotherhood and increased the pressure on all those who traded with either side to share their stance. Islam was adopted by the rulers of Mataram (central Java), South Sulawesi (1603–12), Buton, Lombok, Sumbawa, Magindanao, and southern Borneo. The established Islamic states, notably Aceh, Johor, Patani, Banten, and Ternate, extended their authority to their rural hinterlands, together with their demands for minimal Islamic conformity. The first clear evidence of a community of Muslim scholars writing in Malay dates only from the

1590s, but this Islamic literature quickly reached great heights in the work of Hamzah Fansuri, Syamsud-din as-Samatrani, Nuru'd-din ar-Raniri, and Abdurr'auf as-Singkili. This literary flowering was strikingly contemporary with the appearance of Christian devotional literature in Malay (beginning with Xavier in the 1540s), Tagalog (from the 1580s), and Vietnamese (Rhodes from 1627).

A third scripture-based religion, Theravada Buddhism, had already been accepted by the major Mainland states before 1400, and the changes there were therefore less dramatic. Nevertheless, between 1400 and 1650 the *sangha*, the brotherhood of monks, was reformed into a unified order under royal control and transformed into a popular force far outweighing in spiritual potency any local spirit cult (Tambiah 1970: 375; Keyes 1974; O'Connor 1985, 1989).

Fifteenth-century Vietnam, too, underwent a major shift as the Le emperor Than-tong (1460–98) established Confucianianism as the state ideology, sustained by the examination system and a hierarchy of educated officials (Whitmore 1970: 152–65). Profound though this change was, it did not establish Confucianism as securely as in China, and the civil wars of the sixteenth century may have undermined some of its gains. The experience of the Jesuits, who found animism stronger and Confucianism weaker in Vietnam than in China, seems to bear this out. The French Jesuit Alexandre de Rhodes, unlike his colleagues in China, had little difficulty converting Vietnamese from a belief system which, as he described it, was very close to what I have called Southeast Asian religion.

Confucian orthodoxy was only slowly carried southward by the Vietnamese Nguyen regime in the seventeenth and eighteenth centuries. The first Confucian temple of Cochin-China was not opened until 1697, whereas Buddhist shrines abounded (Li 1992: 150). Vietnamese of both north and south responded enthusiastically to Jesuit and other missionaries, despite royal opposition, and there were an estimated 190,000 baptisms between about 1590 and 1645.

This extraordinary series of changes in religious orientation has not been seriously examined as a whole. There are discrete literatures on the Christianization of the Philippines and the Islamization of the southern half of the region, while work on Buddhism in this period has hardly begun to cope with the difficulty of the sources. Yet the new religions were all scriptural orthodoxies validated by authorities outside the societies in question; they all stressed personal morality; they all claimed universal validity. Although the most profound and extensive change was perhaps the move to Islam, the sources are most abundant for Christianization. The synchronism between the acceptance of these two religions in particular suggests the probability of some broader explanations.

Southeast Asian Religion

> All these Oriental people [Siamese and their neighbours] do not only
> believe that they may be helpful to the dead . . . ; they think also that
> the dead have the power of tormenting and succouring the living; and
> from hence comes their care and magnificence in funerals; for it is only
> in this that they are magnificent. Hence it comes also that they pray to
> the dead.
>
> —La Loubère 1691: 121

Diversity was necessarily the key to a system of belief and ritual that had no written tradition. It was not simply that each district, community, or village had its own religious specialists and values. Individuals were highly pragmatic and experimental in explaining and coping with spiritual forces. As has been said of their modern descendants, they "had only a minimal attachment to the particular soul possession, emotional disequilibrium, taboo infringement, or bewitchment hypothesis they advanced and were all too ready to abandon it for some other" (Geertz 1966: 101; cf. Miles 1966: 5). When the Dutch attempted to investigate the religion of Seram (central Maluku) in 1684, they concluded that "the informants differed so widely that it was impossible to describe the system, and moreover they are so superstitious that it would almost take a book of paper to note the details of each village" (cited Knaap 1987: 71). Modern ethnographers have faced similar difficulties. Fifteen hundred distinct spirits are reported to have been identified by the Ifugao of Luzon, and "perhaps thousands" by the Toraja of Sulawesi (Volkman 195: 34; Fox 1987: 524). In Burma, Borneo, and upland areas of the Mainland, ethnographers have pointed out the impossibility of asserting that there is a single belief or ritual practice even among quite limited groups (Evans 1953: 6; Spiro 1967: 46–47). This has not prevented scholars from seeking underlying principles. The most important such features, which appear to be delineated even in the early literature, are set out here.

As in other pre-modern traditions, there was no distinction between a religious and a secular dimension. The material world was suffused with spiritual forces, and to survive and flourish in it everybody had to know how to manipulate them. In a sense it is modern religion, notably Christianity, Judaism, and modernist Islam, that created the category "primitive religion" by largely abandoning its "functions of explanation, prediction and control" of everyday events and withdrawing to an other-worldly personal piety that does not compete directly with scientific understandings of nature (Horton 1971: 104). Southeast Asian religion, in contrast, can be understood only as an intimate part of every significant event of daily life (for modern explanations, see Volkman 1985: 33 and Hoskins 1987: 139).

Ritual and shamanistic activity was usually designed, therefore, for immediate practical ends. Spiritual forces had to be manipulated to cure illness, ensure fertility, increase power, safeguard the living, particularly at dangerous life crises, and ensure that the dead were assisted through the most traumatic of all transitions into a contented afterlife. Feasting and animal sacrifice ensured the spirits were sympathetic towards "whatever personal matters there might be, the recovery of a sick person, the prosperous voyage of those embarking on the sea, a good harvest in the sowed lands, a propitious result in wars, a successful delivery in childbirth, and a happy outcome in married life" (Plasencia 1589: 191). When Filipinos, for example, wanted to pick fruit from a tree, plant or harvest rice, cross a stream, or pass any major landmark, they would ask permission from the protective spirit and make some appropriate offering (Chirino 1604: 298–99; Ortiz 1731, cited Rafael 1988: 112). Vietnamese believed, at a popular level, "that the life, health, and repose of the family, and all the temporal prosperity of the house, depends on their deceased relatives" (Rhodes 1651: 85). Throughout the region, European observers were struck both by the feasts and offerings to the spirits of the dead to aid the sick and by the attribution of illness and premature death to incorrect ritual or malign manipulation of the spirit world by some enemy (of Laos, Fitch 1591: 307 and Marini 1663: 473; of northern Vietnam, Rhodes 1651: 80–86 and Missions Etrangères 1674: 256; of Cambodia, Miche 1852: 614; of Banjarmasin, Beeckman 1717: 118–22; of Melaka, Hamilton 1727 II: 45–48; of Samar, Alcina 1668 I, iii: 15).

The spirits that bestowed power, health, and wealth were amoral but not indifferent to individual human conduct. Those who were successful in the material world had necessarily been successful in the ritual manipulation of spirits. Far from a theoretical concept of human equality, there was what Fox (1987: 526) calls "a celebration of spiritual differentiation." Many societies even had different creation myths to explain how kings, free persons, and slaves came to earth. The effect of this was not fatalism but an intense competition for status and success, in which spiritual means were at least as important as physical. Highland Makassarese called their pre-Islamic religion *patuntung* from a root that means "to strive," because it was essentially about competitively manipulating spirits to increase status in this world and the next (Martin and Birgit Rössler, conversation with author). Acciaioli (1989: 256) interprets "searching for good fortune" as the primary aim of Bugis ritual. The same point has been made about Ngadju Dayak religion in Borneo: "If one man is richer than another they say it is because he must have sponsored the correct rituals at the right time and was careful in his selection of spirits. . . . The more a man knows about ritual, the more he can do for his own and his family's welfare" (Miles 1966: 5).

Such contemporary observations about local Southeast Asian religions help to explain the reactions of seventeenth-century observers. Spanish missionaries, for example, never complained about the passivity or resignation of the pagans they were attempting to convert. It was rather that they "seemed to have no heart or understanding for anything except the gaining of money" (Aduarte 1640: 238). When a Jesuit explained Christianity to Buddhist monks in Laos in the 1640s, they rejected it on very this-worldly grounds, because "from it one could hope to obtain neither gold, nor silver, nor amusement, nor many wives, and . . . on the contrary it seemed to put faith only in dishonour and insult, . . . it esteemed poverty as treasure and death as gain" (Marini 1663: 471).

The whole material world was animated by spirits that needed sustenance and propitiation. Modern theorists have interpreted this multiplicity of spirits as forming part of a cosmic unity, a single animating principle that Skeat (1900) and others have called "anima" or "animism," Kruyt called first "life fluid," then "soul stuff," and finally "magic power," Alkema and Bezemer (1927) "dynamism," Keyes (1981: 711) "vital essence," and Fox (1987) the "immanence of life." Such global theories were not developed by villagers or at least not reported by early missionaries, but they were a feature of the more abstract thought of the important capitals and courts. In Java, notably, the doctrine of "non-duality," or the essential unity of existence, was widely held in pre-Islamic court and religious circles, and continued into the theological writings of the earliest Muslim mystics of Java (Drewes 1954, 1969; Johns 1965). In Sumatra, too, a radical monism was evident in the earliest Muslim writings (notably those of Hamzah Fansuri and Syamsud-din as-Samatrani). It may be that the Southeast Asian religious tradition, when acted upon by Indian religious ideas, was a congenial environment for more esoteric speculation of a pantheistic or monist sort.

In the African context Horton (1971: 101) has described a two-tier cosmology, in which "lesser spirits" controlled the affairs of the local community while a "supreme being" presided remotely over the cosmos. The supreme being became important to Africans who were drawn out of the local society for reasons such as trade, administration, or enslavement, but had little relevance for those immersed in the settled agricultural community. Most Southeast Asians, too, had a concept of a somewhat remote creator, usually named with reference to Sanskrit terminology—*Batara Guru* (*Betala* in Tagalog) or *dewata*—even though grounded in a specifically local mythology. Christian and Muslim missionaries naturally took special interest in these shadowy notions of a supreme creator god but declined to use them to translate their own awesome concepts. Arabic *Allah* and Spanish *Dios* became the terms for God in Malay and Tagalog, respectively. Rhodes coined in Vietnamese a high-sounding new term, "Lord of Heaven and Earth," which was only a slight variation of the "Lord of Heaven" that his fellow Jesuits had adopted in China.

The magnificence, elaboration, and gaiety of funerals struck observers throughout Southeast Asia. In eastern Indonesia and the Philippines there were complex double burials, with taboos during the mourning period and then much "feasting and drunken revelry" when the final burial was complete. The buried remains were accompanied by rich cloths, pottery, and jewellery, helpful in ensuring status and comfort in the afterlife (Morga 1609: 280; also Paiva 1545: 299–300; Chirino 1604: 327–30). In Siam, Burma, and Laos, Buddhist cremation was already practised for the upper classes, who were first carried around the town in sumptuous funerary biers and feasted for days with music and dancing. These rituals were "pompous and magnificent beyond expression" (Kaempfer 1727: 21–22; also van der Hagen 1607: 30–31; du Jarric 1614: 890; Marini 1663: 455). In pre-Muslim Java and Bali, wives of rulers were expected to commit suttee on the funeral pyres of their husbands (Fei Hsin 1436: 248; Galvão 1544: 93; *Dagh-Register* 1631–34: 179; Fryke 1692: 109–10), while in the Philippines, Sulawesi, Borneo, Nias, Cambodia, and Burma, slaves were often killed to accompany the wealthy in the afterlife. It has been argued that, beneath a veneer of Hindu forms, the real purpose of many Javanese temples of the tenth to fifteenth centuries was to serve ancestor cults (Wisseman 1983: 25–29).

The modern literature on death-ritual in Southeast Asia is extensive and shows considerable variation in both ritual practice and underlying cosmology (Schärer 1946; Uchibori 1978; Huntingdon and Metcalf 1979; Metcalf 1982; Forth 1981; Koubi 1982; Gerdin 1981; Volkman 1985). For Southeast Asian societies still outside the scriptural world religions, the most important and elaborate communal feast continues to be the death ritual, because of the dual convictions that the dead require the rituals of the living for a safe journey to the next life and that the living depend on the cooperation of the dead for their well-being in this world.

Conversion or Adhesion

The Indian religious ideas which had spread "below the winds" for more than a thousand years were not exclusive even in principle. They demanded of adherents the crossing of no boundaries and the renunciation of no previous practices. Although their influence is unmistakable in the monuments and inscriptions of all the classic kingdoms, we cannot know how far they drove out the older religious beliefs even at the court level. Among the majority of the rural population it must be assumed that they represented at most an additional set of rituals and deities that could be turned to for certain purposes.

Some authors have suggested that Islamization followed a similar course, especially in Java, adding no more initially than the *shahada* and other prayers and rituals that could be used for the old purposes (van Leur 1940: 168–69). Before the sixteenth century this was probably a common pattern. Yet as prophetic religions that offered an exclusive path to salvation, Islam and Christianity did require some outward signs of membership in the new community. In principle both demanded a renunciation of the pagan past, the central mark of conversion, as opposed to passive adherence. Even if in practice most "converts" followed their rulers in nominal adherence to the new community, this change required a selective renunciation of past habits.

The major difference in the missionary strategy of the two faiths was the Christian reliance on a celibate and relatively disciplined priesthood to define the boundaries of the new community through baptism, ideally preceded by memorization of a catechism. Lay baptism could and did occur—in the sixteenth century Portuguese traders and fidalgoes baptized the rulers of Solor (Lesser Sundas), Siang, and Sidenreng (South Sulawesi). But since the Catholic church had no mechanism in this period except the European priest to maintain continuity, these communities were eventually lost without one. Because Spanish and Portuguese priests could not marry locally and made little use of Asian colleagues and catechists before 1700, the boundaries of Christianity were naturally defined largely in Iberian terms.

In contrast, Muslim proselytists invariably married locally, and many were local people. In cultural terms, therefore, they were much more accepting of the existing spiritual landscape than were Iberian priests. As against this, the minimal outward signs of adherence were more demanding for Muslim than for Christian neophytes. In particular, the Southeast Asian attachment to pork was a major obstacle to conversion. Pigs were the major meat source and a central element in feasts (Reid 1988: 35). The killing of all domestic pigs (often in one final feast) in itself implied "conversion" in the sense of rejecting as evil the pig-eating past. Circumcision was another major step, expected from the beginning: "Never is a Lutao [of Mindanao-Ternate] found who has not been circumcised, or one who eats pork—and it is this which constitutes their Mahometanism . . . for they do not know what the Koran is" (Diaz 1718: 321; cf. Legazpi 1569: 60–61). In more recent times the external changes of food, dress, and hairstyle expected of converts to Islam have been so great that Islamization has frequently been regarded as a change of ethnic status (Bartlett 1952: 634–36; Geertz 1964: 181–82; Miles 1976: 93; Rodgers-Siregar 1981: 63).

Did this rejection of the evil past extend beyond externals to the system of belief? The best test of this is the extent to which acceptance of Islam or Christianity was accompanied by such explicit breaking of past taboos and destruction of sacred objects as would make the old religion no longer credible or practicable. Here the Catholic proselytists took a tougher stance. Magellan insisted that the ruling circle in Cebu who had agreed to become Christian should burn their four-tusked wooden images, which they were distinctly uneasy about doing (Pigafetta 1524: 41–42). The Jesuits in Maluku made it a matter of deliberate policy to seek out all places of "diabolical cults" and destroy them (Mascarenhas 1570: 595, 610). This was a high-risk policy that aroused great fear in the population and the danger of retribution if disease or crop-failure followed, but it could also bring spectacular quick rewards. In the Philippines after 1570 the Spanish friars were still bolder, since they enjoyed state protection. There were no "temples" of Indianized worship there, but the friars destroyed shelters erected for the spirits as well as ritual objects (Chirino 1604: 294, 299–305; Phelan 1959: 54). In Pangasinan these were chiefly ceramics containing treasured wines used in feasting. The Dominicans there secretly paid informers to advise them where they could find and destroy these (Aduarte 1640: 186, 243–44). Such tactics must often have been sufficiently dramatic to stimulate "conversion" by destroying the credibility of religious specialists and rituals on which the old system rested. Yet there was a difficulty. As Spanish sources implicitly acknowledge, the heart of Southeast Asian religious practice was not in any specific place or object, and hence could not be invalidated at a stroke.

Islamic conversion stories show surprisingly little evidence of this iconoclasm. Hindu-Buddhist temples were eventually destroyed or built over in Malaya and Sumatra (though not in Java, where even lingga-yoni complexes were preserved by Muslims), but there is little evidence that their destruction was part of the initial conversion. Cultural conservatives may have been encouraged by the mystical argument, best expressed in Malay by Hamzah Fansuri (*Al-Muntahi:* 336), that the true believer found God in idols as in all created things. Only the conversion story of Kedah has the newly convinced ruler producing "his idols of gold and silver, porcelain, wood and clay, human figures" for the missionary sheik to destroy (*Hikayat Marong Mahawangsa*,[1] quoted in Jones 1979: 140). The ruler presumably did not yet have the courage to destroy them himself. If this was indeed a common pattern it would have required genuine rejection of a pagan past, at least at the court, where such (presumably Hindu) images had some ritual role.

At a probably later date (early sixteenth century, if the Patani chronicle can be believed), the ruler of Patani accepted Islam. The chronicle relates that "he gave up worshipping idols [*berhala*] and eating pork, but apart from that he did not alter a single one of his *kafir* habits" (*Hikayat Patani:* 75). In spite of the writer's disapproval, this would seem to be a major step if it really implied that the ruler abandoned the religion of his ancestors. The word *berhala*, however, implies a Hindu-Buddhist image alien to grass-roots Southeast Asian religion, so this rejection may only have been of a royal Brahmanic cult. The chronicle says of the time of his successor, who built the first

1. Because this is the least historical in spirit of the Malay chronicles containing conversion stories, a word is needed about using such texts in general. Surviving indigenous accounts of the acceptance of Islam in North Sumatra, Melaka, Java, and Ternate are so remote in time from the events described that they must be seen not as a factual record of events but rather as a description of what seemed plausible or exemplary to their sixteenth-to-eighteenth-century authors. All show elements that may have become conventional—a transaction between an indigenous ruler and a foreign saint, accompanied by dreams and miracles (Jones 1979: 152–58; Brakel 1978: 11–13). Taken together, they indicate what was remembered as important about these early cases on which other evidence is minimal. The absence of stories of destroying temples, for example, is significant. Much more historical attention should be paid, however, to the post-1500 cases of Islamization about which potential data are far richer.

mosque, that the people of the town had given up pork and idols but continued to make offerings to trees, rocks, and spirits (ibid.: 79).

The scraps of evidence we have from before 1500 are frankly inadequate to describe with any confidence the process or extent of Islamization. By 1500 there was a substantial group of Muslims speaking Malay or Javanese in the coastal port-cities on the major trade routes, who claimed among their number the most important port-rulers of Sumatra, the Malayan Peninsula, northern Java, and Maluku. How far the people of their hinterlands practised Islam is far from clear. There is no firm evidence of Islamic writing in Malay or Javanese before the late sixteenth century, which suggests that devout and learned Muslims remained somewhat "quarantined" at that time.

Some Arabs were certainly unimpressed with the Islamic commitment of these early Muslim cities. The famous Arab pilot Ibn Majid (1462: 206) was not flattering about the people of Melaka: "They have no culture at all. The infidel marries Muslim women while the Muslim takes pagans to wife. You do not know whether they are Muslims or not. They are thieves for theft is rife among them and they do not mind. The Muslim eats dogs for meat for there are no food laws. They drink wine in the markets and do not treat divorce as a religious act." Although this may be less than fair, the Melaka chronicle itself accepted a relaxed stereotype for Melaka Malays, making fun of a puritanical Arab scholar worsted in repartee with a drunken Malay nobleman (Sejarah Melayu 1612: 177–78). Even serious drinkers like the Portuguese thought that the Melaka Malays, "in the feastings and rejoicings . . . take too much wine" (Pires 1515: 268).

1540–1600: Polarization and Religious Boundaries

> After some time quarrels arose, and we fought with them [the Portuguese]. We attacked each other, overcame each other as if there would be no end to the holy war. . . .
> When a Muslim died in the holy war nothing was put in the balance against him in the hereafter, but he entered heaven directly.
> —Rijali 1657: 169–70

In the sixteenth century, for which much more satisfactory data are available, large numbers of people both rural and urban were clearly "converting" to Islam, rejecting former ways of life, abandoning pork, accepting Islamic modes of dress, salutation, and ritual, and identifying themselves as part of an international Islamic community.

This explicit identification can be attributed primarily to two factors—the direct and intense shipping links between Southeast Asia and the Red Sea area, and the sharper polarization between the *Dar ul-Islam* and its enemies.

Before 1500, as we have noted, most Maluku spices and almost all Indonesian pepper had been exported to China. The pull of the European market changed both the quantity and direction of exports, until by 1600 more than half of the much increased Southeast Asian pepper crop was being taken to the Middle East and Europe. By the 1530s Muslim traders based in Aceh were sending their own ships to the Red Sea, and by the 1550s they were sailing directly across the Indian Ocean to Arabia (Boxer 1969: 416–19). For the next sixty years, Indonesian Muslims had, for the only time until this century, their own means of direct regular contact with the sacred centres of their faith.

When the first Dutch, English, and French ships arrived in the Archipelago around 1600 they found traders whom they called Turks or "Rumes" (Malay *Rumi*) established in Aceh, Banten, Banda, and Ternate. When Frederik de Houtman wanted to describe how foreign traders were received in Aceh around 1600, he chose as a typical example the arrival of a nakhoda from Mecca, who offered the sultan military assistance from his country (de Houtman 1603: 27–28). This regular commercial connection made possible a flow of pilgrims and scholars between Southeast Asia and Mecca. From the 1550s Catholic sources complain of "casizes" (ulama) from the Middle East, travelling as merchants, who carried the Islamic faith to the remotest islands of the Archipelago (Dias 1556: 245; Osorio 1563: 245; Argensola 1708: 103).

Many of the saints and scholars popularly credited with the advance of Islam were Arabs; others were Southeast Asians who had been in Mecca, such as the founder of Muslim Banten, Sunan Gunung Jati, and the Sufi sheikhs Hamzah Fansuri, Abdurra'uf as-Singkili, and Sheikh Yusuf. Arab scholars journeyed to Aceh and made it their temporary home, preaching, writing (primarily in Arabic), and disputing with one another there. Some, such as Muhammad Azhari of Mecca around 1570 and Abu'l-kheir of Mecca and Muhammad of Yemen in the 1580s, were influential enough to be remembered by Raniri (1644: 33–34) half a century later. Aceh earned its title as "the verandah of Mecca": it was the port and centre where pilgrims and scholars from below the winds awaited the pepper ships that would take them to the Holy Land.

The Iberians had a long tradition of crusading against the Muslims in their homeland, but also one of trading peacefully with them when it was in their interests. The crusading ideology was ideally suited to serve the key Portuguese objective in the Indian Ocean—to take from the Muslims the trade that had supplied Asian spices to Alexandria and Beirut for sale to Venice. In their first two decades the Portuguese identified the wealthy Muslim traders and the rulers who supported them as the enemy to be attacked and plundered at every opportunity. The same commercial interest nevertheless led eventually to pragmatic trading arrangements with Muslims as well as Hindus, so that Asian merchandise was freighted on Portuguese ships and vice-versa. By the 1530s the Portuguese appeared to have found a niche compatible with Asian trade.

In mid century, however, a change of Portuguese strategy led to the abolition of state trading within Asia. Instead, certain leading Portuguese factors were given the monopoly on particular routes—notably those between Coromandel and Portuguese Melaka. This effectively reestablished the official Portuguese regime as an overt rival to Muslim trade in the Bay of Bengal, as it always was to the west of India (Subrahmanyam 1990: 108–13). The shift coincided with a growing cleavage in religious terms, though whether the two were causally connected is not clear.

Little positive action was taken to spread Christianity until the Counter-reformation and the arrival of the first Jesuit in Asia, Saint Francis Xavier, in 1542. Only then did mass conversions occur outside the Portuguese fortresses, notably in eastern Indonesia. This missionary investment interfered to some degree with Portuguese desires to follow commercial opportunities even in Muslim strongholds, causing ultimately irreconcilable conflicts of interest in Maluku in particular. Although the missionaries modified some of the buccaneering violence of the early Portuguese fidalgoes, they also widened the breach between what were increasingly two rival social systems in the Archipelago.

In contrast to the struggling handful of priests working under Portuguese protection, the wealthy Spanish crown sent large numbers of clerics to the Philippines after the occupation of Manila in 1571. There were thirteen missionary priests in those islands in 1576, 94 in 1586, and 267 in 1594 (Phelan 1959: 56). The conversion of the lowland populations of Luzon and the Visayas was essentially accomplished by 1650. In the period 1580–1660 Spanish missionary work was extended southward to Mindanao, northern Sulawesi, and Maluku in a conscious spirit of military and spiritual competition with Islam. After a number of unproductive initiatives in the Theravada countries of the Mainland, the Jesuits began their remarkably successful work in Cochin-China in 1615 and in northern Vietnam in 1626.

The Muslim merchants of Southeast Asia, particularly those involved in the spice trade, had responded to the initial Portuguese onslaught by regrouping around Islamic centres prepared to counterattack the Portuguese. A diaspora of dispossessed Muslim traders from Melaka established themselves in Johor, Pahang, Patani, and above all Aceh, making these cities self-consciously Muslim opponents of the infidel intruders. High-handed Portuguese intervention in Pasai and Pidië drove all the more Islamic, commercial, or simply patriotic elements in northern Sumatra to support the Sultan of Aceh in his ambition to unite that hitherto politically fragmented coast in an explicitly anti-Portuguese sultanate. For more than a century Aceh remained the most consistent enemy of Portuguese Melaka. Its own marriage of ideology and commerce, as the new centre of the Islamic spice route, mirrored that of the Iberians. Following quickly on this triumph, about 1525, a Sumatran known in Java as Sunan Gunung Jati returned from studying in Mecca, allied himself with the thriving port-state of Demak, and established Banten as an Islamic centre in west Java. Since the Portuguese had sought to establish their influence over the previous Hindu occupants of the coast (Pajajaran, with its port at Sunda Kelapa—later Jakarta), the example of Aceh cannot have been far from Muslim minds.

The Ottoman expansion to Egypt, Syria, and the Hejaz in 1516–17, and to Iraq and the Persian Gulf in 1534–38, introduced to the Indian Ocean a first-class military power with an interest in defending the Muslim spice-trading routes. The attacks of Sultans Sulaiman and Selim II upon the Christian powers led by Spain appear to have had a galvanizing effect even as far away as Southeast Asia. The first Turkish fleet to combat the Portuguese in the Indian Ocean was launched by the governor of Egypt in 1537–38. Though it failed dismally, some of its members must have found their way to Southeast Asia, where the Portuguese repeatedly referred to Turks and "Abyssinians" leading the Muslim armies. Pinto (1578: 21, 28, 46–47, 55) insists that Sultan Alau'd-din Ri'ayat Syah al-Kahar, the crusading king of Aceh, sent four pepper-laden ships to the Red Sea in 1538–39, which returned with several hundred Turkish soldiers, in fulfillment of a "treaty arranged by the Pasha of Cairo with the king of Aceh in the name of the Grand Turk, in exchange for which he was granted the exclusive rights to a factory in the [Acehnese] port of Pasai." With these and other foreign Muslim auxiliaries Aceh was able to defeat its non-Muslim Batak neighbours and drive them from the coast.

The better-documented commercial and diplomatic relations between Turkey and Aceh in the 1560s gave a further impetus to the concept of a pan-Islamic counter-crusade against the Portuguese in Southeast Asia. Aceh sent a succession of envoys to Istanbul from 1563, presenting gifts to the Turkish sultan and asking for his help against the Portuguese: "The Sultan [of Aceh] says that he is left alone to face the unbelievers. They have seized some islands, and have taken Muslims captive. Merchant and pilgrim ships going from these islands towards Mecca were captured one night [by the Portuguese] and the ships that were not captured were fired upon and sunk, causing many Muslims to drown" (letter of Sultan Selim II, 1568, in Saffet 1912: 606–08). Turkey responded to these repeated requests by sending gunsmiths and artillerymen, probably in 1564 and certainly in 1568. This stimulated some unprecedented cooperation between Islamic kingdoms involved in the spice trade and an upsurge of *jihad* mentality. Not only did Aceh crusade against the Bataks and against Portuguese Melaka (1568, 1570); in India Bijapur allied with Golconda and other Muslim states of the Deccan to sack the Hindu capital of Vijayanagar (1565) and attack Portuguese Goa (1570) (Reid 1969; Eaton 1978: 83–85). Vijayanagar's main outlet at Pulicat rapidly declined and was replaced by Masulipatnam—the chief port for Muslim Golconda, which was now the dominant power of southeast India. Golconda formed an anti-Portuguese alliance with Aceh, supplying arms and men for its assaults on Melaka (Subrahmanyam 1990: 151–53).

In eastern Indonesia the positions of Islam and Christianity were almost equally tenuous in the mid-sixteenth century. The unstable modus vivendi between the Portuguese and the sultanate of Ternate in the clove trade allowed Christian as well as Muslim missionaries to make some headway amongst the still largely animist Malukans. In the 1560s the Portuguese became increasingly irritated as Sultan Hairun of Ternate proved adept at manipulating them to advance his own authority and that of Islam. In 1570 they treacherously murdered him. Hairun's son Baabullah used the outrage against this act to drive the Portuguese out of Ternate and to compel most of their Christian supporters throughout Maluku to adopt Islam as a sign of loyalty. Baabullah had already been an effective propagandist for Islam during his father's day (Vieira 1558: 239), but now he was able to spread the faith through much of the Ambon area, to Buton, Selayar, some of the coastal kingdoms of east and north Sulawesi, and southern Mindanao. The Portuguese and Spaniards believed that this crusading sultan introduced "a great number of Arabian and Persian false prophets" into Maluku, and sent envoys and missionaries to Brunei, Mindanao, Java, and Aceh to encourage the holy war (Salazar 1588: 68–69; Argensola

1708: 93–94, 103). During Baabullah's reign (1570–83), and until the Dutch arrival in 1600 complicated religious loyalties, there was a stronger sense than before or since that acceptance of Islam was an essential part of loyalty to the ruler of Ternate.

Malay sources, such as the *Sejarah Melayu* and the *Hikayat Tanah Hitu*, reported the arrival of the Portuguese in a neutral or even positive mood. In the second half of the century, however, the Iberians were routinely referred to as enemies and *kafir* (infidel), and descriptions of them entered the discourse of holy war (Raniri 1644: 31–32; Rijali 1657: 169–72). In the same period, Portuguese and Spanish sources, reeking hostility to Islam themselves, left no doubt that the feeling was reciprocated. Mendes Pinto's racy narrative put anti-infidel heroics into the mouths of the kings of Aceh and Demak, and claimed that Pahang would not allow Portuguese to be buried ashore because "the ground would be cursed and . . . nothing would ever grow again because the bodies had not been cleansed of the great quantities of pork consumed" (Pinto 1578: 59; also 30, 48). Pinto is also the main source about Khoja Asem, a Gujarati nakhoda who had sworn vengeance on the Portuguese after three members of his family had died in one of their brutal raids on shipping in the Red Sea. He had assembled a small Muslim fleet to attack Portuguese ships in the South China Sea and was said to have behind him, when the Portuguese eventually killed him in 1540, fifteen hundred Muslims from India as well as from "Luzon, Borneo, Java and Champa." His rhetoric was all jihad, according to Pinto, promising heaven to his men "if we bathe ourselves in the blood of these savage infidels" (ibid.: 106–12).

Spanish envoys reported that the Sultan of Brunei had responded in 1578 to an arrogant letter from Manila by saying, "So this is the way that your people write to me, who am king; while the Castilians are kafir . . . who have no souls, who are consumed by fire when they die, and that, too, because they eat pork" (Blair and Robertson 1903–09 IV: 150, 160–61). Even in the neutral entrepôt of Ayutthaya, two Dominican missionaries who arrived in the 1560s were set upon by a mob of rioting Muslims; one priest was killed, the other was badly injured, and a number of Muslims were sentenced to being trampled to death by the Siamese royal elephants for their unruliness (Sancta Maria 1569).

One should not exaggerate. In most places except Aceh, commercial and personal relations between Muslim and Christian continued to be extensive. But the normally tolerant atmosphere of Southeast Asia was affected for a time after 1540 by what one might call the "great-power conflict" between Spanish-led Christendom and Turkish-led Islam. A cosmopolitan array of Muslims from all around the Indian Ocean were involved in these wars—not only Gujaratis and Turks in Southeast Asia but Indonesians fighting as mercenaries in the wars of India (Voorhoeve 1955. 5). During this period war was frequently waged in the name of spreading Islam (and Christianity), so that the boundaries between Muslim and non-Muslim became clear and often embittered. Bataks, Torajans, Balinese, and others, forging some unity for the first time in the struggle to resist such jihads, began to perceive their identity as having to do with not being Muslim.

In Java, which is sometimes seen as having slipped on a light mantle of Islam almost imperceptibly, war between Islamic and non-Islamic forces was a constant feature of the fifteenth and sixteenth centuries, with most of the interior still resisting Islam in 1600 (see below). The boundaries between the two were clearly perceived. A propagandist of the period writing in Javanese sharply distinguished between acceptable Muslim behaviour and Javanese tradition. He explicitly condemned as unbelief "worshipping idols or participating in the worship of infidels," "making open avowal of infidel devotional practices, or practices resembling those of Javanese hermits [*tupuning yogi*]," or ascribing power to an idol, as well as a host of moral and behavioural deviations ("Javanese Code": 32–37). This rare survival of a sixteenth-century text drew a much clearer line between the new religion and the old than is found in the more abundant Javanese writing of the eighteenth century.

During this period of religio-political conflict the older assumption that Islam need only be firmly established in the port and capital was no longer adequate. The Patani chronicle relates that it was only in the reign of Sultan Mudhaffar (d.1564) that "the Islamic religion spread to all the rural areas [*dusun*] and reached as far as Kota Maligai"—still just 14 kilometres from the coast (*Hikayat Patani*: 78–79). In the late sixteenth century the boundaries of the Dar ul-Islam had to be more sharply drawn.

Those who crossed the boundary in this period can be more readily classified as "converts" than most of their predecessors. The sources are explicit on the conversion of Makassar's rulers in 1605, both as to the moment the rulers of Tallo' and Goa (the two royal lineages of Makassar) pronounced the *shahada* and became Muslims and on how seriously they took up the faith. The Tallo' chronicle recorded of the first royal convert, Karaeng Matoaya, "he was expert at reading Islamic books; from the time he embraced Islam until his death he never once missed the [five times'] daily prayer; only at the time he had a swollen foot and an Englishman treated him by giving him liquor did he omit to pray for eight days" (*Sejarah Kerajaan Tallo'*: 19). Within a generation of this official acceptance of Islam, the trans-vestite ritual specialists (*bissu'*) of the old religion were driven out of Makassar, and Islamic norms had transformed its dress, diet, devotion, literature, and sexual behaviour (Navarrete 1676: 110n; Reid 1981: 13–19). The leaders of the adjacent Bugis states—Wajo', Soppeng, and Bone—were then obliged to pronounce the shahada and renounce pork by the crusading power of Makassar (Noorduyn 1956: 94–98).

By the mid-seventeenth century this sharp distinction between Islam and non-Islam was already fading. The major conflicts were no longer between crusading Catholics and Islam but between the re-ligiously neutral VOC and its allies on one side and those who sought a freer system of trade on the other. The commercial connections be-tween Southeast Asian Muslims and the Middle East were broken, while in the Philippines and elsewhere the enthusiasm of the first generation of Catholic missionaries was replaced by a more defensive spirit. Among both Muslims and Christians the age of crusades around the religious frontiers was over.

The internal consequence of this shift was to encourage the con-viction that the existing society was already Islamic (or Christian), and to ease the concern that those practising the old spirit cults might be actual or potential traitors to the cause. It could be misleading to label the eighteenth century a new phase of domestication of the prophetic religions (Phelan's "Filipinization of Catholicism"), since that process had begun as soon as the new concepts were translated into Southeast Asian languages. The most intense phase of conversion, in the sense of a conscious transformation of individual and social ways of life, how-ever, had ended.

The Attractions of Conversion

The profound change in the mental universe of many insular Southeast Asians during the age of commerce could not have hap-pened if there was not some desire for change, some perceived lack of fit between existing beliefs and the changing world. There was in the sixteenth and early seventeenth centuries (as there would be again in the twentieth) a sense that the present was different from the past, and that some new solutions were necessary. Bugis and Makassarese lead-ers, already heavily involved in international commerce, were por-trayed as having agreed that they must adopt one of the new religions, and it was only a question of which one (Rhodes 1653: 207; Gervaise 1701: 124–29). In weighing the factors that appear to have attracted

Southeast Asians to Islam and Christianity, therefore, some perceived change in the external environment is assumed. Many were seeking not simply to confirm their world-view but to find a new one.

Portability

As Horton (1971) has pointed out for Africa, O'Connor (1989) for northern Tai-speakers, and Hoskins (1987: 146) for modern Sumba, the system of spirit-worship was not readily portable. Once away from their familiar landscape, travellers were at the mercy of unknown spirits manipulated by their enemies. They had to return frequently to their own village to attend to their ancestors. Those who left the village world—for trade, warfare, cash-cropping, or serving a new lord—needed a universally valid faith. As a time when a substantial proportion of Southeast Asians were drawn into the international economy, the age of commerce provided a necessary precondition for conversion on a large scale. Although the pattern was not as neat as Horton (1975) has argued for Africa, the earliest and most thorough converts to Islam tended to be found in the merchant communities of every port in the region. Since the port-cities were also the dominant political and cultural centres of the period, this already provides part of the explanation.

Association with Wealth

Southeast Asians first encountered Muslims and Christians as traders and warriors. Appearing both wealthy and powerful, they were believed to possess important secrets about how to manipulate the spirit world. Observing Islamization at an early stage in the Manila area, a Spaniard wrote, "Some are Moros [Muslims], and they obtain much gold, which they worship as a God. . . . They believe that paradise and successful enterprises are reserved for those who submit to the religion of the Moros of Brunei, of which they make much account. . . . These are a richer people, because they are merchants, and with their slaves, cultivate the land" (de Sande 1576: 67–68; cf. Lavezaris 1574: 267). Apparently even without any proselytism, some Filipinos who observed the Muslim traders imitated their taboo on pork, presumably believing it to be the ritual key to their success (Legazpi 1569: 60–61; "Relation" 1572: 165). A similar phenomenon has been observed among Bataks and Torajans in more recent times (*Adatrechtbundels* IX: 239–40; Hirosue 1988: 85–87).

Military Success

In warfare Muslims and Christians alike were seen as powerful and valuable allies, used as mercenaries even by the Theravada kingdoms. Firearms came to Southeast Asia through Indian, Turkish, and Chinese Muslims, and Europeans employed them yet more effectively. In addition to their better ships and arms, the foreign traders had a more ruthless and determined view of war—partly because they were often desperate minorities with nowhere to retreat to, partly because they were less inclined to see the first casualty as proof of unfavorable omens. In the skirmishing between Muslims and Christians for control of eastern Indonesian waters, therefore, the locals were anxious to choose the winning side not simply for self-preservation but in order to make their own whatever spiritual and practical techniques these warriors possessed.

When Magellan arrived in Cebu in 1521 he made a great display of his superior armour and firearms. Nevertheless he insisted that it was the power of God which helped him win victories and that it would do the same for Cebuano converts. The local elite quickly responded by asking for baptism, though naturally all these "converts" defected as soon as Magellan's defeat and death at Matan gave the lie to Christian invulnerability (Pigafetta 1524: 27, 38–46).

Antonio de Paiva, seeking to buy slaves and sandalwood from the Bugis king of Suppa (near modern Pare-Pare, Sulawesi) in 1544, was asked by the king why the Christians always fought the Muslims. Later he particularly asked about Santiago (Saint James, the patron of Iberians, particularly in their crusades), since Muslim traders had told him that the Portuguese shouted the saint's name in battle. Paiva replied that James was "their apostle and knight of Jesus Christ" and that in battle the Portuguese called on him and "visibly saw him come to their help dressed in full armour and riding upon a fire-breathing steed, as the Moros themselves could testify who also saw him in times of defeat." The king was fascinated by this, and said that he wanted to have as a gift when he became a Christian the altar-piece Paiva had shown him with the saint's image on it (Paiva 1544: 286; also Schurhammer 1963: 523–24). He received baptism from Paiva, though its results were presumably not those he had hoped. Christianity did not long survive among the Bugis.

That Islam was perceived as spiritually and militarily powerful is even more clear in Southeast Asian literature. Javanese traditions, including those unenthusiastic about Islam, took for granted the superior military power of Muslims in the battles of the sixteenth century. Majapahit was portrayed as overcome by magically irresistible Muslim leaders, while even the troops defending Hindu Majapahit were believed to be led by a Muslim brigade loyal to the old order (Raffles 1817 II: 125–26). Among the heroes most enthusiastically adopted from Islamic literature were the world-conqueror Iskandar Dzulkarnain (Alexander the Great) and the warrior hero Amir Hamzah. The chronicles and letters of Sumatran and Peninsula kings—Melaka, Minangkabau, Palembang, Aceh, Deli, Johor, and Pahang—all claimed that their dynasties descended from Alexander (*Sejarah Melayu* 1612: 43–48; Marsden 1783: 338–42; Schrieke 1942: 253). Some chronicles simply asserted that the spiritual potency of the saint was so obvious that no battle was needed, as when the "radiance" of Raden Rahmat was enough to convert the ruler of Jipang in east Java (*Hikayat Banjar:* 420), or when the ruler of Kutai (east Borneo) was defeated in a contest of magical powers by Datu ri Bandang (Jones 1979: 148). There were also rulers such as the raja of Banjarmasin, who like Emperor Constantine promised to convert if the new faith proved its power by winning the civil war for him (*Hikayat Banjar:* 427–30).

The existing religious system would undoubtedly have led Southeast Asians to believe that the victors in any battle had supernatural forces on their side. In principle neither Muslim nor Iberian Christian proselytists disagreed. Both believed that God had commanded them to fight for the faith, and would give them the victory if they proved worthy. There was a difference, however. Their view of the divine purpose had to be a much longer one, since their religious communities had collective memories of many defeats. This both increased their attention to the technical aspect of war and encouraged the development of the doctrine of martyrdom to sanctify failures—something animists could never do. These factors made Muslim and Christian soldiers still more formidable and helped them to spread their faiths through military victories all over the island world.

Writing

The prophetic religions introduced writing to relatively few areas—at most Maluku, the southern Philippines, northern Sulawesi, some islands east of Lombok, and parts of Borneo. For the rest, Indic-derived scripts were already widespread. Where the new Arabic and Latin alphabets came to replace or co-exist with the older alphabet, as in Luzon and the Visayas, coastal Sumatra and south Sulawesi, there seems little doubt that literacy was higher in the old alphabet than the new, and very much so for women (Bartlett 1952: 630–31; Reid 1988: 215–25). Only in Vietnam, where Chinese characters already restricted literacy to an educated male elite, did the introduction of a simpler phonetic alphabet by Catholic missionaries offer new opportunities of literacy to the poor.

What carried weight was the sacred authority of a book. Cambodian legends admitted that the Thais were superior to them in knowledge, but only because they had stolen the Cambodian sacred books (Chandler 1983: 84). In the islands (except Java) the purposes of writing had been largely ephemeral—love poems and messages written on bamboo or palm-leaf. Islam and Christianity each claimed that their authority rested on a book, and moreover on a book written in an alien language that carried the extra sacral weight of impenetrability. The apostle of Sulu presented himself to initially sceptical animists as an Arab who could communicate by writing on paper (Majul 1973: 58). Marsden (1783: 289) tells of a Sumatran spirit-worshipper who challenged a Muslim fellow-countryman to show how his God was any more demonstrably real than the spirits. The apparently persuasive answer was that the truths of Islam were "written in a book." Modern ethnographers have noted a similar persuasiveness inherent in scripture among animists of Borneo and eastern Indonesia, to the extent that some Dayak groups wishing to assert their equality insist that they lost their books during their migrations but memorized the texts (Coomans 1980: 39, 55; Hoskins 1987: 146). Counter-reformation missionaries generally made little direct use of the Bible, but Alexandre de Rhodes made a calculated impact on the Vietnamese crowd attending his public debate with Buddhist scholars in Thang-long (Hanoi) by reading in Latin from his splendidly bound copy of the Vulgate (Rhodes 1651: 147).

Memorization

Both Muslim and Christian proselytists based their authority on their ability to read and explicate sacred texts. At the point of most rapid religious change (1550–1650), moreover, they generated new texts in Southeast Asian languages, designed to convey the essential truths of the new religion in forms that could be memorized and understood by their proselytes. But these texts were for the specialists. The new religious ideas were invariably conveyed orally to new converts, with writing merely assisting the teacher. Prayers and articles of faith were learned by group recitation, usually in a poetic or melodic form.

Saint Francis Xavier was the first Christian evangelist to compose in Malay a version of Christianity that could be memorized:

I taught to the children and native people a "Declaration" which I had written on each article of the faith, in a language that all could understand, adapting myself . . . to what the people of the country newly converted could understand. This declaration I taught instead of prayers, in Melaka as I had in Maluku, to establish in them a basis to believe well and truly in Jesus Christ, ceasing to believe in vain idols. This declaration could be learned in one year, if one taught each day a little, that is about twenty words that they could easily learn by heart (Xavier 1548: 389).[2]

The Spanish had a similar compendium of the essentials of the faith, the *Doctrina Christiana*. Compiled originally in Mexico, this was translated into Tagalog and printed in Manila in 1593. Later versions adapted into Tagalog the very popular *Dottrina Cristiana* (1597) of the Jesuit Cardinal Bellarmine. So that this document could be memorized by new Christians, question-and-answer sessions were held after masses, with the correct responses preferably chanted by the congregation (Phelan 1959: 57–58; Schumacher 1984: 253; Rafael 1988: 39–54).

Muslims also used oral recitation to commit to memory the essential Arabic prayers (*salat*), as well as the Koran. New popular genres of poetry—the *sya'ir* in Malay and the *suluk* in Javanese—were created by the earliest Muslim writers to enable students and initiates to chant the crucial doctrines and mystic steps on the path to God (Pigeaud 1967: 85–87, 94–95; Drewes and Brakel 1986: 34–35). Syamsud-din as-Samatrani wrote an Islamic creed in Malay, the *Mir'at al-Mu'minin* (1601), which used a question-and-answer format no doubt intended to be recited between a teacher and pupils and thus committed to memory. One of the most popular Persian works rendered into Malay and Javanese was the "Thousand Questions" (*Kitab Seribu Masalah*), which provided crucial items of religious dogma and Islamic cosmology in the form of the questions a learned Jew put to the Prophet. Questions and answers were presented in a form that could readily be committed to memory (Pijper 1924: 72–81; Winstedt 1961: 148–52).

Healing

Because illness was always linked to spiritual causes, the new religions could not flourish unless they, too, were seen as having answers to disease. Whatever practical novelties the new religions

2. None of Xavier's Malay writings appear to have survived—see Schurhammer and Wicki 1945 II: 590–94; Jacobs 1974: 14, 35. A Portuguese text of the rhyming catechism referred to here, composed in Ternate, is, however, preserved in Schurhammer and Wicki 1945 I: 355–67. It probably had both Portuguese and Malay versions.

brought in curing disease, they are unlikely to have improved recovery rates. Nor did proselytists set out to be curers, at least until the mid-seventeenth century, when some Christian missionaries began to exploit this option. But the religious climate was one that expected powerful spiritual forces to affect health and disease directly, and so the new religious specialists were also judged in those terms. The Christian missionaries frequently mentioned that times of major epidemics proved extremely advantageous for conversion, even if Christian ministrations did little to stop the deaths (Chirino 1604: 323; Aduarte 1640: 309–10; Velarde 1749: 48–49). In Java there are also legends linking the introduction of Islam to severe epidemics. The connection between disease and mass conversion has been noted in other times and places. The viability of the established religious system appears to be called into question by such massive "shaking of the foundations of social order," as Weber and more recently Geertz (1964: 173) have pointed out.

It was Catholic practice in the sixteenth century to baptize as many as possible of the mortally ill even if uninstructed or indeed unconscious, in the belief that a soul was thereby saved from hell, particularly in the case of innocent children. In the early stages of Christian missions in the Philippines and elsewhere, this was one of the major activities of the priests. Little wonder that Southeast Asians believed baptism to be essentially a curing ritual, the power of which was demonstrated each time someone recovered after it. To the missionaries the more spectacular recoveries were miracles, but to the Filipinos they were simply what was expected of ritual specialists. One such cure in Pangasinan, "made the Indians regard the baptism as something medicinal, and they wished to be baptized whenever they were sick, in order to be cured; but the fathers undeceived them. They made the same mistake about the sign of the cross, and in regard to the cross itself" (Aduarte 1640: 186–87; cf. Phelan 1959: 55; and for Vietnam, Missions Etrangères 1674: 199).

Holy water was treated similarly. The Jesuit Pedro Chirino (1604: 333–34) relates how when an epidemic was ravaging Bohol, "our Christians in their guileless faith took to drinking holy water for medicine, and so protecting themselves not one of them died. . . . Consequently they make frequent use of this holy remedy in all their illnesses, which is a general custom all over the islands." Alexandre de Rhodes (1651: 183–84) described how new Vietnamese Christians, after many miraculous cures from using holy water, "consequently held this water in such veneration that not only do they keep it in their houses, but on voyages they carry it in their bundles like a precious balm, to use it when needed for themselves and for others."

Mainland societies were no different in their conviction that health and illness were determined by spirits, and Buddhist monks were also expected to be active as healers. Catholic missionaries in turn were obliged to respond to demands for healing in Siam, and in the opinion of La Loubère (1691: 158), "it is principally on this account that they [Siamese] suffer them, and love them."

Traditions about conversion to Islam also emphasized disease and its cure. The kingdom of Patani, according to its chronicle, became Muslim as a result of the healing powers of a sheikh from Pasai (Sumatra). Three times the raja suffered a terrible disease that caused his skin to crack and could not be cured by the traditional healers. Three times the sheikh healed him on condition he became a Muslim. Twice he broke his promise to convert if cured, but the third time he kept it (Hikayat Patani: 71–75).

Islamized Southeast Asians retained the belief that disease was caused by dangerous and malign spirits, who were readily accommodated as shaitan and djinn within an Islamic world-view. The new religion and its written formulae were universally acknowledged to be powerful, and traditional healers naturally made use of them. Arabic phrases were soon incorporated into spells for every occasion (Skeat 1900: 581–672), and the Arabic word for blessing or invocation (du'a) had by 1600 become the standard Malay term for such a spell (doa) (Houtman 1603: 107, 165). A story about the most popular saint of Aceh, Abdurra'uf as-Singkili (died c.1693), illustrates how generously Islam may have given of its mystique for healing and other purposes. Whereas an Arab ulama is represented in the story as preaching violently against cock fighting and other forbidden gambling contests, the Acehnese saint gave a passionate cock-fighter the charm he needed to make his rooster invulnerable. This was the Muslim confession of faith, the shahada. Eventually all the rival cock-fighters found the secret and imitated this charm, with equal success, so that the initial petitioner came and asked for another charm. This time he was given the salat, the ritual prayer to be said five times a day. In this way the saint was seen to have spread Islam, by making its power freely available for the charms that everybody needed to control the spirit world in their interests (Snouck Hurgronje 1893 II: 311–12).

A Predictable Moral Universe

It has been said of the Christianization of the Roman Empire that it helped people to cope with the two main threats they faced in life: arbitrary authority and the unpredictable assaults of demons (Hillgarth 1986: 12). The latter at least was true in Southeast Asia. The power of shamanistic possession was palpable even to tough-minded Jesuits, and posed them a considerable challenge. Chirino (1604: 300) chronicled many contests with traditional healers, conceding that though some were fakes, "there are also those who actually have a special pact with the devil, who aids and supports them with very special assistance, which Almighty God in his inscrutable judgement permits." For Iberian priests these unfamiliar supernatural forces could only be categorized as in league with the devil. Alarming as the phenomena often were to them, the friars believed they had to do battle with these powers of darkness, armed with the cross and the sacraments. Sometimes, presumably, they failed, but in their pious narratives are numerous stories of spectacular victories over demons: "Having planted this royal standard of our redemption [the cross] in an island greatly infested by demons, who were continually frightening the islanders with howls and cries, it imposed upon them perpetual silence, and freed all the other [neighbouring] islands from an extraordinary tyranny. For the demons were crossing from island to island, in the sea, in the shape of serpents of enormous size . . . but this ceased, the demon taking flight at the sight of the cross" (Velarde 1749: 71).

In his first weeks in northern Vietnam, Alexandre de Rhodes (1651: 131) also saw himself as the agent of liberation of "a famous magician, who had erected twenty-five altars to demons in his house, by whom he was cruelly tormented." Later, in the age of Descartes and Newton, another pious chronicler knew that his French readers would find difficulty accepting the succession of miracles whereby the priests of the Société des Missions Etrangères cast out demons, cured people of possession, and raised children from the dead in Vietnam. He felt obliged to point out "that the hand of God is not withdrawn, that he can do today in his emerging churches, to validate the faith, something approaching the marvels he performed in the first centuries for the same purpose; and . . . that in the countries where the devil reigns by idolatry, and marks his tyranny by possession, it should appear no more incredible that Jesus Christ wants to overturn his empire there . . . by the ministry of the bishops and priests" (Missions Etrangères 1680: 9).

The assimilation of Southeast Asian spirits to Islamic djinn, both good and bad, presented fewer problems. Even learned ulama did not deny the existence of spirits, but they felt less threatened than others by them. Like Christianity, Islam offered a refuge from the domination of these demanding spirits in a different vision of the cosmos. This was a predictable, moral world, in which the devout would be protected by God from all that the spirits could do and would eventually be rewarded by an afterlife in paradise. The powerless, too, would be rewarded if they lived lives of personal virtue. "The high and the low; the rich and the poor; they will all appear the same," as a Tagalog devotional poem put it (Herrera 1645, quoted Rafael 1988: 176).

This new vision undoubtedly provided "a tremendous increase in distance . . . between man and the sacred" (Geertz 1964: 174), a major step towards what Weber characterized as rationalization of religion (Weber 1951: 226). For those who in the age of commerce were making their way in a wider world of international trade, of large-scale state operations, of the exchange of ideas through literature and debate, this new world-view provided the necessary foundation.

This moral universe depended on a simple but consistent concept of eternal reward and punishment. The older view of the afterlife had been full of dangerous possibilities, against which nobody could ever be sure. By contrast, Islam and Christianity introduced the promise of a heaven that was forever safe and comfortable, "without death, only joy and happiness and life. . . . There is nothing lacking there, every wish will be fulfilled . . . without sorrow and lament, no sadness, no tribulation, nothing that is not glorious," as a seventeenth-century Augustinian wrote in one of the first catechetical poems in Tagalog (cited Rafael 1988: 172–73).

On the Muslim side, Raniri composed in 1636 a popular Malay tract of more than two hundred pages, the *Achbaru'l-Achirat,* on death, judgement, heaven, hell, and the last days (Juynboll 1899: 274–76). Others also portrayed the rewards of paradise for those who recited the Muslim confession of faith (Hamzah *Asraru'l-Arifin:* 238; Syamsud-din 1601: 370; Jones 1979: 148).

Hell was even more persuasive. Chirino (1604: 297) noted that Filipino fears of what evil spirits could do were such that "a well-painted picture of hell has converted a very great number of them.". Writers and preachers of both faiths dwelt on the torments in hell that awaited those foolish enough to prefer earthly pleasures to their eternal welfare and those who rejected the true faith for its rivals (see examples in Xavier 1546: 365; Rafael 1988: 179–84; Hamzah *Poems:* 76, 92, 132; fig. 22).

Some of the finest Malay and Javanese poetry, however, was concerned with a higher state of ecstatic union with God in which heaven and hell themselves were immaterial. A sixteenth-century Javanese Muslim text replicated older Islamic teaching that many would serve God through hope of paradise, or "neither eating or sleeping day or night out of fear of hell," but that the only true reward would be for those who loved God for his own sake (*Javaanse Primbon:* 22–23).

Fig. 22 A Buddhist hell, as represented in a Thai manuscript of 1777

Although the prominence of heaven and hell were new to Southeast Asians, the concepts may not have been. In their desire to find evocative terms to translate the Muslim and Christian visions of heaven, proselytists employed already localized words. Throughout the Archipelago they spoke of the Sanskrit *swarga* (the abode of Siva) for heaven and *naraka* for hell (Malay *syorga* and *neraka*). The Spanish used Tagalog *langit* (sky) or other terms connoting profound peace and contentment when discussing the joys of heaven. When it came to hell, however, the shock of the unfamiliar *infierno* was evidently more effective (Rafael 1988: 170–81).

In a moral universe, the religious specialists were expected to set a moral example. Christian apologists listed the selfless enthusiasm of the early friars, especially in tending the sick, as a factor that eventually attracted Filipinos to them even if they were initially seen as clownishly ineffective (Aduarte 1640: 185, 223; Blair and Robertson 1903–09 X: 107; XVIII: 179). Often, however, the failure of Spaniards to live up to the moralistic doctrine they preached was a source of puzzlement or disgust. One sceptic from Cagayan simply rejected the Christian arguments by saying, "the Castilians have no better sense than we have, since they act as they do, and do not observe that law; say nothing more about it" (Blair and Robertson 1903–09 X: 107; also Chirino 1604: 248; La Loubère 1691: 143).

The ascetism of the Muslim Sufis was of a type familiar to those below the winds who had been exposed to Indian religious models. It was oriented less at self-giving than at self-suppression, the utter indifference to external reality when lost in the ecstatic love of God: "When one's Lord is thus known, then one will be able to be indifferent to all else; whether being clothed [or naked], it is the same to him; whether being rich or poor, it is the same to him; whether being praised or scorned, it is the same to him" (Hamzah *Asraru'l-Arifin:* 280). The closeness of the Sufi saint to God was popularly thought to be evident in his supernatural powers and the bright glow (Malay *cahaya,* personalizing Arabic *nur*) that suffused him. The writers of Southeast Asian texts certainly believed that these self-evident powers were sufficient to convert many (*Sejarah Melayu* 1612: 129; *Hikayat Banjar:* 420), and external sources confirm that at least such outstanding Sufi masters as Hamzah Fansuri, Syamsud-din as-Samatrani, and Abdurra'uf as-Singkili in Aceh, as well as Sheikh Yusuf in Makassar and Banten, were popularly revered even during their lifetime.

Evidence of the power of moral example is clearest in the Mainland Theravada states. Christian missionaries in Cambodia and Siam acknowledged that the reason they made no progress was the extraordinary respect people had for the Buddhist monks: "Their life is so poor and austere, that outwardly they yield in no way to the austerity or the poverty of the most reformed religious in the church. They live entirely on alms, able to have nothing of their own nor to exercise any commerce. They never eat meat, and in the evening they take nothing cooked, but they content themselves with certain raw fruits" (Missions Etrangères 1674: 145; cf. Kaempfer 1727 I: 68).

Spirits remained powerful, and may have grown more so with the retreat of the urban cosmopolitanism of the age of commerce. The scriptural religions offered new ways to tame them through more powerful spiritual forces on the one hand and individual morality on the other.

Difficult Transitions

Sexual Morality

If these factors in some measure explain the attraction of conversion, there were also enormous problems in attempting to adapt Southeast Asian societies to religious systems with contradictory values in many areas. The relations between the sexes were among the most difficult of issues.

Southeast Asian religion was profoundly dualistic, with male and female elements both needing to be present to give power and effect. Female gods of the underworld, of the earth or crops (especially rice), and of the moon balanced the male gods of the upperworld, the sky, iron (that which ploughs the earth, cuts the rice-stalk), and the sun (Schärer 1946: 14–15; Stöhr and Zoetmulder 1968: 31–32, 61–66, 115–20; Hoskins 1986: 139–40; Hamonic 1987: 29–49). Women had as much power in their ritual domains as men had in theirs. In particular, women were prominent as spirit mediums and ritual healers and in preparing offerings to the spirits—indeed, in every aspect of the relations between humans and spirits.

The scriptural religions, in contrast, introduced exclusively male religious specialists ministering to a deity also identified as male. Men who had been prominent ritual specialists in the old religion could be converted to play a similar role in the new. They could use the new external source of divine authority for familiar purposes. Women did not have this option. Islamization in particular involved a transfer of knowledge and commitment from one male to another—father to son, teacher to pupil, conqueror to vassal. Ambonese Muslim men told Gijsels (1621: 29) that their women did not need to come to the mosque "and that they pray[ed] for the women." Banjarese men were reported more crudely: "They say their women have no souls . . . and . . . are only design'd by God to gratify Men's appetite; for which reason the women are never suffer'd to use any divine worship" (Beeckman 1717: 122). From the perspective of the old religion, however, it probably seemed to women that this was simply a male ritual activity not relevant to them.[3]

It is not surprising that resistance by the old religion was often led by women. The Philippines provides the most striking cases, not only because the evidence is better but also because the Spanish friars forced the issue with female shamans, whereas Muslim proselytists ignored them. In Panay, for example, Fray Juan de Alvas "had continual battles with the devil, who by means of the priestesses whom they call *babaylanas* made strong resistance and war against them." Even though Christianity appeared to prevail in the town, these priestesses hid from Spanish authority in the hills, where people from the town would come secretly to seek help when ill (San Agustin 1698: 72–73). After their initial success in Christianizing the Taytay region east of

---

3. Modern explanations of why propitiation of spirits is still primarily women's business may be quite different. Burmese informants gave Spiro (1967: 59) two reasons: The Buddhist answer was that men did not need to be so fearful and respectful of the *nats* (spirits) as women because men occupied a higher level than the nats in the thirty-one abodes of existence, while women were at a lower level. The more practical answer was that the health of the household was the mother's responsibility, so she had to propitiate the nats who determined it.

Manila, the Jesuits faced the sudden revival of "a great plague of idolatry" inspired by female shamans led by one of high birth. They went to great pains to find and destroy all the "idols" of this group (Chirino 1604: 302–05).

Islamic conversion stories provide only one such insight on the role of women. The *Babad Lombok* (17–19) relates that when all the men of Lombok submitted to a superior Javanese force and agreed to be circumcised, the women refused to accept Islam. The leading men feared that this would enrage the Javanese, and so moved their capital away from the coast and back to the ancient Hindu capital, though their commitment to Islam remained. In South Sulawesi a few aristocratic women appear also to have been prominent among the resistance to Islam. Women of ordinary birth, however, were probably under little pressure to abandon domestic ritual activity, and even shamanistic healing. The chief evidence for this is less in the sources than in Southeast Asian religious practice, where such activities survived surprisingly well until this century.

For Christian proselytists, the sensuality and freedom of Southeast Asian women, and the polygamy of male chiefs, constituted major problems. The Lao had many virtues, one Jesuit noted, but were "lamentably tolerant of fornication" (Marini 1663: 454; cf., for Java, Scott 1606: 173). Long after the Philippines were Christianized, missionaries continued to complain that sensuality was its "prince and master vice; . . . so general that . . . it kept these regions aflame with an infernal and inextinguishable fire" (Velarde 1749: 93–94). The Inquisition in the Philippines differed from its counterparts in Latin America and Europe in that its most frequent charges against priests concerned sexual rather than theological lapses, and particularly abusing the confessional to arrange assignations with women (Angeles 1980: 270). Chirino (1604: 313) instanced a lady of high rank in Leyte who refused Christianity solely because of its insistence on the indissolubility of marriage. "She said that it was a hard thing if unhappy with one's husband one could not leave him, as was the custom among them."

There were some roles for women. In spite of the male dress in which Iberian Catholicism came to the islands, Philippine women proved zealous to create their own religious domain in the sodalities of Our Lady and the *Beatarios*, which they formed despite many obstacles (Schumacher 1979: 86–87, 165–68). In Vietnam, which was in the process of enforcing a Confucian ideology of female subordination even harsher than the Iberian, women were prominent among the early converts to Christianity and provided the missionaries with their chief access to the court (Rhodes 1653: 51–52, 60, 113, 152–53).

The struggle of Islam to impose a radically different sexual moral-ity on Southeast Asians was a long one, with rapid change in periods of orthodox emphasis but other periods of relaxation and compromise with the enduring autonomy of Southeast Asian women. Among the elite of the trading cities in the seventeenth century, adultery was punished by death, and women were sometimes, as in Makassar, "en-tirely covered from head to foot, in such fashion that not even their faces can be seen" (Rhodes 1653: 207). Female dress in public was one of the earliest changes with Islam as with Christianity. Social and occupational patterns also changed, though more slowly. The new scriptural ideas came to be seen as "religion" (*agama*) and the old pattern as "custom" (*adat*), a category allowed for in Islam. A modern example of the type of debate that must have occurred time and again as agama gained ground on adat is provided in a Sumatran novel purporting to represent the conflicts around 1900, within three gener-ations of the acceptance of Islam by the southern Bataks. The Muslim spokesman at a meeting argues that adolescent girls should be "penned up in the house so that big sins do not happen" and that no education should be given them except recitation of the Koran. A mother of such a girl gives a spirited response that agricultural work was necessarily divided between the sexes and that men could not possibly do it alone. Moreover, "it has become adat here to let girls free and let them go courting. . . . It is in courting that people can see the behaviour, manners and adat of young people . . . there too one can gauge the firmness of the love one has for the other" (Rodgers Siregar 1981: 71–73).

Death and the Spirits

Even if the scriptural religions loosened the grip of the spirits, people continued to face illness, misfortune, and death. The anger of unsatisfied spirits of the dead were a more immediate and direct explanation of these disasters than scriptural notions of evil, and for most they continued to be influential (Hoskins 1987: 150–51). Ordi-nary Javanese Muslims in Banten told Scott (1606: 172–73) that God was good and would not hurt them, but the devil (by which they meant evil spirits)[4] was constantly doing them harm, so they directed all their ritual activity to him. The early Tagalog catechisms berated

4. Scott's confusion is understandable. As early as 1521 (Pigafetta 1524: 84) South-east Asian Muslims used the term *setan* (Arabic *shaitan*) for evil spirits or demons. The devil of Islam was usually called Iblis.

Christian converts for making offerings to their ugly, malevolent spirits (*anito*) instead of worshipping God and his saints: "Christians, you who have been baptized, why do you despise God? Why do you consult the anito when you get sick? Or when you are suffering? . . . Can the anito relieve you? Can the lifeless give life? Why do you make an offering when you work in the rice fields?" (Oliver 1586: 32–35).

Change in the externals of funerary practice was achieved remarkably quickly. Burial sites of the tenth to sixteenth centuries have yielded valuable ceramics and gold items, buried with the dead in the Philippines and eastern Indonesia to ensure a comfortable passage to the afterlife. These end abruptly with the coming of Islam and Christianity. The pattern of sacrificing slaves to accompany a chief into the afterlife was discontinued, as was widow-burning (suttee) in Java. The elaborate feasting, designed to ensure that the deceased endured this most dangerous transition and would not return to torment the living, was replaced by simple burials within two or three days of death. There were some exceptions. The Banjarese continued to put camphor and other precious things in the grave for more than a century after their conversion, "but now being Mahometans they say they do it only as a mark of respect" (Beeckman 1718: 42). The funerals and tombs of the rulers of Melaka, Aceh, Mataram, and Makassar continued to be of spectacular magnificence, with gold and ceramics now displayed on the graves rather than buried with the corpse (Albuquerque 1557: 136; Davis 1600: 321–22; Gervaise 1701: 140–47; Djajadiningrat 1929). For most Muslims and Christians, however, rapid burials and simple gravemarkers became the norm.

Prayers and offerings for the spirits of the dead, in contrast, were far too deep-rooted to be crushed. They had somehow to be incorporated into the new scheme. In the Philippines the Spanish tried to suppress the practice by force:

The Indios usually believe that the soul of the dead returns to their house on the third day after their death in order to visit the people there, and attend their feast, and for this reason they hold a ceremony called *tibao*, which they cover and hide by saying that they come together in the house of the dead to pray the rosary for [the departed soul]; and if they are told to recite the rosary in the church, they prefer not to because this is not what they really do. For this reason, the Minister shall impede their gathering in the house of the dead after the burial, and shall not permit them to go to the house under some pretext, particularly on the third day (Thomas Ortiz 1731, trans. Rafael 1988: 187–88).

Clerical strictures against any communication with the spirits created a difficult hurdle for new Christians. Alexandre de Rhodes (1651: 140–

41) had no hesitation about sending a sister of the (northern) Vietnamese king away disappointed when she asked him for some means to assist her recently deceased husband towards heaven. In Borneo, a Catholic missionary was reportedly killed by Ngaju Dayaks "because he had not performed his promise of shewing them all their deceas'd friends," which they had understood in an immediate, perhaps shamanistic, sense (Beeckman 1717: 124–25).[5] Some Filipinos rejected baptism because they had no wish to share paradise with Spanish soldiers, while others told the missionaries they preferred to go to hell if that was where their ancestors had gone (Mendoza 1586: 148–49; Vaez 1601, cited Schumacher 1979: 70).

Even if the stern Iberian attitude to the dead created a barrier to conversion, Southeast Asian Christians found ways to adapt Catholic ritual to their needs. Not only was the annual holy day for All Souls celebrated with great feasting at the gravesites, but a daily prayer for the dead, the *anima*, was devised to be said at the sound of the church bell each night (Schumacher 1984: 255).

Though from its origins uncompromising in its condemnation of idolatry, Islam had come to Southeast Asia in a form that incorporated helpful popular compromises with the potential power of the dead. In the years following the fall of Baghdad the Sufi orders (*tariqa*) became the major instruments for the extension of the faith. Although the founders and saints of the Sufi orders had been learned visionaries seeking a direct path to union with God, at the popular level Sufism by the fifteenth century represented a means of linking the individual with the spiritual power (Arabic *barakah*; Malay *berkat*) of holy men, apostles, rulers, and other remarkable people. The power of these dead saints was invoked to help the living through the spiritual genealogy which linked each Sufi teacher to the venerated founder of his order, and through visitations (*ziyara*) to the tombs of holy men, where offerings were frequently made. "The mystic carries out a ziyara for the purposes of *muraqaba* (spiritual communion) with the saint, finding in the material symbol an aid to meditation. But the popular belief is that the saint's soul lingers about his tomb and places especially associated with him whilst he was on earth or at which he manifested himself. At such places his intercession can be sought" (Trimingham 1971: 26).

Southeast Asia, like southern India, was prone to saint-veneration, since the berkat of the dead saints was seen to be able to help the

---

5. Beeckman may have been referring here to the Italian Theatine, Fra Antonio Ventimiglia, who was killed in the Banjarmasin area in 1693 (Coomans 1980: 89–90).

living much as spirits did. Among the tombs at which "sacrifices and rogations" (Dasmariñas 1590: 10) were most popular were those of the apostles thought to have introduced Islam to each area, such as the nine *wali* of Java or Dato ri Bandang in Makassar, certain powerful kings such as Iskandar Muda in Aceh, and the popularizers of the Sufi orders. In the last category were two of the outstanding Indonesian scholars of the second half of the seventeenth century, who had both travelled and studied in Arabia. Abdurra'uf as-Singkili, revered by the Acehnese as Sheikh Kuala, introduced the Shattariya tariqa to Indonesia, while Sheikh Yusuf was the great teacher of the Khalwatiya order, held by Makassarese even in his lifetime "in such love and awe as though he was a second Muhammad" (Hartsingh 1689, cited Andaya 1981: 277). The strength of this saint-veneration as early as the sixteenth century is confirmed by the protest of a strictly orthodox Javanese handbook against it: "It is unbelief to say that the great imams are superior to the prophets, or to put the saints (*wali*) above the prophets, and even above our lord Muhammad" ("Javanese Code": 38–39).

Though they rapidly accepted the form of Muslim funerals, Southeast Asians continued to fear that the dead would trouble them unless ritually satisfied. In Banda in 1599, corpses were quickly buried in a white cloth, as prescribed by Islam, but when the Dutch asked Bandanese why they continued to pray for several days at the gravesite, they were told it was to prevent the dead from "standing up," which would otherwise surely happen, causing great misfortune to all ("Tweede Boeck" 1601: 90). Southeast Asian Muslims enthusiastically adopted the widespread Muslim practice of returning to the gravesite at ritually significant moments, the third, seventh, fortieth, and hundredth days after the burial, to feast at the gravesite (Martin 1604: 49; Gervaise 1701: 140–74; Raffles 1817 I: 327; Ali Haji 1866: 76; Brooke 1848 I: 87–88). "According to the official or learned conception this is done in order to bestow on the deceased the recompense earned by his good work; according to the popular notion it is to let them enjoy the actual savour of the good things of the feast" (Snouck Hurgronje 1893 I: 221). Gervaise (1701: 133) made the point about the Makassarese he encountered in Siam that "they observe an infinite number of ceremonies that are not in use among the Turks, nor among the Indian Mahometans; because they believe them to be practised at Mecca." Most of these had to do with Islamized forms of offerings to the ancestors at various life crises, especially death.

Honouring the dead continues to be a great preoccupation of Southeast Asian Muslims. Whereas in the Arab world the seventh month of the Muslim year is considered most appropriate for such commemoration, in Indonesia it is before and after the fasting month (the ninth) when ancestors are especially remembered, as if the spirits, too, had to be prepared to undergo the great fast. Feasts were (and still are by many) held at gravesites in the week before the fast commences (Koentjaraningrat 1985: 365). This is the period known to Javanese as *nyadran*, a word Pigeaud (1960–63 IV: 424) has traced back to a Tantric ceremony for the dead, *shraddha*, elaborately celebrated in the fourteenth century. The Islamic month of Sha'ban, preceding the fast, is known in Java as *ruwah*, the month of spirits. The week after the fast was again devoted to visiting graves. At the great Idulfitri feast on 1 Shawwal that begins this week it was appropriate to ask the forgiveness of elders—dead as well as living—for sins committed. Although certainly practiced in the seventeenth century (Gervaise 1701: 146–47), the origins of these practices lie in obscurity. They may initially have represented another creative adaptation of Islamic festivals to serve older purposes of propitiating the spirits of the dead (Crawfurd 1820 I: 97; II: 261).

Some of the vocabulary of Southeast Asian religion was used to embody and empower new Muslim concepts. *Ngaji* (and related *kaji*, *mengaji*) is an Austronesian word still used by animists in Flores to describe ritual prayers addressed to the ancestors (Novena 1982: 13–24). It became the everyday word for reciting the Koran, whether for the souls of the departed or for other purposes. Similarly, the normal word for prayer in Southeast Asian Islam, including the public Friday prayer, was not taken from Arabic but from an ancient indigenous term, *sembahyang*, literally "veneration of lord(s) or deity(ies)." More common, however, was the grafting of Arabic terms and prayers onto activities previously associated with the spirit world. Potent graves were referred to by Arabic words that could validate their power in Islamic terms—*kramat* (sacred [grave]), *berkat* (spiritual power), and *ziarah* (pilgrimage—Houtman 1603: 250).

Most crucial of all, the fundamental Austronesian concept of *semangat* (soul-substance or spirit), which animated both the individual and the cosmos and linked the two (Endicott 1970: 28–51), could be reinterpreted as the Sufi concept of *ruh* (plural *arwah*), the spirit of God that animates the universe (al-Attas 1970: 86–90). Although the stern monotheism and legalism of the urban Islam of the jurists appeared a direct contradiction of a spirit-animated world, popular mysticism could see that this was only the "outer" dogmatic expression, not the "inner" mystical truth.

Power and Kingship

In older Southeast Asian belief, all power was spiritual. The powerful chief or ruler was the one who best controlled the cosmic forces, and his authority rested entirely on them. Indian ideas were adapted by the largest kingdoms of the region in a similar spirit, underpinning more grandiose ideas of divine and universal kingship, whereby the ruler not only mediated with the gods but embodied them on earth. Brahmans were retained at the courts of Burma, Siam, Cambodia, Java, and Bali to ensure that the king expressed these divine attributes in a ritually correct fashion.

In relation to such a background, the equality of all believers taught by the new scriptural religions might have seemed extremely subversive. Islam in particular, which was spread by traders and brought with it a commercial ethos, has often been seen as a "bourgeois" force, shifting power to coastal trade centres and undermining for ever the ideological basis on which the hierarchic states of previous eras had held sway (van Leur 1934: 113–15; Lombard 1990: 150–55). That religious authority ultimately lay outside the king's control, with an international orthodoxy represented locally by an influential literate elite, did provide a long-term challenge to royal authority. Why then did kings accept the new religions?

Often they did not. The major Javanese, Lombok, Sumbawa, and Bugis courts were essentially defeated in battle, not in argument, and the same may have been true in earlier cases where the records are lost. A further source of pressure was the plurality of most of the region. If one small northern Tai state threw in its lot with Buddhism, or a Sumatran state with Islam, this posed the danger to more important states that commerce and eventually power would pass to their rivals unless they followed suit. The small state of Perlak preceded Pasai into Islam, Terengganu preceded Patani, and Luwu preceded Makassar. In the succession disputes that frequently tore Southeast Asian states apart, the new religions with their popular or commercial support could be a source of strength for a challenger to the throne.

Nevertheless, Islam and Theravada Buddhism proved to be powerful weapons in the extension of royal power, which was a feature of the age of commerce. Because the claims of the scriptural religions were universal, they could be used to undercut the authority of internal rivals. The traditional authority of spirits and their cults were highly local, but outsiders were in awe of interfering with them. In the name of a universal religion they could be rendered innocuous. The scriptural religions also provided an honourable motive for conquest, to spread the faith ever further. In South Sulawesi a highly developed set of contractual alliances and power-sharing was sanctioned by the powerful authority of the spirit world, and only the acceptance of Islam in 1605 enabled Makassar to subordinate its neighbours in the name of a higher authority.

Buddhist and Muslim rulers had powerful means to domesticate these international religions. First, they alone made the highest religious appointments. The abbots and patriarchs (*mahasangharaja*) in Theravada countries, and the religious judges (*kadi*) in Islamic ones, were appointed by the king, often from among close relatives. In Ternate it was said that the kadi had to be of the king's blood, "because on feastdays he kisses his hand" (Galvão 1544: 87). Rulers resolved religious disputes, exercised censorship, and imposed the religious law. Their patronage of religion through building and endowing religious edifices and supporting scholars gave them enormous authority.

Whatever the theologians might have said to the contrary, Southeast Asian rulers themselves continued to claim divine status. In royal decrees, letters, and chronicles the king was still presented as the ultimate source of supernatural power in the land. To quote an imperfect translation of the Siamese king's titles, he was among many other things "the most divine master of immortal souls, the most Holy who sees all things" (Glanius 1682: 151). Although he was the most orthodox of Aceh's sultans, Iskandar Thani (1637–41) claimed to be "King of the whole world, who is like a god over it, shining like the sun at midday, a king whose radiance is like the full moon, chosen by God" (*Dagh-Register* 1640–41: 6). Malay sultans claimed to be not only the shadow of God on earth but also caliph (successor of Muhammad as commander of the faithful) and deputy of God (Milner 1983: 34–39; Drakard 1993: 211–16).

Far from being in ideological conflict with Islam, kingship found new ways to express its transcendence in Islamic terms. The word *dawla*, which in Arabic had become the standard term for the state (having evolved from the word for "turn" to the alternation of dynasties), was given a more profound and mystical meaning in Malay as the essence of sovereignty. "*Daulat Tuanku!*" became the necessary salutation with which every Malay-speaker repeatedly affirmed the divine authority of the king. This same daulat was endowed with magical power, so that it could strike down enemies and traitors without the ruler having to lift a finger. In Javanese this magical power unique to rulers was expressed by the word *wahyu*, another word taken from the Islamic vocabulary. But the Arabic original (*wahy*) applied not to kings but to that divine inspiration found preeminently in the Prophet.

Kings could use ideas from Islam or Buddhism in this way to enhance their own supernatural pretensions, but they gained no such assistance from Iberian Catholicism. This helps to explain why no significant Christian kingdoms survived below the winds. In spite of the hundreds of thousands of baptisms, and the numerous kings who expressed great interest in embracing Catholicism and allying with the Iberians, no substantial Christian dynasty lasted for more than a generation. Where Islam and Buddhism could be manipulated to help rulers, Iberian Catholicism undermined their authority. Counterreformation discipline required that spiritual authority rested with the priesthood, while Spanish and Portuguese claims to be exclusive patrons of the Asian missions (the *padroado*) ensured that the priesthood was a European preserve. Those kings who became Christian, in eastern Indonesia and Arakan, became involved in Portuguese power plays and lost the hold they had on their own people. The words which Pinto (1578: 94) put into the mouth of one of the great scourges of the Portuguese, the part-Chinese naval warrior Hinimilau, reveal part of this story. Hinimilau had become a Christian in Melaka around 1540 after trading there for some time, but:

after he had become a Christian, he was always treated with deep contempt by the Portuguese, whereas previously, when he had been a heathen, they would all remove their hats when they spoke to him and address him politely as "Kiai Nachoda," which was like calling him "sir captain"; . . . and that he went to Bintang to become a Moslem, and that there, after he was converted, the king of Juntana [Johor] . . . always treated him in the most honorable manner, and the mandarins all addressed him as "brother."

The major populations that remained Catholic did so without their own kings, as subjects of Spain in the Philippines or of Confucian monarchs in Vietnam.

To express the concept of subjection to an all-powerful God, both Islam and Christianity employed the metaphor of slavery: "The relationship between the master and the slave [*aliping*] is similar to that between God and man. We are all slaves of the Lord God, who has made us, as it were, to dwell on this earth first. If we are good and respectful to him, we will be taken by him to his house in heaven when the time comes, where he will treat us like his children and bless us there" (Oliver 1586: 39; cf. ibid.: 31). In adopting the Tagalog, but not the Spanish, terminology of slavery, the Spanish friars were seeking a more persuasive imagery of total submission than would have been conveyed by, for example, "Christ the king." Until the period of absolutism in the early seventeenth century, kings tended to be problematic as focuses of Southeast Asian loyalty. European writers by the sixteenth century seldom used the word *slave* of their own submission to God, despite the precedent of scripture.

Islamic literature used the images of both slave (*'abd*) and kingship to express the submission of man to God, and this passed naturally into the apologetics written in Malay by foreign-born scholars like Raniri (Al-Attas 1986: 90, 96). Local-born mystics like Hamzah Fansuri (*Poems:* 96, 102; *Asraru'l-Arifin:* 295), preferred ambiguous Malay *hamba* to Arabic *'abd*, and emphasized the immanence rather than the transcendent otherness of God:

> He is the greatest of kings . . .
> He constantly conceals himself within a slave . . .
> He is both mother and father . . .
> Now He is a (merchant) traveller
> Now a comrade working the fields
> Now His wealth is of no account
> Always sailing onto the reef
>
> (Hamzah *Poems:* 98)

In spite of these different backgrounds, the scriptural religions tended to oppose private slavery and thereby to strengthen state authority. In the eyes of some Spanish clerics, freeing Filipinos from slavery was "a matter of natural and divine right and clear justice" (Salazar's Council 1581: 330). The abolition of slavery also meant that all Filipinos would become directly subject to the Spanish crown and liable for its taxes.

Islamic law made very clear provision for slaves, much of which was adopted into Southeast Asian law codes. But the distinction between Muslim and kafir tended to override the distinction between freeman and slave, especially where this corresponded with the interests of a centralizing king. If we accept the word of the Makassar chronicle, the people of Bima were initially conquered and enslaved by Makassar, but then progressively freed so as to meet the requirements of Shafi law that forty freemen were needed to celebrate the Friday prayer (Noorduyn 1987: 317–22). A Bugis chronicle records the apostle of South Sulawesi decreeing that some favourite habits of pre-Islamic Bugis—pork, palm-wine, adultery, lending at interest—were absolutely forbidden to Muslims, but in addition "God would reward those who freed their slaves" where these slaves followed the master into Islam. A number of powerful Muslim rulers took the view that their own Muslim subjects could not be enslaved by others and that conquered peoples who became Muslim should be assimilated into the dominant population. Like the Spanish, they thereby increased the numbers of subjects under their direct control (Reid 1983: 169–73).

The Special Case of Java

> *The state of Mahomedanism in Java differs widely from that among the maritime and commercial tribes. . . . Of all the Mahomedans the Javanese are the most lax in their principles and practice, a singularity to be ascribed to their little intercourse with foreign Mahomedans, occasioned by the exclusion of the Arabs in particular, through the commercial jealousy of the Dutch, during a period of two hundred years.*
> —*Crawfurd 1820 II:261*

The continuing strength of *kejawen*, or Javanism, has made the Javanese-speaking area of east and central Java appear unique among Islamic cultures. In modern times (though more in the 1950s than the 1980s) it has not been difficult to find nominally Muslim Javanese aristocrats who believed that the Islamization of the island was a cultural disaster and that an older tradition of meditation and asceticism was a truer way to the sacred than the *shari'a*. Recent scholarship (Ricklefs 1979; Kumar 1980: 12–16; Kumar 1985: 6–7) has shown that the cultural gulf memorably portrayed by Geertz (1960) between kejawen aristocrats and literalist Muslims owed a great deal to Dutch intellectual preferences over the preceding century and to the divisive new moralism of reformist Islam. Java in the seventeenth century was much less a special case than it became in the early twentieth. Nevertheless, in two respects it was at one end of a spectrum. It possessed the most developed Indianized court culture of any of the states which accepted Islam, and its retreat from involvement in the international Islamic network in the seventeenth century was more marked than that of others.

The first of these factors ensured that the major Javanese states would not accept Islam voluntarily. Although there were prominent Muslims identifiable by their gravestones at the Majapahit capital from the fourteenth century, Javanese ruling elites were among the latest in the Archipelago to surrender to the rising new power. Javanese sources on the fifteenth and sixteenth centuries are notoriously obscure, and their convention of placing in 1478–79 (the Javanese year 1400, regarded as appropriate for a new dynasty) the overthrow of Majapahit by Muslim armies is certainly mistaken. Whatever happened in that year was not the final victory of Islam (Noorduyn 1978: 254–55). The earliest and most reliable chronicle begins with this conventional end of Majapahit but mentions Muslims only a century later, when in 1577–78 the "martyrs of Islam" defeated Kediri (*Babad ing Sangkala* 1738: 18–25). Pires (1515: 174–75) reported that there was still a "heathen" king of Java, based at Daha (Kediri), while eighty years later the Dutch reported that the Muslims of Java were only on the north coast and "they are heathens in the interior" (Lodewycksz 1598: 114). The critical period for Java's Islamic revolution was the sixteenth and early seventeenth centuries.

The Muslim enclaves of the north coast were, however, much older. Already during the first decades of the fifteenth century Ma Huan (1433: 93) divided the people of the north coast trading cities into three groups, the Muslims from many countries, the Chinese, many of whom were also Muslims, and the "primitive" pagan Javanese. From the string of ports between Tuban and Surabaya, Majapahit's fleets had sailed to subjugate the other major ports of the Archipelago, including the established Muslim centre at Pasai, whence numerous talented Muslims were brought back in the 1360s to add a strong Malay element to the Muslim minority in Java (*Hikayat Raja-raja Pasai:* 159). Gresik appears to have been the first of these cities to have a Muslim ruler, perhaps one of the Chinese mentioned by Ma Huan (1433: 90). Gresik, the adjacent "holy hill" of Giri, and the Ngampel area of nearby Surabaya probably constituted the first centre where Islam began to be translated into a Javanese idiom and where Majapahit culture began to receive a Muslim dress. From there, in the last quarter of the fifteenth century, a man known to Javanese tradition as Raden Patah moved to Demak, where he led another flourishing Muslim mercantile community (de Graaf and Pigeaud 1974: 37–39). His origins were probably also connected with the Chinese community of Palembang. The *Babad Tanah Jawi* (22–23, 31) rests its case for Demak's claim to legitimate succession to Majapahit on the notion that Raden Patah was the son of the last king of Majapahit by a Chinese princess who gave birth to him in Palembang.

By the first decade of the sixteenth century the balance of power in the Javanese *pasisir* had shifted to Central Java, further from what remained of the Hindu state. The Demak mosque was the meeting-place of influential Muslims presided over by the scholarly Sheikh Bonang, who according to tradition was the son of Raden Rahmat, the great saint of the Surabaya-Gresik area whose origins were in the Muslim trading community of Champa (*Babad Tanah Jawi:* 20–21; de Graaf and Pigeaud 1974: 19–24, 47–50). The warlike Sultan Trenggana ruled Demak (c.1504–46), while the neighbouring port-state of Japara was the strongest naval power of the Java Sea. Trenggana led an Islamic coalition that may have destroyed the major Hindu-Buddhist state, with its last capital in Kediri (*Babad ing Sangkala:* 21; de Graaf and Pigeaud 1974: 53–56; Noorduyn 1978: 255). Far from taking over an established Javanese state (which was probably in an advanced state of disintegration), he returned to the Islamic stronghold in Demak, from where he continued to battle numerous Hindu enemies. The title Sultan, which according to tradition he assumed about about 1524 with authorization brought from Mecca by another wali, Sunan Gunung Jati, indicated the intention to make Demak an Islamic kingdom of a new type in Java (de Graaf and Pigeaud 1974: 50–51). Mendez Pinto (1578: 382–93) portrayed Trenggana in the 1540s as the "Emperor" of Java and all the surrounding islands, yet nevertheless having to crusade against "heathen" kingdoms in eastern Java. Another Portuguese who visited Java at this time warned that "his aim is to Islamicise all the surrounding peoples, so that he himself will become another Sultan of Turkey beside whom [Portuguese] Melaka is nothing" (Pinto 1548: 423).

During the sixteenth century an extraordinary cultural transformation was taking place in the Javanese coastal cities, then the centres of wealth and ideas to which Javanese of talent were attracted. Mosques and holy tombs were built that blended the brickwork and ornamentation of Majapahit and the great wooden pillars of the Javanese *pendopo* with the ritual needs of Islam (figs. 23a, 23b). Javanese performing arts were transformed or created, perhaps in the direction of replacing realistic representations of humans with the stylized *wayang* form less offensive to devout Muslims. Though the history of these developments is largely lost, Javanese tradition surprisingly credits the most illustrious of the semi-legendary walis of Java, Sunan Kali Jaga, with the creation of masked drama—even though its subject matter is pre-Islamic (Pigeaud 1938: 39–52; de Graaf and Pigeaud 1974: 65–71).

Islamic norms were certainly not the only ones in the coastal cities of the sixteenth century. One must imagine a pious core of internationally connected Muslims around the mosques of the harbour cities, a constant influx of non-Islamic Javanese from the hinterland, and courts that attempted to exploit both Islamic and Javanese claims to legitimacy. The earliest Javanese manuscripts extant are Muslim works from these cities, and they indicate a deep interest in exploring the Islamic scholarly tradition of mystical union with God, as well as a determination to uphold the true faith in a pluralistic context ("Javanese Code"; *Javaanse Primbon;* Drewes 1969).

The continuing wars between various Muslim and Hindu states in Java throughout the sixteenth century are attested by the *Babad ing*

Fig. 23a The Masjid Agung of Demak, reportedly built in the late fifteenth century, reflecting the style of a traditional audience-hall (*pendopo*)

Sangkala (18–29), as well as by the Portuguese. The leading position of Demak ended when Trenggana was murdered in 1546. Fighting broke out between candidates for the succession, the city was sacked and burned, and "nothing was left of it that anyone could lay eyes on" (Pinto 1578: 394).

In the warfare that followed to assume the mantle of Demak (and to revive the memory of Majapahit), Surabaya gradually emerged as the strongest of the Muslim port-states, while the locus of power in central Java shifted inland, first to Pajang and then to Mataram (near Yogyakarta). The great builder of Mataram's fortunes was the warrior Senapati, whose career was summed up by van Goens (1656: 186) half a century after his death in 1601:

[Senapati] was the third Pangeran [among fourteen independent rulers in Java] to accept the Mahomedan sect, about the year A.D. 1576, the first being the lord of Bantam and the second of Ceribon; and because his peers in his opinion were stubbornly refusing to accept this religion along with him, he made himself ready for war, having in his own district the might and the means; attacking first the strongest, most populous and fruitful province, named Mataram, which having conquered in a short time, he immediately made away with all the royal dynasty, with their servants,

Fig. 23b Winged gate of the sixteenth-century Sendang Duwur mosque near Tuban, on Java's northeast coast, in a style transitional from that of Hindu-Buddhist Majapahit

with great cruelty, not sparing their wives and children; immediately introducing his newly accepted religion, and established his residence in the Mataram, in a new court. . . . After conquering this province, he made war to the end of his life, having made himself lord and master before his death of the provinces of Purbaya, Blitar, Salaron and Pamalang.

Though it goes too far in ignoring altogether the Islamization sponsored by Demak, this picture indicates that the core of the state inherited by Senapati's grandson Agung in 1613 had been Islamized only very recently and superficially. Senapati was a conqueror who saw the need to ally with the wealthy and militarily advanced Islamic element in the pasisir. Sultan Agung's long reign witnessed the complete eclipse of the pasisir cities, the dominance of the Mataram court in Javanese affairs, and a new religious synthesis of which the king was the central exemplar. It was the achievement of Agung and his court to have established a ritual pattern that was both Islamic and Javanese—at least in its own eyes.

The international mercantile community committed to the shari'a was virtually unrepresented in Mataram, whereas it had had the upper hand in the pasisir. Sultan Agung had ulama at his court (de Graaf 1958: 103, 117), but their only source of influence was the king himself—there was no constituency to support a full application of Islamic law. Hence Sultan Agung's demands on his subjects for Islamic adherence were not especially heavy. They did, however, include certain vital elements. Prominent men had formally to accept Islam and undergo circumcision; the same requirement was made of European and other captives who wished to avoid execution (ibid.: 102–03). Unlike his immediate successors, Agung also sometimes publicly celebrated the Friday prayer and required his officials to accompany him to it.[6] Like other rulers below the winds Sultan Agung made Idulfitri, the feast at the end of the fasting month, a great royal occasion, probably the biggest in the calendar. A Dutch envoy who was there for the feast in 1622 observed the king go to the "temple" to pray and then receive the obeisance of his most important vassals on the *alun-alun* (de Haen 1622: 303–04).

Although Agung was not under pressure from a pious and legalistic international community, there was another tradition of ascetic holy men of great importance throughout Java. These were the *tapa* (ascetics, with their female equivalent *tapi*) who had gathered in the ashramas of Hindu-Buddhist Java to learn techniques of "asceticism, religious vows and meditation, combining them for the well-being of the whole world" but also practised these techniques in forests, on mountaintops, and at holy places all over Java, supporting themselves by alms (*Nagara-kertagama* 1365: 94, cf. ibid.: 36–37, 64, 113–14). Tomé Pires (1515: 177) has a revealing description of these revered figures during the period of transition to Islam:

Tapas means observants, like Beguines. There are about fifty thousand of these in Java. There are three or four orders of them. Some of them do not

6. This is known from a single reference by the Dutch envoy de Haen (1622: 312). The silence of other sources, Dutch or Javanese, about the mosque in Mataram suggests that its construction was not particularly notable. It may have been so like a brick wall–encircled, high-roofed Javanese pendopo that it was not identified as a mosque by visitors (de Graaf 1958: 113–15).

eat rice nor drink wine; they are all virgins, they do not know women. They wear a certain headdress which is a full yard long and . . . where it fits on to the head it has five white stars. . . . And these men are also worshipped by the Moors, and they believe in them greatly; they give them alms; they rejoice when such men come to their houses. They go two and two by law, and they do not go about alone. . . . I have sometimes seen ten or twelve of these in Java.

This is striking evidence of the continuity between Hindu-Buddhist and Islamic patterns of asceticism in Java. In the following century, when Islam was no longer contested as the religion of Javanese, a German surgeon again described a category of "hermits" with a similar long headcloth, living in caves, practising asceticism, guarding places of pilgrimage, and regarded as Muslim saints (Fryke 1692: 147–48). For the most part the tapa appear not to have opposed Islam, at least as it was understood in the interior. Instead they adopted elements of the Muslim mystical tradition, associated with the tombs of Muslim saints, and thereby became accepted by Javanese Muslims as Sufis who went beyond the outer commands of Islam to its inner essence. Even so strict a definition of pasisir Islam as the sixteenth-century "Javanese Code" (15, 18, 22) adopted the word *tapa* to refer to Islamic austerity and self-denial, though warning against those practices clearly Hindu in character (ibid.: 34).

The teachings of the walis celebrated in Javanese tradition, and still more the cult that surrounded their tombs, appear to have led this ascetic tradition in a direction compatible with Islamic mysticism, at least as understood by most Javanese of the period. The tapa came by the eighteenth century to be known as *santri*, students of religion and seekers of gnosis, travelling the holy places of Java and subsisting on the alms of their admirers.

The relationship of ascetics to a hierarchic state would always be problematic. They could both contribute to a royal cult and fatally undermine it.[7] In 1630 a group of such ascetics began a movement threatening to Sultan Agung around Tembayat, the most sacred Muslim tomb of the Mataram region (de Graaf 1958: 198; *Babad ing Sangkala*: 37). The king crushed the movement ruthlessly, but also interrogated survivors about their beliefs. The experience did nothing to shake his faith in the importance of the Tembayat shrine, for in 1633 he made a very public pilgrimage to it and ordered that it be

---

7. Ricklefs (1974: 315–33) has documented an eighteenth-century case in which santri provoked a crisis in Dutch-Javanese relations by conferring magical powers on the king and raising his ambitions to rule all Java.

rebuilt with a splendid stone gateway (de Graaf 1958: 200–04). In effect, he appears to have resolved to link his own royal charisma to the cult of the holiest Muslim shrine of the region he controlled directly.

Further evidence of Agung's determination to establish an effective synthesis of Javanese tradition, Islam, and the cult of kingship was his promulgation of a new court calendar on his return from Tembayat, incorporating the Islamic lunar year with its festivals into the Javanese (Indic) calendar starting from A.D. 78. Probably linked to these moves was the decision to subjugate Giri, the most sacred and obdurate centre of the Surabaya region, which had been defeated militarily in 1625. Agung prepared for this definitive transfer of legitimacy from east to central Java, from the coast to the interior, by his generous treatment of the defeated Surabaya dynasty. Its cultivated crown prince, Pangeran Pekik, was brought to Mataram and given Agung's sister to wed, while Pekik's daughter by an earlier marriage was married to Agung's son and heir. Pekik was then sent to conquer Giri, which represented more a spiritual than a military challenge, and to bring its sacred patriarch to make his obeisance to Agung. This Pekik accomplished in 1636.

In 1624, after conquering more of Java than any ruler since Majapahit, Agung claimed the title Sunan (or Susuhunan), according himself a spiritual status equal to the walis of Islam. In 1641 he obtained from Mecca the title Sultan. Shortly before his death, in 1645, he constructed a grave for himself at Imogiri similar in style to those of the Muslim saints, but grander in conception. The Javanese chronicles subsequently referred to him as *prabu-pandita* (king-priest), thereby granting him another title of the walis, and claimed he possessed such unusual spiritual power that he had magically travelled to Mecca each Friday to pray (*Babad Tanah Jawi:* 122). Agung had achieved the synthesis that had escaped Sultan Akbar in India, enabling all his subjects to call themselves Muslim while enhancing their reverence to himself. A keen Dutch observer noted a few years after Agung's death, apparently unaware of any contradiction, that the Javanese "outwardly consider their king so proudly that they respect him as a God; put such a firm foundation on their Mahomedan faith that they believe their salvation is certain, and curse all others, even mock them as unholy people" (van Goens 1656: 263).

Such a synthesis could not last. As long as there was knowledge of the larger Islamic world and its various currents of legalism and mysticism, there would be attempts at reform. The pressures of international Islam were, however, mediated through the north coast, and the loss of control of that coast after Agung's death led to a deliberate rejection by some of his successors of the world of commerce and of broader Islamic affiliation. The Javanese of the interior remained Muslims, but the waves of reform that washed over other parts of the Islamic world reached them only gently. Other societies that had been led into Islam by their established rulers, notably the Bugis and Makassarese, shared some of this resistance to the full impact of Islamic law and custom. But the additional factor of disengaging from the commercial connections of the pasisir made the Javanese synthesis the most enduring.

A Peak of Islamic Scriptural Influence

> *Uphold the shari'a;*
> *Within the shari'a it is not far to deeper knowledge;*
> *If the rope of your anchor is attached to something other than the*
>   *shari'a,*
> *It will be difficult to reach the harbour of gnosis.*
> —*Hamzah Fansuri*, Poems: 92

The influence on Southeast Asian public behaviour of the legal requirements of Islam reached a peak in the first half of the seventeenth century. A similar phenomenon has been pointed out in India at the same period. It is no coincidence that it occurred in the last stages of the age of commerce, at a time when state absolutism (discussed in chapter 4) was also at its apex. Muslim urban traders were relatively strong in this period, and their international connections remained extensive. Centralizing rulers (leaving aside their personal beliefs) found it useful and necessary to incorporate some of the symbolic and legal requirements of this class into the new state structures they were building. While taking over much of the commercial activity of the traders, the rulers found they needed to incorporate some of their ideas as well. Although it is harder to measure the extent of popular commitment to the observance of Islam, there is some evidence that this was also at a high level in these years.

There was, first, a widespread vogue for rulers and their close relatives to make the pilgrimage to Mecca. This may have begun with the regent of Banten in the period 1608–24, Arya Mangalla, but it peaked in the 1630s when the rulers of Banten, Mataram, and Makassar all sponsored elaborate missions to Mecca, one aim of which was to acquire the additional title Sultan (Schrieke 1942: 242–50).

At home, rulers chose to display their majesty on occasions which also symbolized their commitment to Islam. In Aceh and Ternate there was a weekly procession to celebrate the ruler's participation in the obligatory Friday prayer. From both Malay and European sources it is clear that during the early part of Sultan Iskandar Muda's reign, thousands of men and dozens of elephants were assembled every Friday to conduct the Acehnese sultan to the mosque. In 1613 the procession involved two hundred elephants and more than four thousand men and was followed by prayer, as well as animal contests and other entertainments (Croft 1614: 168–69, 171–72; Reid 1989: 33–35). The pomp and circumstance was even grander for the major annual Islamic feasts—the eve of the fasting month, the night of revelation on 27 Ramadan, the end of the fast (Idulfitri), and the festival of sacrifice during the month of pilgrimage on 10 Dhu al-hijja (Idul Adh). This last was evidently the most spectacular, to judge from Peter Mundy's description of it in 1637, when five hundred buffaloes were slaughtered and thousands of horsemen, soldiers, and elephants marched in procession (*Adat Aceh:* 25–46; Ito 1984: 217–27; Reid 1988: 175–77; Reid 1989: 31–32). These public ceremonies marked the reigns of the first four rulers of Aceh in the seventeenth century but were discontinued under the first of its queens, Taj al-Alam (1641–75).

States were also more inclined in this period to make Islamic orthodoxy an essential test of political loyalty. All Southeast Asian states were pluralistic, with non-Muslim minorities accorded a degree of tolerance in their capitals. When a non-Muslim broke the law or was on the wrong side of a dispute, however, conversion to Islam was frequently the alternative to execution. There is no sign of such a phenomenon in, for example, Melaka before 1511, but it occurs in Aceh from at least 1565, in the Ternate of Sultan Baabullah (1570–84), and in Banten, Mataram, Makassar, and Kedah in the middle of the seventeenth century (Taillandier 1711; Schrieke 1942: 241; de Graaf 1958: 102). Two well-known cases in Aceh, de Houtman in 1601 and a group of Portuguese envoys in 1637, illustrate a sustained attempt at conversion, with Acehnese ulama using a range of intellectual arguments as well as threats and promises (Reid 1993: 173–74).

Although Islamic law prescribed death for apostasy (*murtad*), it was rare to find this applied to Muslim heretics in Southeast Asia. The only well-documented case occurred in the reign of Iskandar Thani of Aceh (1637–41). This was the same devout king who had executed some scores of Portuguese who did not accept Islam in 1637, who excluded Chinese traders from Aceh because for them "pigs are a must" (van der Meulen 1639: 1200), and who abolished the age-old practice of trial by ordeal in favour of witnesses, as prescribed in the shari'a. The Gujarati scholar Nuru'd-din ar-Raniri rushed back to Aceh as soon as this pillar of orthodoxy was enthroned. He publicly attacked the ideas of Syamsud-din and Hamzah Fansuri, had their books burned in front of the great mosque in Aceh, and successfully demanded that the sultan execute those who continued to uphold doctrines he believed he had shown to be heretical—in equating man with God. There was a strong popular reaction against Raniri's excesses as soon as his patron, Iskandar Thani, died in 1641. Raniri narrowly escaped with his life from a vengeful mob (Nieuwenhuijze 1945: 200; Ito 1978; Reid 1993: 174). The most influential ulama of the second half of the century, the Sufi sheikhs Abdurra'uf of Singkel and Yusuf of Makassar, were Indonesians less inclined than Raniri to draw sharp lines around the faith.

Given the disinclination of these absolutist rulers to accept any outside authority, there is surprisingly widespread evidence that the law of God, the shari'a, was applied. Not only do the chroniclers record of some pious rulers that they imposed Islamic law in certain respects (Raniri 1644: 36), but foreign observers confirm that the appropriate penalties were carried out. Shafi'i law imposed the penalty of amputation of the right hand, left leg, left hand, and right leg for first, second, third, and fourth offences, respectively, when an item worth at least a quarter of a dinar (about a gram of gold) was stolen. Its application was obvious enough to be recorded by even casual visitors. It is therefore known that Aceh applied these shari'a penalties throughout the seventeenth century, Brunei in the 1580s, and Banten under Sultan Abdulfatah Ageng (1651–82). Aceh often punished Muslims who consumed alcohol publicly (though some of its rulers set a bad example), and Banten also enforced Islamic penalties on those who used opium or tobacco. When a Eurasian bondservant of a rich Malay in Makassar was executed by kris in 1644 for having reverted to Christianity after converting to Islam, this was explained as not by order of the king but in consequence of Islamic law having to take its course (Santo Ignacio 1644: 59). Even in statecraft, the clearest prerogative of the ruler, the ulama had some success. In mid-century Banten refused to make peace with the infidel Dutch for more than ten years, in accordance with the requirements of the shari'a (Schrieke 1942: 241–42).

In the same period stern Islamic penalties were applied for a number of sexual offences among the urban elite of the same cities and Patani, in marked contrast to the spirit of older Southeast Asian practice (Reid 1988: 143, 157). The structure of surviving law codes, however, suggests that shari'a provisions were often tacked on in a learned footnote rather than replacing the older law. The *Undang-undang*

Melaka (84–85), for example, sets out rather lenient penalties for rape (marry the woman or pay a fine), and then adds, "But according to the law of God, if he is *muhsan* [an adult Muslim], he shall be stoned." The pluralistic cities no doubt had pluralistic legal systems, with the cosmopolitan commercial minorities who spearheaded stricter Islamic observance having the option of using Islamic law among themselves. A Muslim writing in a coastal city of sixteenth-century Java confirmed such pluralism, in a nominally Muslim polity, by insisting, "It is unbelief when people involved in a lawsuit and invited to settle the dispute according to the law of Islam, refuse to do so and insist on taking it to an infidel judge" ("Javanese Code": 37).

The leading sultanates of the seventeenth century, however, did establish official shari'a courts that followed Islamic procedures, to which their Muslim subjects were obliged to submit. The evidence is again clearest for Aceh, where at least one Islamic court operated throughout the first half of the seventeenth century. Beaulieu (1666: 100–02) in fact tells us that there were two, one for offences against the requirements of prayer, fasting, and religious orthodoxy, and the other for matters of debt, marriage, divorce, and inheritance. In 1636 a Dutch observer noted specifically that "the great bishop" (Syamsuddin's successor as kadi) presided over a weekly court in Aceh to judge theft, drunkenness, and offences against royal etiquette (Ito 1984: 155–60). Other sources also note the importance of the kadi in Acehnese affairs as early as the 1580s. Ito shows that while Sultan Iskandar Muda (1607–36) may have set up some of these institutions, his two successors first allowed them to work without constant, arbitrary royal interference.

In Banten, Patani, Ternate, and elsewhere an Arabic-speaking kadi ("bishop" to Europeans) was also prominent at court (van Neck 1604: 218; fig. 24). The only definite evidence for a functioning shari'a court outside Aceh, however, is in Banten under Sultan Ageng. There a resident French missionary reported that "they have two principal judges, of whom one is called the grand Chabandar [Syahbandar], who knows all commercial affairs; and the other carries the name of Thiaria [Shari'a], who extends his jurisdiction over all civil and criminal cases, and who among other crimes, punishes theft and adultery rigorously" (Missions Etrangères 1680A: 93).

On the difficult question of the extent of popular devotion, one can only resort to the impressions of foreigners. In the 1640s the Dutch complained of increased religious observance in Jambi, where the people were "at present so religious that the ordinary man is half like a pope [the usual Dutch pejorative term for an ulama], and the

Fig. 24 The Governor of Banten in council with the kadi in 1596, as represented by a Dutch engraver

nobles wholly so" (quoted Andaya and Ishii 1992: 541). In Makassar it was during the reign of Sultan Hasanuddin (1654–69) that observance of Arab norms of female dress were noted and restrictions placed on the powerful Portuguese Catholic minority.

Southeast Asian devotion did not express itself in mosque attendance. Many orangkaya did patronize a mosque or even build one of their own, but "the meaner sort of people have little devotion: I did never see any of them at their prayers, or go into a mosque" (Dampier 1697: 231; cf. Scott 1606: 172). To outsiders, Muslims seemed at their most devout in their observation of the fasting month, perhaps because it confirmed older ideas about "the deliberate and voluntary seeking of hardship and discomfort for religious reasons" (Koentjaraningrat 1985: 370). Francis Drake was impressed at the rigour with which the Maluku aristocrats who came aboard his ship observed the fast in 1579, refusing even a cup of water during the day and feasting at night (Drake 1580: 72; cf. Gijsels 1621: 28). In Mindanao during Ramadan, "they fast all day and . . . spend near an hour in prayer" (Dampier 1697: 234). In Aceh, according to Raniri (1644: 33, 36), prayer five times a day and strict fasting were imposed on the people by the pious Sultan Ala'ud-din Perak (1577–85), and again by Sultan Iskandar

Muda. Visiting between these two rulers, van Warwijck (1604: 12) thought that no one over twelve was allowed to eat during the day during Ramadan, whereas de Houtman (1601: 86) observed that the fast was celebrated elaborately only at court while "the ordinary man keeps this fast no more than he pleases."

The Muslim Challenge in Mainland Southeast Asia

> [King Ramadhipati of Cambodia] said to the ministers, mandarins, and royal servants of all the service groups, "You must all enter the religion of Allah. Anyone who refuses to enter must leave the royal service." Fearful of royal authority, the dignitaries and all the mandarins agreed to all embrace the religion of Mahomet. . . . The ministers, the mandarins, and all the royal servants all participated, without exception, in the ritual of cutting the foreskin. . . .
> When the king returned to the august royal palace, he ordered, "The king and the members of the royal family must wear a long tunic and always insert a kris in it."
> —Chroniques Cambodge 1981: 190

Given the advances of Islam and Christianity in the Archipelago and the economic and social changes which paved the way for them, the question must be asked whether the same factors operated on the Mainland. To some extent, Theravada Buddhism responded to the same challenges by moving toward state absolutism and personal morality (see below). But in each country there was also a strong challenge from outside the dominant faith. Catholic Christianity made important gains in Vietnam in the first half of the seventeenth century, while Islam reached the apogee of its influence in Champa, Cambodia, and Siam. All these gains were concentrated in commercially involved areas near the port.

Less can be said of Burma, although de Brito's brand of militant Catholicism certainly had supporters among the Mons of the ports. A more intriguing indication of a need for forms of religious expression congenial to commerce is the sect of "Zodis" (perhaps from Pali *joti*, light), observed by Catholic missionaries in eighteenth-century Burma. The sect was fiercely suppressed by King Bodawpaya at his accession in 1782. Mantegazza (1784: 145; cf. Sangermano 1818: 111–12) believed it was essentially the pre-Theravada religion of the Burmese and Shans but had been re-introduced as a Burmese minority sect by a Shan monk at least several reigns earlier. Its adherents had nothing to do with the state, scorning the Buddhist temples and the doctrine of reincarnation. They believed rather in eternal reward or punishment at death for deeds of this life. Mantegazza saw them as completely antithetic to the fatalism he identified with mainstream Burmese Buddhism: "They are mostly merchants and assist each other; they have the spirit of proselytism."[8]

The alliance of king and Confucian literati in northern Vietnam, and of king and Buddhist monkhood (*sangha*) in the Theravada countries, was strong enough to limit and eventually roll back the influence of these aggressive new faiths. Part of this process of containment was, as in Japan, the containment of international commerce, from which the Mainland countries tended to disengage during the seventeenth century.

The rise and fall of Islam in the seventeenth century is sufficiently dramatic to require particular attention. Both the advantages Islam enjoyed in the Mainland and the forces ranged against it shed great light on the earlier process of Islamization in the Islands, where the information is scarce.

The earliest centre of Islamic influence was Champa, strategically placed on the trade routes to China and related through its Austronesian language, ethnicity, and diplomatic interaction to the peoples of Island Southeast Asia. Muslim traders were resident there from at least the eleventh century, and Muslim influence increased after 1471, when Vijaya (Qui Nhon) was captured by the Vietnamese and the Cham capital moved south to the Phan-rang area, where Muslims had always been concentrated. In the late sixteenth century Islam was making rapid advances, and "those who newly profess it are numerous" (San Antonio 1604: 124). The king remained a Hindu until at least 1607, but he was closely allied with the Muslim ruler of Johor against the Portuguese and Spanish, and encouraged the building of mosques and conversion to Islam among his leading orangkaya. In 1611 what remained of Champa's independence was curtailed by further Vietnamese advances, and there is little information on religious affiliation in the Cham "province" of Cochin-China. Muslim influence must have continued to increase, however, since by the 1670s the bulk of the population, including the king, was Muslim (Matelief 1608: 120; Manguin 1979: 269–71).

Neighbouring Cambodia was also linked to the Malay world by

8. Mendelson (1975: 73–77), who like other commentators had seen Sangermano's second-hand account but not Mantegazza's, introduced some confusion into this issue by equating the Zodis with the nineteenth-century Paramats described by Shway Yoe (1882: 147–8). Whereas the Zodis were definitely pre-Bodawpaya and suppressed at the beginning of his reign, the Paramats appear to have been founded later and greatly encouraged by Bodawpaya.

trade and involved in the conflicts that pitted Muslims, Hindu Chams, Khmer, and Vietnamese against one another in the Champa area. In the late sixteenth century, Malay and Cham Muslims, including refugees from Champa, were among the most important commercial minorities in Cambodia, along with Chinese, Japanese, and Portuguese. They played a crucial role in the conflicts that plagued the country during the ensuing half-century. The troubles began in 1594, when the reigning king fled to Laos to escape a Siamese conquest. In the next six years, four successive kings met violent deaths as foreign influences competed in the capital. The fleeing king had encouraged the Portuguese and Spanish at his capital to appeal to Manila for help, and a group of Iberian adventurers eventually reached the Cambodian capital in response to this invitation. They only added to the chaos by quarrelling with Chinese and other traders, killing the Siamese-imposed king, plundering indiscriminately, and then withdrawing from a city they left looking like "Rome burning, Troy annihilated or Carthage destroyed," to quote one Spanish chronicle (San Antonio 1604: 120). The two moving spirits of the Spanish expedition, Blaz Ruiz and Diego Veloso, sailed to Cochin-China, however, whence they made their way to Vientiane to find the exiled Cambodian king. He had died, so they brought down the Mekong to the capital his son, Cau Bana Tan (San Antonio 1604: 132–33; Morga 1606: 72–87, 120–35; *Chroniques Cambodge* 1981: 71–73).

This ruler depended heavily on foreigners for his tenuous hold on the throne. Besides the two leading Europeans, who were made governors of provinces, one of his most formidable allies was a Johor Malay orangkaya who was given the Malay title Laksamana (admiral) and authority over the Cambodian coast at the mouth of the Mekong. He claimed to have four thousand armed Muslim followers, many of them refugees from the power struggles in Champa, as well as "the greatest force of artillery and prahus" in the country (Morga 1606: 128). Tension between the Muslims and Christians in the disturbed country was high, especially when an additional force of European and Japanese desperadoes from Manila and Nagasaki aided the small group of Spaniards and made them more arrogant in their demands for land and position. One of their attacks on the Muslim camp eventually provoked the laksamana to launch a wholesale massacre of the Christian adventurers in Cambodia in 1598.

This left the laksamana as the most powerful figure in Cambodia, and he soon killed the new king, who had tried to move against him. A Malay, he was hardly credible as a Khmer king, but he became an independent Muslim warlord in eastern Cambodia. Within a year the remaining Khmer court officials were able to raise an army and to kill both him and his principal Cham ally, Po Rat. The officials then made peace with Siam and invited a prince who had been held captive in Ayutthaya to assume the throne. With Siamese support a Buddhist monarchy retained some tenuous authority (San Antonio 1604: 141–42; Morga 1606: 126–50, 210–11; *Chroniques Cambodge* 1981: 75–80, 110–11).

The Muslim minority emerged from this crisis with a formidable military reputation, and some claim to be defenders of Cambodian independence. This claim was strengthened by their subsequent resistance to Dutch demands for monopoly privileges in exporting the produce of Cambodia and the Mekong. Malay shippers were the principal rivals of the VOC in providing Indian cloth to Cambodia in exchange for benzoin, deerskins, and lacquer. Meanwhile, conflicts continued among the Khmer elite, with successive usurpers ever less capable of eliciting real support in the country. King Padumaraja (Ang Chan), who seized power about 1640, was particularly ruthless in his execution of leading Khmers and Muslims. There was thus some popular support for another coup in 1642, which brought to power his nephew Cau Bana Cand, who took the title Ramadhipati. When he alienated this goodwill through his own round of executions, he found his power base increasingly restricted to the Muslims who had helped bring him to the throne (*Dagh-Register* 1641–42: 133; *Chroniques Cambodge* 1981: 179–87).

In 1643 conflicts over trade resulted in a massacre of about forty Dutchmen in Cambodia, and the king's need for allies against the fierce Dutch retaliation the following year drove him even closer to the Muslims. He embraced Islam, adopted for some purposes the title Sultan Ibrahim, and established a replica of a Malay court on the Mekong. As in other Muslim states attempting to keep the Dutch at bay, Portuguese (and Japanese Christian) traders and mercenaries also played a large part in the capital (*Dagh-Register* 1643–44: 17–18, 22–24, 42–43; *Dagh-Register* 1656–57: 36–37, 118–19, 146–50; Winkel 1882: 492–500; Buch 1937: 195–225).

The explanation of this dramatic development by the royal chronicles, recorded much later, was that the Muslims possessed powerful magic and love charms, which had been used first to make the king fall hopelessly in love with a Malay woman and finally to embrace her faith (*Chroniques Cambodge* 1981: 188–89). Another text added the plausible motive that the king needed to win the active support of the powerful Muslims, since the Khmers were in any case loyal or passive subjects (ibid.: 350).

This move cannot have been in vain. In spite of the extraordinary turbulence of his earliest years, Sultan Ibrahim retained the throne of Cambodia for another fifteen years, longer than any of his Buddhist predecessors since the previous century. The judgement of the royal chronicle on him was that "the monks . . . of the kingdom were greatly annoyed because the king did not take them into account. . . . The dignitaries and the great mandarins as well as the ordinary people had no desire or love for a king who strayed from the path and entered the Muslim religion and ceased to take into account the Buddhist faith" (ibid.: 191). The dissident princes nevertheless prevailed only by invoking another foreign intervention, this time from the Vietnamese ruler of Cochin-China. After a ruinous Vietnamese invasion in 1658–59, Sultan Ibrahim was taken captive and a half-Vietnamese prince placed on the throne of Cambodia. The Islamic interlude was over, but Cambodia became more than ever a battleground for Vietnamese and Thai ambitions (Maetsuyker 1659: 257–58; *Chroniques Cambodge* 1981: 57, 191–200; Phoen and Dharma 1984).

The same critical period brought Muslim influence to its peak in Siam. Even as early as the 1540s, Persian, Indian, and Malay Muslims had been numerous in Ayutthaya and especially influential in Tenasserim, distinguishing themselves by their resistance to Portuguese demands (Pinto 1578: 306–09). The greatest of the Muslim mystical poets of the Malay world, Hamzah Fansuri, appears to have learned his mysticism among the (mainly Shi'ite) Muslims of the Siamese capital (Drewes and Brakel 1986: 4–7). In the reign of the usurper Prasat Thong (1629–56) Shi'ite Muslims came to dominate the commercial offices of Siam. Prasat Thong's son Narai, according to a Persian writer, as a boy "used to visit the Iranians regularly and he took great pleasure in their social manners and their foods and drink." When Narai made his bid for the throne in 1657, the Persians aided him by using the cover of their annual Hasan-Husein feast to approach the incumbent ruler and attack him with their firearms (Ibrahim 1688: 77, 95–97). Thereafter, Persian Shi'ites were among Narai's closest advisers, especially as commercial counterweights to the more dangerous European companies. Chief among them was a cultivated merchant, Aqa Muhammad Astarabadi, better known by his Siamese title, Okphra Sinnaowarat. He engineered the sending of a Thai embassy to Persia in 1668 and the splendid reception of subsequent Persian and Acehnese ambassadors to Siam, both of whom were said to be hoping that the king would embrace Islam (Ibrahim 1668: 98–100; Missions Etrangères 1674: 11–12). Astarabadi was encouraged to fill the standing army of the kingdom with Persian and Indian Shi'ite Muslims. Various governorships of key ports were placed in Muslim hands; by the late 1670s Tenasserim and Mergui were ruled by Persians, Phuket and nearby Bangkhli by Indians, and Bangkok by a Turk (Pombejra 1990: 134). In return for their services to the state, Muslims were exempted from corvée, which evidently stimulated conversions to Islam among the merchants of the trading ports. In 1686, after the peak of Muslim influence had passed, there were ten thousand such converts in Tenasserim alone, to judge from the yield of a special tax placed on them (Aubin 1980: 110). At the same period in the Siamese capital it was said that two thousand Shi'ites participated in their annual Hasan-Husein processions celebrating the battle of Karbyla, still paid for by the king in gratitude for its role in his accession, and that "a great many Siamese men and women" had been attracted into embracing Islam (Tachard 1686: 214–15; La Loubère 1691: 112).

Quite distinct from the above group were the Sunni Muslims from below the winds, including Malay and Javanese traders and aristocratic refugees from the disasters that befell the great Muslim trading states of the region. The humiliation of the proud Makassarese by the Dutch in the 1660s drove some of the elite to Ayutthaya, but more to Muslim Banten, which was conquered by the VOC in 1682. Because Ayutthaya had had extensive commercial and diplomatic connections with these other great trading cities, it became the principal place of refuge for Muslims in the 1680s. Cham Muslims took refuge there from the Vietnamese advance and from internal conflicts. There were in Ayutthaya three brothers of the embattled king of Champa, by then Muslim, and one was said to be prominent at Narai's court (Manguin 1979: 272–73).

Astarabadi died in 1679, and his sons were too much given to quarrelling among themselves and to high living to enjoy the same influence with the king. King Narai's undoubted interest in Persian civilization was replaced in the 1680s by an even greater fascination with European achievements as mediated especially by the French. The Greek adventurer Constance Phaulkon rose to dominate Ayutthaya's foreign and commercial relations, partly by showing that he could conduct embassies with more commercial profit to the king than the Persians had done. The final blow to Muslim fortunes, however, came in 1686, when some Southeast Asian Muslims in the capital revolted, led by Makassarese and Cham aristocrats and some ulama who felt their faith was being maligned as a result of the new direction in policy. Though only a few hundred in numbers, these desperate men came surprisingly close to seizing the palace. Had European troops not been on hand to help in their suppression, many observers thought they might have succeeded. After this crisis, however, they quickly lost their position as the most important of Siam's minorities (Turpin 1771: 53–64; Anderson 1890: 286–96).

In short, the high tide of Muslim fortunes in the Mainland, as in the Archipelago, was borne along by commerce, by military prowess, and by a readiness to resist the impositions of more arrogant Europeans. Native converts to Islam were made in large numbers. This movement failed in part because the balance of foreign forces was turning against them, and in part because the alliance of king and Buddhist sangha had already created a strong and popular sense of Buddhist identity.

Buddhism and the State

> It is strange to me that the King of France my good friend should so much concern himself in an Affair that relates to God, wherein it would seem God does not at all interest himself, but leaves it wholly to our discretion. For would not the true God that made Heaven and Earth, and all things that are therein, and hath given them so different natures and inclinations . . . if he had pleased have also inspired into them the same sentiments for the religion they ought to follow, and for the worship that was most acceptable to him, and make all nations live and die in the same laws? . . . Ought not one to think that the true God takes as great pleasure to be honoured by different worships and ceremonies, as to be glorified by a prodigious number of creatures.
> —King Narai's response to Louis XIV's invitation to become a
> Christian, Tachard 1688: 223–24

The progress of Theravada Buddhism cannot be explained in the same terms as that of Islam. This Sri Lankan school of Buddhism appears to have been imposed as a state religion by great empire-builders well before the age of commerce—Anawhrata in Burma (1044–77), Jeyavarman VII in Cambodia (1181–c.1220), Mangrai in Chiengmai (1292–1317), and Ramkamheng in Sukhothai (c.1279–98). Chinese observers noted that the celibate, shaven-headed, and saffron-robed monks who were its principal carriers were already numerous in Angkor in the late thirteenth century and in Ayutthaya in the fifteenth (Chou Ta-kuan 1297; Ma Huan 1433: 103). Temples and especially pilgrimage centres were certainly also markets, to the extent that in Laos "the convents seem turned at present into shops and markets" (Marini 1663: 483). The Mons of southern Burma were at once the most commercially active of Mainland peoples and the leading agents of Theravada reforms. Their ports of Thaton, Martaban, and Pegu, with the southern Thai port of Nakhon Sithammarat, were crucial diffusion centres of new doctrines. Nevertheless, Theravada Buddhism was not assisted by international traders in the same direct sense as Islam. Burmese, Thais, and Khmers were not themselves great maritime traders, and not overwhelmed by the case for a universally valid faith. On the contrary, they appeared exemplars of that "miracle of tolerance" which Fernand Braudel found in all great trade emporia, finding it natural that different peoples should have different beliefs.

What did characterize the period was the marked strengthening of a few large states at the expense of local chieftains, for reasons common to Southeast Asia as a whole. The powerful empire-builders of the fifteenth to seventeenth century all favoured "textually-based, externally-validated (often via Sri Lanka) sources of authority over local traditions" (Lieberman 1993: 242), for the same reasons as their island counterparts favoured Islam. They laid claim to relics and Buddha images of unique sanctity and power; they patronized the sangha, sponsoring reforms which invalidated other religious traditions; they grandly celebrated religious festivals as rituals of kingship, with themselves as the central actors. As they gained in power, therefore, the remarkable diversity of spirit cults, rituals, and ascetic practices that marked the region in the fifteenth century gradually gave way to a more uniform understanding of Buddhist orthodoxy.

Because the main sources for Buddhism before 1500 are pious monastic narratives and inscriptions, the extent of this diversity emerges only in glimpses. As O'Connor (1989: 11) notes, the heroes even of Buddhist chronicles were often "magically powerful hermits (rusi) and other charismatic religious leaders." The Shans, who ruled most of Upper Burma until annexed by Bayinnaung, were classified by Burmese chroniclers (though probably not themselves) as unbelievers "converted" by the Burmese conquest. A Shan king was accused of slaughtering 360 monks in Ava in 1540 and pillaging the temples and monasteries of the city. Even the Burmese monks of Upper Burma in this period were conducting ritual animal sacrifices and alcoholic feasting more characteristic of Southeast Asian religion than of their reformed Theravada successors in the seventeenth and eighteenth centuries (Than Tun 1985: xiii; Lieberman 1991: 38).

Another precious, if perhaps embroidered, glimpse of the religious diversity of the Mainland is given by Mendez Pinto's account of his (or someone's) voyage in the train of a Burmese ambassador to the Lao kingdoms on the Mekong in the 1540s.[9] At one famous centre of pilgrimage an annual festival was held at which penitents threw themselves beneath the wheels of carts carrying the sacred image, in a manner reminiscent of the Hindu juggernaut. Nearby were various hermits "leading lives of excessively harsh austerity" in caves. In a kingdom probably identified as Luang Prabang there were said to be "twenty-four different religious sects, among which there is so great a variety and confusion of diabolical errors and precepts, principally in the blood sacrifices they employ, that it is frightful to hear them" (Pinto 1578: 338–47, 362).

The struggle to suppress these cults also appears only in glimpses. The chronicles of Luang Prabang refer to a royal decree in 1527 "to abandon the cult of the spirits, to destroy the great shrine to the titular spirit of the city at the mouth of the Nam Ton river before Luang Prabang, and to erect . . . on this site a pagoda" (cited Pinith 1987: 206–07). Burmese inscriptions and chronicles show King Bayinnaung (1551–81) not only building temples throughout conquered Upper Burma but also outlawing both human and animal sacrifices and unifying the religious calendars of these diverse domains (Lieberman 1991: 40). Bayinnaung dealt with the spirits (nat) as imperiously as with his own subjects, commanding that if they failed to assist him in his wars their shrines should be burned (Than Tun 1985: 7–8). The devout Siamese King Songtham (1611–28) is portrayed as warring against idolatry (van Vliet 1640: 89). Yet animal sacrifices to the spirits

9. Pinto still suffers, like Marco Polo before him, from the initial incredulity with which his immensely colourful posthumous (1614) publication was greeted. The Portuguese have long regarded his *Peregrinacão* as a literary classic, but his reputation among English-speakers has retained something of the mendacious if charming rogue, epitomized by Congreve's epithet: "Mendez Pinto was but a type of thee, though liar of the first magnitude." Part of the problem was the ill-informed Cogan translation of 1663, often reprinted, which has at last been made good by the full modern translation of Rebecca Catz. Pinto's loose way with numbers (e.g., of urban populations and armies) also did his reputation little good. Finally his literary device of personalizing stories as though he heard and recorded conversations between the leading Asian actors must be regarded for what it is, a vivid and often satirical commentary on human weakness and oppression. Time and again serious scholarship has vindicated his knowledge of Asian societies. There is no longer doubt that he was based in Melaka for several years after 1539, and acquired a good knowledge of Malay from his travels in the Archipelago. He appears also to have been based in Pegu for some years in the 1540s, and sprinkles his narrative with Mon terms no longer current. He must either have participated himself in the embassy King Tabinshweihti sent to Laos (also recorded in the Lansang annals), or have listened carefully to people who did. His empire of the Calaminham ("lord of the earth") was almost certainly the otherwise shadowy Lansang kingdom, with its capital then at Luang Prabang (de Campos 1940: 229–30; Catz 1989: 564n; Vickery 1991).

and shamanistic possession by them continued to be common ways of dealing with illness even in the capital (van Vliet 1636: 81–82; Gervaise 1688: 230).

Mon and Thai monks visited various Sri Lankan monasteries periodically from the thirteenth century in search of a purer way. One centre of pilgrimage was Mahavihara, favoured especially by the southernmost Thai trade centre at Nakhon Sithammarat (Wyatt 1982: 51). Only in the fifteenth century, however, did the Mahavihara become dominant in Mainland Southeast Asia as an instrument of centralization of both sangha and state.

According to a northern Thai chronicle, thirty-nine monks from Chiengmai, Lopburi, and the Mon areas of Burma journeyed to Sri Lanka in 1423, where they were reordained into the Mahavihara order. They returned first to the rising port-state of Ayutthaya, whose king was persuaded to give his patronage to their new system of ordination. According to its pious chronicler, the Mahavihara reached Chiengmai in 1430 but found the incumbent king unsympathetic, since he "greatly honoured the votaries of demons" (cited Swearer and Premchit 1975: 28). This king, however, was overthrown in 1442 by his son, Tilokaraja, who formed a close alliance with the Mahavihara reformers. Temples were founded for the new order and existing monks reordained into it. The Mahavihara extended its influence as Chiengmai extended its borders, until it became "coextensive with Tilokaraja's hegemony over northern Thailand" (Swearer and Premchit 1975: 29). Under this king, and his successor, Muang Kaew (1495–1528), Chiengmai unified the northern Tai in the name of a reformed Buddhism, and produced a golden age of Pali scholarship. Tilokaraja's contemporary in Ayutthaya, Trailok, was no less conscious of the political potential of the reformed sangha and had himself ordained in 1465 by a monk invited from Sri Lanka (Kasetsiri 1976: 138–39).

At the same time the Mahavihara was reconstituting the sangha in Pegu. That city's emergence as the centre of an independent Mon kingdom profiting from the flourishing Indian Ocean trade occurred under Queen Shinsawbu (1453–72), and the monk Dammazeidi, whom she selected first as viceroy and then as her successor (1472–92). Both were exemplary Buddhist rulers, building pagodas, endowing monasteries, and issuing decrees famous for their wisdom. According to a lengthy inscription of 1476, Dammazeidi called a council of monks to decide on a major reformation of Buddhism. Two separate parties of monks were despatched to Sri Lanka for study and reordination into the Mahavihara order. On their return the king built for them the Kalyani monastery near Pegu, which became the centre for the reformed discipline. Dammazeidi announced that all monks had to be reordained or leave the sangha and that reordination involved the loss of all seniority gained previously. His inscription also demanded that monks abandon their possessions of "gold, silver, and other such treasure, corn, elephants, horses, oxen, buffaloes, male and female slaves," on pain of defrocking. Nine hundred monks and more than fourteen thousand novices were reportedly ordained. The inscription concluded: "It was in this manner that Dammazeidi purged the religion of its impurities throughout the whole of lower Burma, and created a single sect of the body of the priesthood" (Mendelson 1975: 51–52; Than Tun 1983: 26–27; Than Tun 1985: x–xii; "History of Kings": 55–57).

Most kings of the period were temple-builders. "Every king [of Siam] when he ascends the throne . . . commences a Temple, and some make two or three, to which they give great endowments" (Barros 1563 III, i: 165). Their erecting of monasteries for a favoured order, or stupas to honour sacred relics, also extended the cult of kingship. From the fifteenth century, moreover, ambitious kings tended to build the most important temples within their palace complexes. King Trailok (1448–88) built Wat Putthaisawan within his palace at Ayutthaya, and subsequent rulers extended it to become the spiritual centre of the kingdom (Kasetsiri 1976: 136–37; cf. O'Connor 1985: 6–9). Bayinnaung endowed the capital he built at Pegu in 1566 with a royal temple of stunningly lavish decoration adjacent to the palace (Fredirici 1581: 249; Fitch 1591: 305).

Some Buddha images acquired reputations of particular potency. In Cambodia, for example, the chronicles attributed a defeat by the Thais in the 1580s to the destruction of a Buddha image which had previously protected the kingdom (*Chroniques Cambodge* 1988: 191–94). In the course of the wars of the sixteenth and seventeenth centuries such images became progressively associated with the power of rulers, who brought them to their capitals from conquered territories. The famous emerald Buddha, believed to have been brought from Sri Lanka in the eleventh century by King Anawhrata of Pagan, had become by the sixteenth century the protector of the Lanna kings of Chiengmai. About 1548 the founder of the greatness of the Lansang or Lao kingdom, Setthattirat, who had also ruled Chiengmai for a time, brought the statue to his new capital at Vientiane, where it presided over the fortunes of Laos until seized by the Siamese in 1778 (Tambiah 1976: 92; Thao 1976: 11). With each move, its potency to guarantee the success of its possessor appeared to increase.

The sangha was undoubtedly the crucial institution with which

Buddhist kings had to deal, because of its prestige but also because of its size. In sixteenth-century Cambodia a Dominican missionary thought that the monkhood appeared to be a third of the population (da Cruz 1569: 61).[10] In Laos in the following century there was "hardly any householder who did not have son or brother" in the monkhood (Wusthoff 1669: 44). Van Vliet (1636: 76) estimated that there were twenty thousand monks in the city of Ayutthaya (Schouten 1636: 140 thought thirty thousand), and perhaps eighty thousand in the whole kingdom. The sangha was everywhere respected, but not inherently disciplined or hierarchically unified as a body. Strong kings usually extended their influence by bringing it under their control, but at other times land and people were dedicated to monasteries as a means of escaping from tax and other obligations to the king, so that the number of monks was a direct threat to the ruler.

The reforms of the sangha undertaken by a pious ruler such as Dammazedi could create a disciplined and respected monkhood that was difficult for more headstrong rulers to bend to their will. The powerful Toungoo rulers who unified Burma in the sixteenth century, in particular, had to contend with a sangha which was not only relatively disciplined and highly respected but focused on centres of pilgrimage outside the capital and therefore not immediately controlled by the king. Pinto (1578: 366–77) provides a colourful description of the death of the patriarch of Pegu, whom he situates on an island off Moulmein, and the election of an abbot from Rangoon as his successor. This shows the king, Tabinshweihti, allying himself as far as possible with the prestige of this revered office by providing a lavish funeral, but having only limited control over the successor elected. Even under his powerful successor, Bayinnaung, Fitch (1591: 306) suggests it was "forest monks" outside the city, living "for the most part by the highway's side, and among the trees, and in the woods," who were most respected by the populace.

Though the Toungoo kings were able to unify religious practice to a large degree throughout their Mon, Burman, and Shan domains, the sangha in the Mon area was still independent enough in the 1590s to play a part in overthrowing the dynasty, protesting against King Nandabayin's impositions and finally appealing to Chiengmai to rebel against him (du Jarric 1608–14 I: 626–27; Lieberman 1984: 41–42). Only after the Burmese polity was reconstituted with its capital far inland at Ava was King Thalun (1629–48) able to establish a civil

10. Lieberman (1984: 20n) suggests more soberly for Burma that 1–3 percent of the population may have been in the sangha—still a remarkable proportion.

Fig. 25 A Burmese monastery, from a nineteenth-century Burmese illustrated manuscript

bureaucracy to manage monastic lands and to restrict entry to the
sangha to the adequately educated and motivated (Than Tun 1983: 68–
69; Lieberman 1984: 109–12: Koenig 1990: 126–30; fig. 25).

In Cambodia, too, the monks had won great respect by the sixteenth century—"the common people have a great confidence in
them, with a great reverence and worship" (da Cruz 1569: 61). The
ordeals they endured from Christian and Muslim intervention in the
seventeenth century may have increased their sense of commitment,
for French missionaries in the 1660s were impressed at their strong
discipline both in celibacy and "keeping perfectly a perpetual fast"
(Missions Etrangères 1674: 142–45). This contrasted with the monks
of Laos, who were able to exploit royal patronage and popular reverence to enjoy a good life. They taught that the Buddha had lived in
Laos,

and they glory greatly in this, saying that their God has consequently
blessed them above the Siamese and Cambodians and others, with such
extraordinarily splendid temples and so many holy men (as they call
them) and men of learning. . . . As evidence of this the Cambodian and
Siamese "popes" [monks] come here to study for 10 or 12 years until they

graduate; which is believable not for those reasons but rather it happens purely because the Lao "popes" are esteemed as Gods, for they are provided in abundance with the best of everything they need, and food is brought them daily, and more clothing than they need, and they moreover use women as they please (but with careful appearance that they live a chaste life), which the Cambodians cannot do, and if it came out they would be cast before the judges and made into slaves, and they must also collect or buy their own food; so that each despises the other, the one saying that it is scandalous to run after women, and the other [Lao] replying that they [Khmer] must beg for their upkeep from passers-by, which scandalizes and disgraces their holiness in the eyes of men (Wusthoff 1669: 44–45; cf. Marini 1663: 478, 482–83).

Although this contrast to some extent reflects long-standing national stereotypes, it is possible to interpret it as meaning that the Lao sangha was at an earlier stage of the transition to a disciplined and integrated body under its own national hierarchy. All the great men of Laos patronized different monasteries and religious festivals, though the Lao sun-king Surinyavongsa (1637–94) was beginning to centralize religious as well as secular authority. He prescribed religious feast-days, "corrects their faults, explains theological problems, resolves disputes, regulates rituals" (Marini 1663: 483–84; cf. 477–78). His uncle was installed as patriarch (mahasangharaja) (Wusthoff 1642: 192).

Cambodia already had its mahasangharaja in the sixteenth century, a figure da Cruz (1569: 62) thought more revered than the king. The personage described as Rolim[11] of Mounay by Pinto (1578: 368) appeared also to have the role of patriarch at least in the Mon area, though he was not the king's man and was probably not recognized throughout the vast empire of Pegu. That stage was not reached until seventeenth-century Ava (Mandelson 1975: 358). In Siam the process of imposing a royally appointed patriarch on a diverse set of monasteries and former kingdoms was even slower.

The earliest detailed European report on Siam suggested that Wat Mahathat of Sukhothai was still regarded as the most prestigious temple in the land (Barros 1563 III, i: 164). A century later Ayutthaya had become sufficiently dominant through the centralizing revolution wrought by Naresuan (1590–1605) that only its monasteries were mentioned by foreigners (fig. 26). In one of them an aged uncle of the king was the abbot (sangharaja) in 1606, but even he did not appear to

---

11. Collis (1949: 196n) believes this term to be a corruption of Burmese yahan or rahan, the highest monastic grade. Since Fitch (1591: 306) independently gives the term rowli as chief monk, however, there seems likely to be a more immediate source in Mon.

have national authority (du Jarric 1608–14 III: 890). Van Vliet (1636: 73–76) reported that there were four principle temples in and around the capital, each headed by a sangharaja (Thai *sankharat*) who was authorized to perform ordinations. One of them, the abbot of Wat Mahathat, had "supreme dignity" in his day, though not as an authoritative patriarch. A generation later the abbot of a different monastery outside the city was regarded as the most senior (Pombejra 1984: 91–92), whereas for La Loubère (1691: 114) in the 1680s it was the abbot of the palace monastery.

Although this last shift is indicative of King Narai's determination to maintain control over the sangha, still more so is La Loubère's insistence that "no Superior, nor no *Sankharat*, has authority or jurisdiction over another. This body would be too formidable if it had but one head, and if it acted always unanimously" (ibid.). Narai was perhaps the nearest Southeast Asia afforded to a Renaissance absolutist, personally sceptical but determined to manipulate the sangha in the interests of the state. He continued royal patronage of the monasteries and the grandiose *kathina* processions which publicly demonstrated his devotion to them. Yet he reduced the number of monks, whose tax-exempt status reduced his income, by two means. He implemented celibacy laws harshly to discourage frivolous ordinations, and he had monks regularly examined in the Pali scriptures. About 1687 he expelled several thousand who failed the test. Such discipline was characteristic of many a strong Theravada king, but the fact that it was a young layman of the court who conducted the examination was an unusual humiliation. The more independent (and generally more revered) "forest-dwelling monks" refused to be examined except by one of their superiors (La Loubère 1691: 115; Ishii 1975: 82–83).

These attempts to manipulate the sangha, and still more the privileges given by Narai to French soldiers and Catholic missionaries, eventually went too far for the normally quiescent Buddhist population. The monks of the capital, and the sangharaja of the royal retreat at Lopburi, played an important part in Narai's overthrow in 1688 by Prince Phetracha, who had cultivated his links with them (de Bèze 1691: 87–88; Le Blanc 1692 I: 46–52, 144). Not surprisingly, therefore, the reign of Phetracha was the first in which there is definite evidence of a single patriarch of the Thai sangha, "and his authority is such, that even the king himself is obliged to bow to him" (Kaempfer 1727: 69).

The age of commerce, in short, witnessed great changes in the religious life of Mainland, as of Island, Southeast Asia. Underlying much local variation, commercialization and increased mobility provided conditions that encouraged a "rationalization" of religion in a

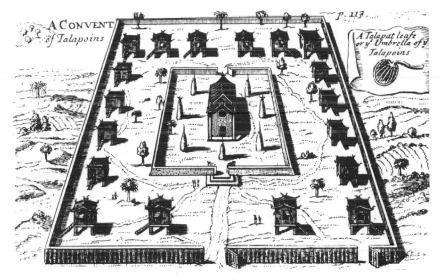

Fig. 26 Seventeenth century sketch of a Siamese monastery, with a prayer hall (*vihara*) surrounded by elevated houses for the monks

Weberian sense, strengthening the appeal of universal moral codes reinforced by scripture and a system of eternal rewards and punishments. Centralizing states allied with this trend by enforcing one of the international orthodoxies. Yet as the period drew to a close and commercial engagement weakened, the need of states for internal unity increasingly took precedence over reformist literalisms.

=== 4 ===

Problems of the Absolutist State

*These Kings which are so absolutely the masters of the fortune and life
of their subjects, are so much the more wavering in the throne. They
find not in any person, or at most in a small number of domesticks,
that fidelity or love which we have for our kings.*
　　　　　　　　　　　　　　　　　　—La Loubère 1691: 106

　　The exalted rhetoric of Southeast Asian rulers was always in
tension with the tenuousness of their power base. The power of master
over servant was great, and kings had power of life and death over their
immediate subjects. All states, however, were in process of formation
by conquest or coalitions among local chiefs and patrons. The personal
ties between lord and vassal were constantly being renegotiated. The
legal and bureaucratic basis of all states was still fragile. There were
few acknowledged boundaries between the ambitions of one ruler and
the next. States rose and fell rapidly in terms of the degree of force,
charisma, and wealth each ruler was able to put together. In this
context the advantages that derived from trade were critical. The trade
boom of the fifteenth and sixteenth centuries transformed the political landscape of the region by endowing some rulers with unprecedented disposable wealth, as well as with ideological and technological innovations they used to advantage.

The Crisis of the Classic States

The wealth which derived from the control of markets and the flow of trade was an essential resource of Southeast Asian states long before the age of commerce. It provided enough military and technical innovation, and leverage over scarce items of foreign import, to allow one centre to prevail over others in symbolic and economic terms. The classic states of Angkor, Pagan, and Java were also dependent, however, on the mobilization of the major concentrations of population created by irrigated areas associated with certain river systems.

These temple-building civilizations were all in crisis in the thirteenth century. Some of the reasons were internal, such as the escalating transfer of landed wealth to the monasteries which followed the adoption of Theravada Buddhism in Burma (Aung-Thwin 1985: 169–98). There were, however, broader factors that affected all of Southeast Asia. Maritime trade was stimulated in the Indian Ocean by the fall of Baghdad and the rise of Cairo's Karimi merchants, and in the South China Sea by the unprecedented mercantile interests of China's Southern Song and Mongol dynasties (Abu-Lughod 1989). New opportunities for private Chinese shippers to visit the sources of production themselves undermined the function of the few southern "empires" such as Sri Vijaya and Angkor to collect produce and ship it to China in the form of a tribute trade (Wolters 1970: 4).

After conquering China the Mongols moved south by both land and sea. In the 1280s they fatally disrupted the Burmese kingdom of Pagan and with less success invaded Vietnam and Champa. The principal beneficiaries of this upheaval were the Tai (a broad ethno-linguistic group including modern Thai, Lao, and Shan), who by 1300 had organized a series of small kingdoms in territories formerly dominated by Burmese Pagan, Khmer Angkor, and Malay Sri Vijaya. Meanwhile, a Mongol fleet invaded eastern Java in 1292, exacerbating a dynastic dispute that ended the kingdom of Singhosari and gave rise to a new kingdom closer to the mouth of the Brantas River at Majapahit.

If the old order of temple-building Hindu-Buddhist empires was in eclipse by 1300, the new order did not become clear for another century. Angkor and Pagan continued to be occupied by shadowy kings with only symbolic power outside the capital. Majapahit was a transitional kingdom, more interested in maritime activity and less in temple-building than its predecessors but continuing the Hindu-Buddhist traditions of earlier regimes. The Straits of Malacca area, long the stronghold of the Sri Vijaya empire was contested between Javanese, Chinese, Tai, and local Sumatran forces.

In the fourteenth century new centres of international trade began to arise that were strong enough to ignore the historical claims of the older empires. Pasai (or Samudra) in northern Sumatra was the earliest of a new type of port-state, a beachhead of Muslim trade on the eastern side of the Indian Ocean. Throughout the fourteenth century it issued coins, sent tribute missions to China, and conducted a vigorous trade but appeared unconcerned with imperial pretensions in the manner of Sri Vijaya. In the Irrawaddy Delta the Mons reclaimed their independence at the end of the thirteenth century and established a kingdom at Pegu that was engaged actively in commerce. Although the strongest Tai kingdoms were far from the sea, at Chiengmai and Sukhothai, a new principality was founded at the major port of Ayutthaya about 1351, and its fortunes rose with its trade.

Between 1400 and 1600 this new form of port-state, directly involved in the expanding international trade, came to dominate Southeast Asia both politically and culturally.

The Port-States in the Fifteenth Century

The rapid growth of port-centred states around 1400 was closely bound up with the unprecedented vigour of Chinese interaction with Southeast Asia under the first Ming emperors. Vietnam was a special case for the reasons outlined in chapter 2. The ability of the early Le emperors to construct a Confucian state under bureaucratic governance must have owed much to the two decades of direct Chinese rule (1407–28) which preceded their regime, but Thang-long (Hanoi) was the only rising capital of the period that did not owe most of its strength to commercial revenues. Its envoys to China travelled by land. Its relation to the Chinese model was direct, in defiantly asserting its equality of status and civilization with the empire whose authority it had thrown off.

Elsewhere a string of maritime principalities arose by taking advantage of the unprecedented Chinese interest in sending and receiving seaborne missions both diplomatic and commercial. Cambodia, Champa, Brunei, Java, and Samudra (Pasai) had sporadically exchanged envoys with earlier Chinese dynasties, but these increased enormously in frequency and intensity with the advent of the Ming in 1368. Immediately the Hongwu emperor sent missions to all known countries of Southeast Asia to emphasize that Chinese te (virtue) had been restored under a Chinese dynasty and all southern kingdoms should flourish under its protection (Wang 1968: 43–48). Missions flowed regularly back and forth to all the above states during this reign. His son the Yongle emperor (1402–24) conducted a still more active policy of sending enormous fleets under the Muslim eunuch Zheng He to ensure that all countries in the south submitted to the impartial protection of the Son of Heaven. Missions in both directions were at their peak in this period (see table 1, above), and the rewards were substantial for rulers able to exploit the Chinese connection.

The great winners were Ayutthaya and Melaka, and perhaps Brunei and Manila. The new Siamese principality of Ayutthaya was one of the states that received the imperial rescript in 1368. It responded with exceptional enthusiasm, becoming the most frequent Southeast Asian sender of tribute over the ensuing two centuries. The Siamese themselves were not seafarers. Although the king sent Siamese envoys with sappanwood and other trade goods as "tribute" (Ma Huan 1433: 107), the missions were transported by Chinese shipowners, many of whom must have made their base at the hospitable Thai capital. Korean and Ryukyuan records also report the arrival in the 1390s of Siamese envoys to these two countries and Japan (Kobata and Matsuda 1969: 53–54). Chinese merchants resident in Ayutthaya must have played a major role in giving the Siamese capital this rapid prominence. They may also have assisted Ayutthaya in extending its authority down the Malayan Peninsula during the late fourteenth and early fifteenth centuries. Ma Huan (1433: 107) reported that the Ayutthaya ruler "constantly despatches his commanders to subject neighbouring countries."

Progress in the interior was slower than in the south, but by 1412 Ayutthaya had made Sukhothai and Phitsanulok its vassals. In 1432 the moribund Khmer capital of Angkor was taken and looted. Under King Boromatrailokanat (1448–88) Ayutthayan government was reorganized as a bureaucratic hierarchy. If the two laws regulating civil and military hierarchies are correctly attributed to him, he gave every member of Thai society a rank expressed in *sakdi na* (literally, field power) points—from five for a slave and twenty-five for an ordinary peasant up to ten thousand for the highest-ranking ministers. The king and the leading officials reinforced their claim to the labour of all adult males (excluding monks and private slaves) for six months in the year. The transformation of Ayutthaya from a warrior chiefdom to the most elaborate bureaucracy in Southeast Asia owed something to techniques taken from Angkor, as is conventionally asserted, but more to the Chinese-dominated trade that brought wealth to its port.

Melaka appears to have been established in about 1400 at the narrowest part of the Malacca Straits, which shipping from Pasai and the Indian Ocean had to pass on its way to China or Java. The first ruler, Paremeswara, despite his claimed descent from the dynasty of Sri Vijaya, could only succeed if he attracted traders from China, Java, Siam, and Pasai to call at his port without being swallowed by one of these established powers. The eagerness of the Yongle emperor to pose as the beneficent protector of all was a godsend to him. By responding correctly and immediately to all the imperial initiatives, Melaka won formal equality with its stronger neighbours in Chinese eyes, as well as a major stake in the tributary trade between Southeast Asia and China. China sent six missions to Melaka in the decade 1403–13, most of them large fleets led by Zheng He. In gratitude for this recognition Melaka's rulers not only joined their neighbours in sending tribute to China; they made the arduous journey to Nanjing or Beijing themselves, spending as long as three years on the return journey, in order to secure their status in Chinese eyes. Between them the first three rulers of Melaka made five journeys to China, in 1411, 1414, 1419, 1424, and 1434 (Wang 1968, 1970). By the time the Ming emperors lost interest in pursuing these overseas adventures, in 1435, Melaka was secure as an entrepôt and local power.

Brunei, though a much older port than Melaka, lacked its strategic advantages. Brunei's ruler distinguished himself in the eyes of the Yongle emperor not by his political importance but by his "loyalty" as the first southern king to present tribute in person, in 1408. He was splendidly received in the capital, and still more splendidly buried at Chinese expense when he died on the way home from his mission (fig. 27). His infant son was sent home with a substantial Chinese retinue, including a commissioner who reportedly governed Brunei during his minority (Wang 1970: 68, 78). That this Chinese intervention was a factor in Brunei's rise was acknowledged in later Brunei legends about a founding king who went to China and married a Chinese princess (Dasmariñas 1590: 4).

The only other "kings" to visit the Chinese capital were from the Sulu area, and they seem to have remained rival chieftains rather than establishing a fifteenth-century kingdom there (Scott 1984: 75–77). Further north, the fine port of Manila Bay, known to the Chinese as Luzon, sent tribute missions in 1405 and 1410. Manila's contact with China appears to have been lost after about 1430, but its contact with Brunei became very close as both cities reoriented their China trade via Melaka. In the sixteenth century Manila was in the process of becoming a Muslim port-state and the biggest trade centre in the Philippines.

The effect of Chinese intervention in states elsewhere is less clear. It may have encouraged a new centre of economic activity in Cam-

Fig. 27 Approach road to the tomb of the King of Brunei, erected in China on his death in 1408

bodia around the confluence of the Mekong and Tonle Sap rivers near modern Pnompenh, but it was well into the sixteenth century before this emerged as a new capital. Palembang, principal centre of the defunct Sri Vijaya empire, began a new life in the late fourteenth century as a centre for Chinese and Muslim freebooters, over whom Zheng He established a locally born Cantonese Muslim in authority in 1407 (Ma Huan 1433: 98–100; Kobata and Matsuda 1969: 138–45). In Java, as noted above, the imperial fleets and individual Chinese traders played a major role in the rise of Gresik, Surabaya, and Demak, the coastal port-states which gradually assumed political and cultural leadership of Java from the Hindu-Buddhist centres of the interior.

Wherever there was trade, there were greater or lesser ports where the produce of the hinterland was gathered for exchange with imported cloths, ceramics, and other goods. The collapse of the ancient empires together with the trade boom gave small river-ports greater independence. By 1500 every natural port or navigable river in Sumatra and the Malayan peninsula had a little port-state with a raja claiming more or less equality with other port-rulers, and more or less symbolic supremacy over the stateless peoples up the river. On the Peninsula, such ports as Patani, Kelantan, Terengganu, Johor, Kedah,

Perak, and Selangor acknowledged the supremacy of Siam in the first half of the century, and of the booming port of Melaka towards its end, but conducted their trade largely independently. In Sumatra a dozen independent ports were becoming effective states, and only those of the southeast sent tribute to Melaka or Java.

Further east the spice trade gave rise to centres where Javanese and Malay traders gathered and sometimes settled, introducing Islam and notions of statehood in the second half of the fifteenth century. The Banda Islands, source of the world's nutmeg, were an extreme case of kingless rule by a commercial oligarchy who controlled the export of nuts. In the clove-producing Moluccas four rajas emerged—Ternate, Tidore, Bacan, and Jailolo—each recognizing the others' legitimacy, and each resting in turn on a string of dependent chiefs. In Borneo, Sulawesi, and the Philippines the formation of states was at a still earlier stage, though port-rulers calling themselves rajas were beginning to arise at every centre of trade.

State Formation in the Long Sixteenth Century

> Without wishing to belittle the role played by individuals and circumstances, I am convinced that the period of economic growth during the fifteenth and sixteenth centuries created a situation consistently favorable to the large and very large state.
>
> —Braudel 1966: 660

When the Portuguese arrived in Southeast Asia in 1509, they found an exceptional, and probably unstable, concentration of trade at a single entrepôt—Melaka. During the previous half-century this port-state par excellence had succeeded so well in creating congenial conditions for trade that most Chinese and Indian shippers chose to collect their cargoes there rather than visiting Java, Maluku, Sumatra, or Burma. By conquering this rich but vulnerable city in 1511, the Portuguese forced a dispersion of the trade to a number of other centres. Patani, Johor, Pahang, Aceh, and Banten were the immediate beneficiaries, all emerging from obscurity to become substantial states in the sixteenth century (map 10). The great increase in trade between 1500 and 1630, and the wealth and new technology that came with it, enabled a great diversity of states to flourish in the interval between the fall of Melaka in 1511 and the rise of Dutch Batavia to a different kind of dominance in the mid-seventeenth century.

Pegu, in lower Burma, rose the highest and fell the hardest. In the second half of the fifteenth century it enjoyed a long period of peace as

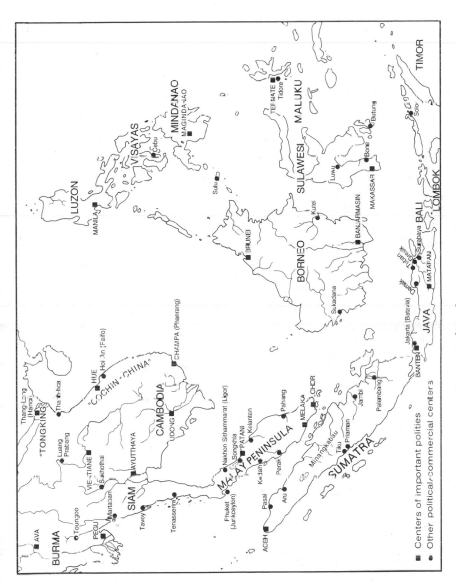

Map 10 Political centres, c. 1600

BURMA

AVA

Toungoo

PEGU

Martaban

Tavoy

Tenasserim

SIAM

Luang Prabang

"TONGKING"

Thang-Long (Hanoi)

Thanh-hoa

Sukhothai

VIENTIANE

AYUTTHAYA

CAMBODIA

UDONG

HUE

Hoi An (Faifo)

"COCHIN-CHINA"

CHAMPA (Phanrang)

Nakhon Sithammarat (Ligor)

Songkhla

PATANI

Kelantan

Phuket (Jurikceylon)

Kedah

Perak

MALAY PENINSULA

Pahang

MELAKA

JOHOR

LUZON

MANILA

VISAYAS

Cebu

MINDANAO

MAGINDANAO

Sulu

BRUNEI

BORNEO

Kutei

SUKADANA

BANJARMASIN

SULAWESI

MAKASSAR

Luwu

Bone

TERNATE

Tidore

Butung

MALUKU

TIMOR

ACEH

Pasai

Aru

Minangkabau

Tiku

Pariaman

SUMATRA

Jambi

Palembang

BANTEN

Jakarta (Batavia)

JAVA

MATARAM

Demak

Tuban

Gresik

Surabaya

BALI

LOMBOK

Sclo

Centers of important polities

Other political/commercial centers

a Mon kingdom. Its Indian Ocean ports of Bassein, Syriam, Martaban, Ye, and Tavoy brought it prosperity and opened it to the reforming influence of Sri Lankan Buddhism. In the 1530s, however, this kingdom was overrun by Tabinshweihti, of the rising Burman dynasty of Toungoo. He had moved swiftly to exploit the opportunities offered by Muslim and Portuguese mercenaries, as well as by superior Portuguese cannon and harquebuses. Having conquered the Mon area he made Pegu his capital, adopted many features of its flourishing Mon culture, and used the wealth of its ports for further conquests. His successor, Bayinnaung (1551–81), turned these advantages to brilliant account, conquering northern Burma, Chiengmai, and Ayutthaya to create one of the strongest empires Southeast Asia has known. Under Bayinnaung's son Nandabayin (1581–99), however, most of this empire was lost and its glittering capital utterly destroyed. A new capital for the Toungoo kings finally took root in Ava in 1632, two months' voyage up the Irrawaddy from the sea.

Arakan, occupying the strip of coast between Burma and Bengal, managed to hold off the powerful Toungoo rulers and direct their aggressions eastward. When the Pegu empire collapsed in 1599 Arakan was a major beneficiary, seizing much of its treasure and some of its Indian Ocean ports. It, too, was exceptionally quick to take advantage both of the expanding trade of its port-capital, Mrauk-u, and of Portuguese mercenaries and military techniques. Its historian (Collis 1925) has pointed out that Mrauk-u enjoyed just a century of brilliant success, from 1540 to 1640, in attracting and organizing international commerce, defending its independence, and building an imposing capital.

Laos, or the Kingdom of Lansang, was as far from the sea as is possible in Southeast Asia but also had its moment of glory in the age of commerce. As the Angkor empire declined in the fourteenth century, a Tai principality emerged at Luang Prabang on the upper Mekong. In the sixteenth century the capital was moved to Vientiane to take advantage of the fertile plains and the long navigable stretch of the middle Mekong of which it is the centre. Further down the Mekong, at Nakhon Phanom, the mid-century Lao kings endowed a celebrated shrine, which became a centre of scholarship, pilgrimage, and trade with the Vietnamese, Khmer, and Thai. The apogee of the state was reached during the long reign of Surinyavongsa (c.1637–94), when the Mekong River road was busy as a crucial link between China, Vietnam, Cambodia, and Siam.

In **Vietnam,** as noted above, the rulers of the northern heartland known to Europeans as Tongking were particularly reluctant to tie their fortunes to foreign commerce. They allowed a dynastic rival, Nguyen Hoang, to become established in Thuan Hoa and Quang Nam, the then unsettled southern frontier, in the second half of the sixteenth century. He responded imaginatively to the strategic position of this coast on the Chinese trade-route south, founded the international port of Hoi An (Faifo), and quickly adopted the military innovations made available by Portuguese and others. By his death in 1613 his domain was effectively a vigorous new state, referred to by Europeans as **Cochin-China**.[1] Nguyen Hoang's successors called themselves lords (*chùa*) rather than emperors, continuing to acknowledge the legitimacy of the powerless Le dynasty, whom they argued the Trinh in Tongking had usurped. Nevertheless, it was an important new model of a Vietnamese state based on flourishing trade and innovative military technology. Le Quy Don (1776: 26) noted that its core area (Quang Nam), "was a place in which ships gathered since ancient times. Since the Nguyen occupied the area, they gained much from the taxes on the shipping trade." In seven wars between 1627 and 1672 Cochin-China drove off the numerically superior armies of Tongking (as well as its Dutch allies in the period 1640–43) and took many captives to help populate the new southern regions being wrested from the Cham. Vietnamese in language and administration, Cochin-China was much like the rest of Southeast Asia in its economic basis and cultural pluralism.

Patani was merely one of several small port-states on the east coast of the Malayan Peninsula until the Portuguese conquered Melaka in 1511. Within a few years much of Melaka's trade had relocated to Patani, where "many ships of the Chinese, Ryukyus and Javanese come, as well as from all the surrounding islands" (Barros 1563 III, i: 183; cf. Kobata and Matsuda 1969: 182). A Malay and Muslim prin-

1. Vietnamese never gave a distinctive name to the southern state, other than the domain of the Nguyen, or the "inner region" (Dang Trong) as opposed to the "outer region" (Dang Ngoai) in Tongking. The Portuguese picked up the Malay term for Vietnam, Kuchi, which was distinguished from the other Kuchi (Cochin in Kerala) by its proximity to China, hence Cochin-China (Pires 1515: 114). Malay Kuchi had in turn derived from the very old Chinese term Jiao zhy (Gao zi in Cantonese and pre-Ming standard Chinese) or its Vietnamese equivalent, Giao chi. The southern kingdom's success in dealing with foreigners is indicated by its having usurped this term originally designating Vietnam as a whole. Tongking, a corruption for one of the names of Hanoi, emerged in the seventeenth century to distinguish the northern state. Most Europeans called the Nguyen kingdom Cochin-China in the seventeenth and eighteenth centuries, though the Dutch preferred Quinam. The French moved the Cochin-China label further south again by using it to describe their colony in the Mekong Delta after 1860—an area still Cambodian in the age of commerce. In spite of this confusion, I use it here in its seventeenth-century sense.

cipality tributary to Siam, it did not, however, gain a permanent advantage over its rivals—Siamese Nakhon Sithammarat (Ligor) and Malay Pahang—until the 1560s. Then more than two thousand Chinese "pirates" made it their commercial base, according to the Ming Annals (Kobata and Matsuda 1969: 180; cf. van Neck 1604: 217). Local Chinese traditions refer to the leader of this group, Lin Daoqian, having seized the city and founded a new dynasty, whereas Malay chronicles symbolize the Chinese role only through a story about their casting cannons there (Skinner 1957: 4–5; Teeuw and Wyatt 1970 II: 224–28). In any event, Patani became the major entrepôt for Chinese trade in the Peninsula during the ensuing century and was perceived by some Dutch writers as effectively a colony of Chinese exiles (van Noort 1601: 124; van Neck 1604: 222–23). Political problems were intense until 1584, when a succession of female rulers was placed on the throne by the mercantile orangkaya. The Dutch and English established lodges there to buy pepper and Chinese wares, and the city remained populous and prosperous until the middle of the seventeenth century, when internal instability gradually drove its trade to Malay Johor and Dutch Melaka. Patani did not fully recover from Siamese conquests in 1674 and 1688.

Aceh was created in 1520–24 by a military campaign that ended Portuguese interference on the north Sumatran coast and united the independent port-states of Baros, Daya, Lamri, Pidië, and Pasai. During the reign of Sultan Alau'd-din Ri'ayat Syah al-Kahar (1539–71) the trade of all these ports was concentrated in Banda Aceh, which became the principal Muslim entrepôt in the Straits of Malacca region, whence Southeast Asian pepper and spices were exported to the Middle East and the Mediterranean. From the 1590s Aceh moved in an absolutist direction that culminated in the harshness of Iskandar Muda's regime (see below). This may have helped Aceh against its rivals militarily, but it did not satisfy commercial interests, which in the 1640s moved to the Patani model of female rulers. Aceh was the only important Archipelago port never to fall under European influence, and though its power waned in the second half of the seventeenth century, it remained a major force.

Banten, at the northwestern corner of Java, was also established as a Muslim port-state in the 1520s. Javanese tradition makes its founder one of the nine walis of Java, Sunan Gunung Jati, a scholar from Pasai who had left that port in disgust at Portuguese activities, travelled to Mecca, and then to Java, where he married the sister of the powerful ruler of Demak, Trenggana. With Trenggana's help he conquered the ports of the Sundanese Hindu kingdom of Pajajaran, making his capital at the strategic harbour of Banten. The inland capital of Pajajaran was not finally conquered until about 1579, but Banten's authority had meanwhile spread to the rich pepper-growing districts of southern Sumatra. Control of these areas gave Banten a power base similar to Aceh's. Whereas Aceh sent its pepper westward, however, Banten supplied the China market. The Dutch from 1596 and the English from 1602 made Banten their Southeast Asian headquarters, partly because Banten was still in the pluralistic, open phase of development from which Aceh had radically departed. The long tutelage of Sultan Abdulkadir, which lasted from 1596 to about 1624, represented an effective, if often turbulent, oligarchy of cosmopolitan orangkayas. Later sultans became progressively more powerful, culminating in the last independent ruler, Abdulfatah Ageng (1651–82).

Makassar was the commonest name for the city and state created by the alliance of two leading chiefdoms of the Makassarese people of southwestern Sulawesi: Goa, more warlike and populous, and Tallo', oriented towards maritime trade. The sixteenth century marked its steady rise to pre-eminence, economically based on its success in becoming the major stapling port of Sulawesi and in developing an exportable surplus of rice. A Malay trading community made its base in Makassar in the mid-sixteenth century, and the port became progressively more attractive thereafter as an alternative to Java in providing rice and other supplies for the Maluku spice trade. The Dutch attempt to monopolize these spices in the seventeenth century made Makassar an essential free port for all other traders, including Malays, Javanese, south Indians, Portuguese, English, Danish, and Spanish. After the Dutch conquest of Portuguese Melaka in 1641 it became for twenty years the principal Portuguese base in Southeast Asia. Makassar was exceptionally avid as a technological borrower. Portuguese military, historical, and mathematical texts were read and sometimes translated, the use of maps and court diaries was pioneered, and cannons, muskets, and armour were deployed by one of the Archipelago's most effective armed forces. Makassar adopted Islam in 1605 and proceeded to conquer the whole of South Sulawesi in its name. Contractual rights and obligations between autonomous states remained a feature of the region, but the period 1610–69 was the only real exception before 1904 to a South Sulawesi tradition of balance among a number of competing states. Elsewhere, Makassar's "empire" extended as far as Buton, Sumbawa, and Timor, on the basis of personal loyalties backed up by the threat of force (Boxer 1967; Reid 1981, 1983A; Bulbeck 1992).

Throughout the Archipelago a variety of lesser states rose to brief pinnacles of power at the end of the sixteenth or the first half of the seventeenth century. Jambi and Palembang in the sixteenth century, and Banjarmasin in the seventeenth, arose as river-ports controlling the export of pepper in their hinterlands. The geography and political traditions of Maluku made a single "clove state" unlikely there. For a brief period between 1570 and 1606, however, the sultanate of Ternate subordinated much of northern and central Maluku and made its port a central market for cloves at which buyers from all quarters competed (van Fraassen 1987 I: 45–48).

Even rulers who lacked this opportunity to parlay control over an export crop into power could profit from the expansion in trade and the introduction of new technologies and ideas. The strongest indigenous state in Philippine history began to consolidate along the Pulangi River in Mindanao in the late sixteenth century. Its capital was initially up-river at Buayan, but dissident elements established a new commercial centre near the mouth of the river about 1606, which soon became the dominant power. The Magindanao sultanate reached its height under Sultan Kudarat (1619–71), who shifted the capital decisively to the coast, triumphing over the autonomy of chieftains with a mixture of religion, force, and economic power similar to that used by the Spanish to his north (Laarhoven 1989, 1990). Even ethnic groups known in the eighteenth and nineteenth centuries for their fragmentation or statelessness tend to remember the age of commerce as a time when they were politically unified under strong kings. In the case of Bali before 1650 and Minangkabau before 1680 foreign sources make clear, at a minimum, that there was a dynasty claiming to rule the whole region from an impressive and populous capital (Dias 1565: 98–101; Lintgens 1597: 98–102; Dias 1684; Vickers 1989: 46–53).

There is more than coincidence in this spate of state building, in Southeast Asia as in other parts of the world. We must turn to the key factors that encouraged the rise of powerful states but also created problems for them.

Trade Revenues

"You stay here in the palace, my Lord, and [leave your rival] Jumaloy
  Alam in Kampung Jawa [the port]
Do not go elsewhere, for the amount of toll-money Your Majesty levies
  is enormous.
My Lord collects the duties on the products of the forest: ten percent of
  the resin and rattan,
And when the vegetable-grower is well-disposed, he gives you onions
  and ginger.

But Jumaloy Alam collects the duties on the sea-borne commerce; over
and over again he rakes in thousands and thousands of bahars.
My Lord is content when he has enough to eat; he does not pursue
riches."
                                        —Hikayat Pocut Muhammad: 60–61

Not all state revenues derived from trade. The needs of the court
for rice and other foodstuffs, for building materials, and above all for
labour were provided without charge by its subjects and dependents.
Such taxes in kind, however, provided no basis for one ruler to rise to
dominance over his peers unless they could be turned into arms or
disposable income. This was the case in Java, the most consistent and
important exporter of rice, where rulers of Mataram in the seventeenth century squeezed the farming population, or at least that which
was close to roads and ports, for a substantial rice surplus. This was
then exchanged for arms and other necessities through export to
Dutch Batavia, Portuguese Melaka, Maluku, and elsewhere (van
Goens 1652: 114).

In the Mainland countries, and particularly in Tongking, monetary taxes on the agricultural population were of some importance, in
the form of a head tax (in Vietnam), a land tax, or both. Tongking levied
a poll tax in money on every adult male, as well as a land tax and
"donations" for a series of annual festivals. When in 1720 a complex
range of earlier imposts was simplified into a uniform head tax, those
aged 20–50 were expected to pay the full tax of 1.2 *quan* (about 28
grams of silver) each year, while those aged 17–19 or 50–60, as well as
students, paid half this. A further 1.2 quan was levied on each taxpayer
in two annual instalments to represent the various "donations" previously levied. Land taxes were a lesser burden, generally about 5
percent of the crop (Le 1971: 260; Li 1992: 112). Rhodes (1654: 28–29)
reckoned the poll tax in his day at 2 écus (about 50 grams of silver), in
addition to donations for four annual festivals, whereas Choisy (1687:
252) thought the Tongkinese paid only 14 écus for a village of one
hundred inhabitants. Either way, there is no question that the Le and
Trinh courts of Tongking drew most of their substantial cash revenue
from their large but poor population of rice-farmers.

In Cochin-China the more extensive junk trade provided considerable revenue, which Li Tana (1992: 95) has estimated at about a third
of royal income in the eighteenth century. In addition, the state's
heavy investment in defense led to exceptional direct demands on its
subjects. The annual poll tax on adult males (aged 20–50) was reported
by the Japanese Christian Fransisco (1642: 121) to be 11 Spanish reals
(about 300 grams of silver) for married men and half that for unmarried

males. Choisy (1687: 252) confirmed that Cochin-Chinese were very heavily taxed, though his figure, 5 écus, was equivalent to Fransisco's for unmarried men. Since Fransisco declared that there were only ten thousand such tax-payers, two-thirds of them married (thus giving revenue of 2.5 tonnes of silver), most Nguyen subjects must have been meeting their obligations in other ways, including direct levies of a third of their produce or their labour when required (Choisy 1687: 254; Li 1992). The core group of Cochin-Chinese subject to the poll tax, however, were probably paying the heaviest single money tax in Southeast Asia.

King Prasat Thong of Siam imposed a tax of 1 *fuang* (0.17 Dutch guilders or less than 2 grams of silver) for each family rice-plot. Van Vliet (1636: 26) considered that this and related taxes on agriculture produced "the greatest revenue" of the king, though some of his countrymen thought trade more important ("Vertoog" 1622: 289). Fifty years later, when royal revenues from commerce had been increased severalfold, La Loubère (1691: 93–95) reported a much higher land tax of one-fourth of a tikal but pointed out that this was levied only on fields actually cultivated, and "only in places where his authority is absolute.... The king of Siam has never been well paid his revenues in lands remote from his court."

Burma appears to have been substantially less monetized. Lieberman (1991: 24) has calculated that 79 percent of agricultural taxes were still paid in kind before 1550, and 58 percent in the period 1600–1752. Farmers closer to the capital understandably tended to have their taxes demanded in foodstuffs, whereas those further afield were expected to pay in silver or export products (Lieberman 1984: 129–30). Various new taxes were levied in silver in the seventeenth century (ibid.: 161), no doubt in response to the silver revolution. The notion that the king's share should be 10 percent of the country's product, whether in agriculture, livestock, or commerce, was well established in Burmese law (Symes 1827 II: 53; Than Tun 1985: 19–20; Koenig 1990: 119–20), though officials often interpreted this to mean the net income received by the crown, exclusive of the various charges they pocketed.

Heavy though these charges and the burdens of military and civil corvée were on the rice-growing population near the capital, at the peak of the age of commerce the bulk of disposable revenue for all states except Tongking came from the commercial sector. Some of this was on internal trade. Royal charges were levied on markets, on ferries, and on river and road traffic. Most rulers monopolized some of the most lucrative items of internal trade, such as salt (in Vietnam) and metals, especially silver and gold. In Narai's Siam there was a tax on every productive fruit tree (La Loubère 1691: 93), and the sale of the areca and betel alone that came into royal coffers was reported to yield a phenomenal 225,000 écus (more than 5 tonnes of silver—Choisy 1687: 182).

Such internal levies increased with the growth of commerce and the greater commercialization and monetization of the economy. The major variable in state revenues, however, was external trade. For the states that successfully plugged into the growing world economy during the age of commerce, this was the key to wealth and power. Moertono (1968: 136) quotes a Javanese ethical saying (*piwulang*): "The soldier is the fortress of the king, the peasant the food of the state, the merchant the clothing of the land," to mean that the riches of the state had to come from trade. The court and its officials both central and regional obtained their subsistence needs through rice deliveries and corvée, but for the items that placed them above their peers—firearms, imported manufactures, horses, luxuries, and novelties—they had to rely on cash revenues from commerce.

In the states most reliant on trade, agriculture contributed little to state revenue. The port-state of Melaka, with scarcely any agricultural hinterland, was at the opposite extreme from Tongking in this respect. Thomaz (1993: 74) has calculated that the sultanate probably received no more than 10 percent of its tax revenue from anything that could be considered land-based, chiefly through tribute from its provinces. The rest, amounting to at least 50,000 cruzados (about 2 tonnes of silver), came from the customs-house, without considering the sultan's own extensive trade.

The share of commerce in the revenue of other Archipelago states, such as Aceh, Palembang, Patani, and Banten, must have been overwhelming. It is difficult to document any substantial land-based revenues in any of these states to set against the array of port duties, export levies, weigh-charges, and market and river tolls (Ito 1984: 335–91). Even the rulers of Siam and Burma appear to have drawn most of their cash income from trade. In the eighteenth century, when Burma's agricultural character was more marked than in the sixteenth, Mantegazza (1784: 103–04, 128) believed that the port of Rangoon provided the largest share of Burmese royal income and thought that the absence of any substantial tax on agriculture was a major failing of the Burmese state. The port revenues of Rangoon in 1797 were 150,000 *kyats* (about 2.5 tonnes of silver) a year, which might be compared to

50,000 kyats from other sources in the Rangoon Province, and an average 56,000 kyats of cash revenue from all sources in the rice-bowl of Kyaukse in northern Burma in 1784–85 (Koenig 1990: 120).

Import and export duties varied with the port and the bargaining position of the traders concerned but seldom were above 10 percent. The exception was Burma, which imposed a 12–20 percent duty on imports, though nothing on exports other than rubies (Pires 1515: 99; Frederici 1581: 253; Hall 1939: 153). Malay ports, in competition with one another for the entrepôt traffic, tended to have similar regulations. Malay Melaka levied a 6 percent import duty on ships from above the winds, though nothing but a weighing fee of 1–2 percent on their exports. Southeast and East Asian ships were free of both import and export duties but were obliged to sell 25 percent of their import goods to the king at 20 percent below market prices, while the ruler paid for the goods in export produce at 20 percent above market prices. This system, known as *beli-belian* (mutual buying), thus amounted to a 5 percent duty on both imports and exports (Thomaz 1993: 74). In Aceh, Indian shipping paid a 5 percent duty on both imports and exports, whereas Europeans were expected by Sultan Iskandar Muda to pay 7 percent (Ito 1984: 341–48). In Makassar, by contrast, no duties were levied until Sultan Hasanuddin (1653–69) imposed anchorage and weighing fees (Macassar General 1665: 260; Navarrete 1676: 114). The English East India Company agreed with delight to present the first sultan, Alauddin, with "some rarity" worth 100 pounds each year, since "if he should exact the usual custom of other places, it would rise to thousands of rials" (Willoughby 1636: 151).

These were, however, the best regulated ports, where duties were fixed and presents relatively modest and predictable. In smaller or more chaotic ports, the arrival of large European ships introduced a process of bargaining. The first English and Dutch ships in Banten paid 1500 reals anchorage and 1 real per bag of pepper exported (thus about 18 percent), whereas fifty years later the English managed through gifts to avoid paying even the 800 reals anchorage demanded (Lancaster 1603: 114–15; Curtis and Chambers 1656: 127; Kathirithamby-Wells 1990: 113). In Patani the Dutch in 1604 ended by paying a 5 percent royal export duty on pepper, as well as a substantial gift to be divided among the queen, the "young Queen," and nine orangkaya (Warwijck 1604: 44). Ten years later the English complained bitterly about duties of 4 percent, as well as 856 reals for the orangkaya (*LREIC* II: 44, 79, 123). Europeans frequently complained of "large gifts being better regarded than good dealing" (Keeling 1612: 529), but it was their own readiness to take advantage of the bargaining power represented by their larger ships that caused most of the uncertainty.

Although the regular port duties provided the cash income which sustained the administration of the port and the capital, the most ambitious rulers all obtained larger incomes from their direct participation in trade. "These kings are all merchants, and are only wealthy to the extent that they engage in commerce" (Le Blanc 1692 II: 154). Those whose dominions produced vital export commodities always regarded at least 10 percent of the product as a tribute, as the Sultan of Ternate did on Malukan cloves (van Neck 1604: 199) or the Sultan of Aceh on forest products (above). Often, however, rulers sought to act as the sole exporters of certain products, in effect monopolising the supply to foreign buyers. A growing trend in this direction during the seventeenth century, which brought unprecedented wealth to such rulers as Prasat Thong and Narai of Siam and Iskandar Muda of Aceh, is examined below.

The Military Revolution

> On arrival at Melaka the [Portuguese] ships forthwith opened fire with their cannon. And the people of Melaka were bewildered and filled with fear at the sound of the cannon, and they said, "What sound is this like thunder?" And when presently the cannon balls began to arrive and struck the people of Melaka, so that some had their heads shot away, some their arms, and some their legs, the people of Melaka were more and more astonished to see the effect of this artillery; they said, "What is this weapon called that is round, and yet so sharp that it kills?"
>
> —Sejarah Melayu 1612: 182

From their earliest encounters, Southeast Asians associated Europeans with advanced military technology. Not only could the newcomers bombard a city or an enemy vessel with their shipboard cannon, but they introduced the effective use of handguns and protected themselves with armour against Southeast Asian arrows, lances, and daggers.

This technological edge was maintained from 1511 onwards. Until the introduction of machine guns and steamships in the nineteenth century, however, it was never more than a slight edge. Gunpowder and firearms were invented in China and had spread throughout Eurasia by 1500. It was in Europe that they were developed to the point where they changed the whole nature of warfare, but this occurred just before the European invasion of Asia. Only in the Franco-Spanish War of 1494–95 was field artillery first used so effectively that it brought forth a new defensive strategy, and only in 1490 did the first European state, Venice, replace its bowmen with musketeers (Parker 1988: 9–17). After their initial surprise the leading Southeast Asian port-states quickly bought, hired, captured, or copied the new techniques and weapons, thereby limiting the power of Europeans largely to the reach of their guns and fortresses. The most profound impact of the new technologies, in Southeast Asia as in Europe, was in strengthening the authority of the regimes which possessed them over their hinterlands which did not.

Despite the surprised tone of the Malay chronicle quoted above, Southeast Asians were familiar with firearms well before the arrival of the Portuguese. China had pioneered metal-barrelled cannon and their use onboard ship in the thirteenth century. Chinese cannons were carried to Java by the Mongol invasion of 1293, and again by the Zheng He expeditions, one of which left behind in Java a still extant cannon dated 1421 (Lombard 1990 II: 178). Vietnam made sure it was not lagging behind its powerful neighbour in this respect. Cannon fire from a Vietnamese vessel killed the Cham king and hero Che Bong Nga in 1389, and the Ming chronicle acknowledged that China had learned some artillery techniques from the Vietnamese during its occupation of the country in 1407–24 (Le 1971: 194; Li 1992: 37). Around 1500 Vietnam was distinguished for its "countless musketeers and small bombards" (Pires 1515: 115). According to Burmese and Thai chronicles of later date, firearms were also used in the fourteenth century in wars between Siam and Cambodia and among the states of Burma—possibly by Chinese auxiliaries in the first case and Indians in the second (Wood 1924: 77; Lieberman 1980: 211).

In spite of what the Malay chronicler of the battle would have us believe, Melaka in 1511 probably had as many firearms as the Portuguese fleet that attacked it. Portuguese chroniclers make extraordinary claims that there were between two thousand and eight thousand guns in the conquered city (Castanheda 1552–54 III: 152–53; Albuquerque 1557: 127–28). Albuquerque stated that a thousand of the guns seized were of iron and two thousand were of bronze, the largest of the latter being a present to the Sultan of Melaka from the zamorin of Calicut, in South India. Pires (1515: 13, 269) described a regular trade in firearms all the way from the Mediterranean to Melaka. The largest cannons did indeed travel eastwards along this route, but Eredia (1613: 32) pointed out that most of the weapons seized in Melaka were not the large guns favoured in the Middle East but small bronze culverins and falconets probably imported from China or from foundries in Siam or Burma influenced by the Chinese. Until the Europeans made their cannons more widely available, the ornamental bronze culverins of Chinese type must have dominated in quantity if not in size.

There is no reason to doubt that gunsmiths were already at work in the Archipelago—probably Chinese at first but soon also local Muslims. The Portuguese reported that in Melaka "the gun founders were as good as those in Germany" (Albuquerque 1557: 128) and that the Japara fleet which attacked Melaka in 1513 was armed with cannons cast in Java (Lombard 1990 II: 178). The Spanish were fired upon when they seized Manila in 1570, and later found that some guns were being cast in a house next to the raja's. "There were clay and wax moulds, the largest of which was for a cannon 17 feet long, resembling a culverin" ("Relation" 1570: 103). Later evidence makes clear that most of the artillery of these Muslims of Manila Bay was imported by Chinese and Japanese from their respective countries—"bronze culverins so excellent and well cast, that I have never seen their equal anywhere" ("Relation" 1572: 143–44, 148; Artieda 1573: 201, 205; de Sande 1576: 76). The expertise for local casting presumably came from the same source.[2]

The evident importance of Chinese models for most Southeast Asian guns is not reflected in local tradition, where the Islamic connections of the Indian Ocean are paramount. As Lombard (1990 II: 179) has pointed out, one of the principal Malay words for cannon, *bedil*, is of Tamil origin, while the other two, *meriam* and *lela*, appear to be Islamic feminine names. The largest guns were created in this Islamic context, and their size and symbolic importance outweighed the numbers and elegance of the Chinese. It is striking, though, that Acehnese, who had profited most from Turkish artillery, were able to tell a French visitor that firearms had been invented in China (Martin 1604: 54).

The oldest of the "giant" Southeast Asian guns to have survived is Ki Jimat, which weighs 6 tonnes and carries an Arabic inscription and a date, 1526/7. According to tradition it was cast in Demak, the leading Muslim state of Java, and brought from there to help establish the new Islamic centre of Banten, where it still rests. Similarly, the rise to prominence of Patani is associated with the casting of three famous guns there, by a Turk in one version and a Chinese in another. One of

---

2. Nevertheless, one must record that some Filipinos told one disbelieving Spaniard that they had learned to make guns from a Fleming and a Spaniard from one of the early Spanish expeditions ("Relation" 1572: 160).

these was taken by the Siamese who conquered Patani in 1785 and remains in Bangkok under the name Phya Tani (Teeuw and Wyatt 1970: 152–54, 164, 224–27; Lombard 1990 II: 179).

The casting of large cannon in Aceh was a consequence of Sultan Alau'd-din Ri'ayat Syah al-Kahar's appeal in the 1560s for military assistance from Turkey against the Portuguese (see chapter 3). As the Aceh chronicler Raniri (1644: 31) put it, "The Sultan of Rum [Turkey] sent various craftsmen and experts who knew how to make guns. It was at that time that the large cannons were cast." The most famous of these guns was known as "a measure of pepper" (lada secupak), because of the legend that the Aceh ambassador was kept so long waiting in Istanbul that he had only this token left to offer the sultan when admitted to make his request for arms. It broke apart while firing during the Aceh civil war of the 1720s (Hikayat Pocut Muhamat: 223). Though at 4.6 metres what remained was not as large as some of the other Turkish-styled cannons of Aceh, it was still revered when the Dutch conquered the Aceh capital in 1873 and carried it as a trophy to the Netherlands (Reid 1969; Crucq 1941). In the 1570s another giant Aceh cannon, "which for greatness, length (and workmanship) is hardly to be found in all Christendome," was presented to Johor to seal an anti-Portuguese alliance (Linschoten 1598: 109). Davis (1600: 150) also found the Acehnese cannons "the greatest that I have ever seen," though they were fired clumsily as they lay upon the ground.

The Spanish captured 170 large and small cannons from Brunei in 1579 (de Sande 1579: 126). Aceh, during its military height in the 1620s, claimed to possess 5000 pieces. Beaulieu (1666: 105) said he could vouch for 1200 bronze ones, 800 of which were large. Johor around 1700 had more than 1000 cannon though only a few were large 12-to-24 pounders (Guerreiro 1718: 121). When the Dutch captured the main fort of Makassar in 1669 they took possession of the mighty bronze cannon of over 5 tonnes known as "anak Makassar," and 11 iron cannons averaging over a tonne each, as well as 34 small bronze cannons averaging 220 kg, and 224 culverins and small guns that averaged less than 100 kg (Maetsuyker 1669: 680; Crucq 1941A: 78).

In the Mainland there was a similar mix of large and small cannon. Champa in the 1590s had 10 large cannons weighing up to a tonne simply lying on the ground, whereas the main effective armoury consisted of 500 small culverins, which were mounted on galleys in time of war (Gonçalez 1595: 259). The Trinh ruler in Tongking had about 60 iron cannons in an armoury, which Dampier (1699: 52) was able to inspect, but just 2 or 3 larger ones. The largest was of bronze and weighed 3.5 tonnes. "It is an ill-shaped thing, yet much esteemed by them, probably because it was cast here, and the biggest that ever they made." It was, he thought, "more for a show than for service." In Cochin-China the Nguyen ruler made better use of his substantial armoury, which comprised 200 cannons in the 1640s and 1200 a century later. Most were probably cast locally, since a gun factory had been established by 1631 and a suburb of the capital became known as *Phuong Duc* (District of [gun] casting). Those that proved most effective in Cochin-China's many wars were made in the 1660s under the supervision of João da Cruz, a skilled Eurasian well paid by the Nguyen ruler, or else bought from the Portuguese in Macao (Navarrete 1676: 381; Poivre 1750: 90; Li 1992: 39–40).

Indigenous perception clearly linked the fortunes of Southeast Asian dynasties with the large cannons they began to make in the sixteenth century. Although the chronicles virtually ignore the role of handguns, they frequently mention the firing of the great guns, each of which was given a name and a kind of personality (*Hikayat Patani*: 89 90; *Hikayat Pocut Muhamat*: 222, 228; Amin 1670: 140–43, 148–51). Like elephants, they became symbols of the supernatural power of kings, able to intimidate and overawe the internal enemies who lacked them. Long after their military role had ceased, these monster cannon were revered as sources of magic and as sacred relics of a glorious age.

The big guns appear not to have killed many in battle and were not manoeuvrable enough to transform warfare in Asia as they did in Europe. Rulers used them effectively to overawe their subjects. At least in Aceh and Mataram, two of the most powerful "gunpowder empires," the great cannons were used to announce public occasions in place of the older gong or drum. In Aceh the fasting month was inaugurated and ended with a deafening thunder of artillery (Ito 1984: 220–21); in Mataram the largest and most revered cannon, Sapu Jagad, was used to summon the people, but also "to show the anger of the Susuhunan, when he wants to get rid of the nobles of his kingdom," and for royal mourning (cited Lombard 1990 II: 348). The casting of Sapu Jagad in 1625 was a triumph for Sultan Agung, then at his peak of power. His ill-starred successor, Amangkurat, attempted a similar feat in 1652, but when he had his gunsmith put a particularly large charge in the finest of his creations, it blew into fragments, one of which narrowly missed the king. "The fright and the setback caused him to decamp, to take the gunmaker prisoner, to curse this beautiful great square [the alun-alun], and to brick up the entrance gates to it forever . . . causing great disruption to his court. That night the king had a very horrible dream and within a few days his whole body swelled up" (van Goens 1652: 123; cf. *Babad ing Sangkala* 1738: 59).

In practical terms, the rulers able to deploy handguns effectively were the ones best able to transform the political landscape in their favour. A type of harquebus was developed in Europe in the fifteenth century, and a musket that could penetrate armour in the mid-sixteenth. Both quickly made their way east as trade items and with Muslim and Portuguese soldiers. Until the seventeenth century they remained much slower than Southeast Asian bows or blowpipes, since they took several minutes to reload. Rulers who could train large numbers of men in their use, however, could deliver a succession of volleys by ranks of soldiers firing in turn, each supported by an assistant with lighted taper and ramrod (fig. 28). Whereas the older weapons were used by the ordinary population, who became experienced with blowpipe, dagger, or bow from childhood, firearms were invariably kept in a centralized magazine and released to soldiers only during training or warfare. This new technology entailed a drastic centralization of military muscle.

The quickest way for ambitious rulers to deploy the new arms was to employ Portuguese or Islamic adventurers already familiar with their use. The constant naval skirmishing in the sixteenth century between Portuguese on the one hand and Turkish, Arab, Gujarati, and Acehnese Muslims on the other produced a floating population of seamen capable of giving a good account of themselves. Rulers of Burma, Arakan, Siam, Java, and Makassar all made effective use of both Portuguese and foreign Muslims as artillerymen, gunsmiths, and trainers. The Portuguese were particularly welcome in Pegu and Arakan, and these two states gained the greatest advantage from them.

The conquests of Tabinshweihti (1531–51) and Bayinnaung (1551–81), which extended to the boundaries of modern Burma and many Tai areas, were the first in which artillery and handguns, introduced through Portuguese (and to a lesser extent Muslim) auxiliaries, played the decisive role. Tabinshweihti eventually relied too heavily on his Portuguese force, led by Diego Suarez d'Albergaria, and was remembered in Burmese chronicles for having abandoned himself to drinking with the Portuguese shortly before he was assassinated (Pinto 1578: 314–36, 411–30; Lieberman 1980: 208–14). Bayinnaung more successfully integrated the new technology into his own vast army. The Italian traveller Frederici reported that although his armour, pikes, and swords were second-rate, "his arquebusses are most excellent, and always in his wars he has 80,000 arquebusses, and the number of them increases daily. Because the king will have them shoot every day at the Plank, and so by continual exercise they become most

Fig. 28 Arms of Javanese warriors of Banten, about 1600, as depicted by a Dutch engraver. On the right, an harquebusier, with bullets in his belt and carrying a taper to light his powder. His assistant at rear reloads.

excellent shot; also he has great ordinance made of very good metal" (Frederici 1581: 248). With this force, in which Portuguese mercenaries had only a specialized minor place, Bayinnaung conquered the Shan states north of Burma, Chiengmai, and eventually his great rival, Ayutthaya, creating an unprecedented if short-lived empire.

In the seventeenth century these skills were more widespread, and muskets became a major item of trade. Cochin-China made most effective use of them, organizing its entire adult male population along military lines. The knowledge that its northern Vietnamese rivals were far more numerous provided the incentive for military innovation, and extensive trading contacts with Portuguese and Japanese provided the opportunity:

The Cochin-Chinese are now become so expert in managing artillery, that they perform it better than the Europeans, practising continually to shoot at a mark, with such success, that being proud of their skill, as soon as any European ship arrives in their ports, the king's gunners challenge ours, who . . . avoid this trial of skill, being convinced by experience, that they will hit anything as exactly with a cannon, as another shall do with a firelock, which they are also very expert at, often drawing out into the field to exercise (Borri 1633: H3; cf. Fransisco 1642: 122).

Although Cochin-China was assisted by individual Portuguese, its strength was a well-trained native standing army. Navarrete reckoned this to number 40,000 men, while Francisco (1642: 121) counted only 4000, though also referring to other forces such as the 15,000 men of the navy. All sources agreed that this was an exceptionally well paid and disciplined force (Missions Etrangères 1680A: 73–75; Li 1992).

Cochin-China's northern antagonists reputedly had upwards of 70,000 professional soldiers armed with handguns (Dampier 1688: 52–53). They were also "good marksmen, and in that . . . inferior to few; and surpassing most nations in dexterity of handling and quickness of firing their muskets" (Baron 1685: 24; fig. 29), but they suffered against the Cochin-Chinese from their wretched pay and lower morale. To the south, Champa had been reported to have a thousand harquebuses in the 1590s, "but it is foreign slaves who deploy them, for they themselves have little taste for that and they use them more to terrify than to have an effect" (Gonçalez 1595: 258). The same pattern was common elsewhere. Siam and the Javanese states did not develop a disciplined native corps of harquebusiers or musketeers, relying instead on traditional massive levies stiffened by some foreign auxiliaries with firearms.

Demak's rise as an Islamic power in sixteenth-century Java was assisted by foreign Muslims, some of whom used firearms. Pinto (1578: 384–94) regarded the best forces of Demak as "three thousand foreign mercenaries from various countries, most of them Acehnese, Turks, and Malabaris," as well as Chams, "Luzons from Brunei," and even a unit of Portuguese. The Javanese chronicle portrays a ruler of Pajang, Demak's successor around 1600, ordering his "slaves, Balinese, Buginese, and Makassarese" to load his guns with gold and silver bullets, as if the traditional Javanese military hierarchy would not stoop to the new weapons (*Babad Tanah Jawi*: 96–97). Firearms remained so marginal to Javanese warfare that the Dutch in 1596 thought (wrongly) that Banten had no guns (Lodewycksz 1598: 117). The better muskets brought by the English and Dutch began to change this. After the English demonstrated during a festival in 1605 how rapidly they could reload and fire, they found themselves constantly annoyed by Banten notables sending their men to try to steal the English muskets (Scott 1606: 100, 163).

Flourishing ports attracted both the foreign mercenaries and the money to pay them, and thereby increased the power of their rulers against the aristocracy and the interior. All the Siamese monarchs of the seventeenth century were dependent on a nucleus of foreign mercenaries. In the first half of the century the most crucial was a unit of

Fig. 29 Detail of military exercises in seventeenth-century Tongking, depicting an exercise for reloading muskets quickly

about a hundred Japanese, but there were more numerous standing forces of Mons, Portuguese, and Malays. Persians and Indian Muslims replaced the over-powerful Japanese in the 1630s, and finally in the 1680s French officers and men were introduced by Constance Phaulkon as the nucleus of a professional army (fig. 30).

Although the Archipelago states were slower to move in this direction, the King of Jambi was not alone in his reliance on his five hundred Bugis in the 1660s (Speelman 1690: 93). Iskandar Muda of Aceh had a crucial royal guard—"about fifteen hundred slaves, mostly foreigners, who do not leave the citadel any more than do his women, and who have no communication with anyone; he uses them for the executions and murders he commits . . . having taken them young and had them train at arms and at firing harquebuses" (Beaulieu 1666: 103).

The acquisition and manufacture of large cannon was a royal prerogative throughout Southeast Asia. What little we know of the local manufacture of harquebuses in sixteenth-century Burma and

Fig. 30 Seventeenth-century Thai sketch of European gunners assisting an assault on a Thai city

Vietnam suggests the same pattern. Yet both the import and manufacture of muskets began to escape the control of weakened rulers in the mid-seventeenth century. Iskandar Muda strictly controlled his vast armoury: "The king provides arms [to his expeditionary forces], of which they keep a register, being obliged to return them when they come back, their wives and children being surety" (Beaulieu 1666: 106). This control broke down during the Aceh succession conflicts of 1637 and 1641. In 1642 a Dutch report could refer to a cargo of three or four hundred flintlocks being sold "among the people" for 6 reals apiece (Willemsz 1642: f513v). The English were especially inclined to sell firearms as a normal trade item, thereby potentially assisting local chiefs and rebels as much as the ruler. By the late seventeenth century muskets had become sufficiently light, manageable, and widespread as to neutralize the advantages initially brought to centralizing rulers by the advent of firearms.

Matchlocks of European type were manufactured in a number of Southeast Asian centres in the seventeenth century, though the more complex mechanisms of flintlocks and wheel locks still had to be imported from Europe. Mataram reportedly manufactured 800 muskets within three months in 1651–52 (van Goens 1652: 123). Makassar had stockpiled 2422 "pieces" by 1615 and began to manufacture its own muskets around the 1620s—perhaps with initial Portuguese help (*LREIC* III: 150; *Sejarah Kerajaan Tallo'*: 16). Makassar was never as absolutist as other Southeast Asian states, and with its defeat by a Dutch Bugis coalition in the 1660s, the art of making and wielding muskets escaped any centralized control. Many Makassarese refugees became soldiers of fortune elsewhere, carrying the art of musketry to Java, Borneo, and beyond. It was the Bugis hero Arung Palakka who made his people a force to rival Makassar, and he learned to make and wield firearms directly from the Dutch while fighting their wars in Sumatra and Sulawesi. After his victory over Makassar he surrounded his capital in Bone with arms manufacturers whom he brought to a very high quality. As Valentijn (1726 III: 120–21) put it, "He was the first among his people to learn to make muskets and various firearms, precisely, and just as fine as we do, which he then taught to his people, so that it then became a general art among them." By the eighteenth century three peoples noted for their lack of centralized authority— the Bugis, the Balinese, and the Minangkabau—made the most beautiful muskets in Southeast Asia (Marsden 1783: 347; Crawfurd 1820 I: 191–92). They were willing to sell them to anyone who could buy. The age of the "gunpowder empires" in Southeast Asia was over.

The armed galley was the other major weapon of absolutist rulers during this period. The major advantage Europeans brought into Southeast Asia was their ability to employ cannon effectively onboard ship. As noted in chapter 1, this was a major factor in the decline of the large Southeast Asian trading junk, which proved unable to defend itself. The response of Southeast Asian rulers was not to copy the advances in ship design of the Atlantic powers but to build more and bigger armed galleys. The relatively sheltered waters of Southeast Asia, like those of the Mediterranean, made oars seem the fastest way to transport large numbers of troops and to position the vessel in order to deploy its firepower. In the short run this strategy greatly increased the power of Southeast Asian rulers both internally and externally, though in seventeenth-century contests with the light, manoeuvrable, but heavily armed ships of Holland and England they were almost always defeated.

The Vietnamese undoubtedly adopted armed galleys before the

European advent. Lacking a tradition of large sailing junks, they adapted the galleys of Chinese and Vietnamese river transport to the needs of warfare against the Chams along the southern coast. Le Thanh Tong was reported to have sent his army against the Chams in 1465 on five thousand galleys, each armed with primitive cannons with wooden or bamboo barrels (Li 1992: 42). The seventeenth-century wars between the two Vietnamese states, together with the lessons of skirmishes with European ships, brought these fast armed galleys to a high level of efficiency.

Of the many laudatory foreign accounts of the Cochin-Chinese fleet, that of a Japanese resident was probably the most accurate. He counted 230–40 galleys, each manned by sixty-four men who were both rowers and soldiers, with one cannon at the front firing a 4–8 pound ball and two smaller culverins (Fransisco 1643: 121; cf. Rhodes 1651: 22; Borri 1633:H3). A fleet of about fifty of these galleys destroyed a Dutch fleet of three warships in 1643, blowing up the flagship with the loss of all aboard and inflicting probably the most humiliating Dutch naval defeat at Asian hands before the 1940s (Buch 1929: 96). The Tongking ruler was thought to have about two or three times as many galleys (fig. 31a). Alexandre de Rhodes accompanied a royal expedition to the south with 200,000 men, 200 war galleys "glistening with gold and decorated with rich paintings," all moving in perfect precision, and followed by 500 more vessels carrying supplies (Rhodes 1651: 134–36; cf. Tavernier 1692A: 185). This was a stunning sight, rivalled only by the river galleys of Siam and Burma, but the galleys proved less effective in artillery duels than those of their southern rivals, who had learned better the lessons of European warfare.

The Chinese example was important in Vietnam, but Mediterranean models, both Turkish and Portuguese, appear to have been more important elsewhere. Of course, craft propelled by a number of oars or paddles had long existed everywhere, with paddlers in eastern Indonesia often sitting on the outrigger supports characteristic of vessels there. But large galleys carrying guns and designed primarily to transport soldiers swiftly appear to have been a new development. The chronicles of Siam and Makassar assert that the first war galleys of each country were built at the beginning of the seventeenth century (*Sejarah Kerajaan Tallo'*: 17; van Vliet 1640: 89). The Makassarese word for the new craft was *gallé*, confirming the influence of the Portuguese then frequenting the city. The term for the fast fighting galleys of Maluku and the Philippines (*korakora*) appears to have derived ultimately from Arabic *kurkur*, while Acehnese *gurab* came directly from the Arabic. The Dutch reported that the war galleys of Banten were built in Lasem, a port near the best stands of Javanese

Fig. 31a Vietnamese galleys in the Red River, as drawn by Samuel Baron

Fig. 31b Two types of armed galley, according to a Dutch engraver about 1600. *At left,* a Madura warship with two decks of spearmen above the rowers; *at right,* the korakora of the King of Ternate, the rowers seated on the outrigger supports, equipped with drums, gongs, and seven small cannon.

teak, "on the instructions of the Turks in Banten" (Lodewycksz 1598: 132).

All these galleys carried small cannon. According to the Dutch, those of Banten carried four on the lower deck, the outriggered korakora of Maluku carried seven on a raised platform, while the large galleys of Madura were packed with up to two hundred men but had fewer oars and just two cannon (fig. 31b). Argensola (1708: 17) described the korakora of eastern waters as having one hundred rowers, six musketeers, and "four or five little brass guns." There were three men to each gun: "the one levels, the other charges, and the third fires it." After each volley these korakora quickly paddled away, returning when ready for the next round. The Filipino equivalent usually had between sixty and a hundred men on the paddles, though a few larger ones are mentioned (Scott 1982: 74–79).

In their replication of the *naga* (dragon) form, in their speed, and in their craftsmanship, these vessels always astonished Europeans. The elaborately decorated galleys of Siam were "the most beautiful there are in the world" (Choisy 1687: 243). Those of Maluku were built "in the style and make of a dragon; the prow at the front is like a dragon's head and the stern is like the tail of a dragon" ("Tweede Boeck" 1599: 58). A Dutch visitor to Makassar claimed that the galleys "are so large and smartly made, that all our carpenters who have been there affirm, that there are no masters in our country who would be able to make them" (van der Hagen 1607: 82). Many of these South Sulawesi vessels were probably made by specialist carpenters from Selayar and the Bira peninsula in the southeastern corner of South Sulawesi, for in the 1660s "these islanders do almost nothing else than make vessels, which they then sell again" (Speelman 1669 II: 24; cf. Stavorinus 1798 II: 260). One of their finest products must have been the elaborately carved royal galley of Tallo', coated in gold leaf and carrying 260 oarsmen, which looked like a "monstrous animal" glittering in the sea (Amin 1670: 116–17). Nearby Buton also made galleys "as beautiful as any in the Indies," and up to 40 metres in length (Coen I: 76; van den Broecke 1634 I: 62).

Aceh took the Mediterranean interest in ever larger galleys to its ultimate extension. Beaulieu (1666: 106) explained that Sultan Iskandar Muda was:

stronger than his neighbours by sea, having about a hundred huge galleys ... all ready; of which a third are without comparison bigger than any one of those they build in Christendom. I saw the keel of one, which was only of medium size, which was a hundred and twenty feet long, all of a piece. They make these galleys very capably, and they are beautiful structures, but they are too heavy, for they are too wide and too high . . . they put only two men on each oar, and they stand upright; the sheathing or planks of these galleys are six inches thick, so that being so heavy, it seems to me that one Christian galley would beat ten of these. They normally have three large cannons . . . along with several falconets which they place at the shoulder and waist [of the vessel]. They normally put six or eight hundred on these monsters.

A giant galley the Acehnese built to attack Melaka in 1629, "the Terror of the Universe," may have been the largest wooden vessel ever built.[3] The Portuguese who eventually captured it claimed it was a hundred metres in length and carried a hundred guns, including a magnificently worked one made of *tembaga* (brass)—"our eyes, although accustomed to being astonished with fine things, were all amazed by this sight" (cited Lombard 1967: 87).

Manguin (1993) has recently shown that there was a dramatic shift towards large fleets of war galleys in Southeast Asia around the middle of the sixteenth century, as a response to the aggressive naval tactics of the Portuguese. By 1600 not only Aceh but also Banten, Johor, Pahang, and Brunei could put a hundred or more armed galleys into battle. This trend, Manguin argues, contributed to the decline of the great trading junks that had previously ruled the seas. It also checked the naval challenge of the Portuguese and accentuated the power of the stronger rulers over their vassals. Yet these galleys proved no match for the Dutch and English warships, which took naval technology to new heights in the seventeenth century.

Diplomacy

> *Maharaja diraja [of Aru] sent an embassy to Pasai; the envoy was Raja Pahlawan. On arrival in Pasai, the letter was borne in procession and brought to the palace. It was duly received by the letter-reader, who then read it. What was written in the letter was "the younger brother presents his greetings [salam]." But what that man read out was, "the younger brother presents his obeisance [sembah] to his elder brother." Raja Pahlawan thereupon observed, "The letter says one thing, but a different thing is read out." . . . When the man again read the letter as before, Raja Pahlawan's anger passed all bounds and he ran amok, killing many of the Pasai men. So the men of Pasai killed Raja Pahlawan and all the men of Aru. Because of that Pasai was at war with Aru.*
>
> — Sejarah Melayu 1612: 145–46

3. Parker (1988: 87) nominates for this honour a Venetian quinquereme of 74 m constructed according to Greek notions in 1529.

Every Southeast Asian ruler was very well aware that he was one among many. Kings may have borrowed the rhetoric of world rulers from Indian epics and used grandiose titles and rituals which compared them more to gods than to other kings. Yet all were constantly in relations of trade, war, or diplomacy with their neighbours. Their chronicles acknowledged that it was a measure of a ruler's greatness that the harbour was full of foreign vessels and the court of foreign envoys.

In international as in domestic affairs the easiest relations were those of inequality. The languages themselves made it difficult to express relations of complete equality, especially between kings who had to be addressed with customary self-abasement.

One model that influenced Southeast Asian practice was that of the Chinese tribute system. All Southeast Asian states recognized that China was larger and stronger than themselves, and in the fifteenth century all were content to have letters of homage written in Chinese in their name. Rulers of some smaller states even travelled themselves to China to present their homage and receive enfeoffment from the emperor. Tribute was the only way to trade legally and safely with China, and it proved extremely lucrative to rulers as well as to those who arranged the missions. The language of tribute to a faraway emperor, expressed in an alien language, did not appear to trouble Southeast Asian rulers, if indeed they knew about it. Even their letters to the small state of Ryukyu, also written in Chinese, often included the same terms of self-abasement and "tribute" (Kobata and Matsuda 1969: 116–17, 141–42). Within the East Asian world of exchanges in written Chinese, trade was legitimate only as an aspect of the formal relations among rulers.

Within Southeast Asia there were replications of this kind of "tribute," often little more than an opportunity to trade at a larger port in return for a symbolic acceptance of its primacy. States in Borneo, South Sumatra, and the Lesser Sundas frequently offered such tribute to Java, while those in the Malayan Peninsula offered the "golden flowers" (bunga emas) of fealty to the court of Siam. In the 1680s even faraway Jambi (Sumatra) was sending the golden flowers to Siam with a "return gift" of pepper for the China trade, in response to the Siamese king's "gift" of saltpetre and sulphur (Pombejra 1990: 137). Only when a neighbouring state was conquered by force of arms did tribute become a one-way flow of goods and manpower to the capital.

In Southeast Asia and around the Indian Ocean there were increasingly extensive relations, which could only be conducted on the always problematic basis of equality. Although the best-documented embassies were the highly political ones, these must be seen against a routine background of trade missions facilitated by royal letters and representatives. As the King of Siam explained to his Ryukyuan counterpart in 1480: "It is praiseworthy that our two countries, from ancient times up to the present, have carried on trade, coming together and separating, and exchanging what we have for what we do not have. Envoys have been continually despatched and never cease to come" (Kobata and Matsuda 1969: 86). A Japanese resident of Cochin-China noted that that country's need for the military essentials, saltpetre and lead, was met by Siam, "from where an ambassador comes every year" (Fransisco 1642: 351). If Chinese emperors tolerated international trade only as an aspect of diplomacy, with Southeast Asian rulers it was inclined to be the other way around. Siam regularly exchanged ambassadors with Golconda and Bengal in India, "with letters full of praisings and compliments and also with small presents. This is done only to promote trade" (van Vliet 1636: 93).

Any distinctiveness in diplomatic protocol in Southeast Asia, as opposed to the Indian Ocean and Sinic spheres with which it interacted, lay in the quality of the royal letter. No matter who its nakhoda was, a visiting ship would have a warm welcome if it carried a royal letter, for it was this which partook of the sovereignty of kings.

An Ambassador throughout the East is no other than a King's messenger; he represents not his Master. They honour him little, in comparison of the respects which are rendered to the Letters of Credence whereof he is bearer. . . . Every one therefore who is the carrier of a letter from the King is reputed an Ambassador throughout the East. Wherefore, after the Ambassador of Persia, which Mr de Chaumont left in the country of Siam, was dead at Tenasserim, his Domesticks having elected one amongst them, to deliver the King of Persia's letter to the King of Siam, he that was elected was received without any other Character, as the real Ambassador would have been (La Loubère 1691: 108).

When a foreign ship arrived, the first question asked was whether it carried a royal letter. If it did, the letter was conveyed in the most honoured place in the procession to the palace. In the Malay world a royal letter was usually carried on the most magnificently arrayed elephant, and in the Mainland on the finest galley. In Laos a galley would carry the letter towards its reception not at the palace but at the impressive That Luang temple (Wusthoff 1669: 36–37). The envoys or nakhodas followed behind, and were honoured in their turn as bearers of the letter rather than as spokesmen for their king.

The Melaka chronicle explains a revealing exception to this rule, as the Melaka court pondered how to send a letter to its older but weaker rival Pasai without having the Pasai court deliberately misread greetings as homage. They decided they would send no letter, but instead a courtier who had memorized the royal message. When he reached Pasai, "the men sent to receive the letter said, 'Where is the letter? Let us take it in procession.' Then Orangkaya Tun Mohammad replied, 'I am the letter, take me in procession'" (*Sejarah Melayu* 1612: 179). This courtier then carefully recited his remembered speech, presenting greetings as from an older brother to a younger, and received in reply the customary royal letter.

Because the royal letter was one of the central aspects of sovereignty, it was worded and embellished with great care. In the Islamic states, borrowing some of the literary traditions of western Asia, the royal seal or the opening words would establish the ruler's relation with previous illustrious kings, sometimes including Alexander the Great. The preamble, often amounting to half the letter's length, established the grandeur of its sender—his vast domains, his beautiful capital, his numerous elephants, his golden regalia and other adornments (e.g., van Vliet 1636: 16–17; Shellabear 1898: 126–29). One of the few surviving royal letters from the age of commerce, that of Sultan Iskandar Muda of Aceh to James I of England, is about a meter in length and beautifully illustrated with floral designs.

European envoys wrote much of their elaborate reception at the more important courts, with the initial reception in the roads (fig. 32), a spectacular procession to the palace for a royal audience and reading of the letter, followed by presentation of honorific clothing, a feast, and entertainment of dancing and contests. Perhaps the most interesting description is the Malay dialogue between a questioner Daud and a local informant Ibrahim, written by Frederick de Houtman as an example of the language needed by merchants visiting Aceh.

D.   Who is it coming on this great elephant, who has such a crowd of people behind him?
I.   It is the Shahbandar with the *Penghulu kerkun* [secretary].
D.   I also see some foreign traders sitting up there. Who are they?
I.   That is a Gujarati nakhoda, who has just come with his ship, and whom they are going to take to salute the raja.
D.   What does it mean, that elephant caparisoned in red cloth, with those people in front of it playing on tamborines, trumpets, and flutes?
I.   The elephant you see and the man sitting in a palanquin upon it, means that a letter is being brought from their raja to our lord. . . .
D.   Who is seated up there?
I.   It is one of the sultan's orangkaya that he has chosen for that.
D.   And what is all that for?
I.   To honour the raja whose letter it is.

Fig. 32 A Danish ship and envoys being greeted in the roads of Banten in 1673. The two vessels flanking the Danish ship are carrying important Bantenese officials, as indicated by the umbrellas. The tallest building on shore represents the great mosque.

D.   And what is that I see, so many men and slaves, each bringing a painted cloth in his hands?
I.   These are the presents which the nakhoda will offer to the king.
D.   Is that the tariff he must pay for his goods, or must he pay another tariff?
I.   No, the tariff is extra, 7 percent.
D.   What honour will the raja give them in return?
I.   Indeed, when they enter the raja's palace, they will be given great honour.
D.   What happens there?
I.   There they eat and drink, all sorts of food and fruits are brought, they play, dance, with all sorts of entertainments, they play on the trumpet, flute, clarinet, and *rebab*, and then the king asks for a garment of our local style to be brought, which he gives to the nakhoda (de Houtman 1603: 17–20).

The nakhoda would then be dressed in "a red silk jacket, a coloured headcloth with gold embroidery, a yellow sarung embroidered with gold, a belt with Arabic letters in gold, a kris with its guard in gold encrusted with precious stones and its hilt of black coral," and entertained with elephant and buffalo fights before being sent back to his ship on an elephant (ibid.: 30–31). Exactly this treatment was given to such European envoys as James Lancaster (1603: 90–96) and Thomas Best (1614: 52–54).

As the seventeenth century increased the level of commerce but reduced the number of diplomatic players to a few stronger states, these all established relations with one another. By mid-century the principal trading states—Ayutthaya, Aceh, Banten, and Makassar—were all in diplomatic contact with one another, as well as with Golconda in India, the Spanish in Manila, and the Portuguese, English, and Dutch. In the Mainland the two Vietnamese states and Siam kept up constant contact with Cambodia and Laos in an attempt to manipulate these states against their more dangerous rivals.

All these diplomatic relations were unstable. The states that gave rise to them were themselves struggling to find their place in an extremely dangerous world. There were long-term and relatively stable tributary relations, such as those with China, but the relations of presumed equality were always being pushed to crisis by the need of each ruler to use foreign contacts to enhance his own status. Royal marriages were particularly sensitive. All kings sought to take wives or concubines from the daughters of tributary rulers. This served at once to manifest the potency of the king and to maintain the loyalty of the vassal. Yet to yield his own daughter in marriage to another king (let alone anybody else) always risked the danger that she might be mistreated or made something less than principal queen, in either case humiliating her royal father.

Negotiations between kings often began with a pragmatic need for trade or military cooperation but ended with a request for a royal daughter. The great king of Laos, Surinyavongsa, had reportedly secured a daughter of the "king" (presumably the Trinh lord) of Tongking around 1640, as the price of his cooperation (Wusthoff 1669: 90). When the Dutch were in the Vietnamese capital in 1659, Lao ambassadors were seeking another royal daughter for their king—presumably from the new Trinh ruler Trinh Tac (Maetsuyker 1660: 308). Such requests could be met by daughters of secondary wives. When the Goa (Makassar) and Mataram courts began to exchange missions to try to coordinate strategy against the Dutch, Mataram soon asked for "one or two" daughters of Sultan Hasanuddin in marriage (Andaya 1981: 48; cf. Ricklefs 1981: 69). Rulers did not like to surrender the daughter of their principal wife, however, except on terms that made the husband a virtual hostage at the wife's court—like the prince of subjugated Pahang who remained at the Aceh court and married Iskandar Muda's daughter (cf. van Vliet 1636: 32 on Burma).

The relations between Siam and Aceh were among the most stable of those between equal powers, as their ambitions on the Malayan Peninsula seldom conflicted. "They never have been a vassal or tributary to each other. To maintain the friendship they often sent to each other their ambassadors with letters full of exaggerated titles and compliments and with presents" (van Vliet 1636: 43; cf. Best 1614: 53). According to the Dutch factor in Siam, the relationship was poisoned when a Siamese ambassador irresponsibly encouraged Sultan Iskandar Muda's hopes for a daughter of the Siamese King Songtham. King Prasat Thong (1629–56) nevertheless renewed the alliance, and the exchange of splendid gifts and letters "engraved on gold" recommenced. But when in 1636 the Sultan of Aceh had his envoys revive the issue of marriage with a Thai princess, the alliance was again thrown into question. The Aceh envoys were imprisoned, according to this source, though a French version of the story had them murdered after a dispute over some women in their party (van Vliet 1636: 43–46; Choisy 1687: 222). Nevertheless, the next Siamese king, Narai, was not long on the throne before the Acehnese again sent an embassy to renew the old ties (Maetsuyker 1662: 421).

Sultan Iskandar Muda encountered other setbacks in his quest for exotic wives. Thomas Best was warmly received in Aceh in 1613, and when leaving he was asked by the sultan to request that the King of England send him two English women. "If I beget one of them with child, and it prove a son, I will make him king of Priaman, Passaman, and of the coast from whence you fetch your pepper, so that you shall not need to come any more to me, but to your own English king for these commodities" (Copland 1614: 213). When this became known in London, a "respectable gentleman" appeared before an East India Company committee to offer his daughter for the role. The company declined to proceed. European women were few below the winds, and the only one known to have entered a royal harem was in Makassar.[4] One of Sultan Alau'd-din's forty wives was a local Portuguese Eurasian. Her son by the ruler, Francisco Mendes, became an invaluable, bilingual, "Portuguese secretary" and cultural broker for the Makassar court in the 1640s and 1650s (Boxer 1967: 17).

In the course of the seventeenth century European patterns of diplomacy became familiar to the major trading states below the winds, if not always accepted. Tavernier (1692 II: 505–06) tells of the Aceh ambassador to Dutch Batavia who was astonished at being asked to eat and drink with Dutch women as well as men, and even at being greeted with an embrace by the governor-general's wife. The Aceh court responded by having the next Dutch envoy embraced in turn by an Acehnese woman. The dignity Europeans demanded for their ambassadors as personal representatives of the king gradually raised their status. When James Lancaster (1603: 91) insisted on giving his letter from Queen Elizabeth personally to the Acehnese sultan rather than to a courtier who would read it, this was allowed. Islamic political theory would also have legitimated the trend. The principal Malay-language guide to Islamic statecraft, the *Taj us-Salatin*, viewed envoys as emanations of royal power (Bukhari 1603: 141–45).

The Portuguese and Spanish occasionally took Asians to Europe, but as exotic tributaries and Christian neophytes, not as representatives of equal sovereigns. The Dutch, at pains to puncture Iberian pretensions to universal authority, began with some enthusiasm to take Southeast Asian representatives back to witness the marvels of the Netherlands. Two Zeeland ships that visited Aceh in 1601 found the sultan exceptionally welcoming because of a recent brush with the Portuguese. He trusted them to take two envoys of Aceh back with them to Holland. The elder of these, seventy-one-year-old Abdul Samat, died soon after his arrival in Middelburg and was buried with much pomp in the Sint-Pieterskerk there, with a tombstone bearing a

4. It is possible that the Portuguese Doña Francisca Sardinha, "one of the most beautiful women of her time," was delivered to the ruler of Minangkabau after being kidnapped during an attack on her shipwrecked compatriots on the west Sumatran coast in 1561 (Dias 1565: 101–02; Couto 1645 VII, ix: 424–25).

Latin inscription. Prince Maurits then asked that the remaining envoy, Sri Muhammad, be brought to an audience with him "with no less dignity than his own person demanded". On 4 September 1603 the envoy solemnly conveyed to the prince two letters written in Portuguese, an ornate kris, and a golden dish containing Sumatran camphor (Wap 1862: 16–29; Veth 1873: 71). Sri Muhammad was sent back to Aceh with gifts in exchange. Though he was subsequently important enough at court to be asked by the sultan to attend Thomas Best (1614: 54), this voyage to a distant country was probably not regarded as a full embassy by the Aceh ruler, and the two envoys can not have been of high status. The equivalent first representative of Banten in Holland turned out to be a China-born slave (*True Report* 1599: 36–37).

Siam was quick to hear about the Aceh envoy, as well as another arranged by the Dutch from Johor. In 1605 the new Siamese king began plans to send full-scale missions both to Portuguese Goa and to Holland, to try to learn the truth about the allegations these two powers were making about each other. The chief envoy, interviewed by the English in Banten, was indignant at the suggestion that the Siamese king wanted to discuss matters of trade—"their king was a great king and needed nothing the Hollanders had . . . ; they go into Holland to see their country, their buildings, towns, and ships, and if they require anything it shall be shipwrights, carpenters, and other handicraftsmen" (*LREIC* I: 7–8). Ayutthaya was not as important a port as it later became, and neither embassy was received with much enthusiasm. The Dutch refused to transport all fifteen members of the mission who arrived at their lodge in Banten. In the end five of them were shipped from Banten in January 1608 and duly received by Prince Maurits the following September (Smith 1974: 68–70).

When Coen took over the VOC's affairs in the East in 1619, he discouraged Southeast Asian rulers from equating themselves with the Stadhouder. The governor-general in Batavia conducted all future Dutch relations with Asian states, to the annoyance of several proud monarchs. The ruler of Makassar, for example, declared that "he would be glad to make peace with Prince Maurits as his brother, but not with the General in Batavia who was only an overseer of merchants" (*Dagh-Register* 1624–29: 80). The two grandest embassies from Southeast Asia, from Banten and Ayutthaya in the 1680s, were sent to England and France, respectively, to seek support against the Dutch.

The young Sultan Haji of Banten was under great pressure from the VOC when he decided to send an embassy to London to seek military supplies and support, against the advice of the English factors, who feared the expense and the possible diplomatic complications. Nevertheless, these two envoys and their twenty-nine retainers were lionized by an East India Company alarmed at Dutch advances and by a sensation-seeking London public. They spent more than three months of 1682 in London at company expense, visiting all the major sights, enjoying the theatre and various musical entertainments, and witnessing technical improvements in printing and warfare. The envoys, Kiai Ngabehi Naya Wipraya and Kiai Ngabehi Jaya Sedana (who had been to Mecca, and also spoke passable English), were entertained by many of the leading men of the city, including the Duke of York, while Charles II not only received them lavishly at Windsor on 13 May but knighted them as Sir Abdul and Sir Ahmad before their departure in July (fig. 33). Sadly, their country was being conquered by Dutch troops in alliance with the unpopular young sultan at the very time of their diplomatic triumph in London, and the letters and gunpowder from Charles II never reached their destination (Foster 1926: 99–112; Jones 1982).

King Narai of Siam conducted an extensive diplomacy, to Golconda and Persia as well as to closer states. His interest in France was aroused by the French missionaries established in Ayutthaya from 1662. Whereas the other European powers increasingly left Asian contacts to their local representatives, the French missionaries were repeatedly able to bring letters from their patron Louis XIV, the first in 1673. Narai sent a mission to Versailles in 1680, which was aborted by shipwreck. In 1684 he sent another mission in an English ship and accompanied by the French missionary Vachet, to learn about France and to request a French embassy to conclude a formal alliance. These envoys dined with Louis XIV at Versailles and with his brother at Saint-Cloud, making a great impression with their exotic dress.

As the able Catholic Constance Phaulkon rose in favour with the Siamese king, the missionaries persuaded Louis XIV that Narai himself might convert if the correct approach was made. The French embassy of 1685 was large and impressive, and led to a commercial and military treaty (fig. 34). The third Siamese mission, in 1686–87, accompanied Ambassador de Chaumont of France on his return home. Since a good reception in France was now assured, three senior officials were sent and lavishly received at Versailles in September 1686 (figs. 35a, 35b). After seven busy months in France, including a tour of Flanders and performances of two Molière plays and two operas by Lully, they travelled home with yet another French embassy. This one, led by Simon de la Loubère in 1687–88, carried twelve Jesuit scholars

His Excellency Kaia Nebbe Nia Nia prupa. Ambass.ʳ Extraordinary from ÿ Sultan of **BANTAM**. To his Majesty of Great Brittain: in the Yeare 1682.

R White sculp.

Sold by R White in Bloomsbury Market.

Fig. 33 Two envoys from Banten to England in 1682, both of equal status despite the rendering here. *Above*, Kiai Ngabehi Naya Wipraya, and *below*, Kiai Wijaya Sedana, who had made the pilgrimage to Mecca.

Fig. 34 King Narai receiving the letter of Louis XIV from Ambassador de Chaumont, who is accompanied by de Choisy and the French bishop to the East, 1686. It was a major change of protocol to allow the ambassador to approach the king in person.

and marked the high point of European scientific cooperation with Southeast Asia, albeit with missionary motives. It also, however, carried several hundred well-equipped soldiers, who contributed much to the justifiable suspicion of French motives that abruptly ended the alliance and caused the fall of Phaulkon and Narai in June 1688 (Choisy 1687; Tachard 1688; de Bèze 1691; Turpin 1771: 41–52; Anderson 1891: 224–52; Smithies 1989).

Squeezing the Lemon

> It was . . . the liberty of commerce which had formerly invited to Siam a great multitude of strangers of different nations; who settled there with the liberty of living according to their customs. . . . But the richest foreigners, and especially the Moors, are retired elsewhere, since the King of Siam has reserved to himself alone almost all the foreign commerce. . . . Commerce requires a certain liberty.
> —La Loubère 1691: 112

Complaints from traders about the exclusive demands of rulers did not begin in the seventeenth century. The first surviving Ryukyuan letter to Siam, from 1425, is a polite complaint that the previous ship's porcelains had to be sold on royal terms, that the Ryukyuan envoys had not been permitted to buy sappanwood on the open market, and that excessive presents had been demanded. "It is enough of a difficulty to go through winds and waves" without such impositions, the king of Ryukyu complained, and the 1424 voyage had therefore been cancelled (Kobata and Matsuda 1969: 55–56).

Although rulers occasionally expressed their disdain for commerce, especially in Vietnam, where this was part of Confucian convention, they were both dependent on it and directly involved in it. The pomp with which they received envoys from a distant king clothed with splendour the mercantile pragmatism through which they took their slice of the trade cake and bargained over its size. This process, they knew, was central to their well-being and power. The tension was constant between the ruler's need to attract the life-giving trade to his port by fairness and relative freedom, and his need to extract from it the profit required for his administration (at best), his wars, his pageantry, his patronage, and his self-indulgence.

Economic change was so rapid in the age of commerce that conventions strong enough to override the whims of monarchs or the muscle of the most powerful foreigners could not be established. Traders descended on the region with disconcerting irregularity—the Chi-

Fig. 35a Luang Kalya Ratchamaitri, one of the Siamese ambassadors to France in 1688.

nese in the early fifteenth century and again in the late sixteenth, the Portuguese in the early sixteenth century, and the northern Europeans and Japanese in the early seventeenth. Each injection changed the ground rules as new ports cut different deals to the advantage of the new traders. The commerce of particular ports grew rapidly at periods

Fig. 35b Reception of Siamese envoys by Louis XIV at Versailles in 1686

when they allowed relative freedom of trade, either as a deliberate ploy against their rivals (Melaka in the early fifteenth century and Makassar in the early seventeenth) or because the crown was too weak to impose its demands over the interests of the trading class (Patani and Banten in the early seventeenth century). Strong kings almost invariably squeezed the merchants and drove many of them away.

At times, certainly, this tension produced agreed rules for the conduct of trade, moving in the direction of security of property and predictability of legal decisions in commercial matters. The most promising conditions for such progress appeared to be after a period of strong personal rule, when a less secure king and a vigorous commercial class agreed to write down what they understood to be the tradition of the reign just passed. This was the atmosphere in which the

Melaka legal codes were drawn up in the reign of Sultan Mahmud (1488–1511)[5] and when the *Adat Aceh* was codified under Aceh's first queen (building on an initial codification at the beginning of Iskandar Muda's absolutist reign—Ito 1984: 8). Such codes were copied and elaborated during subsequent reigns, and their potential for providing the conditions for sustained economic growth should not be over-looked. Nevertheless, the set of conditions that enabled merchants in the cities of northern Europe to establish property rights and predict-able procedures obtained only briefly and partially in some Southeast Asian states.

Evidence for radical increases in the extent of royal monopolies comes largely from the seventeenth century, especially the period 1620–80. In these years states had to become stronger or go under. European traders, and especially the big Dutch and English compa-nies, preferred to do business quickly in large amounts, and if they could not do so to their satisfaction with a strong ruler they would try to undercut him by going to a local chief. From the time of Coen the VOC extended its monopoly of critical trade items to every port that was not strong enough to resist. A mid-century drop in the prices offered for Southeast Asian exports added to the pressure, forcing rulers to squeeze the producers and dealers to maintain state revenues.

The export of key products of the country, especially minerals, had been monopolized by rulers and a key to their wealth long before the age of commerce. In Burma the sale of "amber, gems, gold, [aro-matic] gums and iron" was a royal monopoly (Than Tun 1983: 9); in Siam "sappanwood, tin, lead and saltpeter, which are the principal products of the country, may be sold to foreigners only from his Maj-esty's warehouse" (van Vliet 1636: 26–27). Monopolies on imports were less traditional. It has been argued for Siam that this pattern began with the ban, attributed to the reign of Chakkrapat (1548–69), on anyone except the king buying imported firearms (Ouansakul 1976). The other common items of royal import monopoly were the silver, copper, or cowries used to provide currency.

In Siam, as elsewhere, the king became much further involved in shipping on a large scale in the mid-seventeenth century. From about 1624 royal ships began to compete on the lucrative Coromandel-Mergui run (Subrahmanyam 1990: 215). Van Vliet (1636: 90, 93) laid

5. Stamford Raffles (1837 I: 101) rightly concluded that the Malay rulers' constant attempts at trade monopoly could find no basis in these laws. He was mistaken, however, in concluding that "this pernicious practice has been entirely copied from the monopoly regulations of the Dutch."

most of the blame for the manipulation of the market on the fierce usurper King Prasat Thong (1629–56), under whom "the trade has suffered much by monopolies and other hindrances. . . . As the present king preferred to force the market by his factors . . . and further lays taxes upon them and does not pay market prices, nobody comes to Siam unless compelled to do so." The foreign traders themselves, however, were the principal authors of this undoubted trend. The Dutch East India Company pressed for monopoly contracts with the king wherever possible, including the supply of deerskins from the 1630s and Ligor (Nakhon Sithammarat) tin in 1671 (Pombejra 1984: 39). Chinese, Muslims, and English were eager to man the king's ships, enabling him to compete on favoured terms.

In the reign of King Narai the system of royal trade reached unprecedented heights. Narai restored relations with Japan, which had been ruptured by Prasat Thong, and thereafter ensured that his own junks, manned by Chinese, played the dominant role in that lucrative branch of trade (Innes 1980: 176; Smith 1974: 121). Indian Muslims manned most of his shipping to India until the 1680s, when Europeans were introduced under Phaulkon's patronage. Narai used his advantageous position as a supplier of the European merchants to corner the imports of cloth:

He has carried it to such a degree, that Merchandize is now no more the Trade of particular persons at Siam. He is not contented with selling by Wholesale, he has some shops in the Bazars or Markets, to sell by Retail. The principal thing that he sells to his subjects is Cotton-cloth: he sends them into his Magazines in the Provinces. Heretofore his predecessors and he sent them thither only every ten years, and a moderate quantity, which being sold, particular persons had liberty to make commerce thereof; now he continually furnishes them, he has in his magazines more than he can possibly sell, and it sometimes happens that to vend more . . . he has forced his Subjects to clothe the children before the accustomed age. Before the Hollanders came in the Kingdom of Laos, and into others adjacent, the King of Siam did there make the whole Commerce of Linnen with a considerable profit (La Loubère 1691: 94).

Banten followed a similar pattern. The city was close to being a free market when the Dutch and English first arrived, during the long minority of Sultan Abdul Kadir (1596–c.1624). At the height of Banten's conflict with the ruthless Dutch Governor-General Coen over control of the pepper supplies, however, the regent in 1619 pushed through a policy mandating that foreigners could purchase pepper only through the Banten court (Meilink-Roelofsz 1962: 254). Under Banten's most successful ruler, Sultan Abdulfatah Ageng (1651–82), all the pepper grown in Lampung was delivered to the sultan through a system of forced cultivation administered by the Banten nobility. A rigid royal monopoly was imposed on its sale to foreigners, partly as a weapon in the continuing struggle with the Dutch in Batavia (Kathirithamby-Wells 1990: 115–17). The sultan gradually developed his own fleet of Western-rigged and Chinese vessels, often skippered by foreigners, to trade with ports as distant as Manila, China, Japan, Siam, Coromandel, Surat, and Mocha. Such a concerted campaign may have been Banten's only chance to compete successfully with its formidably organized neighbour in Batavia, which viewed its success as a major threat (de Jonge 1862–88 VI: lxvii–lxviii, 124).

In Aceh, Sultan Iskandar Muda (1607–36) was adept at manipulating the Dutch and English to make monopoly arrangements in which the principal losers were the Acehnese and Gujarati local traders. About 1612 he banned the established Gujarati pepper-buyers from the west coast pepper-producing areas (*LREIC* II: 270; III: 123–24). Both the Dutch and the English were at different times promised a monopoly of the trade of these regions on the sultan's terms, but in the end his own factors and ships dominated the supply. Already in 1615 the English learned that "the King hath engrossed all the pepper into his hands . . . and the Protector and the Shabandar are his merchants" (*LREIC* III: 103). In 1622 he outraged the Dutch by forbidding anyone to sell pepper to the Europeans on pain of death until he had sold his own pepper at the exorbitant price of 25 reals per bahar (Coen 1622: 695). Both Dutch and English were effectively shut out after 1622, the king having sufficiently strengthened his hand to do as he wished with the market. In the 1630s, in common with the rulers of Arakan and Ayutthaya, Iskandar Muda was sending a "great ship" to Coromandel every year, making a great dent in the trade of both the VOC and the Persians of Masulipatnam, who had previously dominated this sector (Subrahmanyam 1990: 335; and see table 5, above).

The same trend appears to have affected most pepper-growing states in the second half of the seventeenth century, as lower prices and Dutch monopoly pressure made it more difficult for rulers to maintain their profits. Jambi and Palembang imitated the practice of Banten in Lampung, appointing royal commercial agents (*jenang*) to exchange cloth and salt for pepper at below-market prices (Andaya 1989: 39). Banjarmasin's ruler began in the 1660s to force growers to sell to his agents at low prices in order to fulfil his contract with the VOC and still make a profit (Coolhaas 1968: 422, 455). During the last decades of the century Sultan Barahaman introduced to Magindanao the practice of monopolizing the supply of export products to foreign ships (Laarhoven 1990: 176).

Even Makassar, the freest of seventeenth-century ports, began to annoy the foreign merchants in the 1650s by giving special advantages to royal ships and trade. The English complained that, "These kings [of Goa and Tallo'] are become unreasonable merchants, for they would have goods at their own prices," and two years later, "the kings, by their avarice in business, are degenerating from their ancestors" (Macassar Factory 1658, 1660). Sultan Hasanuddin (1653–69) was certainly less judicious a statesman than his great predecessors, but the late seventeenth century was a very dangerous time for rulers unless they imitated some of the methods of the relentless VOC.

Absolutism and Its Rivals

> He [King Naresuan] always said, "This is the way you Siamese must be ruled because you are obstinate people of abominable nature and in a rotten state. But I shall do these things to you until I make you a respected nation. You are the grass of the fertile field: the shorter you are mowed, the more beautifully you grow. I will have gold strewn in the streets and let it lie there for months. Whoever looks at this gold with greed will die."
>
> —van Vliet 1640: 83

The powerful rulers of the age of commerce appeared absolute both in theory and in practice. They proclaimed supernatural status in their titles and rituals; they claimed the right to dispose of the land and the wealth of their subjects; and numerous accounts testify to the arbitrary killing and dispossession of vassals who got in their way. Such absolutism found theoretical justification in long-standing Southeast Asian adaptations of Indian ideas of the supernatural king, and there were always foreigners (Brahmans, peripatetic ulama, European adventurers) ready to help ambitious kings give substance to such ideas. But it must be remembered that absolutism had to deal with an underlay not of feudalism, still less constitutionalism, but of autonomous lineages, tribes, and entrepreneurs not yet incorporated into state structures.

The state-creating kings could evoke earlier local models of sublime kingship—the Tai states borrowing ideas from Angkor, the Mon and Burman ones from Pagan, the Malay from Sri Vijaya, and the Javanese-Balinese from Majapahit—even if the reality of these classic states, especially the last two, was far from centralized. Yet the immediate background of all the state-building of the age of commerce (except in northern Vietnam) was intense local autonomy on the one hand and a great diversity of wealthy foreign traders on the other. Although conquest played a role in the rise of each state, there was usually also an element of voluntary but conditional federation between a port and its hinterland areas, or between rivals seeing the need to cooperate against an outside threat. There was always, therefore, great tension between the sublime rhetoric of absolutism and the reality of autonomy, diversity, and contractualism.

Examples of this diversity are easy to find throughout the Islands and, on the basis of much later evidence, in the highlands of the Mainland. In fifteenth-century Melaka, the Portuguese portrayed a situation where royal authority sat lightly upon a population predominately born elsewhere. Even the royal chronicle, more concerned with the elite Malay population and its values, embodies a remarkable social contract between the first ruler and his subjects, as represented by the prototype of the Bendahara lineage. The latter is made to declare that "my descendants are prepared to be the subjects of Your Majesty's throne; they [in turn] must be well treated by your descendants" (*Sejarah Melayu* 1612: 57). While subjects are exhorted to be loyal to the ruler, rulers in turn are warned through the testaments of their dying predecessors about the limits to their power:

You my sons, do not covet the property of others nor lust after the wives of your subjects . . . .
My sons, do not take what belongs to anybody improperly, for the servants of God are all entrusted to you. . . . As for the Malays, however great their offence, do not simply have them killed unless this is prescribed by the law of God (ibid.: 74, 79, 150).

Even more striking is the approval the chronicle gives to Tun Perak, who when questioned by the ruler about some complaint in the Klang Region, which he administered, replied that local government was no business of the ruler, who must either trust him or dismiss him (ibid.: 95).

The state which was in process of formation in the Manila area at the Spanish arrival was still effectively a federation, so that Raja Suleiman could tell Legazpi (when it suited him), "As you already know, there is no king and no sole authority in this land; but everyone holds his own view and opinion, and does as he prefers" (Riquel 1573: 235). Bugis and Makassarese rituals of enthronement reflected an exceptionally well developed concept of federalism, whereby the head of each lineage which had formed the state reiterated its autonomy: "I seek protection from you [the king], but I will conduct my own affairs, I will preserve my manners, I will maintain my custom; only if I need it will I appeal to your advice" (quoted Pelras 1971: 173–74). Even the strongest concentration of authority made possible by the age of commerce in South Sulawesi, the Goa-Tallo' union at the nucleus of the Makassar kingdom, coordinated a range of contractual autonomies that baffled the Europeans who had to cope with it. The Dutch conqueror of Makassar, Cornelis Speelman (1670 III: 117), commented that "The kings of Tallo' and Goa cannot make one false step once outside their own gates." Almost everywhere in the Archipelago, even in Java (except in the reign of Sultan Agung), the Dutch and British were frustrated by the difficulty of finding monarchs who could make decisions binding on their subjects.

The conciliar principle was well established at some port-states the Dutch visited around 1600. At Banten (then under its regency), at Banda, and in Ternate they found that no important commercial or political decision could be made without an assembly of many notables, each having a say (figs. 36a, 36b). A form of oligarchy was institutionalized in eighteenth-century Sulu, long after the high tide of absolutism had retreated. As Forrest (1779: 326) described it, government was in the hands of a council of the sultan and fifteen datu. "The Sultan has two votes in this assembly, and each datoo has one. The heir apparent [raja muda] . . . if he side with the Sultan has two votes; but if against him, only one. There are two representatives of the people, called Manteries, like the military tribunes of the Romans."

The centralizing rulers, armed with new sources of revenue, with new weaponry, and with foreign assistance and example, made drastic changes to this pattern. Siam and Aceh, different regimes in many respects, adapted a similar policy of cutting down the indigenous nobility in the early seventeenth century. According to Simon de la Loubère (1691: 42), Siam previously had a magnificent court attended by "a great number of lords adorned with rich stuffs, and a great many precious stones, and always attended with 100 or 200 slaves and with a considerable number of elephants." He believed that Prasat Thong (1629–56) destroyed this nobility, though earlier sources show that the process began with Naresuan (1590–1605), the great warrior who restored Thai fortunes after the Burmese invasions. Van Vliet (1640: 82–83) portrays Naresuan resisting the nobles' attempts to put him on the throne until they had agreed to obey him in everything. Once enthroned, "his reign was the most militant and severe of any which was ever known in Siam. Many stories and living eye-witnesses report that

Fig. 36a Dutch impression of a meeting of the state council of Banten in 1596

in the twenty years of his rule he killed and had killed by law more than 80,000 people, excluding those who were victims of war. . . . He was the first to make the mandarins come creeping before the king and lie continually with their faces downward, a practice which is still in existence today" (ibid.: 83; see fig. 34, above). He favoured foreigners, wanting to speak to them directly without interpreters and freeing them from all the servility imposed on his own people. "The foreigners at this time were treated with such respect that the officers brought them gifts so that the foreigners would not bring any complaints against them. The mandarins lived in great fear of His Majesty. When they were summoned, they put their homes in order as if they were going to their deaths, for they were always full of dread that they would not return" (ibid.: 84).

The two succeeding kings appear to have continued a policy of favouring foreigners and keeping the indigenous nobility on a tight

Fig. 36b Dutch Vice-Admiral van Neck negotiating with the principal men of Banda, about 1600. The seated figures A and B are the Governor of Ternate and the sultan's brother, while the figures squatting in foreground are orangkaya.

reign. Ekathotsarot (1605–10) was thought to have inaugurated the practice of claiming one third of the estate of every official who died (ibid.: 88; Smith 1974: 71–72). But Prasat Thong took this pressure to new heights:

He was the first who made the mandarins so slavish that they come to court every single day and are . . . not permitted to speak to one another except in a public meeting place . . . this king wants everything. If a mandarin dies, his wives and children are taken into custody. One mandarin will often spy on another in order to discover whether anything is being concealed. Widows and orphans show great gratitude whenever the king extends to them a small section of their properties. It appears that His Majesty cannot consider himself rich until he has gathered all the treasures into his own treasury and has had everything squeezed out of the community (van Vliet 1640: 96).

One of the wealthiest merchants in Ayutthaya, the Muslim Radi Ibrahim, was executed in 1639 on this king's command, and his estate immediately put under royal control (Smith 1974: 109).

This process appears to have reached its height under King Narai, who skilfully used foreigners to advance his commercial interests and kept the nobility under extreme control. One suspect Dutch source claims that he conducted a massive purge of hundreds of his nobility, on the pretext that they were involved in a plot to poison his daughter (Glanius 1682: 136–42).[6] His control over the upper class in the 1680s impressed even French missionaries familiar with the absolutism of Louis XIV: "All the officials can be made destitute at the pleasure of the prince who established them, he deposes them as he pleases; . . . in the distribution of responsibilities they pay most attention to the merits, the experience and the services that one has given, and not to birth; which ensures that everyone applies himself to earning the favour of the Prince" (Bourges 1666: 158–59; cf. Ibrahim 1688: 149).

In Aceh a contemporary of Naresuan, Sultan Alau'd-din Ri'ayat Syah al-Mukammil (1589–1604), carried out a royalist coup against the aristocracy. This ended a period of pluralism and instability in Aceh, in which there had been five kings in ten years, four of them dying violently. During this era, according to Beaulieu (1666: 112): "The orangkayas had beautiful, large solid houses, with cannons at their doors, and a large number of slaves, both as guards and servants. They went out superbly dressed, with large retinues, respected by the people. Such great power very much diminished royal authority." Al-Mukammil, like Naresuan, had been a war-leader under his predecessor. According to Davis (1600: 148), "He ended the lives of more than a thousand Noblemen and Gentlemen, and of the rascall people made new Lords and new Lawes." Forty years after the events, Beaulieu (1666: 112) provided a graphic account of how this massacre was carried out at a feast after his accession. The new ruling class was under much tighter control. If there had been fortified aristocratic compounds in the previous period, as Beaulieu asserted (and as there certainly were in Banten), these disappeared under al-Mukammil: "He doesn't allow anyone to have substantial means; when he is told that someone has something good, he takes it from him; and he finds some pretext for doing this; has it said of him that he has committed some crime, has his hand cut off and himself banished to the islands of Pulau We or Gamispola. . . . The king does not allow anyone to build in stone,

6. The book by the pseudonymous Dutch traveller Glanius appeared in London to exploit the public interest occasioned by the embassy from Banten, though it included no first-hand information on that sultanate. Its most interesting material concerns the Dutch post in Siam and the Genoese expedition to Sumatra, though postdating the Genoese expedition by twenty years to 1669. The resemblance to the account of Jan Struijs, published in Amsterdam in 1686, is great, on which see Subrahmanyam 1990: 286–92.

for fear that they fortify themselves against him" (Martin 1604: 39, 53). Al-Mukammil also resembled his Thai contemporary in that he befriended the English and Dutch, who now appeared, at the expense of Islamic merchants who might have represented a threat (Beaulieu 1666: 113; Warwijck 1604: 14).

Al-Mukammil's powerful grandson Iskandar Muda (1607–36), carried this centralizing policy to new heights, with far greater resources. About his reign, Beaulieu (1663: 63) spoke at first-hand: "He has exterminated almost all the ancient nobility, and has created new ones." Evidence from surviving land grants indicates that Iskandar Muda divided Aceh into *mukim* (Islamic parishes) with grants of land to his war leaders, or *uleebalang* (Ito and Reid 1985: 201–04). Members of this new elite, responsible for raising armies from their territories when required, were made to keep watch, unarmed, in the palace every third night in rotation, as hostages in the event of any conspiracy against the sultan.[7] The inner palace was restricted to women, many of them armed, while the capital was kept under control by a professional praetorian guard composed of foreign slaves, trained in war since their youth in the manner of janisseries (Beaulieu 1666: 103). From 1621 the pepper-producing dependencies of west Sumatra were controlled by the appointment of governors (*panglima*), called to the capital to account for their actions every year and replaced every three (ibid.: 44; Kathirithamby-Wells 1969: 460–61).

Foreign accounts give a picture of a population kept in subjection by a reign of terror. Early in his reign he was reputed to take any woman he chose into his harem, and if the husband objected "then he presently commands her husband's prick to be cut off" (Croft 1613: 176). His depredations among the wealthier class became ever heavier, with numerous orangkaya put to death and their property confiscated: "He draws great profit from those he daily puts to death; ... two causes in particular cost various orangkayas their life; viz. the good reputation they have among the people, and secondly their wealth. ... He has depopulated the whole territory of Aceh and drained everybody of their money, even all the foreigners who have been there" (Beaulieu

7. The *Hikayat Patani* (188) has an interesting story of an attempt to spread this absolutist technique to Patani, noted for the conciliar style of government of the queens. The Acehnese camp-followers of the prince of Johor, brother-in-law of the Patani queen, convinced him that Iskandar Muda's system of controlling the orangkaya, whereby "all the ministers' and officers' wives used to enter the palace in turn to perform guard duty, while their husbands performed guard duty at the audience hall," should be adopted in Patani. The prince and his Acehnese were, however, driven out of the city by the Patani establishment.

1666: 109, 114). Even several decades after his death, the leading men of Aceh remembered Iskandar Muda as "the cruelest tyrant that many ages afforded" (Bowrey 1680: 296).

There were also winners from his policy of ferocious control of the elite. Acehnese tradition makes Iskandar Muda the father of the law, and there is no doubt that law was upheld in his day by a system of four distinct courts—a criminal court, a religious court, a court for settling debts, and another for enforcing commercial laws (*Adat Aceh:* 17; Beaulieu 1666: 31; Ito 1984: 155–67). Subsequent generations have forgotten his cruelties and remember him as the glory of Aceh. His own defence of absolutism, in a speech he made to Beaulieu (1666: 62), is perhaps his best testament:

He said his orangkayas were wicked and cruel, and failed to realise that it was their own wickedness which drew upon them the wrath of God, who made use of him to punish them; that they had no occasion to complain of him, since he had let them live with their wives, children, slaves and sufficient wealth to nourish and sustain themselves, maintaining them in their religion, and preventing neighbouring kings from taking them as slaves from their homes, or foreigners from robbing them; that he had known Aceh formerly as a haven for murderers and brigands, where the stronger trampled on the weak; where one had to defend oneself against armed robbers in broad daylight, and to barricade one's house at night; that the reason they hated him was that he prevented their wickedness, extortion, massacres and theft; that they would like to make kings at their own whim, and have them killed when they grew tired of them.

In Siam and Aceh, but also elsewhere in the region, the seizure of estates of both subjects and foreigners who died without married heirs played a significant part in the shift towards absolutism. The comparable practice of escheat in Europe, whereby medieval lords could sometimes resume the land of vassals, had died out by the sixteenth century, as Roman laws of inheritance were revived to make private property rights almost absolute. In Southeast Asia, in contrast, it became a prominent feature of state policy at just this time. The theory that all land belonged ultimately to the ruler and could be redistributed by him was of long standing, even if it meant little in distant dependencies. Escheat was seldom mentioned in the early sixteenth century and must have become more salient with the fortunes made through trade. In Siam we have noted that the practice of taking a third of the estate was attributed to Ekathotsarot (1605–10), while in Cambodia it was said that the king began to claim the right to the estates of his subjects in the sixteenth century following an unsuccessful rebellion (da Cruz 1569: 62). If there was movement in this direction during this period of absolutism, it can be attributed both to the desire of kings for a larger share of the new wealth derived from trade and to the legitimation provided by Muslim advisers, since escheat was well established in most Muslim states around the Indian Ocean (Wittfogel 1957: 77; Barrington Moore 1966: 322–33).

In Siam, Laos, Cambodia, and Burma it was understood that the king was entitled to reclaim at the death of officials the property they had amassed in official service. King Surinyavongsa of Laos took away the land and property of his officials "sometimes in life but always in death" (Marini 1663: 456). In Siam a law dated 1635 said that the king could take all the estates of officials, but in practice usually only a third went to the crown, a third or more to the heirs, and the rest to funeral expenses ("Vertoog" 1622: 290; Pombejra 1984: 34–36). Burmese practice appears to have been roughly similar (van der Hagen 1607: 33). The estates of all foreigners dying in sixteenth-century Pegu were also divided between the crown, which took one-third, and the heirs, "and there hath never been any deceit or fraud used in this matter" (Frederici 1581: 268).

In the Islamic states in the seventeenth century, at least in Aceh, Banten, and Mataram, the estate of any man dying without male heir usually passed to the king, while widows and unmarried daughters could also be taken into the palace. For this reason many prominent men married their daughters off as young as eight or nine ("Tweede Boeck" 1601: 149; Croft 1613: 176; Pyrard 1619 II: 164; Beaulieu 1666: 108; de Haan 1912 III: 205–06). In sixteenth-century Brunei the sultan shared the inheritance of his subjects equally with their children but took all the property of those who died without issue (Dasmariñas 1590: 5).

The stronger and more ambitious Islamic rulers insisted also on a share of the property of foreign traders who chanced to die in their port. The *Adat Aceh* (74) specified that when a trader of any nationality died, "his room is watched, and the inventory as well as the keys are taken. . . . Then the value of all the property is estimated, and according to the adat for ten tahil, one tahil is taken." According to Beaulieu (1669: 109), however, Sultan Iskandar Muda took all the property of such traders, torturing their servants to discover where property was hidden. In Palembang the same right to the whole inheritance was claimed (de Haan 1912 III: 205). Not only the goods but even the people shipwrecked were often held to be forfeit to the king (Beaulieu 1666: 109; Mantegazza 1784: 118–19). The European companies insisted with some success that their factors be exempt from these practices.

That the trend towards centralized, if personal, government was general is demonstrated by developments in Banten, Mataram, and Makassar between 1600 and 1660, which parallelled the better-documented cases of Aceh and Ayutthaya. In part the phenomenon can be attributed to external pressure from the VOC. The pluralist states, notably Melaka facing the Portuguese and Banda facing the Dutch, were the first to be destroyed militarily even though they had created a congenial environment for commerce. Banten, faced with the constant threat from the VOC headquarters in nearby Batavia, could not allow the same thing to happen. The intensely pluralist Banten of the first decade of the seventeenth century, where Scott (1606: 105) found he could "speake of little else but murther, theft, warres, fire and treason," gave way to the militarily strong Banten of mid-century, where "the prince exercises a more than sovereign power over his subjects . . . he has made himself absolute master of their lives and their property" (Missions Etrangères 1680: 91–92).

Mataram provides another interesting case. The conqueror Sultan Agung (1613–46) destroyed the port-states of the northern coast that had been the base of the flourishing Javanese commercial culture of the previous two centuries. After 1641 he monopolized the supply of Javanese rice to the Dutch. The VOC provided not only a threat to any state less than fully unified but also an opportunity to deal as one monopolist to another, without having to provide opportunities to commercial intermediaries who might have posed a threat to either side. Agung's successor, Amangkurat I (1646–77), took royal monopoly to its most destructive extremes. He forbade his subjects to trade abroad, closed all ports for long periods, and in 1655 requisitioned or destroyed the trading and even fishing vessels of his coastal population. As the principal Dutch envoy to his court explained, "He has forbidden any of his subjects to sail overseas, forcing all outsiders to come to his country for rice. . . . I once made bold to advise the King that he should allow his subjects to sail, to become rich, . . . but was given the reply, 'My people have nothing of their own as you have, but everything of theirs comes to me, and without strong government I would not be king for a day' " (van Goens 1656: 200–01). In the heightened competition of the seventeenth century, the needs of trade for security and for freedom proved irreconcilable. The stronger states made possible by commerce sooner or later fell prey to excesses of personal power which destroyed or alienated the important merchants. Several kings rose to unprecedented pinnacles of personal power, but none could prevent chaos and conflict at their death.

A period of absolutism was probably required, below the winds as above them, if bureaucratic and legal institutions were to emerge strong enough to enable the states to continue to compete with ever stronger rivals. Some progress in this direction did occur in the age of commerce. Two contemporary fifteenth-century rulers, Boromatrailokanat in Siam (1448–88) and Le Thanh Tong in Vietnam (1460–97), were energetic centralizers who promulgated or codified laws that sought to assign all their subjects an appointed place in a bureaucratically organized and harmonious polity. Officials were allotted fixed areas of land in accordance with rank, as a remuneration that they lost at dismissal or death. Subsequent kings in both countries allowed centres of personal power to arise and become hereditary again, but both states retained at least a theory of bureaucratic rule.

The early seventeenth century brought more widespread indications of bureaucratic development, contemporary with the revolutions from above carried out in Siam and Acch. Iskandar Muda's establishment of a legal system, and of ministeriales (*panglima*) replaced every three years, has already been mentioned. Although his tyranny caused a massive reaction, these two innovations outlived him. Further panglimas were appointed, so that in the 1660s there were seven in the various west coast ports, each with a small staff comprising two writers (*kerkun*), a weigh-master (*penghulu dacing*) and a port security official (*penghulu kawal*) (Ito and Reid 1985: 206). In Siam, Naresuan ceased the earlier practice of appointing royal princes to govern as virtual replicas of the king in the leading Siamese dependencies. He kept such princes at court and governed most of the provinces through appointed officials who could be dismissed at will. In addition, he and his successors appointed judges, labour service supervisers, and other officials from the centre to assist these new governors and ensure that the king's policies were carried out throughout his dominions (Nidhi Aewsrivongsc, cited Ishii 1993: 181, 185–86; Lieberman 1980A: 554).

Perhaps influenced by Naresuan's example, the Burmese kings Anaukhpetlun (1606–28) and Thalun (1629–48) carried out their own centralization program, which Lieberman (1980A: 569) has called "the principal watershed in the evolution of Burmese administration" between the country's unification by conquest in the sixteenth century and the advent of the British. In spite of the astonishing success of Bayinnaung's sixteenth-century conquests, he had governed the former royal centres through his closest relatives, who had replicated the insignia, rituals, titles, and functions of kingship. These princes, known as *bayin* (sovereigns) were systematically replaced, after the period of great disturbance in 1595–1608, by lower-ranking *myò wun* (town "ministers") who could not use royal titles and styles. Thalun then sought to control these officials by appointing royal spies (*nà-hkan*), previously used only in the army, to monitor their loyalty. At least in some provincial capitals a range of other officials were appointed from the centre, including secretaries, treasury superintendents, granary chiefs, and revenue ministers (ibid.: 550–59).

The island kingdoms more dependent on their ports, and more exposed to foreign pressures, were generally less successful in such measures. In Mataram, Sultan Agung brought the heads of local lineages to his court to remove them from their power base, while his successor in 1669 appointed royal agents (*umbul*) to oversee the four governors of the rich coastal regions (Ricklefs 1981: 69). The constant upheavals in Mataram from 1670 onward indicate the inadequacy of these measures and how heavily the Javanese state still depended on the forcefulness of the individual at its centre. The problem of arbitrary royal power, moreover, was not solved in any of these states, so that legal security of property was impossible to establish.

Unlike the absolutism of contemporary Europe, that of Southeast Asia was not accompanied by institutions, or even theories, which gave other elements of society a stake in the new accumulation of power. Because kings intervened directly in the market, they did not feel the need to ally with the merchant class in order to destroy baronial power, as happened in a number of European states. If the absolutist kings had allies, they were foreigners, excluded by definition from a role in the polity. And although pluralism was everywhere in Southeast Asian history, it found few champions in the political literature of the region.

As made clear in chapter 3, one political effect of the religious revolution was to encourage kings to ignore traditional constraints upon them. The universalist religions brought their own critiques of arbitrary power, some of which were translated, adapted, and incorporated into the written cultures below the winds. These provided a measure by which good and bad kings could be judged. In the greatest Malay political textbook, the *Taj us-Salatin* [Crown of kings], the qualities of a just king are clearly set out: he must be wise, learned, ready to listen to the ulama, personable, generous, loyal, moderate, and restrained, and he must impose the law of God (Bukhari 1603: 62–63). This manual described the acts of the tyrants known to Islamic history in graphic detail, and quoted the authority of Koranic revelation that such oppressors will be consigned to hell, because "in truth of all men, those who will be most detested by God the Most High, and who will be punished the most severely on the day of judgement, are the kings who have been tyrants" (ibid.: 110). Yet the Islamic treatises left the burden of responsibility on God and the king. There was no theoretical justification for limiting royal power or excluding certain areas from the king's authority, even to the extent that medieval Christianity separated ecclesiastic and civil power. The king *should* do right, but if he did not then it was left to God to punish him.

If rulers quaked before the possibility of divine retribution, they had less to fear on earth from institutional checks to their authority. A few nevertheless regarded the ulama with suspicion simply because they represented an external standard of judgement and an external source of spiritual potency. Amangkurat I assembled two thousand leading ulama of Mataram soon after his accession in 1646 and had them murdered, evidently because he suspected them of supporting rebellion (van Goens 1656: 202).

The concept of the wise king, after the model of Asoka, was also well developed in Buddhist literature. In the sangha, and especially the forest monks less subject to royal control, Buddhism also had a potential alternative locus of spiritual authority. One would like to believe Pinto's engaging account of the speech given by a respected old Burmese monk, himself a relative of the king, before a large crowd, including King Tabinshweihti himself, assembled for the funeral of the patriarch:

God made men to be kings   to be humane to men, to hear men, to satisfy men, and to punish men, but not out of sheer tyranny to kill men. However you, wretched kings, . . . are denying the very nature with which God has endowed you . . . acting like leeches towards some, depriving them bit by bit of life and property . . . while for those who are your favorites . . . you are so lenient in punishing their arrogant deeds and so prodigal in bestowing favours on them at the expense of the poor whom you have despoiled, stripping them of all but skin and bones, that the little people have good cause for accusing you of all these things before God (Pinto 1578: 371).

According to Pinto, these sentiments had some effect, and the king desisted from his cruel military campaign. Even if the story was accurate, however, this was a very different thing from legitimating permanent checks on royal power. The sangha could play a political role, as in the overthrow of King Narai in 1688, but in no sense did it share secular power.

The most promising attempt to limit arbitrary power came not from these imported ideologies but from older indigenous structures. A dual monarchy, of which the most successful example was the union of Goa and Tallo' lineages in Makassar, is a case in point. Originating in the federating model of state-formation for which South Sulawesi showed a particular genius, this became fully institutionalized in 1593 in reaction against the attempt of a king with claims on both thrones to obliterate the distinction between them. For the following half-century, the most successful in Makassar's history, the Goa lineage provided the king and the Tallo' lineage the chancellor, or day-to-day administrator. The chronicles are filled with exhortations to preserve this delicate balance, perhaps just because it was beginning to break down under the last fully independent sultan, Hasanuddin (Reid 1981; Reid 1983A: 134–37).

The concept of a "second king" appears to have been known to all the Theravada countries of the Mainland, but it developed into an active balancing institution only at some periods in Siam. There the "front palace" of the second king (upparat), usually a royal son but not one chosen to succeed, would be more accessible to the population and more engaged in routine affairs than the palace proper. Because much of the official apparatus and the manpower system was directly controlled by the upparat, there was inherent tension between his office and the king's, which was the source of numerous revolts (Rabibhadana 1969: 55–64). In the Malay world a similar division of functions characterized the relationship between the raja and the raja muda (literally, "young king," but usually rendered "underking" by the Dutch). Although the raja muda was typically the crown prince, contractual relations sometimes developed like that in the eighteenth century between the Bugis raja muda of eighteenth-century Riau, who exercised day-to-day authority, and the Malay raja, elevated above the business of government. Contractual relations were also common in Sumatra, Borneo, Sulawesi, and Mindanao between an upstream and a downstream ruler (raja hulu and raja hilir), with different ethnic origins, economic functions, and political and military responsibilities (Drakard 1990; Andaya 1993). Balinese dual kingship appeared to be based rather on an alliance of rival lineages (Geertz 1980: 60–61). The Minangkabau kingdom, though still poorly understood, appears to have rested on a unique combination of sublime royal rhetoric and politicized fragmentation, conventionally simplified as "three kings"—raja alam (king of the world), raja adat (king of custom), and raja ibadat (king of religion) (Drakard 1993: 123–31).

These sources of pluralism qualified the lofty claims of Indic and Islamic kingship. Though tension between these rival authorities was the rule, in the ideal Southeast Asian polity they could be overcome by a process of discussion and consensus. At their best, these institutions of pluralism provided a modest basis for contractualism within state structures. Most often, however, they also inhibited progress towards the bureaucratic institutionalization of state authority.

The most promising attempt to combine an elaborate state apparatus with pluralism at its centre was the experiment with female rule in Patani and Aceh. Both states probably began this experiment—in 1584 and 1641, respectively—because no obvious male candidate was available. The *Taj us-Salatin*, perhaps written in Aceh and certainly known and read there, had counselled strongly against female rule but admitted that a royal daughter could succeed to the throne to prevent still worse eventualities, if no male heir of any kind were available (Bukhari 1603: 53–64). Yet in deciding to perpetuate the female principle for four successive reigns there is no doubt that the orangkaya elite concluded it was the best available way to reconcile the exalted theoretical position of the monarch with the pluralism and security they needed.

The orangkaya class in Aceh had suffered horribly under Iskandar Muda, and it is not surprising that "the very name of a king is longe since become nautious to them, first caused through the tyrannical government of their last king" (Bowrey 1680: 296). Less is known about Patani, but Pinto (1578: 68) portrayed one of the last kings to rule there, Mudhaffar Shah, as given to seizing the estates of merchants by manufacturing charges against them. In the 1680s Gervaise reported the story "that its people were weary of obeying kings who maltreated them, and shook off their yoke" (cited Teeuw and Wyatt 1970 I: 12). These queens were by no means ciphers, particularly the first two in each case who appeared always to have the last say in disputes among the four or five leading orangkaya. There were in fact Elizabethan qualities in the reverence in which the queen was held, the intense rivalry among the leading orangkaya ministers that appeared to leave the queen always unscathed, and the recognition that the satisfactory balance within the state would be jeopardized if the queen were to marry—as happened for a time in Patani.

The female regimes, lasting for more than a century in Patani and for fifty-eight years in Aceh, were relatively benign, orderly, and encouraging to commerce (Reid 1988: 171). In effect they represented an orangkaya oligarchy with the queen as ultimate referee. They enabled the legal and administrative machinery, which in Aceh's case had become quite strong, to operate without disruptions caused by royal whims. But they suffered three fatal weaknesses. First, the authority of the third and fourth queens appeared to diminish to the point where they could no longer adjudicate the disputes among leading orangkaya. In 1688 an Italian visitor to Aceh noted that "in fact it is seven of the nobles who rule the kingdom," not the queen, and ten years later a Frenchman was sceptical whether the queen even existed, since she had no power (Ito and Reid 1985: 207). Chinese reports indicate that towards the end of the century Patani abandoned the hereditary principal for a system in which any baby girl born with auspicious signs could be selected as heir, and her virginity was then protected (Ship 66 of 1694, in Ishii forthcoming). Second, the queens fared badly (though arguably better than their male counterparts elsewhere) in the contest with outside powers. Aceh, pressured by a Dutch blockade in 1647–50, could not prevent the VOC from gaining control of the dependencies that produced the pepper and tin on which its prosperity had been based. Patani's prosperity was declining from the 1650s (see table 10, below) and it lost its autonomy through Siamese invasions in 1674 and 1688. And third, female rule was never legitimate in the eyes of Muslim scholars, and therefore could not serve as a satisfactory model for later generations. The campaign of Acehnese ulama against the queens of Aceh was finally successful after they obtained a letter from Mecca declaring woman rulers anathema.

The power base that had made absolutism possible eroded at the end of the age of commerce. This period left a legacy of legal codification and some of the techniques of bureaucratic rule, but it failed to create any satisfactory model of how government could be strong but also ruled by law, centralized but also constitutional. The subsequent period therefore witnessed a diffusion of practical authority that remained at odds with the memory of past glories.

5

The Origins of
Southeast Asian Poverty

When one compares the old times in Banten, when the European na-
tions first arrived in the Indias, with the present miserable time, then
one must stand still before Almighty God, who creates kingdoms and
brings them down according to his will. . . .
From the greatest place of trade in the East, it has become a home
only of wretches.
—de Rovere van Breugel 1787: 350

The foregoing pages should have removed any notion that the East was unchanging while the dynamic elements of capitalist growth and technological improvements were concentrated in Europe. The rapid development of sixteenth-century Europe certainly changed profoundly the mode of its interaction with the rest of the world, including how Europeans perceived Asians. The same social features that seemed natural or impressive to Portuguese in 1510 may have seemed backward to Dutch writers a century later. Nevertheless, in Southeast Asia itself there were profound changes, which must be understood if we are to perceive the modalities of its entry into the modern era.

Essentially these changes were in the direction of intense interaction with the world economy in the fifteenth and sixteenth centuries and of withdrawal from it in the mid-seventeenth century. Both stages had profound consequences on every aspect of life. The expansive phase, which dominated discussion in earlier chapters, had both similarities and differences from the process in Europe.

To recapitulate briefly, the similarities included integration into world trade, commercialization of production and consumption, the growth of cities, the specialization of economic functions, the monetization of taxation, rapid improvements in military and transport technology, and the growth of absolutist states. As a result of its exceptional exposure to global commerce, Southeast Asia in these respects shared the experience of Western Europe and Japan more closely than did most of continental Asia.

The differences between Southeast Asia and other regions in the early modern era are equally instructive. In relation not only to Europe but to most other parts of Asia, the absence of clear safeguards for private property below the winds inhibited the development of financial institutions and discouraged the accumulation of fixed capital. The rapid development of the market on the one hand, and of royal authority on the other, gave rise to tension rather than to alliance between them. This was resolved in various ingenious ways in the short term, but the exposed strategic situation of all the most advanced commercial centres did not allow them to develop these short-term solutions into alternative routes to sustained economic growth.

Internal Inhibitions to Economic Growth?

By the latter stages of the age of commerce, and still more in the eighteenth century, Europeans had little doubt why Southeast Asians did not become rich. They blamed the rapacity of rulers for the failure of a propertied middle class to develop:

Champa: "They can possess no object of value or price without the king or his nobles immediately taking possession of it, so that they are more like slaves than vassals" (Gonçalez 1595: 259).

Cambodia and elsewhere: "From Champa . . . unto as far as all India there are many unprofitable grounds . . . and the men are generally little curious to get or gather together; for they never gain or get so much but it is tyrannized from them, for that which they have is only theirs as long as the king listeth and no more" (da Cruz 1569: 62).

Tongking: "It is one of the policies of the court not to make their subjects rich, lest they should be proud and ambitious and aspire to greater matters . . . and should [the king] know that any persons were to exceed the ordinary means of a private subject, they would incur the danger of losing all, on some pretence or other; which is a great discouragement to the industrious" (Baron 1685: 6).

Cochin-China: "If he (the *chúa*) learns that a private person has something rare and interesting, he sends soldiers to pillage and seize it all. Hence the little people live in great obscurity. They study how to appear poorer than they are. Each one buries his money and anything finer he has" (Poivre 1750: 111).

Siam: "The estate of the Siamese consist chiefly in moveables. If they have lands, they have not much by reason they cannot obtain the full property thereof: it belongs always to their king.... This is the reason they get as few immoveables as they can, and that they always endeavour to conceal their moveables from the knowledge of their kings" (La Loubère 1691: 52).

Burma: "This inertia or sluggishness from which the country suffers in respect to invention and the progress of the arts may have many causes. But the principal one is the government itself, oppressor of any industry. ... If anyone by his industry makes a fortune above the common level, he will be exposed to envy and to prosecution" (Mantegazza 1784: 103).

Magindanao: "These people's laziness seems to proceed . . . from the severity of their Prince, of whom they stand in awe; For he dealing with them very arbitrarily, and taking from them what they get, this damps their industry, so that they never strive to have anything but from hand to mouth" (Dampier 1697: 223).

Aceh: "It appears that the king does not allow that his subjects become powerful and rich; whoever is so does not dare to show it" (Warwijck 1604: 14).

These observers perceived what they saw as a cultural difference. Rulers and subjects appeared to have different expectations of one another in Southeast Asia than in Europe in the seventeenth century. In consequence, Southeast Asians were less inclined to put their resources into fixed capital, such as buildings, ships, trade goods, or machinery. The more ambitious tended rather to accumulate followers for both security and status, thereby replicating the position of the king at a local level. The small people put what wealth they had into jewellery and fine cloth, which they could hide or carry when they had to flee. The culturally preferred style of light elevated wooden houses, easily destroyed but as easily reconstructed, further discouraged any hoarding of wealth from one generation to the next.

These differences were real, but they were not immutable. The above observations were made at times and places where the market had already been largely defeated by the palace. As we have seen, there were other times and places—Melaka around 1500, Banten and Patani around 1600, Aceh apparently in the 1580s and certainly in the 1650s, sixteenth-century Banda—when the great merchants were secure against arbitrary power and tended to build fortified compounds and brick warehouses. And it is not difficult to think of occasions in European and Japanese history when arbitrary power destroyed private fortunes. Cultural preferences and economic strategies constantly influenced and subverted each other. Asia was no more predetermined than Europe to a particular path of evolution.

One of the most striking differences between Southeast Asia and most other parts of the Eurasian continent was the intimate relation between power and commerce. Rulers and their ministers participated fully in trade, and their literature appreciated its importance. Successful merchants necessarily evolved into power-holders, either by allying with an existing court or forming a new one.

Both van Leur (1934) and Meilink-Roelofsz (1962: 9) have pointed to the absence of a class of large merchants with its own ethos distinct from that of the court as a crucial barrier to capitalism. Yet in societies such as those of India or eastern Europe the compartmentalization between merchant castes or religious minorities and power-holders who despised them has also been seen as an inhibition to sustained growth (Subrahmanyam 1990: 298–99). Rulers for whom foreign commerce was utterly unworthy of interest could be even more inimical to its interests than those who wanted a bigger share of it. In the right historical circumstances, the fluidity of social arrangements in Southeast Asia—the constant interplay between economic and political power—could be a strength rather than a weakness.

In the event, the seventeenth century was decisive in pushing Southeast Asians off the path of intense involvement with international commerce. Military and political forces contributed to that result as much as economic factors. One cannot know where the path would have led had the balance of forces in the seventeenth century differed so that some battles were won instead of lost. It could not have been in the same direction as capitalist Western Europe, nor of isolationist but prosperous Japan, but would have produced a Southeast Asia very different from that which was conquered by European capital and military technology in the late nineteenth century.

Critical Military Encounters with Europeans

> *The kingdoms of Siam, of Tongking and the others pay us tribute every year and have no evil intentions. It is only the Europeans who are to be feared as they are the most evil and intractable of men. . . .*
>
> *[The Dutch in particular] when they arrive in a country, they first examine by what means they can master it. . . . Their ships are irresistible, because of their heavy armament and ability to withstand any wind.*
>
> *—Petition to Chinese emperor, quoted in Mailla 1717: 11–12*
>
> *Listen, Gentlemen, to my request*
> *never make friends with the Dutch*

they behave like devils
when they are about no country is safe.

—Amin 1670: 214

Most of the leading centres of Southeast Asian maritime trade were either physically destroyed or occupied by a hostile force at some time in the sixteenth and seventeenth centuries. Most of these crucial defeats were at European hands, either singly or in alliance with Asian forces. The Portuguese, and the northern Europeans after them, realized that they enjoyed a critical advantage in military technology and organization, and they used it without hesitation to gain commercial objectives otherwise far beyond them. As Pierro Strozzi put it at the very beginning of this encounter, "It seems to me [Asians] are superior to us in countless things, save with sword in hand, which they cannot resist" (cited Subrahmanyam 1990: 256).

Part of this advantage was the ruthlessness learned in the hard school of European warfare, which sometimes enabled Europeans to defeat larger Asian forces even in hand-to-hand fighting. Given the overwhelming numbers of their potential antagonists, however, the Europeans were able to alter the balance of power below the winds only through three factors: superior firepower, particularly on shipboard; fortresses, which they could make virtually impregnable; and Asian allies. With some exceptions—notably the Spanish in Luzon and the Dutch in Java—this meant that the Europeans were strong only at sea and in concerted naval attacks on specific coastal targets. Agriculturally based inland states had little to fear from them; but the point about the age of commerce was that its centres of growth were accessible by sea.

The Portuguese immediately targeted the port-city at which the whole of the Southeast Asian export trade appeared to be concentrated. "The trade and commerce between the different nations for a thousand leagues on every hand must come to Melaka. . . . Whoever is lord of Melaka has his hands at the throat of Venice" (Pires 1515: 287). Melaka in 1511 was also one of the world's most pluralistic cities; the bulk of its population consisted of Javanese, South Indians, Gujaratis, Chams, Tagalogs, and people from every port in Asia. The Portuguese were able to seize the city because they concentrated on it an intensity of firepower unprecedented below the winds, because of the element of surprise, and because much of the city's population quickly deserted the sultan. They were able to hold it, in spite of a dozen massive sieges during the ensuing century, because they constructed a fort that Southeast Asian military strategy did not find a way to breach. Although the fall of Melaka was a major event, it disrupted Southeast Asian trade only temporarily, dispersing the commerce and the merchants of Melaka to half a dozen different ports.

The Portuguese moved quickly to Maluku once they discovered that it was the true source of clove and nutmeg. But whereas Albuquerque had come to Melaka with thirteen ships and twelve hundred men, Serrão was sent to Maluku on a single ship, which was wrecked near Ambon. The Portuguese thus arrived at the principal centre of clove export, Ternate, as a small band of useful allies rather than as conquerors. They quickly became involved in the complex set of antagonisms and alliances that comprised Maluku, usually on the side of Ternate, where they built their central fort (1522). Such technical advantages as they enjoyed (armour and firearms) were neutralized by the arrival of a few Spaniards, beginning with Magellan's expedition, who in their resistance to Portuguese claims to the "Spice islands" allied with the rival sultanate of Tidore. The Portuguese could never control more than a fraction of Malukan spices, let alone any other product. They could win temporary military victories, but they never had enough ships in Southeast Asia to sustain blockades or enforce an effective *cartaz* system as in western India. When in 1570 they provoked the Ternatans against them by treacherously murdering Sultan Hairun, no reinforcement was sent to the besieged fortress for four years, and its small garrison was obliged to flee the unprecedentedly unified sultanate. The overall effect of the Portuguese had been to strengthen rather than weaken Southeast Asian trading states.

The sustained Spanish presence in Southeast Asia began with Legazpi's expedition, which landed on Cebu and claimed it for Philip II in 1565. Although a role in the spice trade was a part of Spanish aims, the Christianization and permanent occupation of the Philippines took priority. Manila was seized from Raja Suleiman by Legazpi in 1571, foreclosing any further evolution of a Tagalog trading state on Islamic lines. From there, expeditions were mounted against the nearest centres of Muslim commerce. Brunei, to which Muslim Manila had been linked by marriage and alliance as well as trade, was razed in 1578, as was the then minor Muslim centre at Sulu. Expeditions were sent unsuccessfully against Ternate in 1582, 1585, 1593, and 1603. The consequence of these actions was to diminish Brunei's importance as both a commercial and a political centre and to encourage the concentration of anti-Spanish Muslim corsairs in Sulu, a highly decentralized sultanate that built an economy largely based on raiding Christian communities in the Philippines.

The Portuguese had seen little alternative than to fight the entrenched Muslims if they were to gain a stake in Asian trade. The Spain of Philip II was at least as serious about anti-Muslim crusading but lacked the same urgent economic motive. Although the Spanish achieved few economically significant victories beyond the Philippines, their commercial base was ready-made in American silver, for which Asian traders beat a path to Manila. China had fortuitously begun licensing junks in 1567 to trade legally in the south, and by 1588 sixteen junks a year were voyaging to Manila, ensuring its prosperity. The galleon trade in American silver ensured that the trade boom of 1570–1630 helped to sustain not an Asian maritime state in the Philippines but a Spanish one.

The extraordinary monopoly Portugal had exercised on shipping around the Cape of Good Hope was breached in the last decade of the century, and a flood of northern European vessels followed. After de Houtman's pioneering expedition returned to Holland in 1597 with a cargo of spices from Banten, twenty-two Dutch ships set off for Southeast Asia in the following year. When these returned with some rich cargoes but reports of conflict, the States-General decided that competition between Dutch ventures was harmful—a unified structure should be forged to pursue both commerce and the fight against the Iberian powers in Asian waters. In 1602 all Dutch interests were merged into the Verenigde Oost-Indische Compagnie (VOC) with an exclusive right to trade east of the Cape. Amsterdam had become the most efficient money market with the lowest interest rates in the world. It launched the VOC as the most advanced corporate institution of its day with the unprecedented capital of 6.5 million guilders. By contrast, the English East India Company was chartered in 1600 with only one-tenth the capital, and the Danish in 1616 with one-fourteenth. The VOC proved able to send to Asia over twelve ships in each of its first three years, and seldom fewer than six ships and four thousand men in any year throughout the century—a marked contrast to the Portuguese and all other competitors. In the second decade of the century, the VOC had an average of 117 ships at its disposal, in the third decade 148, and in the 1660s a peak of 257 (Romano 1978: 203). This novel concentration of economic power had its greatest impact in Southeast Asia, where the Dutch (like the English, Danish, and French) focussed their quest for pepper and spices, bypassing the centre of Portuguese strength on the west coast of India.

In spite of much initial misunderstanding and violence, the initial competition between these newcomers and the older-established buyers was a boon for Southeast Asian export centres. The VOC had, however, been created and armed to establish a monopoly wherever possible. Its first targets were the remaining Portuguese strongholds in Maluku. In 1605 the Dutch joined the local Muslims of Hitu to expel the Portuguese from Ambon, and in return they obtained a monopoly of the now considerable quantities of cloves being grown there. Ambon's Fort Victoria became the base of the first governor-general, Pieter Both, appointed in 1610 to oversee all the company's "forts, places, factories, persons and business" in Asia.

With the appointment of Jan Pieterszoon Coen as governor-general in 1619, Dutch policy hardened into a strategic use of the force it could concentrate at various points to establish strongholds and eventually trading monopolies. In 1618 the VOC had burned most of Japara and all the vessels in its harbour. At the same time it fortified its lodge in the Banten dependency of Jakarta over the protests of its governor. In May 1619, after a four-way contest between the regent of Banten, the governor of Jakarta, the English, and the Dutch, Coen descended on the town with seventeen ships, burned all the houses, and drove out the remaining population. This was to be the base where he would build an impregnable fortress from which to control the trade of Asia.

Coen was appalled to learn that a treaty had been signed in Europe in July 1619 whereby the English and Dutch were to cooperate in the East, sharing equally the burden of military actions, with each taking half the available pepper and the English one-third of Malukan spices. Since Dutch forces in Indonesian waters were predominant and Coen was determined to use them to maximum advantage, the treaty failed to halt Dutch-English conflicts. In January 1621 Coen took a fleet of twelve ships to conquer the cluster of five tiny islands that constituted Banda. The islands represented a remarkable form of pluralist government through a council of orangkaya representing each of the nutmeg-producing islands. Having tired of negotiating with so many, Coen decided to eliminate them altogether. Almost the whole population, estimated at fifteen thousand, were killed, taken into slavery in Batavia, or left to starve in isolated places. Coen then repopulated this source of the world's nutmeg with Dutch planters and their slave workers, who delivered all their product to the VOC.

If there was a turning point in the struggle between the rising absolutist trading states of Southeast Asia and European maritime power, it was 1629. The two greatest concentrations of power in the Archipelago, Iskandar Muda's Aceh and Sultan Agung's Mataram, both suffered bitter defeats in that year from which they never recovered. Economically, too, this was about the end of the period of rapid growth in Asian trade. The high tide of the age of commerce was reached in the 1620s, and the decades that followed were mainly a story of defeats and rearguard actions on the part of the trading powers.

Portuguese Melaka had been the great enemy of Aceh since the sultanate's beginnings in the sixteenth century. The two were natural competitors in the trade across the Indian Ocean, as well as rivals to attract the produce of the Malay states around the Straits of Malacca. Iskandar Muda's reign can be seen as one long build-up to achieve what his predecessors had been unable to accomplish: the final expulsion of the Portuguese. After an initial abortive attack on Melaka in 1616, the sultan proceeded more systematically to surround the fortress while building up his own forces. He took Pahang in 1618, Kedah in 1619, and tin-rich Perak in 1620. Johor he repeatedly sacked, though this only embittered its Malays against him. In 1629 his preparations were complete, and he despatched "the finest fleet that had ever been seen in Asia, full of great and small cannon," with nearly twenty thousand men and 236 vessels, including the monster galley referred to above (Carreiro 1630: 113). The force besieged Melaka for three months by land, erecting stockades and cannon within an harquebus shot of the city's walls (fig. 37), but it failed completely to stop the supply of the city by sea. Numerous skirmishes around the walls were bloody but indecisive, and when a large Portuguese relief fleet arrived, the siege was lifted. This fleet, aided by 150 Malay vessels from Johor and Patani, completely turned the tables by bottling the Acehnese fleet up in the small river that was its base. The whole mighty Acehnese force was killed, captured, or dispersed through the Malayan jungle (ibid.; Pinto da Fonseca 1630). Thereafter Aceh's actions were fundamentally defensive attempts to check the gradual dismemberment of its over-extended empire.

The Portuguese believed that Iskandar Muda had sent envoys to Mataram to halt the flow of Javanese rice to Melaka and to coordinate action against the infidels (Pinto da Fonseca 1629). But Sultan Agung worried not about the Portuguese but about their enemies the Dutch. As early as 1619 the English reported that "he hath said many times unto his nobility that Jakarta hath a thorn in her foot, which he himself must take the pains to pluck out, for fear the whole body should be endangered. This thorn is, the castle of the Hollanders, who have now so fortified themselves (through bribery) that they regard not the king, nor his country, but set him at defiance" (Pring 1619: 292). He, too, proceeded methodically, first conquering the independent port-states of the northern coast. After the last and strongest of them, Surabaya, was destroyed in 1625, Agung turned to Batavia, as the

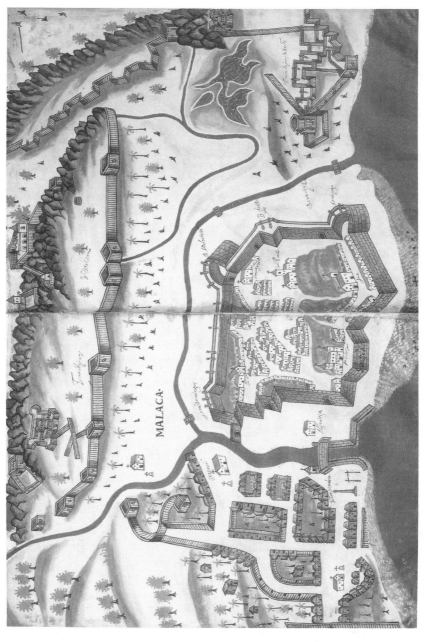

Fig. 37 The Acehnese siege of Melaka in 1629, with stockades and artillery dominating the Portuguese fort

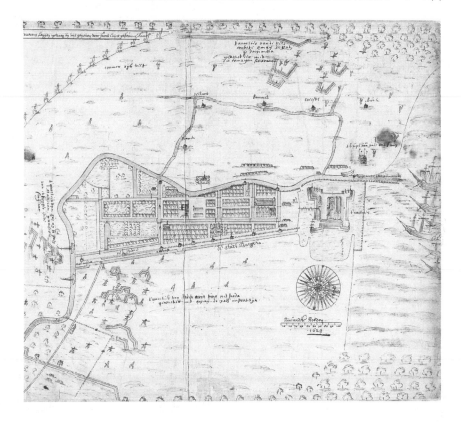

Fig. 38 Mataram's seige of Batavia in 1629, with the sea and the north to the right

Dutch had renamed their headquarters. In August 1628 he launched a combined naval and land attack on Batavia, which was closer to falling than at any time until the British invaded in 1811. Agung ordered the unsuccessful siege lifted in December, after having hundreds of his officers executed. The following year he sent an even larger army (fig. 38), but this disintegrated from hunger and disease after the Dutch destroyed its supplies, so that it posed little danger to the fortress.

The VOC's position in Java was never again seriously threatened. This meant that Sultan Agung's vision of unifying Java could never be fulfilled. Rather it was the VOC which, by controlling Java's external relations and the technological improvements that came with it, would eventually fill that role. During the 1630s the Mataram court concluded that Dutch Batavia could not be destroyed and therefore had to be accommodated somehow into a Javanese world-view. Sultan

Agung's successor, Amangkurat, made peace with the VOC at the beginning of his reign in 1646, in a treaty that he probably regarded as an agreement with a powerful vassal ruling lucrative but uncivilized coastal districts.

After establishing its monopoly of nutmeg through Banda, the VOC next targeted cloves. The inconvenient English "allies" were removed from direct competition when all the members of their factory in Ambon were imprisoned and twenty-one of them executed in 1623 for allegedly plotting against the Dutch. VOC strategy thereafter would be to concentrate clove-growing in the Ambon area it best controlled and try to destroy cloves elsewhere. Such a monopoly attacked the interests of both producers and traders, and the Dutch had to fight a series of bitter wars to make it work.

Ternate was dominated by the VOC from the 1620s, and the Spanish fortress in nearby Tidore could do little to help its opponents. Portuguese Melaka, a major entrepôt for non-Dutch spices travelling westward, fell to a Dutch siege in 1641. A new centre for all those opposing the VOC monopoly emerged in Makassar. The English and Danish companies, a large colony of Portuguese, and representatives from Golconda and Aceh all did their clove-buying there, while Muslim traders going by the general ethnic label "Malay" ran the Dutch blockades to bring cloves to the city. In Maluku resistance focussed around the Muslim centre of Hitu in north Ambon in 1641–46, and in the Ternatan colony of Hoamoal in 1650–56. By 1656 the VOC had effectively suppressed all this armed resistance. The population of Hoamoal was removed and all its clove trees were destroyed. The Sultan of Ternate was bound to a treaty that stipulated his cooperation in the destruction of all clove trees outside VOC control in Ambon. The monopoly was complete.

Many who had resisted this Dutch conquest, including its chronicler from the Muslim side, Rijali, took refuge in the metropolis of Makassar. That city's trade was of course weakened by its great difficulty in obtaining cloves after 1656. It remained a major actor in the long-distance trade, however, relaying Indian cloth to Manila and China, as well as throughout eastern Indonesia. It had always been a thorn in the VOC's side, but too strong to be challenged directly on the battlefield. Makassar's exceptionally astute leadership in its earlier years weakened under Sultan Hasanuddin (1653–69), however, and both its Bugis subjects and the VOC were alternately provoked and placated. In 1660, when Hasanuddin was busy coping with rebellions in Bone and Mandar, a VOC fleet attacked and seized Panakkukang, one of the forts guarding the southern approaches to the city (fig. 39), and used it to enforce its commercial demands.

Fig. 39 The Dutch attack on Makassar in 1660, showing the fort of Panak-kukang, on lower point, under attack, and the royal boatsheds above it in flames. The main citadel of Sombaopu is between river outlets at the top centre.

Bugis dissatisfaction was led by a prince known as Arung Palakka, who received refuge in Batavia in 1663 after leading an unsuccessful Bugis rebellion against Makassar three years earlier. The Dutch tested the mettle of his group of followers in one of the wars against the Minangkabau centre of Pau in 1666 and were impressed at the results. Later the same year they were ready to launch a major assault against Makassar. A fleet of twenty-one ships, with only six hundred Dutch soldiers but large numbers of Ambonese and Arung Palakka's Bugis, defeated in January 1667 a far larger Makassarese expeditionary force that was besieging Buton. The Bugis, who made up almost half the Makassar army, began defecting to Arung Palakka in large numbers. The campaign was then carried to Makassar itself, where the Makassarese were again defeated after hard fighting and forced to sign the humiliating Bungaya Treaty in November 1667. The English, Portuguese, and other Europeans had to leave, Makassar was forced to pay a large indemnity, overlordship of most non-Makassarese territories was surrendered, and the VOC was permitted to occupy the Ujung Pandang fort that guarded the northern approach to the capital—which the Dutch commander Speelman strengthened and renamed Fort Rotterdam after his birthplace. This peace did not hold, and in June 1669 the alliance launched a furious attack on the main Makassar stronghold of Sombaopu. Dutch soldiers fired thirty thousand musketballs in that engagement and tunnelled underneath the wall to blow up a segment of it, but it was Arung Palakka's Bugis who inflicted most of the casualties (Andaya 1981: 130–33).

This was the end of the last Asian-controlled emporium east of Java. Like Melaka before it and Banten after it, Makassar was reduced to a VOC outstation of purely local importance. The English, Portuguese, and Muslim long-distance traders had to fall back to Banten, Cambodia, or Ayutthaya. With control of Malukan spices completely in VOC hands, the next target was the supply of pepper, much harder to monopolize because it was spread among a dozen major and minor ports.

The favoured VOC tactic in this quest was to find a "Company's king" who could be bullied into consigning to the Dutch the sole right to purchase pepper exports at low prices and to import Indian cloth at high ones. The Sultan of Palembang agreed to such a treaty under pressure in 1642, but did not like its consequences. Dutch ships were attacked and factors killed in Palembang in 1657, and the VOC responded in 1659 by destroying the city, reestablishing the Dutch post, and tightening the Dutch monopoly. This in turn directed more of the upland pepper to Jambi, where an English presence kept prices higher until 1679, when the town was in turn destroyed in an attack by Johor. Turbulence continued in Jambi until 1687, when the VOC sent a force to seize the town and install a new "Company's king" on the usual monopoly terms.

The real prize was Banten, the largest pepper-exporting port of the mid-seventeenth century, and a constant challenge to nearby Batavia. Under the forceful Sultan Abdulfatah Ageng (1651–82) Banten was an alternate centre for the long-distance trade, as well as an inspiration for all those resisting VOC commercial dominance. Banten, however, was internally divided, with one court faction supporting the crown prince and a policy of accommodation with the Dutch. In 1680, as the sultan's relations with Batavia reached open warfare, the disaffected prince imprisoned Ageng in his residence and took over the government. His supporters were nevertheless a minority, and with every concession he made to the VOC in return for their help, his internal opponents multiplied. In March 1682, at a point when the old sultan had effectively resumed power, the VOC finally intervened, on condition the young prince become a complete Company's king. It was a long and bitter war before Sultan Ageng surrendered in March 1683. Banten's independence was now a mere token, with its pepper pledged exclusively to the VOC.

Sultan Ageng seemed the embodiment of the spirit of independence, commercial enterprise, and technical innovation, especially after the dramatic manner of his destruction at Dutch hands. Like his contemporary Narai of Siam, his elaborate diplomacy and dramatic fall aroused European sympathy. Ageng was the hero of a classic Dutch tragedy of 1769, probably the first Southeast Asian to be so celebrated (Zwier van Haren 1769; Lombard 1990 I: 40). One of the leading colonial historians of the nineteenth century paused in his narrative of the Dutch rise to pay a rare tribute to "the ruler who had sought to keep his country free from foreign influence and foreign monopoly, . . . who fell for his principles, who was the last of the independent rulers of Java" (de Jong 1862–68 VII: clxviii).

The Dutch could never control the international pepper market fully. Chinese continued to buy pepper from independent ports in the Malayan Peninsula and Borneo, as well as from the VOC in Batavia, and the English retained a share of the European market by shifting their base of operations from Banten to the southwestern coast of Sumatra. But the destruction of the cosmopolitan trading cities of Banten and Makassar was immensely important for the evolution of the societies of which they were the heart. From having been the most progressive centres in the Archipelago, where new ideas were translated and adapted into Indonesian forms, they became embittered backwaters, periodically venting their frustration in rebellion against the Dutch yoke but no longer interested in "modern" ideas when presented in the dress of the conqueror.

The Eclipse of Mon and Javanese Shipping

To conclude that the apparently inexorable rise of the Dutch East India Company was a sufficient explanation of the collapse of the Southeast Asian urban and maritime traditions would be simplistic. Aceh and the trading cities of the mainland were not conquered by Europeans—their more complex evolution will be dealt with below. Such major victories as the VOC had would have been impossible without Asian allies. In the most critical changes, European involvement did no more than tip the balance between contending Asian forces. The role of the Europeans in the two most profound long-term setbacks to Southeast Asian commerce, in particular, was no more than indirect. These were the virtual disappearance from international trade of two of the region's most dynamic commercial actors—the Mons of Pegu and the Javanese of the *pasisir* (Java's north coast).

The importance of these two groups in Southeast Asian long-distance trade at the time of the first Portuguese descriptions was made clear in chapter 1. The largest fleet of ocean-going junks was in Javanese hands, including the Javanese of Melaka. Many junks were built in the ports of Pegu from good Burmese teak. The Mons of these ports sailed their own large junks to Melaka, sometimes to sell them there, sometimes to return with cargoes. During the heyday of Pegu as the capital of King Bayinnaung's vast empire, it conducted an even larger trade in the Bay of Bengal. In 1574 the king was recorded as ordering the construction of seven great ships, "each 63 cubits long and 16 cubits wide" (roughly 30 by 8 metres), to conduct his overseas trade (Lieberman 1984: 32n). Few large junks of the 500-tonne class were being built by the end of the century, for reasons already discussed, but the Mons (or Peguans, as they were known to foreigners) were still taking their ships as far as Aceh and Banten.

Under the disastrous rule of Nandabayin (1581–99) the great wealth of Pegu and its ports in the Bay of Bengal was dissipated in ruinous campaigns to retain Bayinnaung's overextended empire. The chronicler U Kala (1711: 103) believed that the king fell as a result of his own ruthless oppression: "He neither respected the monks nor valued the life of his subjects." The ports of Cosmir [Bassein] and Martaban first rebelled against the labour demands of Nandabayin and were utterly destroyed and depopulated. To escape service in Nandabayin's armies, thousands of Mons fled to neighbouring countries; there were said to be 120,000 in Laos, 20,000 in Arakan, and over 100,000 in Siam (du Jarric 1608–14 I: 623, 626). In the last three years of the century the imperial city of Pegu was besieged by the neighbours Nandabayin had attacked, and the countryside was completely devastated. In 1599 Pegu finally fell before an alliance of Toungoo and Arakan, and the two armies took home all that was moveable of the remaining population and wealth of the coastal region.

The Jesuit Boves reported of the area around the former capital in 1600: "It seems that the whole country is nothing but desert, and that there is nobody left in this kingdom of Pegu; all the streets, especially those which lead to the temples, are scattered with skulls and with the corpses of these wretched Peguans who have died partly of hunger, partly from their own faults, massacring each other; partly also killed by the command of the King, who had them thrown in the river, which is hardly navigable any more even by a small boat because of the multitude of the corpses" (cited du Jarric 1608–14 III: 842). The Burmese chronicler conceded that Nandabayin "became suspicious of all Mons" and set out to persecute them (U Kala 1711: 93), while a Portuguese contemporary believed that he had set out to eliminate all the Mons. The result was that "the wretched inhabitants being slain, the former seats of great and powerful lords became the abodes of tigers and other wild beasts, without any more trace being left at all, but the horrid cinders, and a greater silence on earth than human thought can imagine" ("Kingdom of Pegu" 1605: 111). At second or third hand, Floris (1615: 52–55) believed that these events had "cost the lives of many millions of Pegu-ers," largely through the famine and disease that followed the horrors of war.

The King of Arakan left behind one of his Portuguese mercenary captains, Felipe de Brito, as commander of Syriam, which had become the most important port of the Mon region. But de Brito fortified himself in the port and until 1613 held it as an independent city-state with a little help from the Portuguese in Goa. During this period trade with the interior appears almost to have ceased, and the control of the lucrative routes across the peninsula to the Gulf of Thailand seems to have passed to Siam and its Indian Muslim factors. The Mons of Pegu were no longer mentioned as a factor in maritime trade outside their region.

The thriving ports of Java's north coast had exported Javanese rice and other foodstuffs throughout the Archipelago, in exchange especially for Indian cloth from Aceh and Melaka and for spices from Maluku. The VOC often attacked this Javanese shipping directly, notably when they destroyed everything in the harbour of Japara in 1618. Far more important was the impoverishment of the pasisir ports by the systematic Dutch attempt to cut their commercial arteries in order to promote the Dutch monopoly in Maluku and isolate Portuguese Melaka. During the 1620s Makassar replaced Gresik and Surabaya as the principal provisioning and trade centre for eastern Indonesia.

But the major threat to the pasisir towns, as to the Mon centres, came from the interior. Sultan Agung of Mataram (1613–46) was determined to establish a united polity centred on his capital near modern Yogyakarta. He conquered and devastated Lasem in 1616, Pasuruan in 1616–17, and Tuban in 1619, taking control of the teak forests and shipyards where most Javanese ships had been built. Madura was subdued in 1624, and after a campaign of several years the flourishing complex of ports on the Straits of Madura—Surabaya, Gresik, and Sedayu—was conquered in 1625. For the first time in two centuries the commercial centres of the coast were ruled by an inland dynasty that had no interest in trade. "I am a prince and a soldier," said Agung, "not a merchant like the other princes of Java" (cited Masselman 1963: 313).

Unlike his successors, however, Agung was interested in maritime power. He continued to maintain a substantial navy, with which he conquered Sukadana (West Borneo) in 1622 and threatened Batavia on a number of occasions. He was also interested in monopolizing rice exports through Japara as a political weapon he could use with Dutch Batavia and Portuguese Melaka. His successor, Amangkurat I (1646–77), as we noted above, preferred to ordain the destruction of all Javanese shipping in 1655 rather than see it conceivably strengthen his internal enemies. Javanese traders of course transferred their operations to such other centres as Banjarmasin, Banten, Palembang, Patani, and Makassar, where they tended to assimilate to the "Malay" community. In their homeland of east and central Java, however, it was reported in 1677 that the Javanese, "besides their great ignorance at sea, were now completely lacking in vessels of their own" (cited Schrieke 1925: 79).

That year, 1677, was critical for the dynasty of Mataram. The capital at Plered fell to rebels led by Trunajaya; Amangkurat I died in exile in Tegal. His son Amangkurat II (1677–1703) agreed to everything the Company could require in order to obtain their military backing to regain his throne. This included a complete monopoly on the import of cloth and opium, such that no cloth would be admitted without the VOC mark; a complete monopoly on the export of rice and sugar, with 4000 koyang (9500 tonnes) of rice to be delivered at market prices each year; the exclusion from Java of all other traders, be they European or Asian; and the cession to the VOC of Semarang absolutely and of the other north coast ports until the war debts were repaid from their revenues (Hageman 1859: 323–25; Ricklefs 1981: 72–73).

Of course, none of this could be implemented without the VOC having to fight repeatedly to enforce it. As the Company did enforce its authority gradually in the coastal pasisir, commercial activity revived there after decades of devastating war and oppression. But Javanese would henceforth be distinguished below the winds for their disinclination for seafaring, the weakness of their trading class and the hierarchic nature of their society.

The "Crisis" of the Seventeenth Century

The retreat of Southeast Asian trade in the seventeenth century is usually explained in terms of the military and economic victories of the VOC, to which is sometimes added the rise of interior, agrarian-based states less interested in commerce. These factors appear specific to the historical situation of Southeast Asia and particularly the Archipelago, where Dutch power was concentrated and the indigenous regimes were particularly vulnerable to monopoly pressure. Yet the parallels in other parts of the world cannot be ignored. After three decades of vigorous interaction with the world outside, Japan in the 1630s forbade its people to sail overseas and limited foreign trade to Chinese and Dutch ships at Nagasaki. China experienced a drastic period of famine, population decline, and internal disintegration in the 1630s and 1640s, culminating in the collapse of the Ming dynasty in 1644 and its replacement by the Qing. England, France, Germany, Spain, and Turkey were all convulsed by ruinous civil wars in the period 1620–50, and the last three of these regions at the same time lost their former prosperity and status in the world. The population of England, which had risen at between 0.5 and 1.0 percent per annum throughout the expansive sixteenth century, slowed markedly from 1600 and went into dramatic decline from 1656 to 1686 (Schofield 1983: 268). Though population is less well documented elsewhere, there is little doubt that it declined significantly in France, Holland, Denmark, and Germany, as in China, in the second half of the century, while the setback occurred somewhat earlier in Italy and Spain. These reverses to population in different parts of the world were accompanied by a decline in prices for grain and other essentials after a long period of price inflation through the "long sixteenth century."

This remarkable coincidence in many parts of the world of sixteenth-century expansion followed by seventeenth-century crisis has led to a growing scholarly industry attempting to provide some general explanation. The earliest theories focussed on political phenomena— for Roland Mousnier the conflict of nobility and bourgeoisie, and the undermining of supra-national ideas of both empire and church by the rising power of nationalism; for Hugh Trevor-Roper (1959) the top-heavy absolutism of the "Renaissance state" with its enlarged army, bureaucracy, and taxation demands. For a number of Marxist-influenced scholars, of whom Eric Hobsbawm (1954) is the most explicit but Perry Anderson (1974) and Barrington Moore (1966) are the most wide-ranging, these were the birth-pangs of the modern world, when "capitalism at last burst through the chrysalis of the old feudal order" (Schöffer 1978: 88). Robert Mandrou and others have looked to cultural factors, seeing the Baroque era as an indication of the "romantic agony" of European civilization in crisis. More recently Jack Goldstone (1988) has argued for three diverse countries—England, Turkey, and China—that it was the pressure of rapidly rising population on limited grain resources which pushed prices up in the sixteenth century and correspondingly down in the seventeenth.[1]

Many of these points are suggestive in relation to the Southeast Asian evidence. In particular Trevor-Roper's thesis that there was inherent instability in the greatly expanded resources taken by the absolutist state provides an interesting comparative insight on Siam, Aceh, and Banten. Only two of the theories advanced appear sufficiently general and sufficiently measurable, however, to enable us to say with any confidence whether more than coincidence is at work. The first of these focusses on the depression in global trade and financial indices in the period 1620–50, caused in part by the reduced supply of lubricating silver and gold. The other is the increasing body of data on global climatic change, which makes clear that there was a major cooling of the earth's surface in the seventeenth century.

Trade Decline

Although debate continues about the precise critical point, a marked downturn in global trade in the first half of the seventeenth century is inescapable. This is best documented by some of the vital indices of European trade: the shipping of Seville went into steady decline from 1622; Dutch shipping to the Baltic from 1620; the trade of Danzig from 1623; Venetian trade and cloth production from about 1610; production of Leiden textiles and Amsterdam soap from 1620; English wool exports from 1614; English real wages from about 1590; and so forth. European prices, which had been rising for a century, generally declined from around 1640 (Brown and Hopkins 1956: 302; Braudel 1966: 894, 1240–42; Romano 1978).

One specific cause of the downturn in trade was the renewed outbreak of war between Spain and the Netherlands in 1621, which decimated Dutch trade to the Peninsula and the Mediterranean and plunged Spain further into depression (Israel 1989: 124–56). A more

---

1. Much of the debate on this issue is conveniently reprinted or summarized in Aston 1965 and Parker and Smith 1978. For Asia a special issue of *Modern Asian Studies* 24:4 (1990) debates the evidence for China, Japan, Southeast Asia, and South Asia.

profound cause may have been an agricultural crisis which only Holland and England managed to avoid and which ensured that the Mediterranean and German economies did not recover quickly from the 1620s (Romano 1978: 202–03). A critical phenomenon whose existence is no longer in doubt, though its effects are much debated, was the collapse after 1630 in the output of silver from Potosí (in what was then Spanish Peru). Even when the more stable output of Mexican mines is added, American production of silver declined 0.3 percent a year throughout the period 1628–97, contrasting with a spectacular growth before this period and a steady expansion after it (Garner 1988: 900–02).

Outside Europe and its New World in the Americas, the effects of this economic downturn are less clear. Dermigny (1964 I: 99) has pronounced that "in the general depression which characterized the world of the seventeenth century, the Chinese crisis was the most profound of all," and there is little doubt that the drastic decline in imports of silver to fuel an overheated economy was a cause (Atwell 1986). A case can be made that the effects were at least as profound on Southeast Asia, but that region's more favourable ecological situation meant that the effects showed less drastically in population declines than in turning away from commercial involvement.

Since both Spanish and Japanese silver flowed to China through Southeast Asia, the effect on ports below the winds was profound. Whereas an average of more than 23 tonnes of specie had been shipped from Mexico to Manila each year in the 1620s, this fell to 18 tonnes in the 1630s and 10 tonnes in the following decade, as we saw in chapter 1. Although this decline can be attributed in part to the reduced number of Chinese ships that reached Manila during the final crisis of the Ming dynasty, the shipments did not return to the peak levels of 1610–30 when China revived—indeed, not until well into the eighteenth century.

Portuguese trade and remittances of specie to Asia declined even more rapidly after 1600, and the Southeast Asian branch of this trade centred in Melaka was in deficit by 1630 (Disney 1978: 51–54). Even the VOC, the undoubted "winner" of the seventeenth-century crisis in Asia, took less bullion to the east in the period 1630–60 than it had in the 1620s. In 1652, admittedly an exceptional year, the VOC in fact acquired more than 80 percent of its silver and gold needs from Asia (Glamann 1981: 59). Until 1668 the greatest source of silver for the VOC, as for Asia in general, was Japan. The output of the mines on Sado Island was curiously parallel to that of Potosí, rising spectacularly in the same period, 1590–1630. Japanese exports of silver are believed to have peaked at 150 metric tonnes a year in the 1620s, only to decline to less than half that amount by the 1640s (see table 2, above), while silver export was prohibited altogether in 1668. As explained in chapter 1, this remarkable boom and bust directly affected the Southeast Asian ports where Japanese silver was exchanged for Chinese silk and local deerskins and spices. The prohibition of Japanese trading abroad in 1635 and the resumption of direct (if tightly controlled) China-Japan exchange through Chinese junks trading to Nagasaki had a severe effect on the economy of all these Southeast Asian cities. The privileged access of the VOC to Japanese minerals after 1639 through its factory at Deshima was critical to the success of the Dutch world-economy in Asia.

The Chinese trade to Southeast Asia, which had contributed much to the boom of 1570–1630, was also in a slump during China's mid-century troubles. Whereas 117 junks had been licensed to sail to the south in 1597, and probably more than that in the following decade (see chapter 1), only 39 passes were issued when the licensing system was revived briefly in 1639. Of these, two-thirds were for the European enclave ports—16 for Manila and 8 for Batavia. Of the Asian ports only Cochin-China (8) was allocated more than 2 (van Diemen 1639: 1). Yet 1639 was a good year for the mid-seventeenth century. In that year, thirty-four arrivals from the Chinese mainland or Taiwan were recorded in Manila (Chaunu 1960: 148), which suggests that the officially sanctioned junk trade may have been about half the total. After this the collapse was unremitting. An average of only 7 vessels a year from Chinese ports reached Manila in the period 1644–81, and fewer than 5 reached Batavia, which had become the principal Chinese destination in the southern islands (Chaunu 1960: 148–75; Blussé 1986: 115–20).

Although most sections of the world economy faltered in this period, Southeast Asia was especially hard hit as its share in the shrinking pie was reduced. The region benefitted more than most from the trade boom of 1570–1630. International competition for its products reached a peak in the 1620s, when Southeast Asian pepper and spices accounted for more than half of the value of Dutch, English, Portuguese, and French homeward cargoes from Asia, while most of the trade between China and Japan also took place in Southeast Asian ports. In 1635 the Japanese stopped coming altogether, while Chinese demand was reduced drastically by the crisis of the 1640s. For Europeans the initial concentration on Archipelago spices and pepper was replaced by other Asian interests, notably Indian cloths and indigo. Malukan spice and Southeast Asian pepper together dropped from 68

Table 9. Imports of Manila, in five-year annual averages in reals

	Cargo entered	Customs charged
1601–05	179,168	43,037
1606–10	239,832	42,982
1611–15	474,866	70,356
1616–20	615,599	51,437
1621–25	no figures available	
1626–30	492,866	25,720
1631–35	567,135	42,194
1636–40	577,813	31,037
1641–45	566,208	22,075
1646–50	379,535	14,316
1651–55	192,094	7,504
1656–60	214,904	6,676
1661–65	277,736	4,858
1666–70	186,177	3,884

percent of Dutch homeward cargoes in 1648–50 to 23 percent in 1698–1700, and from the bulk of English cargoes before 1640 to about 2 percent after the loss of access to Banten in 1682 (Chaudhuri 1978: 508–10; Bruijn, Gaastra, and Schöffer 1987: 192).

Of all Southeast Asian ports only Dutch Batavia grew in stature in the second half of the century. Although Spanish Manila was subject to fewer pressures than most Asian entrepôts, its trade also declined markedly, as the series of Chaunu (1960: 78, 82) amply demonstrate (table 9).

The downturn in Manila, as in the Asian-ruled ports, was not made good by an improvement in Chinese trade after its nadir in the 1640s and especially after the defeat of the anti-Manchu Zheng (Koxinga) rebels and the opening of trade in 1684. As will be discussed below, the Chinese junk traders fared better than other Asians in the second half of the seventeenth century. Nevertheless, the only branch of this for which reliable figures survive, the junk trade that the Japanese permitted under tight conditions to Nagasaki, declined from Cambodia and Patani after 1660, from Cochin-China after 1680, and from Ayutthaya after 1689 (table 10).

The effective monopoly established by the VOC over nutmeg and mace in 1621, and progressively over cloves between 1640 and 1653, were the most serious blows to Southeast Asian trade, even though the quantities involved were much less than for pepper. These items had been staples of the "long-distance trade" for centuries, passing through

Table 10. Junk trade from Southeast Asia to Nagasaki

	Tongking	Cochin-China	Cambodia	Siam	Patani	Banten	Asian total	Dutch ports
1651–60	15	40	37	28	20	1	141	2
1661–70	6	43	24	26	9		108	14
1671–80	8	41	10	26	2	1	88	38
1681–90	12	25	9	31	9		86	23
1691–1700	6	29	23	19	7	1	85	18
1701–10	3	12	1	11	2		29	2

Source: Derived from Li Tana's reading of the figures compiled by Iwao Seiichi in Li 1992: 70

dozens of hands as they travelled from producers in Maluku to markets in Java, Makassar, or the Malacca Straits, and thence progressively to India, the Middle East, Europe, or China. Both prices and quantities for these spices had been at their maximum in the first quarter of the seventeenth century, as the northern Europeans competed for supplies with each other and with the older-established Chinese, Portuguese, and Muslim buyers. Until this period, the fact that clove and nutmeg grew only in eastern Indonesia drew wealth eastward, invigorating a dozen ports along the trade routes. Once the Dutch monopoly was established, prices to the growers were fixed at minimum levels, and all Asian intermediary traders and ports were eliminated from a share in profits. By the mid-seventeenth century the Dutch were able to sell spices in Europe at about seventeen times, and in India at about fourteen times, the price for which they had bought them in Maluku, with none of the profit passing into Asian hands (Masselman 1963: 459; Knaap 1987: 253).

The mid-seventeenth century can undoubtedly be considered a period of crisis for the trade of Southeast Asia. In difficult times of lower prices and reduced demand from both China and Europe, there was not room for more than one winner. The VOC was that winner. Its profits were at peak levels in precisely the period of crisis in other parts of the global economy. The prices of VOC shares on the Amsterdam stock exchange were high throughout the period 1640–71, with record prices in 1648 and 1671 (Israel 1989: 186, 255, 330). But because of its very high military and administrative overheads, the VOC was able to make such profits only by using its power selectively to establish monopoly conditions. All other actors in the Southeast Asia trade lost out in this period—Spanish, Portuguese, Gujaratis, Bengalis, Chinese, Japanese, and English, and above all the Southeast Asian trading groups. The VOC itself suffered a period of stagnation somewhat later, as its homeward cargoes from Batavia dipped in the period 1660–1700 (Bruijne, Gaastra, and Schöffer 1987: 176–79, 190), and this can be attributed at least in part to the impoverishment of the Southeast Asian trade on which it had previously relied.

Climate

The most truly global explanation of the "general crisis" is also the least understood—that is, the gradual decline in temperatures during the seventeenth century (perhaps caused by the Maunder minimum of solar activity), which reached its nadir in many parts of the northern hemisphere in about 1690 before the modern warming trend began. Evidence has been accumulating recently to substantiate both the global nature of the cooling process and the negative effects of such cooling on harvests and grain yields in the northern temperate zone (Braudel 1979 I: 46–51; Lamb 1982: 201–30, 272–309; Galloway 1986). Equally important is the evidence that it is precisely at such periods of global cooling that climatic conditions vary the most (Lamb 1982: 219–20; Galloway 1986: 20). Parallel research on the effects of short-range fluctuations has demonstrated a correlation between El Niño events and droughts in Java (Quinn et al. 1978). Although too little is yet known about the interaction of short-term and long-term cycles in tropical areas such as Southeast Asia, there can no longer be any doubt that global climatic factors do influence both disease mortality and famines induced by drought.

The effects of the little ice age on the humid tropics remain unclear, though they probably include a greater variability of short-term changes in the weather. There are few systematic runs of climatic data in Southeast Asia that can help establish whether the seventeenth century was also climatically difficult for Southeast Asia. The best is Berlage's remarkable series of tree-rings from the teak forests of east-central Java, which provides relative rainfall levels for every year between 1514 and 1929 (Lamb 1977 II: 603–04). This shows 1598–1679 to be the worst substantial period for rainfall in the 415 years recorded. Of the 82 years in that dry period, only 13 reached the mean level of rainfall over the four centuries. Not a single year between 1643 and 1671 did so, marking these out as much the most critical decades (see fig. 39, above).

Both distinguishing long-term from short-term fluctuations and drawing conclusions for neighbouring areas from data on this Rembang area of Java are fraught with difficulty. Other sources do suggest a correlation between the Berlage data on dry periods in Java and crisis events in a broader area of the Archipelago. We might indeed expect that in those areas of the eastern Archipelago where survival depended on a delicate balance between wet and dry monsoons, these years of low rainfall would lengthen the dry season dangerously, giving rise to crop failures, famines, dry and polluted wells, and epidemics.

The first critically dry period in Berlage's series was 1605–16. Each of these years was markedly below average, and 1606 was the second driest year (after 1603) recorded since 1580. Although descriptive sources are not abundant in this period, both Dutch and Malay sources note the years 1606–08 as ones of exceptional famine in Aceh (partly caused by war), from which many people died (Verhoeff 1611: 242; Raniri 1644: 34). This bad period may also help explain the epidemic said to have reduced Kedah's population by two-thirds in 1614, and the "great reduction in population" in northern Maluku, which Reael (1618: 87) attributed mostly to warfare.

Although there was a bad rice crop in Makassar in 1624 and there were terrible epidemics in Java in 1624–25 (Reid 1988: 60), the 1620s appear relatively benign, according to the Java tree-ring data. The next bad patch in Berlage's series is a shorter one from 1633 to 1638, with 1634 and 1637 the worst years. This may be connected to the rice shortage reported for Bali in 1633,[2] the drought in Maluku in 1635 (Gardenijs 1636: 152), and the terrible epidemic in Makassar in 1636, in which sixty thousand were said to have died in forty days (Reid 1988: 61). Although Siam also experienced a prolonged drought and crop failure in 1633, this should probably be seen as part of a different weather cycle.

As mentioned above, the most dramatic feature of the whole Berlage series is the severe dry period it shows from 1643 to 1671. The importance of this data is confirmed by the drought in Banten in 1657 (*Dagh-Register* 1656–59: 155) and "the great drought" of 1660–61 recorded in southern Borneo, in Ambon, and "most quarters of the Indian Archipelago," in Palembang, where the Musi River was so low that Dutch vessels could not pass (Coolhaas 1968: 321). The grim nadir of this period came in 1664 and 1665, the driest of any years in the four-hundred-year series of Java tree-rings. In the second and worst of these years there occurred probably the most disastrous epidemic of the century, affecting most of the Archipelago. The population of both the Makassar area and Java was said to have been "very much less-

---

2. For this and other disaster events, the source for which is not otherwise attributed in the period 1624–61, I am grateful to Peter Boomgaard, one of whose unpublished papers surveyed data for these years recorded in the *Dagh-Register*.

ened" by it, and Bali and the west coast of Sumatra were also affected (Reid 1988: 61).

The tree-ring data, finally, reveal another shorter bout of very dry seasons in 1673–75, which also shows up well in Dutch observations. Mataram suffered famine and illness throughout the years 1674–76. The rice crops of Jambi, Sumbawa, and South Sulawesi failed in 1674, and in South Sulawesi (again) and Palembang in 1675, while the Musi River again dropped too low for navigation. Mataram suffered famine and illness throughout the years 1674–76, and Maluku in 1675 (Coolhaas 1971: 2, 3, 21, 38, 84, 110; Ricklefs 1981: 70). Although Dutch factors tended to record these crises only when their own people or allies died, or when the high price of rice in a particular area affected their commercial calculations, there is enough confirming evidence to show that the exceptionally dry weather recorded in the tree-rings did seriously increase mortality.

The continental masses of northern Southeast Asia cannot be expected to follow the rainfall patterns of Java in any simple fashion. But the fact of global cooling does appear to have created conditions of unusual variability in other parts of Asia. In the whole period 1626–40 China experienced exceptional difficulties, "with extreme droughts being followed by major floods." Some estimates show Chinese population dropping 40 percent in consequence between 1585 and 1645 (Wakeman 1985 I: 7–8). Detailed local records exist for coastal southern China (Guangdong and Fujian), which interestingly do show severe drought in the worst years of the Java tree-rings—1664 and 1665. The most sustained dry periods in south China, however, were in the 1640s and again in the 1680s (Zhongyang Qixiang 1981: 323–26), which understandably correlate better with Vietnamese crises than those elsewhere in Southeast Asia. The most severe drought-induced famine in Tongking appears to have come in 1641, whereas the Nguyen chronicles suggest that the period 1641–1700 was particularly severe in Cochin-China, with twenty crisis years recorded.[3]

Burma and western Siam appear to have had a long-term climatic pattern more similar to that of southeast India than to that of the rest of the region. In India as a whole, the worst years were 1630 and 1631, representing "almost certainly the most destructive Indian famine of the early modern era," and killing about three million people in Gujarat alone (Disney 1984; cf. Raychaudhuri 1962: 38–39). This spread to the east coast of India and beyond into Southeast Asia, where many

<hr>

3. I owe these Vietnam data to Li Tana, whose recent thesis on Cochin-China in the seventeenth and eighteenth centuries has involved a close reading of both Vietnamese and Chinese sources. See also Li 1992: 15–18.

people were said to have died in Burma and Arakan in 1631–32 (Hall 1939: 140–41), and a prolonged drought destroyed most of the 1633 rice crop in Siam. In 1660–61 another appalling drought struck South India, and particularly Tanjore, where "famine has so increased that whole villages, towns and hamlets have been depopulated, and hardly anyone remains, the dead lying in dried-up tanks" (Maetsuyker 1661: 355). This, too, had some effect in Burma, where 1661 was noted for very high rice prices.

By the standards of seventeenth-century India, China, and Europe, weather-induced famines appear to have been relatively moderate in Southeast Asia. As pointed out in volume 1 (Reid 1988: 19), Europeans thought the region blessed by its climate and its abundance of alternative food supplies even if rice crops failed. The above indications of exceptional crisis mortality, particularly in 1640–75, would therefore not seem a plausible factor to explain broader political and economic setbacks were it not for strong evidence of population decline in the same period. When each case of population loss is looked at separately, warfare usually appears the likeliest cause. Yet the overall demographic record shows such a conjuncture between different Southeast Asian areas and the broader global pattern that it becomes necessary to look for climatic as well as economic explanations.

The demographic data for the seventeenth century are sparse, and the best derive from the areas of greatest European control, which for that reason may not be typical. The Spanish kept lists of the numbers of Filipino *tributos* from whom they claimed labour and tax in Luzon and the Visayas, which can be totalled as follows (each *tributo* perhaps corresponding to four or five people):[4]

1586	146,700
1591	166,903
1608	125,196
1621	130,938
1655	108,277
1686	121,000
1742	184,814

4. I owe these figures to Norman Owen, who wisely traced the better-known figures given by Phelan (1959: 100) back to their sources in Blair and Robertson. Phelan appears to have applied different multipliers in different periods to convert tributos to population, perhaps from a sense that these large population losses were not believable.

Jesuit reports on the tiny Christian island of Siau off northeast Sulawesi show the same pattern of population: *1588*, 2,400; *1612*, 3,000; *1631*, 7,000; *1645*, 3,000; *1676*, 5,500 (Jacobs 1987).

Table 11. Central Maluku population

	Ambon	Lease	Total
1634	22,670	18,565	41,235
1671	19,338	15,973	35,311
1674 (lowest)	17,609	16,596	34,205
1680	18,486	17,288	35,774
1685	19,262	18,847	38,109
1690	21,075	21,142	42,217
1695	22,167	20,940	43,107
1708	21,140	21,343	42,483

Source: Knaap 1987: 99–109

Some of this loss may be explained by Filipinos fleeing Spanish exactions into the uncontrolled hills, but the 35 percent loss between 1591 and 1655 is too great to be accounted for by this alone. It contrasts markedly with the rapid subsequent growth in Philippine population, which on these figures would be 0.35 percent a year after 1655 and 0.76 percent after 1686. The Spanish conquest, followed by the heavy taxation needed to sustain the war with the Dutch (1609–48) and the collapse of the China trade in the middle of the century, may have played a part in this striking mid-seventeenth-century population dip. But the chronological fit with the climatic data is difficult to ignore.

Additional population figures (table 11) are available for Ambon and the Lease Islands, in Central Maluku, relatively meticulously supervised by the VOC, which concentrated all its clove cultivation there. Knaap attributes this mid-century drop to the terrible wars fought by the Dutch for control of the clove-growing islands (1641–56) and to a major epidemic, perhaps of malaria, in 1656–58. Although these must be factors, they do not explain why population continued to decline after the *pax neerlandica* was established in 1656, reaching its nadir in Ambon in 1674, in the "western" Ambonese Islands in 1673, and in the Lease Islands in 1672. A rapid population expansion of about 1 percent a year then restored the population of the Ambon area during the next two decades (Knaap 1987: 109).

These are the only two data series that are reasonably reliable at regular intervals through the seventeenth century, and the coincidence between them must give rise to speculation about both economic and climatic factors (fig. 40). There are also striking indications of population decline in larger states, though the figures are not precise or systematic enough to say with confidence when it occurred.

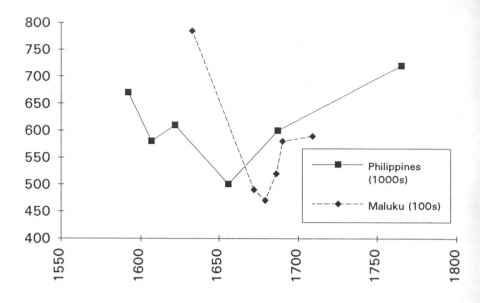

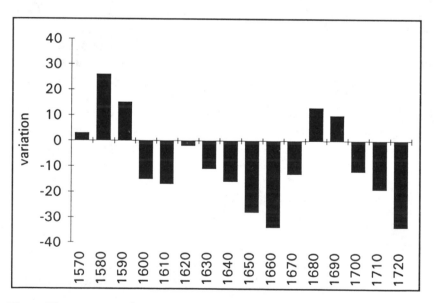

Fig 40 The seventeenth-century crisis as reflected in population and climatic indicators: *(a)* population of Philippines (thousands) and Ambon area
(hundreds); *(b)* tree-ring growth in Java, in terms of variation by decade from
a four-hundred-year mean, in decades beginning in the years indicated

The core area of Mataram (most of modern central and east Java, without the pasisir) was reckoned by a tax registration in 1631 to be 500,000 *cacah* (taxable households), perhaps 3 million people. At the division of the realm in 1755, there appeared to be only 172,500 cacah. The first of these figures is obviously conventionalized at best and not to be taken seriously. But Ricklefs (1986) has convincingly shown that conventionalized local figures revised between 1651 and 1755 showed a consistent downward trend, beginning with a major decline reported in 1678. After the Gianti peace of 1755 there was the same population boom as had begun earlier in the Philippines (and temporarily in Maluku).

In the relatively crowded Red River delta, the Vietnamese heartland known to foreigners as Tongking, tax records (Li 1992: 27) show some remarkable rises and falls in the number of villages recorded for revenue purposes:

1417	3,385
1490	7,950
1539	10,228
1634–43	8,671
1730s	11,766
1810	10,635

Because we cannot be sure that administrative villages remained of comparable size throughout the period, these figures are not an adequate indicator. Nevertheless, the rapid growth (0.5 percent a year) during the prosperous and peaceful fifteenth century is striking, as is the decline after 1539. Other evidence makes it probable that most of the decline occurred during the period of ferocious civil war between the Trinh and the Mac (1545–92), which in turn was connected with the worst series of disaster years recorded in the annals—1559, 1561, 1570, 1571, 1572, 1586, 1588, 1589, 1592, 1594, 1595, 1596, 1597. Crop failure, starvation, and disease in each of these years killed large proportions of the population in certain areas and drove others to migrate to the southern frontier or elsewhere (Le 1971: 248–49; Li 1992: 15–18). While one would have expected the population to rise again after this appalling period, its failure to do so in the seventeenth century (if the record of villages corresponds to population) suggests that rural conditions continued to be very much worse than they had been before 1539.

A combination of factors, including a much less favourable global commercial climate, Dutch monopoly pressure, military defeats, and a relatively unstable climate with a high incidence of drought, combined to produce an unusually severe crisis for Southeast Asia in the middle of the seventeenth century. The reduced opportunities for trade became ever more apparent between 1630 and 1650, while the climate was probably at its worst in the 1650s and 1660s. The effects of the crisis are observable in the demographic record, such as it is, but their most important long-term effect may have been to shift many Southeast Asian societies towards greater self-reliance and distrust of the international market.

Retreat from the World Economy

> Commerce does not yield much profit,
> even if you grow pepper, my friends.
> If there is no rice in the country . . .
> What good are purple headcloths or daggers with golden handles?
> If there is no rice in the country,
> rulers and princes will lose their stature . . .
> Even if you have quantities of gold, what use is it if you are starving?
> —Hikayat Pocut Mohamat: 166–67

Ironically, those with the most precious resources were the first driven to conclude that they should have nothing more to do with cultivating these resources. Just as Filipinos stopped exploiting their gold when they saw that it brought the unwonted attention of predatory Spaniards (Loarca 1582: 51, 53; Morga 1609: 261), spice growers discovered in the seventeenth century that they were possessors of a very mixed blessing. The Banda Islanders suffered worst—they were virtually wiped out as a people in 1620–23 by the Dutch determination to control their precious nutmeg trees. The people of Ternate, Tidore, Bacan, and Makian in northern Maluku, who had monopolized the world's supply of cloves until the sixteenth century, turned against the spice in the early seventeenth. The ferocity of the war between Spanish-backed Ternate and Dutch-backed Tidore in the first two decades of that century was the primary reason the Malukans abandoned clove cultivation, in the hope that they could escape destruction (Meilink-Roelofsz 1969: 216). The VOC, in addition to buying cloves at below market price, caused a fivefold increase in the price of rice after it took over supplying goods to the islands from the highly competitive Javanese and Malays. The result was a wholesale shift out of cash-cropping in northern Maluku: "With our own eyes we see them everywhere plant whole fields with rice, beside their gardens, which they preferred not to do in the time when they had commerce with foreigners, for these people . . . paid with cloves for rice and sago, the bread of these islands, at a civil price and easily obtained; whereas now to avoid the high prices they either plant, as with rice, or go and look for it in other places, as happens with sago, which they get from Sula, Taliabu, as well as the islands of Bacan" (Reael 1618: 89). Although Ambon made good the decline in clove production in northern Maluku, it, too, soon suffered from warfare and the drive for monopoly. Population fell, as we have seen, and so did the clove harvest (Knaap 1987: 234).

Others drew the obvious lesson. When a Dutch factor visited Magindanao in 1686, he was told: "Nutmeg and cloves can be grown here, just as in Maluku. They were not there now because the old Raja had all of them ruined before his death. He was afraid that the Dutch Company would come to fight with them about it" (Brouwer, cited Laarhoven-Casino 1985: 368; cf. Dampier 1697: 218).

Pepper-growing, too, lost its attraction when it became clear that the high prices of the period 1616–50 had ended. Between 1650 and 1653 the price paid for pepper in Southeast Asian markets dropped by half. In the 1670s supply outran demand even more severely, the pepper price in Holland dropped temporarily by four-fifths, and prices paid in Southeast Asia were only a quarter of what they had been in the 1640s (Coolhaas 1971: 275; see fig. 41).

Some rulers decided to ban pepper cultivation because they felt the need for greater self-sufficiency in dangerous times. Early in the century (probably during the famines of 1606–08) the Sultan of Aceh had already ordered the destruction of pepper vines in the vicinity of the capital because his subjects "amused themselves with nothing else, and neglected the cultivation of the ground, so that every year there was great scarcity of victuals" (Beaulieu 1666: 98–99; cf. van den Broecke 1634 I: 174). The English believed that Banten cut down its pepper vines around 1620 in the hope that this would encourage the Dutch and English to leave the sultanate in peace (Guillot 1992: 43), though self-sufficiency must have been an additional reason.

Several states were forced to shift from cash crops to staple foods by shipping blockades, the favorite weapon of the VOC against cities dependent on food imports. Banten was the most frequently affected port, and in the 1630s there was a widespread move to rice-growing. Not all could change their livelihood, and the English complained that "the long desistance from planting of pepper here, which commodity was the only trade of this place, hath so empoverished this people that many of them hath no other manner of living, but stealing" (Willoughby 1635: 154). The Sultan of Magindanao told the Dutch in 1699 that

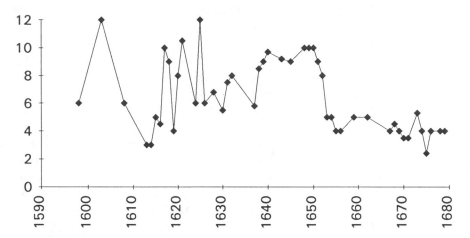

Fig. 41 Prices paid for pepper in Southeast Asia, in reals per pikul. *Sources:*
1599–1620, Meilink-Roelofsz 1962: 248–49, 260, 281, 393–94; van den
Broecke 1634 I: 178; *LREIC III*: 227, *after 1620*, Coolhaas 1960, 1964, 1968,
and 1971, as well as Mundy 1667: 338 and *SP* for the period *1630–32*

"he had forbidden the continued planting [of pepper] so that he did not
thereby get involved in war, whether with the [Dutch] Company or
with other potentates" (Silver 1699: 110). Other rulers squeezed so
hard on the dwindling profits of pepper-growing that they killed the
supply altogether. The Sultan of Palembang's desperate efforts to monopolize supplies of pepper to stop prices falling in the 1670s gravely
reduced the supply from growers (Coolhaas 1968: 882, 902, 920). The
similar policies of Jambi and Banten have already been noted.

The disenchantment with pepper-growing by the end of the century was made very clear in Malay writing, which reflected the anxiety
of court elites threatened by the instabilities of cultivating pepper. In
Banjarmasin the court chronicle pleaded:

Let people nowhere in this country plant pepper, as is done in Jambi and
Palembang. Perhaps those countries grow pepper for the sake of money, in
order to become wealthy. There is no doubt that in the end they will go to
ruin. There will be much intrigue and food will become expensive. . . .
Regulations will be in disorder because the people of the capital will not
be respected by those of the countryside; officers of the king will not be
feared by the highlanders. . . .
If more [pepper than was needed for household uses] should be planted, for
the purpose of making money, this would bring misery over the country
. . . instructions from above would not be executed because the people
would be emboldened against the king (*Hikayat Banjar:* 330, 442).

Similar sentiments were expressed in eighteenth-century Aceh, as quoted at the beginning of this section. Not only did the court elite seek a return to greater self-reliance in view of the dangers and instabilities of the market; they also sought a more stable social order, in which newly rich cash croppers and traders did not pose a threat to their status.

Pepper was by far the most valuable Southeast Asian export in the age of commerce. When prices were still high, in the 1640s, this crop alone probably earned the equivalent of about 25 tonnes of silver, most of which was spent on imports. Production continued to rise despite lower prices until about 1670, when more than 8000 tonnes of pepper were being exported each year. Thereafter the quantity as well as the price dropped sharply, and Southeast Asian growers began to return to subsistence crops on a much larger scale. The loss of Malukan spice profits was felt earlier, and the China-Japan trade was in crisis in the 1640s. The effect of this reduction in export revenue was apparent in the declining ability to buy imported Indian cloth.

Southeast Asian imports of cloth peaked in the period 1620–50 (chapter 1), at around a million and a half pieces per year and a value (in Coromandel prices) equivalent to about 40 tonnes of silver. In the second half of the century textile prices rose markedly in India, just as pepper prices dropped in Southeast Asia. On the Coromandel Coast, the main source, purchase prices rose 45 percent between 1665 and 1700 (Lieberman 1984: 160). Because of the VOC's near-monopoly in many Archipelago ports, the rise in prices was greater there. Not surprisingly, the VOC was selling 20 percent less in the Archipelago in 1703 than in 1652 (Laarhoven 1988). VOC sales to vessels from Archipelago ports visiting Batavia to buy Indian cloth dropped more precipitately, by 43 percent between 1665–69 and 1679–81, and even more rapidly in the subsequent twenty years (Nagtegaal 1988: 181–82; Rontoandro 1988: 61). Because Gujarati, Bengali, English, and Portuguese supplies all dropped drastically in the middle of the century, there is no doubt that overall Southeast Asian consumption of Indian cloth was in sharp decline.

Dutch and British factors complained with increasing frequency that the peoples of the Archipelago were so impoverished by the loss of their export trade that they could no longer afford Indian cloth. After two decades of Dutch blockades and interruptions of its pepper trade, the population of Banten, "formerly so opulent and prodigal in its daily clothing, now made a very impoverished and desolate [impression]" in 1634, and its people had been obliged to weave their own cloth (Philip Lucasz, 1634, cited Meilink-Roelofsz 1962: 258; cf. Hoare 1632: 89). In Central and east Java in 1684, "The Javanese, having become poor and indigent as a result of the endless wars and upheavals, have been forced to resort, more than they otherwise would, to weaving their cloths themselves, not only for their own use, but also to sell these in other places" (Camphuys 1684: 673; cf. Coolhaas 1971: 711; Coolhaas 1975: 287, 427). In the 1670s and 1680s, after the VOC conquered Makassar and ended its spice trade, the Bugis and Makassarese had reportedly resumed their weaving because they could no longer afford to buy Indian cloth (Coolhaas 1971: 139, 246, 336, 715). Both Javanese and Makassarese took to selling their cheaper cloths around the Archipelago, increasing the popularity of Selayar check-cloth and Javanese batik and providing cheaper alternatives for the impoverished populations . The populations of Jambi and Palembang began to buy Javanese cloth in the 1690s and to weave their own, because they could no longer afford the Indian cloth of which the Dutch had monopolized the supply by 1683 (Coolhaas 1975: 754; Andaya 1989: 38–40).

The *Hikayat Banjar* (330) expressed this shift in ideological terms, as part of its rejection of the market economy: "Whenever people follow the style of dress of other countries, evil will certainly befall that country." A Dutch governor-general put the problem another way:

The weaving of their own clothes has been in practice for the convenience of the ordinary people since olden times among the Javanese and most eastern people; but since these countries flourished more formerly than now, most of these peoples sought Coromandel and Surat cloths [for everyday use], not as luxuries, and gave large amounts of money for that. . . . Now most of the surrounding countries are impoverished, and the [Coromandel] Coast and Surat cloths have become limited to the use of the wealthy (van Outhoorn 1693: 639).

A few years later another Dutch official pointed to the impossibility of preventing the Javanese from growing cotton and weaving cloth rather than buying from the Dutch: "It is nothing but poverty that is the true reason that the traffic in the finest [Coromandel] Coast and Surat cloth declines daily while by contrast their own weaving has increased more and more through the multiplication of poor people" (Chastelein 1704, cited Rouffaer 1904: 3).

As the trade that had given life to the great maritime cities ebbed from them, the cities lost population and centrality. Every major city except the Vietnamese capital was conquered and pillaged at some point in the sixteenth and seventeenth centuries (see map 5, above). Thang-long was a special case as capital of the most centralized Southeast Asian state and the one least interested in international trade. Yet even it appears to have declined from its fifteenth-century peak—for reasons usually described in purely political terms (Nguyen 1970: 111–13; *Hanoi* 1977: 40–52). Of the other important cases only Ayutthaya, devastated by the Burmese in 1569, regained its previous population size. The disasters that befell the remaining cities can be seen as crises in an underlying trend against maritime trade–based cities, so that the urban populations of the age of commerce were not recovered.

Melaka was reduced to about a quarter of its population as a result of the Portuguese conquest in 1511 and has only regained its former dimensions in our own times. Brunei was substantially smaller after its destruction by the Spanish in 1579, even though the conquerors did not stay. Pegu was never again a major city after its terrible ordeal of 1598–99, and observers in subsequent centuries could only marvel at the dimensions of its ruined walls. Surabaya, thought to have had a population of 50,000 before its destruction by Mataram in 1621–25, did not again reach this level until the nineteenth century; Makassar and Banten, conquered by the Dutch in 1666–69 and 1682, respectively, lost their economic and political raison d'etre, and declined to no more than a quarter of their previous populations.

The economic function of these entrepôts was assumed in part by the European enclave cities that took over the most lucrative long-distance trade of the region. Because they played a minimal role as political and cultural centres for their hinterlands, and because they discouraged the influx of Asian dependents that the older cities had attracted or forced to them, they were much smaller than their predecessors. Portuguese Melaka never rose above thirty thousand inhabitants, and even Batavia had scarcely thirty thousand people dwelling within its walls in the second half of the seventeenth century, when it dominated the maritime trade of Asia. The commercial life and urban values that flourished behind the walls of these colonial cities had minimal influence on the majority populations of Southeast Asia.

The urban-centred world of Southeast Asia described in chapter 2 had vanished by 1700. When census data became available in the late nineteenth century, the region was one of the world's least urbanized.

Responses to the Loss of Trade Revenue

The Mainland states and Aceh were strong enough militarily, or uninteresting enough commercially, to avoid the fate of Makassar and Banten. All retained their independence and their freedom to trade with whomever they wished. Yet they, too, suffered crises in the seventeenth century that caused them to draw back from their dependence on foreign, especially European, commerce. After the destruction of Pegu in 1598–99 and the subsequent adventure of Felipe de Brito in Syriam, the restored Toungoo kings of Burma shifted their capital definitively to Ava, in the rice-growing heartland of upper Burma, in 1635. Ayutthaya in its "1688 revolution" expelled French traders and imprisoned French missionaries, limited contacts with other Europeans, and surrendered its place as one of the leading trade centres of Asia. The two Vietnamese states put greater obstacles in the way of European trade at the end of the century. Laos, like Aceh, fell into disunity after its brief golden age of the early seventeenth century. Champa's autonomy ended and Cambodia's was severely compromised by repeated military intervention from its neighbours.

Earlier European writers tended to see these developments negatively, as self-defeating attempts at isolation from the modern world. According to Hall (1955: 378), "No [Burmese] king after Anaukhpetlun [1606–29] appreciated the value of overseas intercourse. . . . So the dynasty surrendered to traditionalism and isolationism." Hutchinson (1940: 192) had no better view of the "spirit of blind and arrogant self-sufficiency" in Siam after 1688. For a number of reasons these developments have recently been reevaluated in a more positive light (Lieberman 1991, 1993; Pombejra 1993).

First, a broader consideration of how states responded to the crisis of the seventeenth century can leave little doubt that Japan was the most successful survivor in Asia, just as Holland was in Europe (Atwell 1986: 226–27). Curiously, 1635, the year of Burma's "retreat" to a stronghold in Ava, was also the year when Japanese were forbidden to travel abroad, one of a series of moves ordered by the Tokugawa shoguns in the 1630s to restrict contacts with the outside world. Recent historical work has demonstrated both that trade and cultural contact did nevertheless continue and that the conditions of internal peace and a unified market created by the Tokugawa were favourable for the accumulation of capital and increases in productivity (Innes 1980; Smith 1988; Hayami 1989). Some degree of withdrawal from foreign trade became politically desirable, in other words, once that trade became associated with the military-backed demands of Europeans— for religious freedom or privilege on the part of the Iberians and the French; for monopoly on the part of the Dutch and English companies.

Second, the concentration by Western writers on relations with Europeans tells only half the story. Although the major European actors were expelled from the Mainland states or gave up trying to surmount the obstacles put in their path, Chinese private trade revived everywhere at the end of the century. The Chinese factor was most important in the countries around the South China Sea, especially in the two Vietnams, where silks were the preferred dress and there had never been much interest in the Indian cottons brought in from the west. How damaging was the seventeenth-century crisis for the economy of such states?

In Vietnam the major impact of the boom period had been the Japanese-Chinese trade taking place at Hoi An in Cochin-China in 1600–35. The halting of this by the Tokugawa in the 1630s must have been an important setback. The Dutch were admitted in both Vietnams because they replaced the Japanese, importing Japanese silver, copper, and copper coinage and exporting silk to Nagasaki. The VOC had a factory in Cochin-China in 1633–41 and 1651–54, as well as a longer-standing one in Tongking in 1637–1700. The almost constant warfare between the two states in the period 1627–79 created another source of interest in foreign imports, with the Portuguese providing guns for the Nguyen and the Dutch for the Trinh. The Dutch complained bitterly about the difficult conditions for trade in both states, as did the English during their brief experiment with Tongking in 1672–97. The Vietnamese must have found the Western barbarians troublesome and demanding; they preferred to deal with Chinese traders for essentials. The junk trade remained strong and perhaps even increased after 1684, but the collapse of other branches of trade removed the largest sources of state revenue and left the Vietnamese states more dependent on one source of goods and ideas.

Vietnamese historians, generally following the chronicles, portray the first half of the eighteenth century as a series of disasters, famines, and peasant rebellions that led to the collapse of both Trinh and Nguyen regimes before the storm of the great Tay-son rebellion (Le 1987: 303–12; Nguyen 1987: 109). The fundamental reasons for these disasters remain obscure. In the north the Trinh regime appeared to lose the capacity to mobilize the population effectively to maintain the dykes. In the south the decline of trade revenue induced the Nguyen to increase impositions on land and on upland tributaries, which they could not in the long run sustain. Even though the two Vietnams exhausted each other in warfare for much of the seventeenth century, war may have provided them with a discipline and a stimulus to innovate which peace did not.

In Burma there is no question that the seventeenth century was a bad time for maritime commerce. Not only did the English withdraw their factory in 1657 and the VOC remove theirs in 1679 after one decade and four decades, respectively, of struggling against restrictive practice and unprofitable trade. The destruction of Mon overseas trade was permanent, and the flight of thousands more Mons into Siam during further bouts of rebellion and suppression in the 1660s and 1750s decimated Burma's merchant class. Lieberman (1984: 156–57; 1991: 14–15) estimates that overseas trade with Burma's delta ports recovered somewhat in the 1660s but that it was not until after 1800 that this trade regained its sixteenth-century levels.

Lieberman nevertheless refutes Hall's (1955: 380) concept of "a long period of stagnation" in Burma from the mid-seventeenth century. Although the maritime regions of the delta were in disarray, the population of the core region of upper Burma slowly expanded, its market towns grew in number and size, and an internal market economy based on silver grew in sophistication. Finally, there was a growth in the China trade, not by sea as in Vietnam but over caravan routes into Yunnan. By 1830 this trade may have come to represent one-half to two-thirds the level of the maritime trade, and Burmese had begun to wear Chinese silk on a considerable scale (Lieberman 1991: 15–16).

If Lieberman is right, some of the arguments made about Japan in this period may be applicable to Burma's withdrawal from intense maritime interaction with the outside world. Unlike Japan, however, Burma did not increase its production faster than its population. In spite of the much greater concentration on agriculture after 1600, crop failure and famine became increasingly frequent in the period 1661–1740, as royal authority was no longer sufficient to see that irrigation channels were maintained (Lieberman 1984: 152–54, 176–77).

Ayutthaya's revenues undoubtedly suffered greatly in the 1640s from the cessation of direct Japanese shipping and the drastic reduction in shipping from China. Nevertheless, Siam had a late period of exceptional prosperity under King Narai (1656–88), whose capital remained a great independent port largely through his increasingly desperate balancing of one foreign group against another. As the other major Asian entrepôts of the long-distance trade, Makassar, Banten, and Aceh, fell to Dutch pressure, Ayutthaya became ever more important for all non-Dutch traders. After Makassar's first defeat by the Dutch-Bugis coalition in 1660, the English factors there recommended moving to Ayutthaya, where the Portuguese and Muslims were already heading. "Since the late wars in Cambodia have removed all commerce out of that barbarous hole, it is devolved thither [Siam] and the wealthiest of the Portuguese and Malayans [of Makassar] intend that as their station" (cited Boxer 1967: 28).

By 1664, when the VOC blockaded the capital to force on Narai a monopoly of his lucrative deerskin exports to Japan, the danger posed by the European companies was clear. Narai looked to both English and French as counterweights to Dutch monopoly pressure. Around

1680 it looked as if the English East India Company might provide this, especially when the talented Greek Constance Phaulkon (originally Constantin Hiérachy) rose rapidly in Siamese service as an English protégé. The English proved impossibly quarrelsome, however. The two factors trusted by Phaulkon and the Siamese—Samuel White and Richard Burnaby—left the service of the East India Company and became ever more embittered with its official representatives in Madras. In 1683 Burnaby was appointed Siamese governor of Mergui, with White as syahbandar (harbourmaster), as part of Phaulkon's plan to organize Narai's royal trade to India with European expertise. In 1687 Fort St. George in Madras had grown so frustrated with its two errant sons that it declared war on Siam and abortively tried to seize Mergui (Anderson 1890).

This left Phaulkon little alternative but Louis XIV of France, to whom he had offered Songkhla in 1685 as the price of support against the Dutch and English. In 1687 a French fleet of six warships sailed for Siam to back the new alliance. Unknown to the Thais, the French had decided that they needed Bangkok (gateway to the capital and its river) rather than Songkhla, as well as a garrison at Mergui. Phaulkon was now exasperated with the English, and his marriage to a pious Japanese Catholic had reconciled him to the church and particularly to the hope of French Jesuits eventually to obtain the conversion of the king. He therefore persuaded Narai to accept these unpopular French demands. With six hundred French soldiers in the country and Phaulkon seemingly directing the king's policy, resentment against the Europeans reached unprecedented levels.

Reaction came in the form of a coup in April 1688, during the king's terminal illness. Because Narai had no son, the succession was unclear. The master of the royal elephants, Okphra Phetracha, profited from the anti-foreign sentiments of the Buddhist sangha and elements of the urban populace to make his move. In April he seized the royal palace at Lopburi (Louvo) and had Phaulkon and the king's two brothers (and possible heirs) killed. When Narai died in July, Phetracha succeeded to the throne. The French garrisons were quickly besieged and by the end of 1688 were forced to leave, though with such little grace as to unleash a further round of violence against foreigners, especially Catholic missionaries (de Bèze 1691; Le Blanc 1692; Turpin 1771; Pombejra 1993: 252).

The change of dynasty marked a reversal in foreign policy; for the remainder of the Ayutthaya period Siam kept aloof from European entanglements. It did not deliberately seek isolation. The court still needed the revenues and goods derived from trade, and it continued to employ Muslim Indians and (increasingly) Chinese to conduct commerce. Trade did continue, but it both declined in overall volume and shifted towards the East Asian pattern of overwhelming dependence on the Chinese junk trade.

After 1688 only the VOC remained among large European traders, and it complained constantly about trade prospects, closing its office temporarily in 1705 and 1741 (Pombejra 1993: 266). Indian Muslim trade continued the downward path it had begun in the 1680s. Even the Chinese branch of trade slumped during the reign of King Phetracha (1688–1703), before growing to new heights in the eighteenth century.[5] The tribute trade to China was suspended entirely during that reign, and the *Tosen* (Chinese) shipping in Chinese junks between Ayutthaya and Nagasaki declined. Ayutthaya had become the principal Southeast Asian entrepôt for Tosen ships towards the end of Narai's reign, attracting shipping away from its rivals Cambodia and Patani. In the 1690s, however, the Tosen ships deserted Ayutthaya again for Cambodia on a large scale (see table 10). The royal trade continued to use Chinese on voyages to the east and Indian Muslims to the west, but the king and his son managed to send just four ships to China (plus two to Manila and one to Tongking) in the period 1689–97, and none thereafter. In the last years of his reign Phetracha's ships concentrated on diplomatic ventures to Batavia (1702 and 1703) and Surat (Pombejra 1993: 261–62).

The reality appears to be that even the general increase in Chinese shipping to Southeast Asia after 1684, when the imperial ban on overseas trade was lifted, could not prevent a collapse in Ayutthaya's trade during Phetracha's reign. The country was troubled by war and rebellion in Khorat, Patani, and Ligor. Around 1700 the ruin of commerce was noted by a French missionary—"the traders are reduced to great misery, foreigners no longer come: one has seen here this year only 3 or 4 Chinese junks with not much merchandise" (cited Pombejra 1993). A clear indication of the decline in foreign trade was the acute shortage of silver throughout this reign. Although rice exports in the reign of King Thaisa (1709–33) lifted the Chinese junk trade to new heights, Ayutthaya was then an outpost of the Chinese trading net-

5. Sarasin Viraphol (1977: 54–55) has argued that a rapid expansion of the Chinese junk trade compensated for the decline in European and Indian trade after 1688. His figures, however, show a steady decline from 14–15 Chinese junks a year in 1689 to just 1 in 1701, before a recovery in the eighteenth century. Dutch reports list about 10 junks a year visiting Ayutthaya in 1658 and 1659 (Coolhaas 1968: 193, 257), about 20 in 1695, and again 10 in 1697 (Pombejra 1993: 263). Firm data are lacking for the last years of Narai, but Chinese trade was likely then to have been at its seventeenth-century peak.

work rather than a major international entrepôt. Even Chinese junk captains complained in this reign of a general impoverishment and decline in trade in the ports of Mainland Southeast Asia (Ships from Siam and Cambodia, 1717, in Ishii forthcoming).

How this retreat affected internal developments is more difficult to assess. The parallel with Burma and northern Vietnam is striking, however, in the way Siam progressively lost its ability to control its labour during the first half of the eighteenth century, leading to weakness and factionalism at the centre (Rabibhadana 1969: 34–38; Wyatt 1982: 129–30). The institutions of central control built up during the time of absolutism were not strong enough to survive the loss in external revenues—again in striking contrast to Japan.

The options of withdrawing from dependence on international trade or relying on the less dangerous Chinese junks were not available to the Archipelago states. Most had been created by trade and had few alternative resources to survive without it. When the most lucrative long-distance trade was lost to the VOC, the consequence was a diffusion of power among local dynasties.

In Java, the unified empire of Sultan Agung had disintegrated by the end of the tyrannical reign of Amangkurat I in 1677. Warfare was constant, with the VOC playing a large part, until in 1755 a permanent division of Java was imposed by a "Dutch" peace. In Bali, the single kingdom with which foreigners dealt in the first half of the century, with its impressive capital at Gelgel, began to break up around 1650, and by 1700 there were eight distinct kingdoms with only a token recognition of the spiritual seniority of one of them—the Dewa Agung (Creese 1991). The rapid progress towards imposing the single political authority of Ternate on Maluku in 1580–1600, and that of Makassar on South Sulawesi in 1600–60, was thrown into reverse after the Dutch domination of these capitals.

Myriad other river-ports had grown into substantial states through the trade revenue of the age of commerce, notably Aceh, Palembang, Jambi, Banjarmasin, Brunei, Johor, Patani, and Magindanao. During the seventeenth century most of these lost the capacity to overawe their hinterlands and to attract or force shipping to their major port for the produce of the whole region. All continued as significant sultanates—the aura of past glory helped to compensate for the lack of real political control.

It would be a mistake to label this process "re-feudalization" or to consider it a return to an older political bedrock. Most of these states had not existed before the age of commerce. They did exist after it. Identities had been permanently created. Even the constituent chiefdoms that in practice went their own way by 1700 were frequently the creations of the brief period at which the harbour principalities had flourished. Royal servants rewarded for service to the unified state in the form of a benefice of land turned themselves into hereditary chiefs but continued to value that original appointment by a mighty king. All spoke the same language, literally and metaphorically; all acknowledged that they were the common heirs of a valid tradition which ought in an ideal world to be unified.

The Archipelago state most successful in maintaining both its freedom of action and its status as a major international port was Aceh. Its fate is exemplary, though to some extent extreme, because it had never been based on a single river system. The centralized system of government did for a time outlive the death of its founder, Iskandar Muda, in 1636. Up to the crippling series of Dutch blockades in the 1650s, Aceh continued to channel west coast pepper and Perak tin to its capital, confirming its position as the premier port on the eastern side of the Bay of Bengal. By the end of that decade the VOC effectively controlled Perak's tin output, and in 1663 it prised away the west coast Minangkabau ports, which had always resented Acehnese control. Dobbin (1983: 73–83) has shown that even those few Minangkabau commercial brokers who initially gained by throwing in their lot with the Dutch had by the end of the century been destroyed by the VOC monopoly and the reversion of the Minangkabau area to a more self-sufficient economy. Finally, the east Sumatran state of Deli revolted against Aceh control in 1668 (Coolhaas 1968: 665, 723).

The reign of Aceh's first queen, Taj al-Alam (1641–75), was notable for its peacefulness and prosperity in a troubled time, but it also institutionalized the diffusion of power that marked the following two centuries. The war-leaders (uleebalang) whom Iskandar Muda had rewarded with grants of land in order to replace the power of established commercial orangkaya became entrenched local satraps during Taj al-Alam's reign. They now treasured their original temporary grants (sarakata) from Iskandar Muda as charters of hereditary entitlement. At the death of each of the subsequent queens, various combinations of these uleebalangs caused uproar in the capital as they attempted to advance their candidate for the throne—in opposition to the urban orangkayas' preference for another queen. Their eventual success in restoring male rule in 1699 did not improve stability. A major civil war for the succession rent the country in the 1720s, and when peace returned in the 1730s the authority of certain uleebalang "to enthrone and dethrone sultans" had become established. The transition from a "harbour autocracy" to a diffusion of power with resemblances to feudalism had been accomplished in less than a century. The devolution of power was expressed culturally in the sudden flowering of literature in Acehnese (the oldest extant manuscript in which is dated 1663–64), whereas in its political and literary heyday Aceh expressed itself only in Malay, the language of commerce and Islam (Ito and Reid 1985: 205–08).

This pattern was repeated in a number of states, and not only in the Archipelago. The kingdom of Lansang (Laos) collapsed with exceptional suddenness at the death of its great king Surinyavongsa in 1694. After a series of bitter succession disputes, the kingdom was permanently divided by 1707 with dynasties at Luang Prabang, Vientiane, and later Champassak. The internal unity of Arakan did not long outlast the loss of trade in the 1660s. For the whole period 1684–1710 the throne was the plaything of the royal guard of foreign Muslim archers, and it never regained its internal coherence before the Burmese conquered it in 1785. Cambodia's history before 1660 had been tormented, but it became more so when its river port declined into insignificance, internal division multiplied, and consequent Siamese and Vietnamese intervention kept the country on its knees.

It is too easy to portray this shift in a negative light, as though strong centralized politics with wealthy rulers were the only measure of well-being. On balance the eighteenth century was more peaceful than the seventeenth in Southeast Asia, and the departure of the absolutist rulers was not universally regretted. The age of commerce had given rise to much cultural innovation and borrowing, but the period of less profound interaction with the outside world that followed was marked by some of the most brilliant art and literature of Siam, Burma, Vietnam, and Java. The important point is that there was a change of direction in the seventeenth century that was not reversed until the twentieth.

Chinese Commerce and Ethnic Polarization

> *The Chinese are in Asia, like the Jews in Europe, dispersed into every place where there is some profit to be made. . . . The Chinese have a habit of saying in the form of a proverb, that all the other nations are blind in matters of commerce; that the Dutch alone have one eye; but that they themselves have two.*
>
> —*Savary 1723 I: 1174*

The only sector of the long-distance trade in Asia in which the Europeans failed to established themselves was that to China. Apart from the Portuguese enclave at Macao, a minor factor for most periods, Europeans were resolutely refused trading access to the Middle Kingdom. Even when Canton was finally opened to Westerners in 1684, discriminatory tariffs against European-rigged ships ensured that Chinese junks continued to carry the overwhelming majority of Chinese trade for another century. In addition, with the closing of Japan to all but Dutch and Chinese shipping in 1635, the junk trade had a great advantage in access to Japanese minerals. For these reasons Chinese trade was largely unaffected by European competition. After a slump in mid-century as a result of the collapse of the Ming and the long struggle by the new Manchu dynasty to gain control of the southern maritime provinces, Chinese trade to Southeast Asia recommenced its upward path in the 1680s. At about the same time, Europeans and Western Asians were almost squeezed out of the trade of Ayutthaya, Cambodia, and the two Vietnamese states.

Already in the early 1600s Chinese were the largest group of foreign traders in the Vietnamese states, the Philippines, Patani, and Banten. In Ayutthaya they were probably more numerous, though less wealthy, than the Indian Muslims at the beginning of the century, and they were by far the most important group at its end. Seventeenth-century estimates put the number of adult Chinese males in Ayutthaya and Banten at about 3000. In Manila numbers fluctuated in response to official policy, but had reached 23,000 in 1603, when most Chinese were killed during an appalling massacre. In the Cochin-China port of Hoi An there were perhaps 5000 in the 1640s and more at the end of the century (Fransisco 1642: 122; Chen 1974: 16–17).

As the seventeenth century advanced, those Chinese who stayed behind in the ports of Southeast Asia penetrated further and further into the hinterlands of the great emporia. In Banten around 1600 the Chinese had already begun to buy up pepper in the interior after the harvest, to resell not only to the Chinese but to anyone else who would pay a good price (Scott 1606: 136; Meilink-Roelofsz 1969: 246–47; fig. 42). In the 1620s the same thing was happening in Jambi and Palembang. Chinese, typically aided in the market by their Sumatran wives, would take imported cloth to the interior to exchange with the growers for pepper. By 1636 the Dutch factors thought Minangkabaus would never again bring their own pepper to the Jambi market, being "now so spoiled by having the Chinese bring the goods to them" (Brouwer 1636: 541; cf. Andaya 1989: 36–37). By 1700 Chinese were established in market towns all over the Philippines (de la Costa 1965: 74–75). In the northern Cambodian river market of Sambok (near modern Kratie) in 1641, Wusthoff (1642: 157) found the population:

Fig. 42 Dutch engraver's impression of Chinese merchants in Banten, 1596, with a principal merchant, *left*; his Javanese wife, *centre*; and *at right*, a trader who buys pepper from the inland cultivators. These Chinese wear the Ming top-knot, not the pigtail of fig. 43, imposed by the Manchus in 1644.

less Cambodian than Chinese, who hold most of the trade in the surrounding country, such as deerskins which come to perhaps 20,000 pieces a year . . . which the Chinese go in carts and boats and buy up by sniffing about, since little is brought onto the market. . . . [They buy] gold, rhinocerus-horn and ivory in exchange for salt, Chinaware, iron and small bronze gongs. . . . But these people pay a heavy price for their great profit of 9 or 10 percent with severe illness and looking like ghosts, through the unhealthiness of the place and the bad water.

The Europeans at first resented the competitive advantages this network gave the Chinese as buyers of export goods. By the third decade of the century, however, the Dutch and English had begun to establish a symbiosis with locally domiciled Chinese, who made their bulk long-distance trade possible by accumulating local goods in exchange for cloth. Even the local shipping networks that served the European enclave cities became increasingly dominated by Chinese. The hundreds of small boats that carried east Java salt to Dutch Melaka were 40 percent Chinese-owned and 46 percent Indonesian-owned in 1699–1700. Thirty-six years later these proportions were 53 percent and 28 percent (Knaap and Nagtegaal 1991: 140).

In the cities Chinese residents also became highly valued as craft-workers. At the end of the seventeenth century, when they were permitted to trade in Aceh, Dampier (1699: 94–95) described the numerous "Mechanicks, Carpenters, Joyners, Painters, etc" who came with the Chinese ships and turned the Chinese quarter into the busy heart of the city during the two or three months they were there. Chinese also came to the region as miners and smelters, of silver in northern Burma and copper in northern Vietnam. In the eighteenth century they began to dominate the mining of tin and gold in the Malay world, activities previously the preserve of locals.

Did this input of skills and energy serve to stimulate or to stifle the indigenous economy? The question cannot be answered categorically for Chinese any more than for Europeans. The answer appears to depend very much on the extent of assimilation or barriers to it. As shown by the example of the Southeast Asian junk (chapter 1) and by numerous other commercial and technical borrowings of the fifteenth and sixteenth centuries, urban and commercial culture gained enormously from its encounter with emigrant Chinese. As long as Chinese married into the local society and shared its religious and social norms, they helped to build a vigorous urban and commercial culture in Southeast Asia. This trend was markedly on the decline, however, in the late seventeenth century.

The movement of Chinese traders and craftsmen to Southeast Asia was particularly strong in the last decades of the seventeenth century. Departure for the south was eased by the legalization of foreign trade in 1684, but many also left who had supported Zheng Chenggong (Koxinga) in his long sea-based resistance to the Manchu regime and refused to accept its defeat. Previous bursts of Chinese migration, such as that resulting from the state trading expeditions under the Yongle emperor (1402–24), had been cut off from their Chinese roots and assimilated into the Southeast Asian urban trading elite within a generation or two. But there were new reasons why this did not take place on this occasion. First, the Qing relaxation of the ban on overseas trade meant that it was now possible to return to China, at least in theory, while contact with new migrants was more or less continuous. Second, many Ming loyalist supporters of Zheng Chenggong saw in his stand a kind of legitimation, for the first time, of a separate Chinese identity outside China. Last, the European port-enclaves provided a milieu that discouraged assimilation.

The first two of these reasons applied particularly to the Indo-Chinese peninsula and western Borneo, where a series of small Chinese-led commercial principalities were established. In 1679 there arrived in the Cochin-China port of Hoi An some seventy junks and three thousand soldiers of the defeated Zheng forces who had decided to serve the Nguyen ruler of southern Vietnam rather than the Manchus. The Nguyen king sent them to the Mekong delta area, which he was just beginning to wrest from Cambodia. They settled the Saigon and My-Tho areas and turned them into bustling markets much frequented by Malays, Cambodians, and Europeans, as well as Vietnamese. In effect, they formed an autonomous satrap, which was not fully absorbed into the Nguyen administration until 1732 (Chen 1979: 1535–37; Le 1971: 267).

Further west on the Cambodian coast a similar role was played by Mac Cuu, who had fled his native Guangdong in 1671 to serve as a commercial official of the court at Pnompenh. About 1700 he obtained from the Khmer ruler the farm of gambling revenues at the port of Ha Tien, then something of a piratic frontier. He flourished, attracted many other Cantonese as well as Vietnamese and Khmers fleeing dynastic troubles, and built a little state that embraced a string of ports along the eastern shore of the Gulf of Siam. In 1708 Mac Cuu transferred his loyalty to the rising power of Cochin-China, but he retained his own armed force and administrative structure until his death in 1735. His Sino-Vietnamese son Mac Thien-tu continued the tradition, minting coins, building fortresses, laying out markets, and even conducting an independent foreign policy generally opposing Siam and frequently intervening in Cambodia. In his capital he insisted on Ming-style dress for his officials, built in a Chinese style, and established a Confucian temple and schools. Only with the victory of the Tayson rebels in 1777 was he driven from Ha Tien (Chen 1979: 1537–43).

In the Archipelago the Portuguese in the 1510s had encountered a trade-oriented elite of coastal Javanese and Malays who had a strong admixture of Chinese blood that derived from the immigration of a century earlier. They did not perceive a culturally distinct group of Chinese residents. By contrast, the Dutch and English around 1600 found a large colony of Chinese in Banten, as well as smaller groups elsewhere, which had formed after the Ming began to license voyages to the south in 1567. About three thousand strong, they lived in a separate quarter outside the city wall to the west, in brick houses quite different from the Javanese style; they had their own temple, funerary customs, language and writing, opera groups and various other performers; they dressed in distinctive gowns, keeping their hair long and wrapped in a knot on the head; they reportedly sent much of their profits back to China. There was considerable social tension between them and the local population (Lodewycksz 1598: 124–25; Scott 1606: 174–76). Although these Chinese, too, acquired concubines or temporary wives among the Indonesian population, they expected to leave them eventually and return home. Many still did adopt Islam, but this was now a deliberate step from one culture and loyalty into another. As Scott (1606: 174) put it, Chinese were never too proud to accept any profitable work, "except they turne Javans (as many of them doe when they have done a murther or some other villanie)." They then cut their hair, changed their dress, became as haughty as the Javanese, and abandoned any thought of returning to China.

Separateness was encouraged by the Dutch in Batavia and its satellites, as it was to a lesser but still marked extent by the Spanish in Manila. The Dutch celebrated ethnic difference, with separate quarters, dress, administrative structures, and religions for each group. As Hoadley (1988) has shown in the case of Cirebon, it became difficult to remain culturally ambivalent once the Dutch had the upper hand. The *peranakan* category of assimilated Muslim Chinese disappeared. Those who wished to remain commercially active had to call themselves Chinese, those who wished to hold office, Javanese.

The Spanish did expect the leading Chinese in the Philippines to become Christian and adopt Spanish styles (fig. 43). But it was convenient for them, too, that the Chinese should remain distinct, useful as intermediaries and unlikely to form a combined resistance against the tiny number of Europeans. The arrival of the Westerners moved the interaction between Southeast Asians and outsiders towards a more dualistic one, in which the economic activity of Europeans and Chinese increasingly diverged from that of Southeast Asians. It was from the environs of Manila that the earliest European complaints attributing the "laziness" and dependence of both Filipinos and Spaniards to the industry of Chinese were voiced (de Rojas 1586: 270; Morga 1609: 225).

Both Manila and Batavia depended on Chinese traders for the import of consumer goods, but also on local Chinese as craftsmen, labourers, market-gardeners, bakers, and practically every other productive role. In Batavia the Chinese were allowed to settle inside the city walls, where they represented 39 percent of inhabitants in 1699; in Manila they were obliged to concentrate in the Parian outside the walls. The Dutch, and even more the Spanish, who had experienced Chinese attacks, were profoundly ambivalent about their dependence on the industry of the Chinese colonists. Tensions erupted in horrific anti-Chinese pogroms in both cities (six in Manila, one in 1740 in Batavia). But as Morga (1609: 225) noted after the Manila pogrom of

Fig. 43 Categories of Chinese in the Philippines. *From left:* a Christian Chinese who has assimilated to Spanish dress and removed his pigtail, a prominent "heathen" Chinese, a fisherman, and a coolie with his carrying-pole.

1603, "The city found itself in distress, for since there were no Sangleyes [Chinese] there was nothing to eat and no shoes to wear." The Europeans knew that their cities could not have been built, their trade maintained, nor their everyday needs supplied without the Chinese. Chinese had the great merit of being not only industrious but peaceful. Northern Europeans compared their deference towards the proud Southeast Asian aristocracies to that of Jews in Europe—"like Jews, [the Chinese] live crouching under them, but rob them of their wealth and send it to China" (Scott 1606: 174; cf. Pyrard 1619 II: 163).

For the Chinese, European-controlled ports held a twofold attraction. They were convenient new centres of international trade, particularly as sources of the American and Japanese silver much needed in China. And they provided a relatively stable environment in which Chinese could grow wealthy and even influential without ceasing to be Chinese. Batavia, Manila, and their satellite cities (Dutch Melaka, Makassar, and Semarang; Spanish Ilo-Ilo and Zamboanga) became the centres of Chinese commercial networks, which encouraged even those Chinese living in Asian-ruled states to maintain their Chinese identity.

The major concentrations of Chinese under indigenous control, in Ayutthaya and Hoi An, were big enough also to remain culturally distinctive, but their leaders knew that they had to become to some extent Thai or Vietnamese and take office as court officials in order to protect and develop their interests. The ethnic identification of Chinese with trade and Southeast Asian with office-holding was therefore never so sharp under indigenous rule, but it nevertheless slowly took hold.

A major step towards this sharp functional separation according to ethnicity was the introduction of a system of farming state revenues to Chinese tax farmers. Up to the mid-seventeenth century Southeast Asian states granted areas of economic responsibility to officials, including many foreign ones, but the revenues from these areas were expected to flow to the king—minus a percentage and various additional gifts and perquisites. A tax-farmer, in contrast, retained the port duties, market tax , or salt, opium, and gambling revenues, after having given a fixed sum in advance to the ruler. This offered a tolerably efficient way for rulers to draw revenue in advance from Chinese business without having to concern themselves with the mysteries of commerce. Since it also gave enormous economic power to the Chinese tax-farmer, however, the system tended to marginalize indigenous traders.

The Dutch had developed one of the most efficient systems of revenue farming in Europe, which limited corruption by annually auctioning the farm to the highest bidder. They introduced this system in Southeast Asia, and local Chinese appear to have relished the opportunity it offered to govern their own economic affairs for a fixed fee. Within Batavia's first two decades as a Dutch town, a system developed whereby the monopoly right to operate tolls, markets, weigh-houses, gambling-dens, theatres, taverns, and numerous other remunerative city services was bid for annually by the leading Chinese. This produced 59,000 guilders for Batavia in 1639, and 211,000 guilders by 1656 (Coolhaas 1964: 5–6, 60–61). As the Dutch extended their sway to other ports in the Archipelago, this system went with them.

This model of the financial relation between political authority and Chinese business also offered great advantages to native rulers whose bureaucratic apparatus was even less adequate than the VOC's for levying such taxes directly. In Java the critical point was the beginning of the reign of Amangkurat II in 1677–78, when the new ruler was entirely dependent on the VOC to regain his kingdom, and mortgaged the revenues of his ports to the company to pay for its help. Thereafter, these revenues were all farmed to Chinese in the Dutch manner (Carey 1984: 24–25; Nagtegaal 1988: 84–85). Tax farming was attractive to impoverished Javanese rulers, who spread it inland. In 1700 internal toll-gates began to be established and farmed out to Chinese as a further device for raising revenue (de Haan 1912 III: 182).

Chinese traders themselves must have carried this system to other Asian-ruled states, notably Siam and Cambodia. In eighteenth-century Siam, port revenues, gambling, tin-mining, and even the governorships of productive provinces in the south were farmed by Chinese in return for an annual payment to the crown (Skinner 1957: 20).

This development made it easier for rulers to withdraw entirely from commercial concerns. The Chinese revenue farmers became valued visitors at court and to that extent had to acquire the dress, language, and politenesses acceptable in high society. They were classic cultural brokers between the otherwise autonomous worlds of the indigenous courts and the urban Chinese commercial communities. Their wealth and economic power offered no direct threat to rulers. In the long term, however, Chinese revenue farming undoubtedly widened the gulf between the indigenous population and large-scale commerce. It may be significant that those peoples of Southeast Asia among whom the entrepreneurial spirit best survived were little affected by Chinese tax farming, either because of remoteness, like the Minangkabaus, Bataks, and Torajans, or because of religious and cultural hostility, like the Acehnese, Bugis, and Tausug.

The Last Stand of Islamic Commerce, 1650–88

I find the Malayans in general are implacable enemies of the Dutch; and all seems to spring from an earnest desire they have of a free trade, which is restrained by them, not only here [Sumatra], but in the Spice-Islands, and in all the other places where they have any power.
—Dampier 1699: 83

The turning of the age of commerce had come with the defeats of Aceh and Mataram in 1629; from 1650 its decline was observable to all; the 1680s witnessed its final death-throes. With a monopoly of clove and nutmeg and a string of forts from Melaka to Ambon, the VOC was by mid-century the dominant commercial and naval power of Southeast Asia. Those states with important agricultural hinterlands adjusted to this in the ways we have seen: European sea-power was not a direct threat to them. For those who had lived exclusively by trade—the merchant-aristocrats of the port-cities, the nakhodas, the pepper growers and dealers—the conflict was direct. Since these were the most explicitly Muslim elements in the population, they expressed their defiance in largely Islamic terms. To the Dutch it seemed there were conspiracies of "popes" everywhere. Yet only the VOC acted in a unified manner; its opponents talked of cooperation but never achieved it.

Aceh was a natural focus for such movements. Although the queen and her chief minister had been pressured by the VOC in 1650 into giving the Company half the tin of Aceh's vassal Perak, this humiliating treaty proved extremely unpopular in the city. The Laksamana led a coup in 1651, removing the chief minister, the Bendahara Sri Maharaja, depriving him of "all his weapons and elephants," and shooting his son-in-law and chief supporter as he rode to court on an elephant. Having eventually taken power, the anti-Dutch party conducted a purge of officials in the west coast pepper-districts, all of whom were suspected of having collaborated with Dutch and English demands for direct trade (Reniers 1651: 511–15, 519–21). An attack on the Dutch lodge in Perak the same year, when twenty-nine VOC employees were killed, was probably connected with these events.

VOC-Aceh relations remained stormy for most of the 1650s, but Aceh was not alone. Shortly after coming to the throne of Goa (Makassar), Sultan Hasanuddin told a Portuguese envoy that the kadis of Mecca had written in 1654 to the Muslim kings below the winds— Aceh, Johor, Mataram, Banten, and Makassar—to exhort them to act together to punish the Dutch for all the harm they had inflicted on Muslims. The Sultan of Banten had sent an embassy to Hasanuddin the following year, advising that although Mataram was cool on the proposal, Banten intended to attack Batavia and Aceh to besiege Dutch Melaka. For his part Hasanuddin would continue to harass the Dutch in Maluku (Cabral 1655; Macassar Factory 1655). A Malay nakhoda arrived in Banten from Aceh with the news that Aceh, Patani, Perak, and Johor had all agreed to expel the Dutch, while Banten and Makassar would soon follow (Bantam Agency 1656). Even Amangkurat I of Mataram, who had massacred most of the ulama in his own kingdom, was moved by prophecies that God would give the victory to the Muslim states if they united against the Dutch. He closed his ports to Dutch ships in 1655–57 and exchanged ambassadors with Makassar but was in no position to take stronger action (de Graaf 1961: 103–05).

This was the last occasion when the Muslim rulers had a chance to collaborate before their very survival as commercial powers came into question. Subsequent attempts to defend the Southeast Asian trading communities, particularly against the VOC, were the work of an increasingly marginalized group of exiles, traders, and ulama. This phase of Islamic reaction must therefore be distinguished from the peak of state identification with Islam around the 1640s, discussed in chapter 3.

The diaspora of proud and warlike Makassarese was at the centre of most such movements after the final Dutch-Bugis conquest of their homeland in 1669. The obvious place of refuge for Makassarese was Banten, which had worked with Makassar to keep the Islamic spice-trading network alive. Among the aristocrats given hospitality there in 1671, the most influential and revered figure was the Muslim scholar Sheikh Yusuf, who had studied with the leading ulama of Mecca for some twenty years before returning in the 1660s to rally the spirit of Makassar. In Banten, too, he was respected sufficiently to be allowed to marry Sultan Abdulfatah Ageng's sister, and he continued to inspire Banten's resistance to the VOC until his capture and exile to Ceylon in 1684. The leading Makassarese warriors, however, quarrelled with the Banten court about matters of status and left the city in 1673–74 eventually to find another refuge in the eastern salient of Java, a frontier of conflict among Javanese, Balinese, and Madurese.

There they quickly found employment as the allies and shock troops of Raden Trunajaya, a prince of Madura who was in the process of galvanizing all the elements alienated by the tyrannical policies of Amangkurat I of Mataram. Trunajaya, whose country had been conquered by Mataram and whose father had been murdered at Amangkurat's court, fled the capital for the nearby holy place of Tembayat, long a centre of religious opposition to the court. The spiritual leader of this region was now Raden Kajoran, who prophesied a glorious future for Trunajaya and gave him his daughter in marriage. This ensured Islamic support for the growing rebellion. The collapse of Amangkurat's kingdom was indicated when even his son and crown prince secretly joined the conspirators in 1670 in order to speed his father's demise (Ricklefs 1981: 69–70).

The rebellion of Trunajaya peaked in 1675, when the Makassarese razed the major east Javanese ports, including Surabaya, leaving them defenceless for Trunajaya's Madurese to occupy. The principal Muslim authority of the pasisir, the lord of Giri, gave the rebellion his blessing on the grounds that Mataram was compromised by the infidel Dutch. Trunajaya's forces destroyed the Mataram army sent against him in October 1676, leaving Amangkurat I with no resort except the VOC. The humiliating alliance he signed with the Company in February

1677 sharpened the Islamic and millenarian qualities of the rebellion—especially as the century ended in March 1677, according to the Javanese calendar, leading to expectations of a change of dynasty. An echo of this Islamic and millenarian impulse was felt in the Malayan Peninsula, where a Minangkabau "miracle-worker" was proclaimed king by the small states surrounding Dutch Melaka and besieged the fortress there in 1677 with a force of three thousand Malays (Kathirithamby-Wells 1970: 50).

The Dutch began their help for Amangkurat by taking the city of greatest importance to themselves—Surabaya. This did nothing to help their protégé, who was forced to flee his capital in June and died the following month in Tegal. The crown prince, seeing that he stood no chance of dominating the victorious Trunajaya, had no choice but to become a "Company's king" as Amangkurat II. The VOC, with its Bugis, Ambonese, and Javanese allies, launched a long and difficult campaign on his behalf, succeeding eventually in capturing Trunajaya at the end of 1679. They delivered him to Amangkurat II, who krissed him personally in January 1680. VOC forces had already killed Raden Kajoran of Tembayat in September 1679. Islamic resistance then focussed around the holiest place of Java—the hill of Giri near Surabaya. After a fierce battle, the spiritual lord of Giri and most of his family were killed by the Dutch-led force in April 1680 (Ricklefs 1981: 72–73).

Sympathy for Trunajaya's movement was strong at Banten, as at other Islamic centres, but the sultanate did not openly attack the VOC until 1680, when the Madurese leader had been removed from the scene. The humiliation of Banten at VOC hands in 1682, and the cruel slaughter visited by the vengeful young sultan and his Dutch and other allies on Bantenese patriots produced a resentment as deep in Banten as formerly in Makassar. "The Javans [of Banten] could hardly bear the Hollanders for a great while, and truly their antipathy against us was not without some grounds. . . . They . . . had no other way to show their spite and resentment than by making mouths as they passed by, and sometimes spitting upon them. To break them of that ungainly custom, we made a resolution amongst us, never to let any pass that did so, whether old or young, man or woman, without giving them a good box on the ear" (Fryke 1692: 74). For years after the conquest, Dutch were subject to *amok* attacks or sudden ambush around Banten, provoking yet more grisly punishments by the Dutch-supported king. Batavia itself was disturbed by a series of surreptitious attacks and alleged conspiracies against Dutchmen (ibid.: 71–73, 81, 121, 147, 151; Tachard 1688: 101–02).

This was the background for the last and most pathetic phase of Islamic resistance, particularly in the south Sumatran area most influenced by Banten. It may have been stimulated further by the unexpected arrival in Aceh of a high-level embassy from the sharif of Mecca in 1683, which had originally been intended for the Mughal Emperor Aurangzeb but was much better received below the winds (Snouck Hurgronje 1888), but its origins lay in the very concrete losses the mercantile Muslims had sustained. In 1685 one of those magically powerful adventurers common in Southeast Asian history began to attract Makassarese, Minangkabau, Bantenese, and Malay supporters to his base on the island of Belitung. He called himself Ahmad Shah bin Iskandar and Yang dipertuan Raja Sakti ("the sacred king who is called lord"), and claimed to be rightful king of Minangkabau and a direct descendent of Iskandar Dzulkarnain (Alexander the Great in his potent Islamic form). From Belitung he won the support of the rulers of Palembang and Jambi—both hard-pressed by Dutch monopoly pressure. He wrote to the rulers of Aceh and Mataram, to the coastal chiefs of west Sumatra and southern Borneo, and even to the King of Siam inviting their support in his sacred mission to drive the Dutch from the Archipelago (Kathirithamby-Wells 1980: 51–55).

Quickly he mobilized support, said to number four thousand men and three hundred vessels in 1685. Amangkurat II of Mataram, chafing under the debilitating terms of his alliance with the VOC, replied to the letters by inviting Ahmad Shah to come to Kartasura to lead the holy war. Seriously alarmed, the Dutch in June 1686 despatched to Belitung a force of their own troops and those of their protégé, the young ruler of Banten. When this failed to find him another expedition pursued the messianic ruler throughout southern Sumatra in late 1686 and early 1687. This found the local population very supportive of Ahmad Shah, no doubt partly because of his sacred aura, but partly too because he challenged the harsh pepper-monopoly the VOC imposed through Banten. For the same reason the British gave him shelter when in March 1687 he arrived at their new pepper-collecting base of Bengkulen in southwestern Sumatra. Ahmad Shah's greatest successes came in Jambi, where the ruler took over the Dutch lodge at his instigation, only to be ousted from power by a VOC expedition in September 1687; and in the Lampung port of Silebar, where his force in January 1688 expelled or killed all the representatives of the pro-Dutch Banten regime (Kathirithamby-Wells 1970: 57–61; Andaya 1993: 18).

Raja Sakti's movement gradually petered out in Sumatra during the early 1690s, as it became immersed in various local conflicts in which opposition to the Dutch was only one thread. Meanwhile, the greatest scare he gave the VOC was to win to the rebel cause one of the most trusted Indonesian warriors on the VOC payroll, the Muslim Ambonese Captain Jonker. Jonker had been the head of the Company's Ambonese units since 1665 and distinguished himself against such Dutch enemies as Makassar, Banten, and even Trunajaya, whom he had personally arrested. But in August 1689 the Dutch found evidence that Jonker had become a devout member of the Raja Sakti cult and was heading a conspiracy among Makassarese, Bugis, Balinese, and Ambonese in Batavia to massacre the European population of the city. Amangkurat II was also thought to be a party to this conspiracy but not strong enough to do much to promote it. Once again the movement, if such it was, quickly fell victim to Dutch repression. Captain Jonker was pursued and killed, and his head was displayed on a pole in Batavia to discourage any who might follow his example (Kathirithamby-Wells 1970: 62–63; Ricklefs 1981: 80–81).

Doomed as this series of movements was, it had repercussions in various parts of the region. At its peak, in 1688, the second queen of Aceh, Inayat Shah, died, and a tumult arose in the streets of the capital between the cosmopolitan establishment and those who sought a purer Islamic form of government. A Franciscan mission had been tolerated there since 1668 to cater for a hundred foreign Catholics. Suddenly it became the object of popular hostility: the priest was seized, whipped, and nearly beheaded, and he and the leading Christians had to hide on ships until the furore subsided and a new queen was on the throne (Meersman 1967: 123–30).

It would seem curious that Raja Sakti should have addressed himself to a Buddhist king, Narai of Siam, save that Ayutthaya had become after the fall of Banten the refuge of many of those Muslims and others who sought to keep alive an active Southeast Asian role in the long-distance trade. As noted in chapter 3, some Makassarese and Cham aristocrats were the leading figures in a Southeast Asian Muslim community that played a prominent role at Narai's court and sustained a viable Malayo-Muslim written culture in the Siamese capital. Such men were probably the links to carry and perhaps inspire Ahmad Shah's letter. Perhaps the letter itself, and certainly the atmosphere of messianic expectation that lay behind it, would have played a role in stimulating "the revolt of the Makassars" in 1686, which might have captured the Siamese palace if French troops had not intervened against it (see chapter 3).

The grisly display in the devastated Makassarese quarter of the rebel leaders' heads did not stop contacts between the remaining

Southeast Asian capitals with a role in trade. An ulama from Surat, said to have been a tutor of the Mughal emperor Aurangzeb, visited Siam as well as Johor, Jambi, and Java in 1687, and the Dutch thought he was stimulating a spirit of Islamic resistance to the VOC. Soon thereafter Amangkurat II wrote to King Narai in the same spirit, if Dutch spies can be believed. Narai was indeed concerned about the commercial and military power in VOC hands, but the Makassarese revolt had alienated him completely from Malays and Muslims and had driven him closer to the French. In January 1688 the King of Johor wrote to him expressing surprise "that a king as wise as he should have called to his country foreigners whom he could not get rid of when he wished," and offering to help to chase the French troops out. The same month a Siamese Malay tried desperately to obtain an audience with King Narai to offer proofs that the French and Phaulkon were conspiring against the king, liberty, and religion of Siam. He was tortured and thrown to the tigers in the middle of the Malay quarter to stamp out any similar thoughts (Le Blanc 1692 I: 26–30).

The positive interaction between international trade, scriptural religion, and expanding Southeast Asian monarchies was at an end—and with it the age of commerce.

Continuities and Changes

The age of commerce remade Southeast Asia and enabled it to play a leading role in global commerce. The lands below the winds were well positioned to take advantage of the great expansion of global trade that marked the "long sixteenth century." Their clove, nutmeg, pepper, and aromatic woods were the key items of long-distance trade; their geography exposed them exceptionally deeply to maritime commerce; their political systems were unusually open to outside influences.

Not surprisingly, the beginning of this period is less well documented than its end. Yet the jump in the arrival of Malukan spice in the Mediterranean, the sending of massive Chinese fleets to Southeast Asia, and the beginning of large-scale pepper exports all appear to mark a significant turning point around 1400. The peak of these expansive commercial indices can be placed in 1570–1630 with much greater confidence. After 1600, however, the continued expansion of exports and imports accompanied a series of military setbacks for indigenous commercial centres—the destruction of Pegu in 1599 and of the Javanese ports in 1620–25; Dutch seizure of the nutmeg-producing archipelago of Banda in 1621; the spectacular defeats in 1629 of the most ambitious attempts to expel the Europeans from Melaka and Batavia. Since the trade indices also go into decline around 1630, I have suggested 1629 as the most appropriate turning point of the age of commerce, even if its death throes do not occur until the 1680s.

During this age the region was utterly transformed. For most of it the direction of change was towards ever greater commercialization, urbanization, state centralization, and moralistic, externally validated religion. This is of course the scale of generalization valid only on a large canvas and during the *longue durée*, often contradicted by eddies and currents of specific events. By any measure, however, the overall pace of change was extraordinary. New cities and states flourished, most Southeast Asians were brought within the ambit of scriptural and universal faiths, and large proportions of the population became dependent on international trade for their livelihood, their clothing and everyday necessities, and even their food.

Marxism and nationalism made common cause a generation ago to argue that there was a "natural" evolution of Asian societies towards capitalism, which was interrupted some time in the early modern era by the distorting agency of colonialism. Happily, it has become less common to regard capitalism as a stage through which all societies must aspire to pass. Divorced from the feudalism of Europe and the socialism of Marxist prophecy between which it was conventionally set, capitalism loses most of its utility as a category. As Braudel (1979 II: 239) has pointed out, capitalism (a term Karl Marx never used) existed in no pre-industrial society except as "a world apart, different from and indeed foreign to the social and economic context surrounding it." The adjective is in fact more useful—there were more or less capitalist actors (notably in the long-distance trade), capitalist institutions, and capitalist methods in Southeast Asia as in Europe and elsewhere, interacting with a variety of other forms of dealing and producing. Viewed in this light, Southeast Asia at the peak of the age of commerce had gone further than most parts of the world down the path of reliance on maritime trade but less far towards the accumulation and mobilization of capital in private and corporate hands.

On the other hand, the most effective capitalist institution of seventeenth-century Southeast Asia, and probably the world, was the Dutch East India Company. The spices in world demand, which had stimulated commercialization through most of the age of commerce, also encouraged that first capitalist world power to make its primary Asian base in Java. Southeast Asian maritime traders were not alone in being worsted by capital-rich and cohesive Dutch commerce in the first half of the seventeenth century; the same fate befell much of Europe (Israel 1989). Their defeat was more permanent, however, precisely because maritime trade played such a large role below the winds.

Ironically, there were similarities between the trading cities at the mouth of the Rhine in the sixteenth century and cities such as Melaka (before 1511), Patani, Japara, Demak, and Gresik. Their trade wealth had enabled them to dispense in practice with the authority of larger empires, even if occasionally sending them tribute as insurance. The miracle of the Dutch cities, however, was their combination of decentralization and cohesion; they could act with unprecedented unity of purpose externally, notably in Asia, while pooling capital and labour in a complex legal structure at home. Southeast Asian cities had some of the same interests in a smoothly functioning market, security of property, and the rule of law, but their heterogeneity made it far more difficult to achieve these goals. They had no chance of surviving the fierce competition of the seventeenth century except by merging into stronger states with different interests.

The age of commerce ended in the crisis of the seventeenth century, when the Asian-ruled trading cities lost their place both in world trade and within their societies. That crisis was far more permanent in Southeast Asia, and probably in Asia as a whole, than it was in Europe. It has been calculated that Asia's role in the long-distance intercontinental trade dropped in both the seventeenth and eighteenth centuries, whereas Europe's only stagnated in the seventeenth and rose again in the eighteenth (Wallerstein II: 17–18). The effect was strongest below the winds since Indian cloth and Chinese tea were the growth exports of Asia after 1650, while Southeast Asian spices slumped.

The most important shift in the long term, however, was not any absolute decline in trade but the reduced importance of commerce, merchants, urbanism, and cosmopolitanism in Southeast Asian life. The age of commerce had been marked by constant innovation, by repeated adaption and incorporation of new ideas. The multi-ethnic market cities had set the pace of that change and had kept Southeast Asians for better or worse involved with the world of commerce. The seventeenth century marked not only a retreat from reliance on the international market but also a greater distrust of external ideas. The absolutist hierarchies forged in the crucible of competition for trade, arms, and men resorted increasingly to symbolic assertions of their primacy in areas where competition was less severe.

The most obvious, but also the most profound, changes of the age of commerce were in the areas of religion and mentalité. Changes in religious loyalties were more or less permanent. Communities remained Muslim, Christian, Theravada Buddhist, or Confucian, and at one level these identities divided Southeast Asians from one another and united them with coreligionists elsewhere in the world. If we look behind the labels to what people believed or practised, however, there is in the age of commerce an unmistakable disenchantment with the material world, a growth in the distance between the human and the sacred, and a rise in external standards of personal morality, as well as a more obvious alliance between expanding states and external religious norms.

In these complex areas of human understanding, as in the outward dimension where commerce and power intersected, the crisis of the seventeenth century marked a change of direction that was not reversed until another period of crisis in the mid-twentieth century. To begin with the more measurable areas, cosmopolitan trading cities did not dominate the life of Southeast Asians, whether demographically, economically, or culturally, between the late seventeenth century and the mid-twentieth, as they did before or since. The restoration of the control of indigenous states over the major resources and trade arteries of the region was not achieved without enormous upheavals within my own lifetime, but it eventually resulted in another period of rapid economic growth, urbanization, state centralization, and changes in ways of life and mentalities. The changes in belief and values in our own day, though taking place within established religious loyalties, are no less profound than those of the age of commerce. Once again external norms of personal morality are gaining ground against the enchanted spirit world; once again the expanding state has created an alliance with these external norms—not only scriptural religion but also modernity, science, hygiene, development, nationalism—to incorporate a myriad of diverse identities.

It has not been my purpose to glamorize the age of commerce or to portray its ending as defeat or failure. The less intense engagement with the world's dominant commercial and intellectual systems in the eighteenth century, and even in the nineteenth despite its colonial overlay, preserved the wonderful diversity of Southeast Asia and may well have enabled its people to live more peaceful and satisfactory lives. A disparity in living standards between Southeast Asia and Europe did not become apparent until the nineteenth century. What was clear before the end of the seventeenth century was that Southeast Asia would not continue along the path of strong states determined to claim their share of world commerce.

Because it has now resumed that path (again for better or worse), the first age of commerce is now more immediately relevant. As

Southeast Asians dramatically reshape their present, they need not be inhibited by their immediate past, with its memories of political diffusion, social stratification, and resignation to others of the high economic ground. An earlier period offers abundant evidence of a variety of creative responses to rapid economic change, a variety of social forms, a variety of political and intellectual possibilities.

Appendix: Major Ruling Dynasties of the Age of Commerce

Dates at left are those of accession

BURMA

Mon Dynasty of Pegu

1	1453	(Queen) Shinsawbu
2	1472	Dammazeidi; a monk, later married to daughter of 1
3	1492	Binnyaran; son of 2
4	1526	Takayutpi; son of 3

Pegu conquered by Toungoo Dynasty of Burma, 1539

Toungoo Dynasty of Burma

5	1486	Mingyinyo; conquered central Burma
6	1531	Tabinshweihti; son of 5; conquered Pegu, 1539, and made it his capital, 1546
7	1551	Bayinnaung; brother-in-law of 6
8	1581	Nandabayin; son of 7; interregnum, 1599–1606
9	1606	Anaukhpetlun; grandson of 8; killed, 1628
10	1629	Thalun; brother of 9; capital to Ava, 1635
11	1648	Pindale; son of 10

AYUTTHAYA (SIAM)

1	1409	Intharacha
2	1424	Boromaracha; son of 1
3	1448	Boromatrailokanat; son of 2
4	1488	Intharacha; son of 3
5	1491	Ramathibodi; son of 3
6	1529	Paramaracha; son of 5
7	1533	Prince Ratsada; infant son of 6; killed by 8
8	1534	Chairacha; son of 5
9	1546	Prince Yot Fa (aged 11); poisoned by mother
10	1548	Khun Worawongsa; usurper; killed
11	1548	Chakkraphat; son of 5
12	1569	Mahin, son of 11 and his regent since 1565; captured in Burmese seizure of Ayutthaya, 1569
13	1569	Maha Thammaracha; Burmese client until 1584
14	1590	Naresuan; son of 13
15	1605	Ekathotsarot; son of 13
16	1610/11	Songtham; son of 15
17	1628	Chettharacha; son of 16; killed by 19
18	1629	Athit; son of 16; killed by 19
19	1629	Prasat Thong; cousin of 16; usurper
20	1656	Chao Fa Chai; son of 19; killed
21	1656	Suthammaracha; brother of 19; killed
22	1657	Narai; son of 19
23	1688	(to 1703) Phetracha; foster-brother of 22

CAMBODIA

(most dates problematic)

1	1417	Bana Yat; abdicated
2	1463	Narayanaraja; son of 1
3	1468	Sri Raja; son of 1; exiled to Siam
4	1486	Dhammaraja; son of 1
5	1504	Sugandhapada (Bana Tamkhattiya); son of 4
6	1512	Kan; usurper; killed by 7

at Lovek

7	1529	Candaraja; son of 4
8	1568	Paramaraja; son of 7
9	1579	Paramaraja II (Brah Sattha); son of 8; fled Siamese to Laos, 1594; d. 1595

at Srei Santhor

10	1594	Ram Mahapabitr (Ram Joen Brai); killed by Spanish, 1596
11	1597	Paramaraja III (Cau Bana Tan'); killed by Muslims
12	1599	Paramaraja IV (Cau Bana An); killed by outraged husband
13	1600	Kaev Hva (Cau Bana Nom); son of 9; killed by 14
14	1601	Paramaraja V (Sri Suriyabarn); abdicated

at Oudong

15	1619	Jayajettha; son of 14
16	1627	Sri Dhammaraja (Cau Bana Tu)
17	1632	Ang Dan Raja (Cau Bana Nu)
18	1640	Padumaraja (Ang Nan)
19	1642	Ramadhipati (Cau Bana Cand); Raja Ibrahim
20	1659	Paramaraja V (Ang Sur)
21	1672	Padumaraja II (Sri Jeyajetth)
22	1673	(until 1677) Kaev Hva II (Ang Ji)

VIETNAM

Le Dynasty

1	1428	Le Loi; began revolt, 1418; expelled Chinese by 1428
2	1433	Le Thai Tong; son of 1
3	1443	Le Nanh Tong, infant son of 2, killed by 4
4	1459	Le Nghi Dan; son of 2; killed
5	1460	Le Thanh Tong; son of 2
6	1498	Le Hien Tong; son of 5
7	1505	Le Tuc Ton; son of 6; overthrown by 8
8	1509	Le Tuong Duc
9	1516	Tran Cao
10	1516	Le Chieu Ton; suicide ordered by Mac, 1527
11	1533	Le Trang Ton; restored as powerless figurehead, like his Le successors until 1804

Mac dynasty

1	1527	Mac Dang Dung; as emperor
2	1530	Mac Dang Doanh; son of 11; as emperor
3	1540	Mac Phuc Hai; in Tongking
4	1546	Mac Phuc Nguyen; in Tongking
5	1562	Mac Mau Hop; in Tongking

Macs driven from Hanoi by Trinh, 1592

Trinh family (ruling Tongking in name of Le)

1	1539	Trinh Kiem; Nghe-an and Thanh-hoa only
2	1569	Trinh Coi; Nghe-an and Thanh-hoa only
3	1570	Trinh Tong; captured Hanoi, 1592
4	1623	Trinh Trang
5	1657	Trinh Tac
6	1682	Trinh Con

PATANI

1	c1540	Sultan Mudhaffar Syah; killed attacking Ayutthaya
2	1564	Sultan Manzur Syah; brother of 1
3	1572	Sultan Patik Siam; son of 1; aged 9, under regency of aunt; killed
4	1573	Sultan Bahdur; son of 2; killed
5	1584	Queen Raja Ijau; daughter of 2
6	1616	Queen Raja Biru; daughter of 2
7	1624	Queen Raja Ungu; daughter of 2; married Sultan Pahang
8	1636	Queen Raja Kuning; daughter of 7; first married Sultan Johor, then his brother; probably ruled to 1650s, after which much confusion

MALAY RULERS OF MELAKA AND JOHOR-RIAU

1	c1390	Paremeswara; moves to Melaka from Singapore
2	1414	Sultan Megat Iskandar Syah; son of 1
3	1423/4	Sri Maharaja (Sultan Muhammad Syah)
4	1444	Sri Paremeswara Dewa Syah; son of 3; killed while a child under guardianship of Raja of Rokan
5	1446	Sultan Muzaffar Shah; son of 3
6	1459	Sultan Mansur Shah; son of 5
7	1477	Sultan Ala'ud-din Ri'ayat Syah; son of 6
8	1488	Sultan Mahmud Syah; son of 7; lost Melaka to Portuguese, 1511; capital in Banten until taken by Portuguese, 1526; died a refugee in Kampar
9	1530	Sultan Alau'd-din Ri'ayat Syah II; son of 8; capital at Johor; died a captive in Aceh
10	1564	Sultan Muzaffar; son of 9
11	1580	Sultan Abdu'l Jalil Syah; grandson of 9
12	1580	Sultan Ali Jala Abdu'l Jalil Ri'ayat Shah; son-in-law of 9
13	1597	Sultan Alau'd-din Ri'ayat Syah; son of 12
14	1613	Sultan Abdu'llah Ma'ayat Syah; son of 12
15	1623	Sultan Abdul Jalil Syah; son of 13
16	1677	Sultan Ibrahim Syah; grandson of 14

ACEH

1	1515	Sultan Ali Mughayat Syah; son of Sultan Syamsu Syah
2	1530	Sultan Salahu'd-din; son of 1
3	1539	Sultan Alau'd-din Ri'ayat Syah al-Kahar; son of 1
4	1571	Sultan Ali Ri'ayat Syah; son of 3
5	1579	Sultan Muda; infant son of 4; killed
6	1579	Raja Seri Alam; son of 3; killed
7	1579	Raja Zainal 'Abidin; grandson of 3; killed
8	1580	Sultan Alau'd-din Perak (Mansur Syah); killed
9	1586	Sultan Ali Ri'ayat
10	1589	Sultan Alau'd-din Ri'ayat Syah Sayyid al-Mukammil; aged Laksamana; deposed
11	1604	Sultan Ali Ri'ayat Syah; son of 10
12	1607	Sultan Iskandar Muda Johan Berdaulat (Perkasa Alam); grandson of 10
13	1636	Sultan Iskandar Thani of Pahang; husband of 14
14	1641	Queen Taj al-Alam Safiyyat ad-din; daughter of 12
15	1675	Queen Nur al-Alam
16	1678	Queen Inayat Syah Zakiat ad-din
17	1688	Queen Kamalat Syah

(CENTRAL) JAVA

Demak

1	c1480	A Chinese Muslim, perhaps Cek Ko-po
2	c1490	Arya Sumangsang (Chinese name Cu-cu); son of 1; known to Portuguese as Pate Rodim
3	1504	Trenggana, Sultan of Demak; d. 1546

Pajang

4	1581	Sultan Jaka-Tingkir; son-in-law of 3(?); d. 1587?

Mataram

5	1584	Panembahan Senapati Ingalaga; conquered Pajang, 1587, and Demak, 1588
6	1601	Panembahan Seda Ing Krapyak; son of 5
7	1613	Panembahan Agung; took title Susuhunan, 1624, and Sultan, 1641
8	1646	Susuhunan Amangkurat I; son of 7
9	1677	(Until 1703) Susuhunan Amangkurat II; son of 8

BANTEN

1	1525	Nurullah of Pasai (Sunan Gunung Jati)
2	1552	Hasanuddin; son of 1
3	1570	Molana Yusuf; son of 2
4	1580	Molana Muhammad; aged 9; son of 3
5	1596	Sultan Abdul Kadir; aged 4; son of 4; took title Sultan, 1638
6	1651	Sultan Abdulfatah Ageng (Sultan Tirtayasa); captured by VOC, 1683
7	1680	Sultan Haji; son of 6; contested by 6 until conquest by VOC in 1682; d. 1687

MAKASSAR (GOA/TALLO')

		GOA			TALLO'
G1	1511	Tumaparisi' Kallona			
G2	1548	Tunipalangga; son of G1	T1	1547	Tumenanga ri Makkoayang, chancellor of Goa, 1566–77
G3	1566	Tunibatta (I Tajibarani); son of G1; killed in war			
G4	1566	Tunijallo'; son of G3; killed by slave	T2	1577	I Sambo; daughter of T1; wife of G4
G5	1590	Tunipasulu'; son of G4 and T2; claimed also to rule Tallo'; overthrown			
G6	1593	Tumenanga ri Gaukanna (Sultan Alauddin); son of G4 and T2	T3	1593	Karaeng Matoaya (Sultan Awwal-al-Islam); son of T1; chancellor of Goa, 1593–1637
G7	1639	Ripapan Bature (Sultan Mohammad Said); son of G6	T4	1637	Tumananga ri Timore (Sultan Muzhafar); son of T3
G8	1653	Tumenanga ri Balla Pangkana (Sultan Hasanuddin); resigned after Dutch conquest, 1669	[1639		Tumenanga ri Bontobiraeng (Karaeng Pattingalloang); son of T3; chancellor of Goa, 1639–54;]
			T5	1641	Tumenanga ri Lampanna (Sultan Harun al-Rashid)

Guide to Reading

My method in this book has been to refer to primary sources whenever possible and to cite them in a shorthand form that indicates the original author and date rather than the work of editors. This has given me little opportunity to discuss or acknowledge the work of predecessors and colleagues in this field, without whom none of my work would have been possible.

Expert editors and translators of Southeast Asian language material are indispensable intermediaries between the historian and indigenous sources. Most surviving texts date from the nineteenth century, and painstaking work is required to authenticate, reconstruct, and render meaningful the likely original sources. For my own purposes the labours have been especially valuable of Drewes, Pigeaud, and Ricklefs on Javanese texts; of Brakel, Brown, Iskandar, Kassim Ahmad, Matheson, Naguib Al-Attas, Ras, Skinner, Teeuw, and Winstedt on Malay texts; of Drewes and Siegel on Acehnese texts; of Abdurrahim, Ligtvoet, Matthes, and Noorduyn on South Sulawesi texts; of Frankfurter, Notton, and Wyatt on Thai texts; of Furnivall, Than Tun, and U Khin Soe on Burmese texts; of Mak Phoeun and Khin Sok on Khmer (Cambodian) chronicles; and of Rafael and Rosales on Tagalog Catholic works.

Indispensable Chinese sources on Southeast Asia have also been made available to the nonspecialist by Groeneveldt, Mills, Rockhill, Wang, and Wheatley, while Geoffrey Wade has recently undertaken the massive job of translating the *Ming Shi Lu* passages that deal with the region. The Ryukyuan documents have been translated by Atsushi Kobata and Mitsugu Matsuda (1969). Reports of the Chinese junks arriving in Nagasaki in the period 1640–1740 have been edited by Ren'ichi Ura, and many of them recently translated by Yoneo Ishii (forthcoming).

European sources have been edited and published in greater volume. Most of the Portuguese and Spanish chroniclers have received modern editions, though of the Portuguese only the best—Tomé Pires, Mendes Pinto, and Galvão—have been translated into English. An extremely useful compilation of Spanish material in English is the fifty-five-volume work *The Philippine Islands*, translated by Blair and Robertson (1903–09). Missionary letters from Asia have been lovingly edited by Artur de Sá (1954–58), Querbeuf (1781), Wicki (1950), and Jacobs (1974).

From 1596 Dutch records provide the most detailed and extensive reporting on the region, particularly for commercial matters. The early voyages were first collected for publication by Isaac Commelin in *Begin ende Voortgangh* (1646) and are now being professionally re-edited by the Linschoten-Vereniging. The thirty-one volumes of the Batavia *Dagh-Register* provide superb reports of ship movements for the period 1624–82. Thirteen volumes of excerpts from the VOC archives were edited by J. K. J. de Jonge (1862–88). The correspondence of Jan Pieterszoon Coen was published by H. T. Colenbrander (and later W. Ph. Coolhaas) in seven fat volumes (1919–53). Coolhaas is also responsible for the first eight volumes of the *Generale Missiven* (1960–85), covering the period 1610–1729.

English documents on Southeast Asia are satisfactorily published only for the first two decades, as *Letters Received by the East India Company from Its Servants in the East*, ed. F. C. Danvers (1896–1902—herein abbreviated as *LREIC*). Much information can nevertheless be culled from the *Calendar of State Papers, Colonial Series*, ed. W. N. Sainsbury (herein abbreviated *SP*), and of course from the voyages published by the Hakluyt Society.

Our understanding of the history of the region has been advanced by the appearance recently of a number of professional national histories. Particularly useful for this enterprise is the work of Wyatt (1982) on Thailand, Lieberman (1984) on Burma, Chandler (1983) on Cambodia, Ricklefs (1981) on Indonesia, de la Costa (1965) on the Philippines, and Le Thanh Koi (1971) on Vietnam. More fine-grained, pioneering studies of particular societies have also begun to appear: Andaya on South Sulawesi (1981); Lombard (1967) and Ito (1984) on

Aceh; de Graaf (1958, 1961, 1962) and later Nagtegaal (1988) on Mataram; Kathirithamby-Wells (1990) and Guillot (1989) on Banten; Knaap (1987) on Ambon; Chen Chingho (1974) and Li Tana (1992) on Cochin-China.

Remarkably little work integrates the history of the region other than around essentially colonial themes. The major ongoing debate has revolved around the relation between the economic systems of the Asian region and the rise of capitalism in Europe. Two Dutch sociologists, B. J. O. Schrieke (1925, 1942) and J. C. van Leur (1934), launched the debate into Indonesian waters before the war, in work that became more widely known in English translation in the 1950s. Whereas Schrieke pointed to the collapse of Javanese shipping in the seventeenth century, van Leur was more anxious to minimize the impact of the Portuguese and the VOC and to argue for a continuity in Asian trade well into the eighteenth century. Yet he characterized Asian trade as essentially undifferentiated "peddling," with large numbers of traders carrying small amounts of luxury goods. These themes were examined empirically by M. A. P. Meilink-Roelofsz (1962), who concluded that Asian traders were more varied than van Leur had allowed, that they did decline in importance in the seventeenth century, but that even at their height they lacked such critical advantages of their European counterparts as the legal protection of property.

Subsequent work on this theme has been either at a more local level (such as much of that above) or at a broader one that spans the Indian Ocean. Outstanding examples of bringing the quantification of the *Annales* school to bear on Asia are Magalhães-Godinho (1969), Chaunu (1960), and Chaudhuri's two books on the English Company (1965, 1978). A number of works using the rich VOC records—Steensgaard (1973), Glamann (1958), Bruijn, Gaastra, and Schöffer (1979–87), Wills (1974), and Blussé (1986)—have tended to emphasize the changes introduced to Asian trade by the Dutch world-system. Much greater sophistication has been brought to Indian maritime history by the recent work of DasGupta (1982), Prakash (1979), Raychaudhuri (1962), Arasaratnam (1986), and Subrahmanyam (1990), the last three of whom have looked at the trade of the Coromandel Coast that was closely linked to Southeast Asia. Because of such works it is now much clearer how Southeast Asia interacted with the global economy through a long-term pattern of expansion and contraction, though little has been done to draw conclusions for the history of the region.

Although Schrieke and van Leur both sought to link Islamization with economic changes, the religious/intellectual and economic literatures subsequently parted company. Johns (1961) put most forcefully the case suggested by the corpus of early Islamic works in Malay and Javanese that the chief agents of Islamization were peripatetic Sufis. Fatimi (1963) took this further, and pointed to the importance of Cham and Chinese Muslims in the Islamization of the Archipelago. The maximal case for the importance of the Chinese role can be found in a controversial work by de Graaf and Pigeaud (1984). The data is much richer for the Philippines, where Majul (1973) and de la Costa (1967) provide alternative perceptions on Muslim-Christian rivalry in Mindanao. Phelan's (1959) description of the Christianization process there is still persuasive, though Schumacher (1968) has extended it while the sophisticated nationalism of Rafael (1988) has raised numerous new questions.

Some of the most interesting work on the Archipelago is being done by the group associated with the journal *Archipel* in Paris, notably Denys Lombard, Claude Guillot, and Pierre-Yves Manguin. Important special issues of *Archipel* were devoted to commerce and shipping (no. 18, 1979) and to cities (nos. 36, 1988, and 37, 1989). Lombard's three-volume study (1990) has now appeared, and represents the most ambitious attempt so far to integrate the study of cultural history and *mentalités* with the changing economic and political environment. Although ostensibly limited to Java, it has much broader implications.

Abbreviations

AHR	*American Historical Review*
ANU	Australian National University
ARA	Algemene Rijksarchief, The Hague
BEFEO	*Bulletin de l'Ecole Française d'Extreme-Orient*, Hanoi and Paris
BKI	*Bijdragen tot de Taal-, Land-, en Volkenkunde*, published by the KITLV, Leiden
CSSH	*Comparative Studies in Society and History*
CUP	Cambridge University Press
EIC	East India Company
EFEO	Ecole Française d'Extrême-Orient, Hanoi and Paris
ENI	*Encyclopedie van Nederlandsch-Indië*, 4 vols., The Hague, Martinus Nijhoff, 1899–1905
IOL	India Office Library, London
JAS	*Journal of Asian Studies*, Ann Arbor
JBRS	*Journal of the Burma Research Society*, Rangoon
JEEH	*Journal of European Economic History*
JMBRAS	*Journal of the Malayan/Malaysian Branch, Royal Asiatic Society*, Singapore and Kuala Lumpur
JRAS	*Journal of the Royal Asiatic Society*, London
JSEAH	*Journal of Southeast Asian History*, Singapore
JSEAS	*Journal of Southeast Asian Studies*, Singapore
JSS	*Journal of the Siam Society*, Bangkok
KITLV	Koninklijk Instituut voor Taal-, Land-, en Volkenkunde, Leiden
LREIC	*Letters Received by the East India Company from Its Servants in the East*, ed. F. C. Danvers, 6 vols., London, Sampson, Low, Marston, 1896–1902

MBRAS	Malaysian Branch, Royal Asiatic Society
OUP	Oxford University Press
RIMA	*Review of Indonesian and Malayan Studies*, Sydney
SP	*Calendar of State Papers, Colonial Series, East Indies, China and Japan*, ed. W. N. Sainsbury, 5 vols., London, Longman, 1862–92
T.Aard.G.	*Tijdschrift van het Aardrijkskundig Genootschap*
TBG	*Tijdschrift voor Indische Taal-, Land-, en Volkenkunde*, published by the Koninklijk Bataviaasch Genootschap voor Kunsten en Wetenschappen, Batavia
VBG	*Verhandelingen van het Bataviaasch Genootschap*
VOC	Vereenigde Oost-Indische Compagnie

References

Abu'l-Fazl 'Allami 1596. *The A'in-i Akbari,* trans. H. Blochman, 1871. Reprinted Delhi, Naresh C. Jain, 1965.

Abu-Lughod, Janet L. 1989. *Before European Hegemony: The World System A.D. 1250–1350.* New York, OUP.

Acciaioli, Gregory 1989. "Searching for Good Fortune: The Making of a Bugis Shore Community at Lake Lindu, Central Sulawesi." Ph.D. diss., ANU, Canberra.

Adat Aceh. Adat Aceh dari Satu Manuscript India Office Library, romanized by Teungku Anzib Lamnyong. Banda Aceh, Pusat Latehan Penelitian Ilmu-ilmu Sosial, 1976.

Adatrechtbundels. 45 vols. The Hague, Nijhoff, 1910–55.

Aduarte, Diego 1640. *Historia de la Provincia del Sancto Rosario . . . en Philipinas,* in Blair and Robertson 1903–09 XXX: 113–226.

Aelst, A. van 1987. "Japanese Coins in Southern Vietnam and the Dutch East India Company, 1633–1638." *Oriental Numismatic Society Newsletter* 109.

Al-Attas, S. M. Naquib 1970. *The Mysticism of Hamzah Fansuri.* Kuala Lumpur, University of Malaya Press.

——— 1986. *A Commentary on the Hujjat al-Siddiq of Nur ul-Din ul-Runiri.* Kuala Lumpur, Ministry of Culture.

Albuquerque, Braz de 1557. *The Commentaries of the Great Alfonso Dalboquerque,* trans. W. de Gray Birch, Vol. III. London, Hakluyt Society, 1880.

Alcina, Francisco 1668. "The Munoz Text of Alcina's History of the Bisayan Islands (1668)," preliminary trans. Paul S. Lietz, pt. I, books 3 and 4. Typescript, Department of Anthropology, University of Chicago.

Alfian, T. Ibrahim 1979. *Mata Uang Emas Kerajaan-kerajaan di Aceh*. Banda Aceh, Proyek Rehabilitasi dan Perluasan Museum Daerah Istimewa Aceh.

Ali Haji ibn Ahmad, Raja 1866. *The Precious Gift (Tuhfat al-Nafis)*, trans. Virginia Matheson and Barbara Andaya. Kuala Lumpur, OUP, 1979.

Alkema, B. and T. J. Bezemer 1927. *Concise Handbook of the Netherlands East Indies*, trans. Richard Neuse. New Haven, HRAF, 1961.

Alves, George 1989. Paper presented at Conference of the Social Science Research Council, Lisbon.

Amanna Gappa 1676. "Ade Allopi-loping Ribitjaranna Pa'balu'e" [Rules for commercial sailing], in Tobing 1961: 41–64.

Amin, Entji 1670. *Sja'ir Perang Mengkasar* in Skinner 1963: 65–221.

Andaya, Barbara 1989. "The Cloth Trade in Jambi and Palembang Society during the Seventeenth and Eighteenth Centuries," *Indonesia* 48: 27–46.

—— 1993. "Cash-Cropping and Upstream-Downstream Tensions: The Case of Jambi in the Seventeenth and Eighteenth Centuries," in Reid 1993: 91–122.

Andaya, Barbara, and Yoneo Ishii 1992. "Religious Developments in Southeast Asia, c. 1500–1800," in *Cambridge History of Southeast Asia*, ed. Nicholas Tarling. Cambridge, CUP, I: 508–71.

Andaya, Leonard 1981. *The Heritage of Arung Palakka: A History of South Sulawesi (Celebes) in the Seventeenth Century*. The Hague, Nijhoff for KITLV.

Anderson, John 1826. *Mission to the East Coast of Sumatra in 1823*. London. Reprinted Kuala Lumpur, OUP, 1971.

Anderson, John 1890. *English Intercourse with Siam in the Seventeenth Century*. London. Reprinted Bangkok, Chalermnit, 1981.

Anderson, Perry 1974. *Lineages of the Absolutist State*. Thetford, Verso edition, 1979.

Angeles, Delor 1980. "The Philippine Inquisition: A Survey." *Philippine Studies* 28: 253–83.

Arasaratnam, S. 1986. *Merchants, Companies and Commerce on the Coromandel Coast, 1650–1740*. Delhi, OUP.

Araujo, Rui de 1510. Letter from Malacca, 6 February 1510, in de Sá 1954–58 I: 20–31.

Argensola, Leonardo 1708. *The Discovery and Conquest of the Molucco and Philippine Islands*. London. Reprinted Ann Arbor, University Microfilms, 1982.

Artieda, Diego de 1573. "Relation of the Western Islands Called Filipinas," in Blair and Robertson 1903–09 III: 190–208.

Ashtor, Eliyahu 1969. *Histoire des prix et des salaires dans l'Orient médièval*. Paris, SEVPEN.

—— 1976. *A Social and Economic History of the Near East in the Middle Ages*. Berkeley, University of California Press.

—— 1979. "The Volume of Mediaeval Spice Trade." *JEEH* 8: 753–63.

Aston, Trevor (ed.) 1965. *Crisis in Europe, 1560–1660*. London, Routledge and K. Paul.

Atwell, W. S. 1986. "Some Observations of the Seventeenth Century Crisis in China and Japan." *JAS* 45, ii: 223–44.

Aubin, Jean 1973. "Francisco de Albuquerque: un juif castillan au service de l'Inde Portugaise (1510–1515)." *Arquivos do Centro Cultural Português* 7: 175–202.

———— 1980. "Les Persans au Siam sous le regne de Narai (1656–1688)," *Mare Luso-Indicum* 4: 95–126.

Aung-Thwin, Michael 1985. *Pagan: The Origins of Modern Burma*. Honolulu, University of Hawaii Press.

Aymonier, Etienne 1885. *Notes sur le Laos*. Saigon, Imprimerie Coloniale.

Babad ing Sangkala 1738. Trans. M. C. Ricklefs, in *Modern Javanese Historical Tradition: A Study of an Original Kartasura Chronicle and Related Materials*. London, SOAS, 1978, pp. 16–147.

Babad Lombok. Ed. Lalu Wacana. Jakarta, Departemen Pendidikan dan Kebudayaan Republik Indonesia, 1979.

Babad Tanah Jawi. *Babad Tanah Djawi. Javaanse Rijkskroniek. W. L. Olthofs vertaling van de prozaversie van J. J. Meinsma lopende tot het jaar 1721*. Rev. ed. by J. J. Ras. Dordrecht, Foris for KITLV, 1987

Bantam Agency 1656. Letter to Court, 9 March 1656, IOL G/10/1, p. 138.

Barbosa, Duarte 1518. *The Book of Duarte Barbosa: An Account of the Countries Bordering on the Indian Ocean and Their Inhabitants*, trans. M. Longworth Dames. 2 vols. London, Hakluyt Society, 1918.

Baron, Samuel 1685. "A Description of the Kingdom of Tonqueen," in *A Collection of Voyages and Travels*, Vol. VI. London, A. and W. Churchill, 1732.

Barros, João de 1563. *Da Asia*. Four Decades in 9 vols. Lisbon, Regia Officina 1777. Reprinted Lisbon, 1973.

Bartlett, H. H. 1952. "A Batak and Malay Chant on Rice Cultivation." *Proceedings of the American Philosophical Society* 96: 629–52. Reprinted in Bartlett, *The Labors of the Datoe*, Ann Arbor, University of Michigan Center for South and Southeast Asian Studies, 1973.

Bassett, D. K. 1958. "English Trade in Celebes, 1613–1667," *JMBRAS* 31, i: 1–39.

Bayly, C. A. 1983. *Rulers, Townsmen and Bazaars: North Indian Society in the Age of British Expansion, 1770–1870*. Cambridge, CUP.

Beaulieu, Augustin de 1666. "Memoires du voyage aux Indes orientales du Général du Beaulieu, dressés par luy-mesme," in *Relations de divers voyages curieux*, ed. Melchisedech Thévenot, Vol. II. Paris, Cramoisy.

Beeckman, Daniel 1718. *A Voyage to and from the Island of Borneo in the East Indies*. London. Reprinted London, Dawsons, 1973.

Begin ende Voortgangh 1646. *Begin ende Voortgangh van de Vereenighde Neederlandtsche Geoctroyeerde Oost-Indische Compagnie*, ed. Isaac Commelin. Amsterdam. Reprinted Amsterdam 1974.

Best, Thomas 1613. Letter from Aceh 12 July 1613, in Foster 1934: 255–58.

———— 1614. "A Journal Kept on Board the *Hosiander* by Thomas Best," 1 February 1612 to 15 June 1614, in Foster 1934: 1–92.

Bèze, Claude de 1691. *Memoir*, trans. E. W. Hutchinson, in *1688: Revolution in Siam*. Hong Kong, University Press, 1968, pp. 1–124.

Blair, E. H., and J. Robertson, eds. 1903–09. *The Philippine Islands, 1493–1803*. 55 vols. Cleveland, Arthur H. Clark.

Blussé, Leonard 1986. *Strange Company: Chinese Settlers, Mestizo Women and the Dutch in VOC Batavia.* Dordrecht, KITLV.

Blussé, Leonard, and Zhuang Guoto 1991. "Fuchienese Commercial Expansion into the Nanyang as Mirrored in the 'Tung Hsi Yang K'ao'," *Revista da Cultura* 13–14: 140–49.

Bochier, Francisco dal 1518. "Referir de Francesco dal Bochier, quando ando in India," in Aubin 1973: 189–202.

Boomgaard, Peter 1989. *Children of the Colonial State: Population Growth and Economic Development in Java, 1795–1880.* Amsterdam, Free University Press.

Borri, Cristoforo 1633. *Cochin-China,* trans. R. Ashley. London, Richard Clutterbuck. Reprinted London, da Capo Press, 1970. (Pagination by letters.)

Bouchon, Geneviève 1979. "Les premiers voyages portugais à Pegou (1515–1520)," *Archipel* 18: 127–58.

Bougas, Wayne 1988. *Islamic Cemeteries in Patani.* Kuala Lumpur, Malaysian Historical Society.

Bourges, M. de 1666. *Relation du voyage de Monseigneur l'evèque de Beryte, vicaire apostolique du royaume de la Cochinchine, par la Turquie, la Perse, les Indies, et jus'qu'au royaume de Siam.* Paris, Denys Bechet.

Bowrey, Thomas 1680. *A Geographical Account of Countries round the Bay of Bengal,* ed. R. C. Temple. Cambridge, Hakluyt Society, 1905.

Boxer, Charles 1953. *South China in the Sixteenth Century.* Cambridge, Hakluyt Society.

—— 1964. "The Achinese Attack on Malacca in 1629, as Described in Contemporary Portuguese Sources," in *Malayan and Indonesian Studies: Essays Presented to Sir Richard Winstedt on His Eighty-fifth Birthday,* ed. John Bastin and R. Roolvink. Oxford, Clarendon, pp. 105–21.

—— 1967. *Francisco Vieira de Figueiredo: A Portuguese Merchant-Adventurer in South East Asia, 1624–1667.* The Hague, Nijhoff for KITLV.

—— 1968. *Further Selections from the Tragic History of the Sea, 1559–1565.* Cambridge, Hakluyt Society.

—— 1969. "A Note on Portuguese Reactions to the Revival of the Red Sea Spice Trade and the Rise of Atjeh, 1540–1600." *JSEAH* 10, iii: 415–28.

—— 1969A. *The Portuguese Seaborne Empire, 1415–1825.* London. Reprinted Harmondsworth, Penguin, 1973.

Boxer Codex. See Dasmariñas 1590.

Brakel, Lode 1978. "Problems of Wahrheit and Dichtung: Islamic Historiography in Malay." Unpublished paper.

Braudel, Fernand 1966. *The Mediterranean and the Mediterranean World in the Age of Philip II,* trans. S. Reynolds. 2 vols. New York, Harper Colophon, 1976.

—— 1967. *Capitalism and Material Life, 1400–1800,* trans. Miriam Kochan. London, Weidenfeld and Nicolson, 1973.

—— 1979. *Civilization and Capitalism, Fifteenth–Eighteenth Century,* trans. Siân Reynolds. 3 vols. New York, Harper and Row, 1985.

Broecke, Pieter van den 1634. *Pieter van den Broecke in Azië,* ed. W. Ph. Coolhaas. 2 vols. The Hague, Linschoten-Vereeniging, 1962–63.

Brooke, James 1848. *Narrative of Events in Borneo and Celebes down to the*

Occupation of Labuan: From the Journals of J. Brooke . . . . by Captain Rodney Mundy. 2 vols. London, John Murray.

Brouwer, Hendrik et al. 1636. Letter to Heren XVII, 4 January 1636, in Coolhaas 1960: 507–50.

Brown, E. H. P., and S. V. Hopkins 1956. "Seven Centuries of the Price of Consumables Compared with Builders' Wage-Rates." *Economica* 23: 296–314.

Bruijn, J. R., F. S. Gaastra, and I. Schöffer 1987. *Dutch-Asiatic Shipping in the Seventeenth and Eighteenth Centuries.* The Hague, Nijhoff for Rijks Geschiedkundige Publicatiën.

Brunei expedition 1579. "Testimony and Proceedings in Regard to the Expeditions to Burney, Jolo, and Mindanao," in Blair and Robertson 1903–09 IV: 149–303.

Buch, W. J. M. 1929. *De Oost-Indische Compagnie en Quinam: de betrekkingen der Nederlanders met Annam in de XVIIe eeuw.* Amsterdam, H. J. Paris.

Bukhari Al-Jauhari 1603. *Taj us-Salatin,* ed. Khalid Hussain. Kuala Lumpur, Dewan Bahasa dan Pustaka, 1966. [French trans. Aristide Marre, *Makhota radja-radja, ou la couronne des rois,* Paris, 1878.]

Bulbeck, David 1992. "A Tale of Two Kingdoms: The Historical Archeology of Gowa and Tallok, South Sulawesi, Indonesia." Ph.D. diss., ANU, Canberra.

Cabral, Jaõa 1655. Letter from Goa, in Jacobs 1988: 135–40.

Camphuys, Joannes et al. 1684. Letter from Batavia 19 February 1684, in Coolhaas 1971: 651–78.

Campos, J. de 1940. "Early Portuguese Accounts of Thailand." *JSS* 32, reprinted in *Selected Articles from the Siam Society Journal* 7, Bangkok, Siam Society, 1959, pp. 211–38.

Carey, Peter 1984. "Changing Javanese Perceptions of the Chinese Communities in Central Java, 1755–1825." *Indonesia* 37: 1–48.

Carreiro, Roque 1630. "Narrative of the Great Victory which the Portuguese Won against the King of Achem," trans. in Boxer 1964: 109–14.

Castanheda, Fernão Lopes de 1552–4. *História do Descobrimento y Conquista da India pelos Portugueses.* Coimbra, Imprensa da Universidade, 1924–33.

Catz, Rebecca (ed.) 1989. *The Travels of Mendez Pinto.* Chicago, University of Chicago Press.

Cense, A. A. 1978. "Maleise Invloeden in het Oostelijk Deel van de Indonesische Archipel." *BKI* 134: 415–32.

——— 1979. *Makassaars-Nederlands Woordenboek.* The Hague, Nijhoff for KITLV.

Chandler, David P. 1983. *A History of Cambodia.* Boulder, Westview.

Chang, Pin-tsun 1991. "The First Chinese Diaspora in Southeast Asia in the Fifteenth Century," in Ptak and Rothermunde 1991: 13–28.

Chaudhuri, K. N. 1965. *The English East India Company: The Study of an Early Joint-Stock Company, 1600–1640.* London, Frank Cass.

——— 1978. *The Trading World of Asia and the English East India Company, 1660–1760.* Cambridge, CUP.

———— 1982. "Foreign Trade," in Raychaudhuri and Habib 1982: 382–407.

Chau Ju-kua, c.1250. *His Work on the Chinese and Arab Trade in the Twelfth and Thirteenth Centuries, entitled Chu-fan-chi*, trans. Friedrich Hirth and W. W. Rockhill. St. Petersburg, n.p., 1911. Reprinted Taipei, 1970.

Chaunu, Pierre 1960. *Les Philippines et le Pacifique des Ibériques (XVIe, XVIIe, XVIIIe siècles): introduction methodologique et indices d'activité.* Paris, SEVPEN.

Chen, Chingho A. 1974. *Historical Notes on Hôi-An (Faifo).* Carbondale, Southern Illinois University Center for Vietnamese Studies.

———— 1979. "Mac Thien Tu and Phraya Taksin: A Survey of Their Political Stand, Conflicts, and Background," in *Proceedings, Seventh IAHA Conference, 22–26 August 1977.* Bangkok, Chulalongkorn University Press, pp. 1534–75.

Chirino, Pedro 1604. *Relación de las Islas Filipinas: The Philippines in 1600,* trans. Ramón Echevarria. Manila, Historical Conservation Society, 1969.

Choisy, Abbé de 1687. *Journal du voyage de Siam fait en 1685 et 1686,* ed. Maurice Garçon. Paris, Duchartre et Van Buggenhoudt, 1930.

Chou Ta-kuan 1297. Trans. Paul Pelliot in *Mémoires sur les coutumes du Cambodge de Tcheou Ta-Kouan.* Paris, Maisonneuve.

Chronique de Xieng Mai. Trans. Camille Notton, in *Annales du Siam,* Vol. III. Paris, Paul Geuthner, 1932.

Chroniques Cambodge 1981. Chroniques royales du Cambodge (de 1594 à 1677), trans. Mak Phoeun. Paris, EFEO.

———— 1988. *Chroniques royales du Cambodge (de 1417 à 1595),* trans. Khin Sok. Paris, EFEO.

Clark, Walter 1643. Letter from Aceh to Surat, 17 December 1643, India Office Library E/3/18, f.282.

Clercq, F. S. A. de 1890. *Bijdragen tot de kennis der Residentie Ternate.* Leiden, Brill.

Coen, Jan Pieterszoon 1614. Letter to Heren XVII, 10 November 1614, in Colenbrander 1919: 52–96.

———— 1619. Letter to Heren XVII, 19 January 1619, in Colenbrander 1919: 416–44.

———— 1619A. "Memorie van verscheyden Cleden . . . van de custe van Coromandel geeyscht wort," 16 July 1619, in Colenbrander 1920: 580–83.

———— 1621. Letter to Heren XVII, 8 January 1621, in Colenbrander 1919: 606–22.

———— 1622. Letter to Heren XVII, 21 January 1622, in Colenbrander 1919: 688–700.

———— 1623. Letter to Heren XVII, 20 January 1623, in Colenbrander 1919: 755–806.

Colenbrander, H. T. (ed.) 1919. *Jan Pieterszoon Coen: bescheiden omtrent zijn bedrijf in Indie,* ed. H. T. Colenbrander. Vol. I. The Hague, Nijhoff.

———— 1920. *Jan Pieterszoon Coen: bescheiden omtrent zijn bedrijf in Indië,* Vol. II. The Hague, Nijhoff.

———— 1921. *Jan Pieterszoon Coen: bescheiden omtrent zijn bedrijf in Indië,* Vol. III. The Hague, Nijhoff.

———— 1922. *Jan Pieterszoon Coen: bescheiden omtrent zijn bedrijf in Indië,* Vol. IV. The Hague, Nijhoff.

Collis, Maurice 1925. "Arakan's Place in the Civilization of the Bay." *JBRS* 15, i: 41–45.

—— 1943. *The Land of the Great Image.* New York, New Directions.

—— 1949. *The Grand Peregrination, Being the Life and Adventures of Fernão Mendes Pinto.* London, Faber and Faber.

Compostel, Jacob 1636. "Origineel daghregister van de voyagie, handel en resconter met 'tschip d'Revengie naer Atchin," in ARA KA 1031 (voc. 1119), ff. 1198–1229.

Coolhaas, W. Ph. (ed.) 1952. *Jan Pieterszoon Coen: bescheiden omtrent zijn bedrijf in Indie,* Vol. VII. The Hague, Nijhoff.

—— (ed.) 1960. *Generale missiven van Gouverneurs-Generaal en Raden aan Heren XVII der Verenigde Oostindische Compagnie.* Vol. I: *1610–1638.* The Hague, Nijhoff.

—— 1964. *Generale missiven van Gouverneurs-Generaal en Raden aan Heren XVII der Verenigde Oostindische Compagnie.* Vol. II: *1639–1655.* The Hague, Nijhoff.

—— 1968. *Generale missiven van Gouverneurs-Generaal en Raden aan Heren XVII der Verenigde Oostindische Compagnie.* Vol. III: *1656–1674.* The Hague, Nijhoff.

—— 1971. *Generale missiven van Gouverneurs-Generaal en Raden aan Heren XVII der Verenigde Oostindische Compagnie.* Vol. IV: *1675–1685.* The Hague, Nijhoff.

—— 1975. *Generale Missiven van Gouverneurs-Generaal en Raden aan Heren XVII der Verenigde Oostindische Compagnie.* Vol. V: *1686–1697.* The Hague, Nijhoff.

Coomans, Michael 1980. *Evangelisatie en kultuurverandering: onderzoek naar de verhouding tussen de evangelisatie en de socio-kulturele verandering in de adat van de Dajaks van oost-Kalimantan (bisdom Samarinda), Indonesia.* St. Augustin, Steyler Verlag.

Copland, Patrick 1614. "The Narrative of the Rev. Patrick Copland," in Foster 1934: 207–14.

Cortemünde, A. J. P. 1675. *Dagbog fra en Ostindiefart, 1672–75,* ed. H. Henningsen. Kronborg, Handels-og sjøfartsmuseet.

Cortesão, Armando (ed.) 1944. *The Suma Oriental of Tomé Pires.* London, Hakluyt Society.

Costa, H. de la 1965. *Readings in Philippine History.* Manila, Bookmark.

—— 1967. *The Jesuits in the Philippines, 1581–1768.* Cambridge, Harvard University Press.

Coulson and Ivy 1636. Letter from Makassar to East India Company, 20 December 1636, IOL E/3/15, ff. 293–4.

Couto, Diego do 1645. *Da Asia.* Nine Decades. Lisbon, Regia Officina Typografica, 1778–88. Reprinted Lisbon, 1974.

Crawfurd, John 1820. *History of the Indian Archipelago.* 3 vols. Edinburgh, A. Constable.

Creese, Helen 1991. "Balinese *Babad* as Historical Sources: A Reinterpretation of the Fall of Gèlgèl," *BKI* 147: 236–60.

Croft, Ralph 1613. "A Journal Kept on Board the Hosiander, Begun by Ralph Standish and Continued by Ralph Croft, 3 February 1612 to 29 August 1613," in Foster 1934: 93–182.

Crucq, K. C. 1941. " Beschrijving der kanonnen afkomstig uit Atjeh thans in het Koninklijk Militair Invalidenhuis Bronbeek." *TBG* 81: 545–52.

—— 1941A. "De geschiedenis van het heilig Kanon van Makassar." *TBG* 81: 74–95.

Cruz, Gaspar da 1569. "Treatise in Which the Things of China Are Related," trans. C. R. Boxer, in Boxer 1953: 45–239.

Curtis, William, and John Chambers 1656. Letter from Banten 20 July 1656, IOL G/10/1, pp. 127–29.

Dagh-Register. Dagh-Register gehouden in 't Casteel Batavia, 1624–1682. 31 vols. Batavia and The Hague, Bataviaasch Genootschap, 1887–1931.

Dakers, C. H. 1939. "The Malay Coins of Malacca." *JMBRAS* 17, i: 1–12.

Dam, Pieter van 1701. *Beschrijvinge van de Oostindische Compagnie*, ed. F. W. Stapel. The Hague, Nijhoff.

Dampier, William 1697. *A New Voyage Round the World*, ed. Sir Albert Gray. London, Argonaut Press, 1927.

—— 1699. *Voyages and Discoveries*, ed. C. Wilkinson. London, Argonaut Press, 1931.

DasGupta, Arun Kumar 1962. "Acheh in Indonesian Trade and Politics, 1600–1641." Ph.D. diss., Cornell University.

DasGupta, Ashin 1982. "Indian Merchants and the Trade in the Indian Ocean," in Raychaudhuri and Habib 1982: 407–33.

Dasmariñas, Goméz Peréz 1590. "Berunai in the *Boxer Codex*," trans. John Carroll. *JMBRAS* 55, ii (1982): 2–16.

Davis, John 1600. "The Voyage of Captain John Davis to the Easterne India, Pilot in a Dutch Ship; written by himselfe," in *The Voyages and Works of John Davis the Navigator*, ed. A. H. Markham. London, Hakluyt Society, 1880, pp. 129–89.

Day, A. 1983. "Islam and Literature in South-East Asia," in Hooker 1983: 130–59.

Dermigny, Louis 1964. *La Chine et l'Occident: le commerce à Canton au XVIIIe siècle, 1719–1833.* 3 vols. Paris, SEVPEN.

Deyell, John 1983. "The China Connection: Problems of Silver Supply in Medieval Bengal," in Richards 1983: 207–27.

Dias, Balthazar 1556. Letter from Melaka 19 November 1556, in de Sà II: 234–72.

Dias, Henrique 1565. "Voyage and Shipwreck of the Great Ship Sâo Paulo," in Boxer, 1968: 58–107.

Dias, Thomas 1684. Letter from Melaka, 18 November 1684, in F. de Haan, "Naar midden Sumatra in 1684," *TBG* 39 (1897): 336–57.

Diaz, Casimiro 1718. *Conquests of the Filipinas Islands*, trans. in Blair and Robertson 1903–09 XXXXI: 317–24.

Diemen, van, et al. 1639. Letter from Batavia, 12 January 1639 in Coolhaas 1964: 1–6.

Disney, A. R. 1978. *Twilight of the Pepper Empire: Portuguese Trade in Southwest India in the Early Seventeenth Century.* Cambridge, Harvard University Press.

—— 1984. "Portuguese Goa and the Great Indian Famine of 1630–31." Paper presented at the Fifth Biennial Conference of the Asian Studies Association of Australia, Adelaide.

Djajadiningrat, Hoesein 1913. *Critische Beschouwing van de Sadjarah Banten*. Ph.D. diss., Leiden. Haarlem, Joh. Enschede.

Dobbin, Christine 1983. *Islamic Revivalism in a Changing Peasant Economy: Central Sumatra, 1784–1847*. London, Curzon Press.

Douglas, Carstair 1873. *Chinese-English Dictionary of the Vernacular or Spoken Language of Amoy*. London, Trubner.

Drakard, Jane 1990. *A Malay Frontier: Unity and Duality in a Sumatran Kingdom*. Ithaca, Cornell University Southeast Asia Program.

——— 1993. "A Kingdom of Words: Minangkabau Sovereignty in Sumatran History." Ph.D. diss., ANU, Canberra.

Drewes, G. W. J. 1954. *Een javaanse primbon uit de zestiende eeuw*. Leiden, E. J. Brill.

——— 1978. *An Early Javanese Code of Muslim Ethics*. The Hague, Nijhoff for KITLV.

Drewes, G. W. J., and Lode Brakel (eds.) 1986. *The Poems of Hamzah Fansuri*. Dordrecht, Foris for KITLV.

Dulaurier, Edouard 1845. "Institutions maritimes de l'archipel d'Asie," translated into French from Malay and Bugis texts, in *Collection de lois maritimes antérieures au XVIIIe siècle*, ed. J. M. Pardessus. 6 vols. Paris, Benjamin Duprat VI: 361–480.

Eaton, Richard 1978. *Sufis of Bijapur, 1300–1700: Social Roles of Sufis in Medieval India*. Princeton, Princeton University Press.

Edwards, E. D., and C. O. Blagden 1931. "A Chinese Vocabulary of Malacca Malay Words and Phrases Collected between A.D. 1403 and 1511(?)." *Bulletin of the School of Oriental Studies* 6, iii: 715–49.

Elson, Robert 1984. *Javanese Peasants and the Colonial Sugar Industry*. Singapore, OUP.

Empoli, Giovanni da 1514. Letter to Lionardo, his father, in *Lettera de Giovanni da Empoli*, ed. A. Bausani. Rome, Istituto Italiano per il Medio ed Estremo Oriente, 1970, pp. 107–61.

Endicott, K. M. 1970. *An Analysis of Malay Magic*. Oxford, Clarendon.

English Factories in India, 1668–1669, The, ed. William Foster. Oxford, Clarendon, 1927.

English Factories in India, The, n.s., Vol. II: 1670–77, ed. Sir Charles Fawcett. Oxford, Clarendon, 1952.

Eredia, Manoel Godinho de 1613. "Eredia's Description of Malacca, Meridional India, and Cathay," trans. J. V. Mills. *JMBRAS* 8, i (1930): 11–84.

Evans, I. H. N. 1953. *The Religion of the Tempasuk Dusuns of North Borneo*. London, CUP.

Evelyn, John 1955. *The Diary of John Evelyn*, Vol. IV: 1673–1689, ed. E. S. de Beer. Oxford, Clarendon.

Evers, H. D. 1988. "Chettiar Moneylenders in Southeast Asia," in Lombard and Aubin 1988: 199–219.

Fairbank, John K. (ed.) 1968. *The Chinese World Order*. Cambridge, Harvard University Press.

Fairbank, John K., and Ssü-yu Teng 1960. *Ch'ing Administration: Three Studies*. Cambridge, Harvard University Press.

Farrington, Anthony 1992. "English East India Company Documents relating to Hien and Tonking." Paper presented to Symposium on Pho Hien, at Hai Durong, Vietnam.

Fatimi, S. Q. 1963. *Islam Comes to Malaysia.* Singapore, Malaysian Sociological Research Institute.

Fei Hsin 1436. "Hsing ch'a sheng lan," in Rockhill 1915: 246–50.

Fernandez, Bartolome 1579. "Testimony," Manila 19 April 1579, in Blair and Robertson 1903–09 IV: 219–30.

Ferrars, Max and Bertha 1900. *Burma.* London, Sampson, Low, Marston.

Fitch, Ralph 1591. "The Voyage of M. Ralph Fitch marchant of London . . . begunne in the yeere of our Lord 1583, and ended 1591," in Hakluyt 1598–1600 III: 287–321.

Florentine Letter 1513. "Lettera . . . scripta in Lisbona e mandata a fra Zuambatista in Firenze," 31 January 1513, in *Storia dei viaggiatori nelle Indie Orientali.* Livorno, Franc. Vigo, 1875, pp. 364–98.

Floris, Peter 1615. *Peter Floris, His Voyage to the East Indies in the "Globe," 1611–1615,* ed. W. H. Moreland. London, Hakluyt Society, 1934.

Forbes, A. D. W. 1988. "The Role of Hui Muslims in the Traditional Caravan Trade between Yunnan and Thailand," in Lombard and Aubin 1988: 289–94.

Forrest, Thomas 1779. *A Voyage to New Guinea and the Moluccas from Balambangan.* 2nd ed. London. Reprinted Kuala Lumpur, OUP, 1969.

——— 1792. *A Voyage from Calcutta to the Mergui Archipelago Lying on the East Side of the Bay of Bengal.* London, J. Robson.

Forth, G. L. 1981. *Rindi: An Ethnographic Study of a Traditional Domain in Eastern Sumba.* The Hague, Nijhoff for KITLV.

Foster, William 1926. *John Company.* London, Bodley Head.

——— (ed.) 1934. *The Voyage of Thomas Best to the East Indies, 1612–14.* London, Hakluyt Society.

Fox, J. J. 1987. "Southeast Asian Religions," in *The Encyclopedia of Religion,* Vol. 13. New York, MacMillan.

Fraassen, Ch. F. van 1987. "Ternate, de Molukken en de Indonesische Archipel. Van Soa-organisatie en vierdeling: een studie van traditionele samenleving en cultuur in Indonesie." 2 vols. Ph.D. diss., Leiden University.

Fransisco 1642. "Declaratie vande gelegentheijt des Quinamsen rijcx," in Buch 1929: 120–23.

Frederici, Cesare 1581. "The voyage and travell of M. Caesare Fredericke, Marchant of Venice, into the East India, and beyond the Indies," trans. T. Hickocke, in Hakluyt 1598–1600 III: 198–269.

Fryke, Christopher 1692. "A Relation of a Voyage made to the East Indies by Christopher Fryke," in *Voyages to the East Indies,* ed. C. Ernest Fayle. London, Casse, 1929.

Fujiwara Seika. Letter to Nguyen Hoang, lord of Cochin-China, c.1600. Trans. in *Sources of Japanese Tradition,* ed. Ryusaku Tsunoda, W. Th. de Bary, and Donald Keene. New York, Columbia University Press, 1958, pp. 347–48.

Gaastra, F. S. 1982. "Merchants, Middlemen and Money: Aspects of the Trade between the Indonesian Archipelago and Manila in the Seventeenth Century," in *Papers of the Dutch-Indonesian Historical Conference, 1980,* ed. G. Schutte and H. Sutherland, Leiden and Jakarta, pp. 301–14.

Gaelen, Jan Diresz 1636. "Journael ofte voornaemste geschiedenisse in Cambodia," in Muller 1917: 61–124.

Galloway, Patrick 1986. "Long-term fluctuations in Climate and Population in the Preindustrial Era," *Population and Development Review* 12, i: 1–24.

Galvão, Antonio 1544. *A Treatise on the Moluccas (c.1544), Probably the Preliminary Version of Antonio Galvão's lost História das Molucas*, trans. Hubert Jacobs, S.J. Rome, Jesuit Historical Institute, 1971.

Gardenis, Arend 1636. "Cort Verhael," in Knaap 1987: 141–54.

Garner, Richard 1988. "Long-term Silver Mining Trends in Spanish America: A Comparative Analysis of Peru and Mexico," *AHR* 93, 4: 898–935.

Garnier, Francis 1870. *Voyage d'exploration en Indo-Chine*. 2nd ed. Paris, Hachette, 1885.

Geertz, Clifford 1960. *The Religion of Java*. Glencoe, Free Press.

—— 1964. "'Internal Conversion' in Contemporary Bali," in Geertz 1973: 170–89.

—— 1966. "Religion as a Cultural System," in Geertz 1973: 87–125.

—— 1973. *The Interpretation of Cultures: Selected Essays by Clifford Geertz*. New York, Basic Books.

—— 1980. *Negara: The Theatre State in Nineteenth-Century Bali*. Princeton, Princeton University Press.

Gerdin, Ingela 1981. "The Balinese Sidikara: Ancestors, Kinship and Rank," *BKI* 137: 17–34.

Gervaise, Nicolas 1688. *Histoire naturelle et politique du royaume de Siam*. Paris, Claude Barbin.

—— 1701. *An Historical Description of the Kingdom of Macassar in the East Indies*. London, Tho. Leigh. Reprinted Farnborough, 1971.

Gijsels, A. 1621. "Grondigh Verhael van Amboyna," in Knaap 1987: 20–76.

Glamann, Kristof 1958. *Dutch-Asiatic Trade, 1620–1740*. The Hague, Nijhoff, 1981.

Glanius 1682. *A New Voyage to the East Indies*. 2nd ed. London, H. Rodes.

Goens, Rijklof van 1652. "Het vierde gezantschap, 1652," in de Graaf 1956: 98–125.

—— 1656. "De samenvattende geschriften," in de Graaf 1956: 173–269.

Goens, Rijklof, et al. 1679. Letter from Batavia, 13 February 1679, in Coolhaas 1971: 262–308.

Goitein, S. D. 1967. *A Mediterranean Society: The Jewish Communities of the Arab World as Portrayed in the Documents of the Cairo Geniza*, Vol. I. Berkeley, University of California Press.

—— 1973. *Letters of Mediaeval Jewish Traders*. Princeton, Princeton University Press.

Goldstone, Jack 1988. "East and West in the Seventeenth Century: Political Crises in Stuart England, Ottoman Turkey, and Ming China," *CSSH* 30, 1: 103–42.

Gonçalez, Blas Ruiz de Hernan 1595. "Relation des affaires du Campa," trans. Pierre-Yves Manguin, *BEFEO* 70 (1981): 255–59.

Gould, James 1956. "Sumatra—America's Pepperpot, 1784–1873," *Essex Institute Historical Collections* 92: 83–152, 203–51, 295–348.

Goüye, P. 1692. *Observations physiques et mathematiques, pour servir à l'histoire naturelle . . . envoyées des Indes et de la Chine à l'Academie Royale des Sciences à Paris, par les Peres Jesuites.* Paris, Imprimerie Royale.

Graaf, H. J. de 1956. *De vijf gezantschapsreizen van Rijklof van Goens naar het hof van Mataram, 1648–1654.* The Hague, Nijhoff for Linschoten-Vereeniging.

—— 1958. *De Regering van Sultan Agung, Vorst van Mataram, 1613–1645, en die van zijn voorganger Panembahan Séda-ing-Krapjak, 1601–1613.* The Hague, Nijhoff for KITLV.

—— 1961. *De Regering van Sunan Mangku-Rat I Tegal-Wangi, vorst van Mataram, 1646–1677,* Vol. I. The Hague, Nijhoff for KITLV.

Graaf, H. J. de, and Th. G. Th. Pigeaud 1974. *De eerste moslims vorstendommen op Java: studiën over de staatkundige geschiedenis van de 15de en 16de eeuw.* The Hague, Nijhoff for KITLV.

—— 1984. *Chinese Muslims in Java.* Melbourne, Monash Papers on Southeast Asia.

Groslier, Bernard P. 1958. *Angkor et le Cambodge au XVIe siècle d'aprés les sources portugaises et espagnoles.* Paris, Presses Universitaires de France.

Guerreiro, Tavarez de Vellez 1718. "Jornada," trans. Hughes, in *JMBRAS* 13, ii (1935): 111–56.

Guillon, Emmanuel 1989. "Les villes du Pégou aux XIVe et XVe siècles," *Archipel* 37: 107–18.

Guillot, Claude 1989. "Banten en 1678," *Archipel* 37: 119–51.

—— 1992. "Libre entreprise contre économie dirigée: guerres civiles à Banten, 1580–1609," *Archipel* 43: 57–72.

Gullick, J. M. 1958. *Indigenous Political Systems of Western Malaya.* Reprinted London, Athlone Press, 1965.

Haan, E. de 1912. *Priangan: de Preanger-Regentschappen onder het Nederlandsche Bestuur tot 1811.* 4 vols. Batavia, Kolff.

—— 1922. *Oud Batavia.* 3 vols. Batavia, Kolff.

Habib, Irfan 1963. "Usury in Mediaeval India," *CSSH* 6: 393–419.

—— 1982. "Population," in Raychaudhuri and Habib 1982: 163–71.

—— 1982A. "Monetary System and Prices," in Raychaudhuri and Habib 1982: 360–81.

Haen, Dr de 1622. "Journael ende geschiedenissen op de reyse naer den Mataram ofte Pangaran Angalagga," June 1622, in de Jonge 1862–88 IV: 284–321.

—— 1623. "Journael van't gepasseerd op de reyse naer den Mattaram," 26 December 1623, in de Jonge 1862–88 V: 30–39.

Hageman, J. 1859. "Geshied en aardrijkskundig overzigt van Java op het einde der achttiende eeuw," *TBG* 3, 3, afl.1.

Hagen, Steven van der 1607. "Oost-Indische Reyse," in *Begin ende Voortgangh* 1646.

Hakluyt, Richard (ed.) 1598–1600. *The Principal Navigations, Voyages, Traffiques, and Discoveries of the English Nation,* Everyman's ed. 8 vols. London, J. M. Dent, 1907.

Hall, C. J. J. van, and C. van der Koppel (eds.) 1946–50. *De Landbouw in den Indischen archipel.* 3 vols. in 4. The Hague, van Hoeve.

Hall, D. G. E. 1926. "English Relations with Burma, 1587–1686." *JBRS* 17, i.

———— 1928. *Early English Intercourse with Burma, 1587–1743*. 2nd ed. London, Frank Cass, 1968.

———— 1939. "The Daghregister of Batavia and Dutch Trade with Burma in the Seventeenth Century." *JBRS* 29, iii: 139–56.

———— 1955. *A History of South-East Asia*. 3rd ed. London, Macmillan, 1968.

Hamilton, Alexander 1727. *A New Account of the East Indies*. Edinburgh, John Mosman, Vol. II. Reprinted London, Argonaut Press, 1930.

Hamonic, Gilbert 1987. *Le langage des dieux: cultes et pouvoirs pré-Islamiques en pays Bugis, Célèbes-sud, Indonésie*. Paris, CNRS.

Hamzah Fansuri. *Asraru'l-Arifin* [The secrets of the Gnostics], in Al-Attas 1970: 233–96 (Malay), 354–415 (English).

———— *Al-Muntahi* [The adept], in Al-Attas 1970: 329–53 (Malay), 448–72 (English).

———— *Poems*. In Drewes and Brakel 1986: 42–143.

Hanoi 1977. *Hanoi, Vol. I: From the Origins to the Nineteenth Century*. Hanoi: Vietnamese Studies no. 48.

Hayami Akira 1986. "A Great Transformation: Social and Economic Change in Sixteenth- and Seventeenth-Century Japan." *Bonner Zeitschrift für Japanologie* 8: 3–13.

———— 1989. "Preface," in *Economic and Demographic Development in Rice Producing Societies: Some Aspects of East Asian History, 1500–1900*, ed. A. Hayami and Y. Tsubouchi. Tokyo, n.p., pp. 1–5.

Heemskerck, J. van 1600. "Memorie," in de Jonge 1862–88 II: 448–52.

Heers, Jacques 1955. "Il commercio nel Mediterraneo alla fine del sec. XIVe nei primi anni del XV," *Archivio Storico Italiano* 113: 157–209.

Heren XVII 1621. Letter to J. P. Coen, 4 March 1621, in Colenbrander 1922: 481–508.

Hikayat Banjar. In J. J. Ras, *Hikajat Bandjar: A Study in Malay Historiography*. The Hague, Nijhoff for KITLV, 1968, pp. 228–521.

Hikayat Hang Tuah. Ed. Kassim Ahmad. Kuala Lumpur, Dewan Bahasa dan Pustaka, 1966.

Hikayat Patani. In Teeuw and Wyatt 1970 I: 68–145.

Hikayat Pocut Muhamat. *Hikayat Potjut Muhamat: An Acehnese Epic*, trans. G. W. J. Drewes. The Hague, Nijhoff for KITLV.

Hikayat Raja-raja Pasai. Ed. A. H. Hill, in *JMBRAS* 33, ii (1960).

Hikayat Ranto. *Two Acehnese Poems: Hikajat Ranto and Hikajat Teungku de Meuké'*, ed. G. W. J. Drewes. The Hague, Nijhoff for KITLV, 1980, pp. 6–41.

Hillgarth, J. N. (ed.) 1986. *Christianity and Paganism, 350–750: The Conversion of Western Europe*. Philadelphia, University of Pennsylvania Press.

Hirosue Masashi 1988. "Prophets and Followers in Batak Millenarian Responses to the Colonial Order: Parmalim, Na Siak Bagi and Parhudamdam, 1890–1930." Ph.D. diss., ANU, Canberra.

"History of Kings." "Slapat Rajawan Datow Smin Ron: A History of Kings," trans. R. Halliday. *JBRS* 13, i (1923): 1–67.

"History of Syriam." Trans. J. S. Furnivall. *JBRS* 5 (1915): 1–11, 49–57, 129–51.

Hoadley, Mason 1988. "Javanese, Peranakan, and Chinese Elites in Cirebon: Changing Ethnic Boundaries." *JAS* 47, iii: 503–17.

Hobsbawm, E. J. 1954. "The Crisis of the Seventeenth Century," *Past and Present* 5, reprinted in Aston 1965.

Hooker, M. B. (ed.) 1983. *Islam in South-East Asia*. Leiden, Brill.

Horridge, Adrian 1981. *The Prahu: Traditional Sailing Boat of Indonesia*. Kuala Lumpur, OUP.

Horton, Robin 1971. "African Conversion." *Africa* 41: 85–108.

——— 1975. "On the Rationality of Conversion." *Africa* 45: 219–35, 373–99.

Hoskins, Janet 1987. "Spirit Worship and Conversion in West Sumba," in Kipp and Rodgers 1987: 136–80.

Houtman, Frederick de 1603. *Le "Spraeck ende Woord-boek,"* ed. Denys Lombard. Paris, EFEO, 1970.

Hugo, Graeme 1982. "Population Mobility and Development in Asia." Paper presented at the Fourth Biennial Conference of the Asian Studies Association of Australia, Melbourne.

Huntingdon, Richard, and Peter Metcalf 1979. *Celebrations of Death: The Anthropology of Mortuary Ritual*. Cambridge, CUP.

Hutchinson, E. W. 1940. *Adventurers in Siam in the Seventeenth Century*. London, Royal Asiatic Society.

Ibn Majid, Ahmad 1462. "Al-Mal'aqiya," trans. G. R. Tibbetts, in *A Study of the Arabic Texts Containing Material of South-east Asia*. Leiden and London, 1979, pp. 99–206.

Ibrahim, ibn Muhammad 1688. *The Ship of Sulaiman,* trans. from Persian by J. O'Kane. London, Routledge and Kegan Paul, 1972.

Innes, R. L. 1980. "The Door Ajar: Japan's Foreign Trade in the Seventeenth Century." Ph.D. diss., University of Michigan.

Ishii Yoneo 1971. "Seventeenth-Century Japanese Documents about Siam." *JSS* 59, ii: 161–74.

——— 1975. *Sangha, State, and Society: Thai Buddhism in History,* trans. Peter Hawkes. Honolulu, University of Hawaii Press, 1986.

——— 1993. "Religious Patterns and Economic Change in Siam in the Sixteenth and Seventeenth Centuries," in Reid 1993: 180–94.

——— (ed.) forthcoming. "The Junk Trade from Siam, Cambodia and the Peninsula, 1679 to 1723: Translations from the *Kai-Hentai*." Singapore, Institute of Southeast Asian Studies.

Israel, J. I. 1989. *Dutch Primacy in World Trade, 1585–1740*. Oxford, Clarendon.

Ito Takeshi 1978. "Why Did Nuruddin ar-Raniri Leave Aceh in 1054 A.H.?" *BKI* 134: 489–91.

——— 1984. "The World of the Adat Aceh: A Historical Study of the Sultanate of Aceh." Ph.D. diss., ANU, Canberra.

Ito Takeshi and Anthony Reid 1985. "From Harbour Autocracy to 'Feudal' Diffusion in Seventeenth-Century Indonesia: The Case of Aceh," in *Feudalism: Comparative Studies*, ed. Edmund Leach, S. N. Mukherjee, and John Ward. Sydney, Sydney Association for Studies in Society and Culture.

Iwao Seiichi 1976. *Kaigai Koshoshi no Shiten, 2: Kinsei* [Views on overseas contacts, Vol. 2: Modern times]. Tokyo, Nihon Shoseki Kabukishiki Kaisha.

────── 1976A. "Japanese Foreign Trade in the Sixteenth and Seventeenth Centuries." *Acta Asiatica* 30: 1–18.

Jacobs, Hubert (ed.) 1974. *Documenta Malucensia I, 1542–1577*. Rome, Jesuit Historical Institute.

────── (ed.) 1986. *The Jesuit Makasar Documents, 1615–1682*. Rome, Jesuit Historical Institute.

────── 1987. "The Insular Kingdom of Siau under Portuguese and Spanish Impact, Sixteenth and Seventeenth Centuries." Paper presented at European Conference of Indonesian and Malaysian Studies, Passau.

Jansz, Hendrick 1616. Letter from Patani 31 October 1616, in Coolhaas 1952: 208–22.

Jarric, Pierre du 1608–14. *Histoire des choses plus memorable advenues tant ez Indes Orientales, que autres pais de la descouverte des Portugais*. 3 vols. Bordeaux, Millanges.

Javaanse Primbon. Trans. G. W. J. Drewes, in Drewes 1954: 10–95.

"Javanese Code." *An Early Javanese Code of Muslim Ethics*, trans. G. W. J. Drewes. The Hague, Nijhoff for KITLV, 1978, pp. 14–57.

Johns, A. H. 1961. "Sufism in Indonesia." *JSEAH* 2, ii: 10–23.

────── 1965. *The Gift Addressed to the Spirit of the Prophet*. Canberra, ANU Press.

────── 1979. *Cultural Options and the Role of Tradition: A Collection of Essays on Modern Indonesian and Malaysian Literature*. Canberra, ANU Press.

Jones, E. L. 1981. *The European Miracle: Environment, Economies and Geopolitics in the History of Europe and Asia*. Cambridge, CUP.

Jones, Russel 1979. "Ten Conversion Myths from Indonesia," in Levtzion 1979: 129–58.

────── 1982. "The First Indonesian Mission to London." *Indonesia Circle* 28: 9–19.

Jonge, J. K. J. de (ed.) 1862–88. *De opkompst van het Nederlandsch Gezag in Oost-Indië*. 13 vols. The Hague, Nijhoff.

Jourdain, John 1617. *The Journal of John Jourdain, 1608–1617, Describing His Experiences in Arabia, India, and the Malay Archipelago*, ed. W. Foster. Cambridge, Hakluyt Society, 1905.

Juynboll, H. H. 1899. *Catalogus van de Maleische en Sundaneesche handschriften der Leidsche Universiteits-bibliotheek*. Leiden, Brill.

Kaempfer, E. 1727. *The History of Japan, Together with a Description of the Kingdom of Siam*, trans. J. G. Scheuchzer. Vol. I. Glasgow, James Maclehose, 1906.

Kala, U 1711. *Mahayazawingyi* [Great chronicle], ed. Saya U Khin Soe. Vol. III. Rangoon, Hanthawadi Pidakat Ponneik Taik, 1961 [translated for me by Maung Maung Nyo].

Kasetsiri, Charnvit 1976. *The Rise of Ayudhya: A History of Siam in the Fourteenth and Fifteenth Centuries*. Kuala Lumpur, OUP.

Kathirithamby-Wells, J. 1969. "Achehnese Control over West Sumatra Pepper up to the Treaty of Painan of 1663," *JSEAH* 10, iii: 453–79.

────── 1970. "Ahmad Shah Ibn Iskandar and the Late Seventeenth Century 'Holy War' in Indonesia." *JMBRAS* 43, i: 43–63.

———— 1977. *The British West Sumatran Presidency, 1760–85: Problems of Early Colonial Enterprise.* Kuala Lumpur, Penerbit Universiti Malaya.

———— 1990. "Banten: A West Indonesian Port and Polity during the Sixteenth and Seventeenth Centuries," in Kathirithamby-Wells and Villiers 1990: 107–25.

Kathirithamby-Wells, J., and John Villiers 1990. *The Southeast Asian Port and Polity: Rise and Demise.* Singapore, Singapore University Press.

Keeling, William 1612. "A Journal of the Third Voyage to the East India," in Purchas 1905: 502–49.

Kern, R. A. 1939. *Catalogus van de Boegineesche, tot den I La Galigo-cyclus behoorende handschriften der Leidsche Universiteit.* Leiden, Universiteitsbibliotheek.

Keyes, Charles 1974. "A Note on the Ancient Towns and Cities of Northeastern Thailand." *Tonan Ajia Kenkyu* 11, iv: 497–506.

———— 1981. "Southeast Asian Tribal Religions," in *The Perennial Dictionary of World Religions*, ed. Keith Crim. New ed. San Francisco, Harper and Row, 1989, pp. 709–13.

"Kingdom of Pegu" 1605. " 'A Brief Account of the Kingdom of Pegu,' trans. from Portuguese by A. Macgregor, I.C.S. Retd., with a note by D. G. E. Hall." *JBRS* 16, ii: 99–138.

Kipp, Rita, and Susan Rodgers (eds.) 1987. *Indonesian Religions in Transition.* Tucson, University of Arizona Press.

Klein, P. W. 1986. "De Tonkinees-Japanse zijdehandel van de Verenigde Oostindische Compagnie en het inter-Aziatische verkeer in de 17e eeuw," in *Bewogen en bewegen: de historicus in het spanningsveld tussen economie en cultuur*, ed. W. Frijhoff and M. Hiemstra. Tilburg, Gianotten, pp. 152–77.

Knaap, Gerrit 1987. *Kruidnagelen en Christenen: de Verenigde Oost-Indische Compagnie en de bevolking van Ambon, 1656–1696.* Dordrecht, Foris for KITLV.

Knaap, Gerrit (ed.) 1987. *Memories van overgave van gouverneurs van Ambon in de zeventiende en achttiende eeuw.* The Hague, Nijhoff for RGP.

Knaap, Gerrit, and Luc Nagtegaal 1991. "A Forgotten Trade: Salt in Southeast Asia, 1670–1813," in Ptak and Rothermund 1991: 127–58.

Kobata, Atsushi, and Mitsugo Matsuda 1969. *Ryukyuan Relations with Korea and South Sea Countries.* Kyoto, Atsushi Kobata.

Koenig, William J. 1990. *The Burmese Polity, 1752–1819: Politics, Administration, and Social Organization in the Early Konbaung Period.* Ann Arbor, University of Michigan Center for South and Southeast Asian Studies.

Koentjaraningrat 1985. *Javanese Culture.* Singapore, OUP.

Koubi, Jeannine 1982. *Rambu Solo', "La fumée descend": le culte des morts chez les Toradja du sud.* Paris, CNRS.

Kreemer, J. 1922–3. *Atjèh.* 2 vols. Leiden, Brill.

Kumar, Ann 1980. "Javanese Court Society and Politics in the Late Eighteenth Century: The Record of a Lady Soldier, Part I." *Indonesia* 29: 1–46.

———— 1985. *The Diary of a Javanese Muslim: Religion, Politics and the Pesantren, 1883–1886.* Canberra, ANU Faculty of Asian Studies.

Laarhoven, Ruurdje 1988. "Textile Trade out of Batavia during the VOC Period." Paper presented at the Seventh National Conference of the Asian Studies Association of Australia, Canberra.

—— 1989. *The Magindanao Sultanate in the Seventeenth Century: Triumph of Moro Diplomacy*. Quezon City, New Day.

—— 1990. "Lords of the Great River: The Magindanao Port and Polity during the Seventeenth Century," in Kathirithamby-Wells and Villiers 1990: 161–86.

Laarhoven-Casino, Ruurdje 1985. "From Ship to Shore: Magindanao in the Seventeenth Century (from Dutch Sources)." Ph.D. diss., Ateneo de Manila University.

Lajonquière, Lunet de 1901. "Vieng-Chan." *BEFEO*: 99–118.

La Loubère, Simon de 1691. *A New Historical Relation of the Kingdom of Siam*. London, Tho. Horne, 1693. Reprinted Kuala Lumpur, OUP, 1969.

Lamb, H. H. 1977. *Climate: Present, Past and Future*, Vol. II. London, Methuen.

—— 1982. *Climate, History and the Modern World*. London, Methuen.

Lancaster, James 1603. *The Voyage of Sir James Lancaster to Brazil and the East Indies, 1591–1603*, ed. Sir William Foster. London, Hakluyt Society, 1940.

Lane, Frederick 1933. "Venetian Shipping during the Commercial Revolution." Reprinted in Lane 1966: 3–24.

—— 1940. "The Mediterranean Spice Trade: Its Revival in the Sixteenth Century" (*AHR* 45). Reprinted in Lane 1966: 25–34.

—— 1966. *Venice and History: The Collected Papers of Frederick C. Lane*. Baltimore, Johns Hopkins University Press.

Lapidus, Ira 1967. *Muslim Cities in the Later Middle Ages*. Cambridge, Harvard University Press.

La-uddin 1788. "Memoirs of His Father, Nakhoda Muda," trans. William Marsden, as *Memoirs of a Malayan Family, Written by Themselves*. London, J. Murray, 1830.

Lavezaris, Guido de 1574. "Reply to Fray Rada's Opinion," in Blair and Robertson 1903–09 III: 260–71.

Le Blanc, Marcel 1692. *Histoire de la révolution du roiaume de Siam, arrivée en l'année 1688*. Lyon, Horace Molin.

Legazpi, Miguel López de 1569. "Relation of the Filipinas Islands, and of the Character and Conditions of Their Inhabitants," July 1569, in Blair and Robertson 1903–09 III: 54–61.

Le May, Reginald 1932. *The Coinage of Siam*. Bangkok, Siam Society.

Le Quy Don 1776. *Phu Bien Tap Luc*, extracts translated by Li Tana in Li Tana and Anthony Reid (eds.), *Southern Vietnam under the Nguyen: Documents on the Economic History of Cochinchina (Dang Trong), 1602–1777*. Singapore, ISEAS, 1993, pp. 98–126.

Le Roux, C. C. F. M. 1935. "Boegineesche zeekaarten van der Indische Archipel," *T. Aard. G.*: 687–714.

Le Thanh Koi 1971. *Histoire du Vietnam, des origines à 1858*. 2nd ed. Paris, Sudestasie, 1987.

Leur, J. C. van 1934. "On Early Asian Trade," trans. J. S. Homes and A. van Marle, in van Leur, *Indonesian Trade and Society*. The Hague, Nijhoff, 1955, pp. 1–144.

——— 1940. "The World of Southeast Asia," in ibid.: 157–245.

Levtzion, Nehemia (ed.) 1979. *Conversion to Islam*. New York, Holmes and Meier.

Lieberman, Victor 1980. "Europeans, Trade, and the Unification of Burma, c. 1540–1620." *Oriens Extremus* 27, ii: 203–26.

——— 1980A. "Provincial Reforms in Taung-ngu Burma." *BSOAS* 43: 548–69.

——— 1984. *Burmese Administrative Cycles: Anarchy and Conquest, c. 1580–1760*. Princeton, Princeton University Press.

——— 1991. "Secular Trends in Burmese Economic History, c. 1350–1830, and Their Implications for State Formation." *MAS* 25, i: 1–31.

——— 1993. "Was the Seventeenth Century a Watershed in Burmese History?" in Reid 1993: 214–49.

Ligtvoet, A. 1880. "Transcriptie van het dagboek der vorsten van Gowa en Tello, met vertaling en aanteekeningen." *BKI* 4: 1–259.

Linschoten, J. H. van 1598. *The Voyage of Jan Huyghen van Linschoten to the East Indies*, ed. A. C. Burnell and P. A. Tiele. Vol. I. London, Hakluyt Society, 1885.

Lintgens, Aernoudt 1597. "Verhael vant tgheene mij opt eijllandt van Baelle medevaeren is," in *De eerste schipvaart der Nederlanders naar Oost-Indië onder Cornelis de Houtman, 1595–1597*, ed. G. P. Rouffaer and J. W. Ijzerman, Vol. III. The Hague, Linschoten-Vereeniging, 1929, pp. 73–103.

Li Tana 1992. "The Inner Region: A Social and Economic History of Nguyen Vietnam in the Seventeenth and Eighteenth Centuries." Ph.D. diss., ANU.

Loarca, Miguel de 1582. "Relation of the Filipinas Islands," in Blair and Robertson 1903–09 V: 34–187.

Lodewycksz, Willem 1598. "D'eerste Boeck: historie van Indien vaer inne verhaelt is de avontueren die de Hollandtsche schepen bejeghent zijn," in *De eerste schipvaart der Nederlanders naar Oost-Indië onder Cornelis de Houtman, 1595–1597*, ed. G. P. Rouffaer and J. W. Ijzerman, Vol. I. The Hague, Nijhoff for Linschoten-Vereeniging, 1915, pp. 139–56.

Lombard, Denys 1967. *Le Sultanat d'Atjéh au temps d'Iskandar Muda, 1607–1636*. Paris, EFEO.

——— 1990. *Le carrefour javanais: essai d'histoire globale*. 3 vols. Paris, Editions de l'Ecole des Hautes Etudes en Sciences Sociales.

Lombard, Denys, and Jean Aubin (eds.) 1988. *Marchands et hommes d'affaires asiatiques dans l'Océan Indien et la Mer de Chine 13e–20e siècles*. Paris, EHESS.

Lontara'-bilang Gowa. Trans. in Ligtvoet 1880: 1–259.

Luang Prasoet chronicle. "Events in Ayudha from Chulasakaraj, 686–966," trans. O. Frankfurter. *JSS* 6, iii (1909): 3–19.

Macassar Factory 1658. Letter to Banten, 23 July 1658, IOL, G/10/1, p. 149.

Macassar General 1665. Letter to Banten, 31 May 1665, IOL G/10/1, pp. 260–65.

Maetsuyker et al. 1659. Letter from Batavia, 16 December 1659, in Coolhaas 1968: 247–91.

———— 1660. Letter from Batavia, 16 January 1660, in Coolhaas 1968: 292–313.

———— 1661. Letter from Batavia, 26 January 1661, in Coolhaas 1968: 354–70.

———— 1662. Letter from Batavia, 26 December 1662, in Coolhaas 1968: 403–51.

———— 1669. Letter from Batavia, 17 November 1669, in Coolhaas 1968: 676–708.

Magalhães-Godinho, Vitorino 1969. *L'économie de l'empire portugais aux XVe et XVIe siècles.* Paris, SEVPEN.

Ma Huan 1433. *Ying-yai Sheng-lan: "The Overall Survey of the Ocean's Shores,"* trans. J. V. G. Mills. Cambridge, Hakluyt Society, 1970.

Mailla, P. de 1717. Letter from Peking, 5 June 1717, in Querbeuf 1781, 19: 5–72.

Majul, Cesar A. 1973. *Muslims in the Philippines.* 2nd ed. Quezon City, University of the Philippines Press.

Manguin, Pierre-Yves 1979. "L'introduction de l'Islam au Campa." *BEFEO* 66: 255–69.

———— 1980. "The Southeast Asian Ship: An Historical Approach." *JSEAS* 11, ii: 266–76.

———— 1984. "Relationship and Cross-Influences between Southeast Asian and Chinese Shipbuilding Traditions." *Final Report, SPAFA Consultative Workshop on Maritime Shipping and Trade Networks in Southeast Asia.* Bangkok, SEAMEO Special Project on Archeology and Fine Art, pp. 197–212.

———— 1985. "Late Mediaeval Asian Shipbuilding in the Indian Ocean: A Reappraisal." *Moyen Orient et Océan Indien* 2, ii: 1–30.

———— 1993. "The Vanishing *Jong:* Insular Southeast Asian Fleets in Trade and War (Fifteenth to Seventeenth Centuries)," in Reid 1993: 197–213.

Mantegazza, G. M. 1784. *La Birmanie.* Rome, Ed. A.S., 1950.

Marini, Gio Filippo de, S.J. 1663. *Delle missioni de padri della Compagnia di Giesu nella Provincia de Giappone, e particolarmente di quella di Tumkino.* Rome, Nicolò Angelo Tinassi.

Marsden, William 1783. *The History of Sumatra,* 3rd rev. ed. London, 1811. Reprinted Kuala Lumpur, OUP, 1966.

Martin, François 1604. *Description du premier voyage faict aux Indes Orientales par les françois en l'an 1603.* Paris, Laurens Sonnius.

Mascarenhas, Pero, S.J. 1570. Letter from Ambon, 15 June 1570, in Jacobs 1974: 595–611.

Masselman, George 1963. *The Cradle of Colonialism.* New Haven, Yale University Press.

Matclief, Cornelis 1608. "Historische verhael vande treffelijcke reyse, gedaen naer de Oost-Indien ende China," in *Begin ende Voortgangh* 1646.

Maximilianus Transylvanus 1522. "De Moluccis Insulis," trans. J. A. Robertson, in Pigafetta, *First Voyage Around the World.* Manila, Filipiniana Book Guild, 1969, pp. 109–30.

Meersman, A. 1967. *The Franciscans in the Indonesian Archipelago, 1300–1775.* Louvain, Nauwelaerts.

Meilink-Roelofsz, M. A. P. 1969. *Asian Trade and European Influence in the Indonesian Archipelago between 1500 and about 1630.* The Hague, Nijhoff.

Mendelson, Michael 1975. *Sangha and State in Burma: A Study of Monastic Sectarianism and Leadership.* Ithaca, Cornell University Press.

Mendoza, Juan Gonzalez de 1586. *Historia . . . de la China,* trans. in Blair and Robertson 1903–09 VI: 134–50.

Metcalf, Peter 1982. *A Borneo Journey into Death: Berawan Eschatology from Its Rituals.* Philadelphia, University of Pennsylvania Press.

Meulen, Jan van der 1639. Letter from Aceh. ARA, KA 1040 (VOC 1131), ff. 1194–1204.

Miche, Monsignor 1852. "Notice of the Religion of the Cambojans." *JIAEA* 6: 605–17.

Milaan, P. W. van 1942. "Beschouwingen over het seventiende eeuwse Mataramse wegennet," *Sociaal Geographische Mededeelingen* 4: 205–39.

Miles, Douglas 1976. *Cutlass and Crescent Moon: A Case Study in Social and Political Change in Outer Indonesia.* Sydney, Sydney University Centre for Asian Studies.

Mills, J. V. 1979. "Chinese Navigators in Insulinde about A.D. 1500." *Archipel* 18: 69–93.

Milner, A. C. 1983. "Islam and the Muslim State," in Hooker 1983: 23–49.

Ming Shi Lu. Ming Shi Lu Chong Zhi Dong Nan Ya Shi [Southeast Asia in Ming dynastic chronicles], ed. Chiu Ling-yeong, Chan Hok-lam, Chan Cheung, and Lo Wen. 2 vols. Hong Kong, Hsuehtsin Press, 1968.

Missions Etrangères 1674. *Relation des missions des evesques françois aux royaumes de Siam, de la Cochinchine, de Camboye, et du Tonkin, &c.* Paris, Pierre le Petit.

———— 1680. *Relation des missions et des voyages des evesques vicaires apostoliques, et de leurs ecclesiastiques, és Annees 1672, 1673, 1674 et 1675.* Paris, Charles Angot.

———— 1680A. *Relation des missions et des voyages des evesques vicaires apostoliques, et de leurs ecclesiastiques, és Annees 1676 et 1677.* Paris, Charles Angot.

Moertono, Soemarsaid 1963. *State and Statecraft in Old Java: A Study of the Later Mataram Period, Sixteenth to Seventeenth Century.* Ithaca, Cornell Modern Indonesia Project.

Moloughney, Brian, and Xia Weizhong 1989. "Silver and the Fall of the Ming: A Reassessment," *Papers in Far Eastern History* 40: 51–78.

Moore, Barrington 1966. *Social origins of Dictatorship and Democracy: Lord and Peasant in the Making of the Modern World.* Harmondsworth, Penguin.

Morga, Antonio de 1609. *Sucesos de las Islas Filipinas,* trans. J. S. Cummins. Cambridge, Hakluyt Society, 1971.

Mouhot, Henri 1864. *Travels in the Central Parts of Indo-China (Siam), Cambodia, and Laos during the Years 1858, 1859, and 1860.* 2 vols. London, John Murray.

Muller, Hendrik 1917. *De Oost-Indische Compagnie in Cambodja en Laos: verzameling van bescheiden van 1636 tot 1670.* The Hague, Nijhoff for Linschoten-Vereeniging.

Mun, Thomas 1621. *A discourse of Trade, from England unto the East-Indies: Answering to diuerse Objections which are usually made against the same.* London. Reprinted in *East Indian Trade: Selected Works, Seventeenth Century.* London, Gregg, 1968

Mundy, Peter 1667. *The Travels of Peter Mundy in Europe and Asia, 1608–1667,* ed. R. C. Temple, Vol. III. London, Hakluyt Society, 1919.

Museum Nasional 1980. *Selected Collection of the National Museum.* Vol. I. Jakarta, Proyek Pembangunan Museum Nasional.

—— 1984–85. *Selected Collection of the National Museum.* Vol. II. Jakarta, Proyek Pembangunan Museum Nasional.

Nagara-kertagama 1365. "The Nagara-kertagama by *Rakawi* Prapanca of Majapahit 1365 A.D.," trans. Theodore G.Th. Pigeaud, in Pigeaud 1960–63, vol. 3.

Nagtegaal, Lucas 1988. "Rijden op een Hollandse Tijger: de noordkust van Java en de V.O.C., 1680–1743." Ph.D. diss., University of Utrecht.

Navarrete, Domingo 1676. *The Travels and Controversies of Friar Domingo Navarrete, 1618–1686,* trans. J. S. Cummins. 2 vols. Cambridge, Hakluyt Society, 1962.

Neck, Jacob van 1599. "Reisverhaal," in *De tweede schipvaart der Nederlanders naar Oost-Indië onder Jacob Cornelisz van Neck en Wijbrant Warwijck, 1598–1600,* ed. J. Keuning. Vol. I. The Hague, Nijhoff for Linschoten-Vereeniging, 1938, pp. 1–111.

—— 1604. "Journal van Jacob van Neck," in *De vierde schipvaart der Nederlanders naar Oost-Indië onder Jacob Wilkens en Jacob van Neck (1599–1604),* ed. H. A. van Foreest and A. de Booy. Vol. I. The Hague, Linschoten-Vereeniging, 1980, pp. 166–233.

Needham, Joseph 1971. *Science and Civilisation in China.* Vol. 4, pt. 3: *Civil Engineering and Nautics.* Cambridge, CUP.

Netscher, E., and J. A. van der Chijs 1864. *De Munten van Nederlansche-Indië.* Batavia, *VBG* 31.

Nguyen Gian Thanh 1508. "Spring in the Royal City." *Hanoi* 1977: 138–40.

Nguyen Khac Vien 1987. *Vietnam: une longue histoire.* Hanoi, Foreign Languages Publishing House.

Nguyen Thanh-Nha 1970. *Tableau économique du Vietnam aux XVIIe et XVIIIe siècles.* Paris, Cujas.

Nieuhoff, Johan 1662. "Voyages and Travels in Brasil and the East-Indies," in *A Collection of Voyages and Travels.* 4 vols. London, Awnshawm and John Churchill, 1704 II: 1–369.

—— 1682. *Voyages and Travels to the East Indies.* Reprinted Singapore, OUP, 1988.

Nieuwenhuijze, C. A. O. van 1945. *Samsu'l-din van Pasai: bijdragen tot de kennis der Sumatraansche Mystiek.* Leiden, Brill.

Noguettes [1685]. *Relation du voyage et des missions du royaume de Siam, és années 1681 et 1683.* Chartres, Estienne Massot, n.d.

Noorduyn, J. 1955. *Een achttiende-eeuwse kroniek van Wadjo': Buginese historiografie.* The Hague, Smits.

—— 1956. "De Islamisering van Makasar." *BKI* 112: 247–66.

———— 1978. "Majapahit in the Fifteenth Century." *BKI* 134: 207–74.

Noort, Olivier van 1601. "Beschrijving vande Voyagie ghedaen door Olivier van Noort," in *De reis om de wereld door Olivier van Noort, 1598–1601*, ed. J. W. Ijzerman. The Hague, Nijhoff for KITLV, 1926, I: 1–157.

Novena, Albert 1982. "Tradition and Catholicism: Prayer and Prayer Groups among the Sikkanese of Flores." Lit.B. thesis, ANU.

Nurhadi and Armeini 1978. *Laporan Survei Kepurbakalan Kerajaan Mataram Islam (Jawa Tengah)*. Jakarta, Pusat Penelitian Purbakala dan Peninggalan Nasional.

O'Connor, Richard 1983. *A Theory of Indigenous Southeast Asian Urbanism*. Singapore, Institute of Southeast Asian Studies.

———— 1985. "Centers and Sanctity, Regions and Religion: Varieties of Thai Buddhism." Paper presented at Conference of the American Anthropological Association, Washington, D.C.

———— 1989 "Sukhothai: Rule, Religion and Elite Rivalry," Paper presented at the Forty-first Annual Conference of the Association for Asian Studies, Washington, D.C.

O'Connor, V. C. Scott 1907. *Mandalay, and Other Cities of the Past in Burma*. London, Hutchison.

Oliver, Juan de 1586. "Explanation of the Commandments of the Law of God," trans. Antonio-Ma. Rosales, in *A Study of a Sixteenth-Century Tagalog Manuscript on the Ten Commandments: Its Significance and Implications*. Quezon City, University of the Philippines Press, 1984, pp. 26–67.

Osòrio, Fernão de 1563. Letter from Ternate, 15 February 1563, in Jacobs 1974: 364–79.

Ouansakul, Panne 1976. "Trade Monopoly in Ayudhya." *Social Science Review* (Bangkok): 1–27.

Outhoorn, van 1693. Letter to Heren XVII, 8 December 1693, in Coolhaas 1975: 605–49.

Paiva, Antonio de 1545. Letter to the bishop of Goa, in Hubert Jacobs, "The First Locally Demonstrable Christianity in Celebes, 1544." *Studia* 17 (1966): 282–302.

Pallu, Francois 1668. *Relation abregée des missions et des voyages des evesques francois, evoyez aux royaumes de la Chine, Cochinchine, Tonquin, et Siam*. Paris, Denys Bechet.

Panikkar, K. M. 1953. *Asia and Western Dominance: A Survey of the Vasco da Gama Epoch of Asian History, 1498–1945*. London, Allen and Unwin, 1974.

Parker, Geoffrey 1988. *The Military Revolution: Military Innovation and the Rise of the West, 1500–1800*. Cambridge, CUP.

Parker, Geoffrey, and Lesley Smith (eds.) 1978. *The General Crisis of the Seventeenth Century*. London, Routledge and Kegan Paul, 1985.

Pelras, Christian 1971. "Hiérarchie et pouvoir traditionnel en pays Wadjo'," *Archipel* 1: 169–91.

Phelan, J. L. 1959. *The Hispanization of the Philippines: Spanish Aims and Filipino Responses, 1565–1700*. Madison, University of Wisconsin Press.

Phoen, Mak, and Po Dharma 1984. "La première intervention militaire vietnamien au Cambodge." *BEFEO* 73: 285–318.

Pigafetta, Antonio 1524. *First Voyage Around the World*, trans. J. A. Robertson. Manila, Filiniana Book Guild, 1969, pp. 1–108.

Pigeaud, Th. G. Th. 1938. *Javaanse volksvertoningen: bijdrage tot de beschrijving van land en volk*. Batavia, Volkslectuur.
—— 1960–63. *Java in the Fourteenth Century: A Study in Cultural History*. 4 vols. The Hague, Nijhoff for KITLV.
—— 1967. *Literature of Java*. Vol. I. The Hague, Nijhoff for KITLV.
—— 1968. *Literature of Java*. Vol. II. The Hague, Nijhoff for KITLV.
Pijper, G. F. 1924. *Het boek der duizend vragen*. Leiden, Brill
Pinith, Saveng 1987. *Contribution à l'histoire du royaume de Luang Prabang*. Paris, EFEO.
Pinto, Fernão Mendez 1578. *Peregrinação*, trans. in Catz 1989.
Pinto, Manoel 1548. Letter from Melaka, 7 December 1548, in J. Wicki (ed.), *Documenta Indica*. Vol. II. Rome, Jesuit Historical Institute, 1950, pp. 419–28.
Pinto da Fonseca, Antonio 1629. Letter from Melaka, 9 June 1629, reproduced in *Kerajaan Aceh dalam Dokumen Sepanyol*, ed. Abue Bakar. Banda Aceh, Pusat Dokumentasi dan Informasi Aceh, 1982.
—— 1630. Letter from Melaka, 19 February 1630, trans. in Boxer 1964: 114–20.
Pires, Tomé 1515. *The Suma Oriental of Tomé Pires*, trans. Armando Cortesão. London, Hakluyt Society, 1944.
Plasencia, Fr. Juan de 1589. "Customs of the Tagalogs," 21 October 1589, in Blair and Robertson 1903 09 VII: 173–85.
Poivre, Pierre, 1750. "Voyage de Pierre Poivre en Cochinchine: description de la Cochinchine, 1749–1750," *Revue de l'Extrême-Orient* 3, i (1885): 81–121.
Polo, Marco 1298. *The Travels of Marco Polo*, trans. Ronald Latham. Harmondsworth, Penguin, 1958.
Pombejra, Dhiravat na 1984. "A Political History of Siam under the Prasatthong Dynasty, 1629–1688." Ph.D. diss., London University.
—— 1990. "Crown Trade and Court Politics in Ayutthaya during the Reign of King Narai, 1656–88," in Kathirithamby-Wells and Villiers 1990: 127–42.
—— 1993. "Ayutthaya at the End of the Seventeenth Century: Was There a Shift to Isolation?" in Reid 1993: 252–72.
Prakash, Om 1979. "Asian Trade and European Impact: A Study of the Trade from Bengal, 1630–1720," in *The Age of Partnership: Europeans in Asia before Dominion*, ed. Blair King and M. N. Pearson. Honolulu, University of Hawaii Press, 1979, pp. 43–70.
Premare, P. de 1699. Letter from Canton, 17 February 1699, in de Querbeuf 1781 XVI: 338–72.
Pring, Martin 1619. Letter from Sunda Straits, 13 March 1619, IOL, E/3/6/, ff. 286 94.
Ptak, Roderich, and Dietmar Rothermund (eds.) 1991. *Emporia, Commodities and Entrepreneurs in Asian Maritime Trade, c. 1400–1750*. Stuttgart: Franz Steiner Verlag.
Purchas, Samuel 1905. *Hakluytus Posthumus, or Purchas His Pilgrimes*. Vol. II. Glasgow, Hakluyt Society.
Pyrard, Francis 1619. *The Voyage of Francis Pyrard of Laval to the East Indies, the Maldives, the Moluccas and Brazil*, trans. A. Gray. 2 vols. London, Hakluyt Society, 1887–89.

Qabus Nama 1082. *A Mirror for Princes: The Qabus Nama by Kai Ka'us ibn Iskandar*, trans. Reuben Levy. London, Cresset, 1951.

Querbeuf, Y. M. H. de (ed.) 1781. *Lettres edifiantes et curieuses, ecrites des missions etrangères (de la Compagnie de Jesus)*. 14 vols. Paris.

Quinn W. H., D. O. Zopkf, K. S. Short, and R. T. W. Kuo Yang 1978. "Historical Trends and Statistics of the Southern Oscillation, El Niño, and Indonesian Droughts." *Fishery Bulletin* 76, iii: 663–78.

Rabibhadana, Akin 1969. *The Organization of Thai Society in the Early Bangkok Period, 1792–1873*. Ithaca, Cornell University Southeast Asia Program.

Rafael, Vicente 1988. *Contracting Colonialism*. Ithaca, Cornell University Press.

Raffles, Thomas Stamford 1817. *The History of Java*. 2 vols. London, John Murray. Reprinted Kuala Lumpur, OUP, 1965, 1978.

Raniri, Nuru'd-din ar- c.1644. *Bustanu's-Salatin, Bab II, Fasal 13*, ed. T. Iskandar. Kuala Lumpur, Dewan Bahasa dan Pustaka, 1966.

Raychaudhuri, Tapan 1962. *Jan Company in Coromandel, 1605–1690: A Study of the Interrelations of European Commerce and Traditional Economies*. The Hague, Nijhoff for KITLV.

Raychaudhuri, Tapan, and Irfan Habib 1982. *The Cambridge Economic History of India*. Vol. I. Cambridge, CUP.

Reael, Laurens 1618. Letter from Makian, 20 August 1618, in Coolhaas 1960: 87–94.

Reid, Anthony 1969. "Sixteenth Century Turkish Influence in Western Indonesia." *JSEAH* 10, iii: 395–414.

———— 1980. "The Structure of Cities in Southeast Asia: Fifteenth to Seventeenth Centuries." *JSEAS* 11, ii: 235–50.

———— 1981. "A Great Seventeenth Century Indonesian Family: Matoaya and Pattingalloang of Makassar." *Masyarakat Indonesia* 8, i: 1–28.

———— (ed.) 1983. *Slavery, Bondage and Dependency in Southeast Asia*. St. Lucia, University of Queensland Press.

———— 1983A. "The Rise of Makassar." *RIMA* 17: 117–60.

———— 1987. "Low Population Growth and Its Causes in Pre-Colonial Southeast Asia," in Owen 1987: 33–47.

———— 1988. *Southeast Asia in the Age of Commerce*, Vol. I: *The Lands below the Winds*. New Haven, Yale University Press.

———— 1989. "Elephants and Water in the Feasting of Seventeenth Century Aceh." *JMBRAS* 62, ii: 25–44.

———— 1990. "An Age of Commerce in Southeast Asian History." *MAS* 24, i: 1–30.

———— 1992. "The Rise and Fall of Sino-Javanese Shipping," *Looking in Odd Mirrors: The Java Sea*, ed. V. J. H. Houben, H. M. J. Maier, and W. van der Molen. Leiden, Vakgroep Talen en Culturen van Zuidoost-Azië en Oceanië, pp. 177–211.

———— (ed.) 1993. *Southeast Asia in the Early Modern Era*. Ithaca, Cornell University Press.

"Relation" 1570. "Relation of the Voyage to Luzon," May 1570, in Blair and Robertson 1903–09 III: 73–104.

"Relation" 1572. "Relation of the Conquest of the Island of Luzon," 20 April 1572, in Blair and Robertson 1903–09 III: 141–72.

Reniers et al. 1651. Letter from Batavia, 19 December 1651, in Coolhaas 1964: 480–554.

Rhodes, Alexandre de 1651. *Histoire du royaume de Tonquin.* Lyons, Devenet.

—— 1653. *Rhodes of Vietnam: The Travels and Missions of Father Alexander de Rhodes in China and Other Kingdoms of the Orient*, trans. S. Hertz. Westminster, Md., Newman Press, 1966.

Richard, Abbé 1778. *Histoire naturelle, civile et politique du Tonquin.* 2 vols. Paris, Moutard.

Richards, John F. (ed.) 1983. *Precious Metals in the Later Mediaeval and Early Modern Worlds.* Durham, N.C., Carolina Academic Press.

Ricklefs, M. C. 1974. *Jogjakarta under Sultan Mangkubumi, 1749–1792: A History of the Division of Java.* London, OUP.

—— 1979. "Six Centuries of Islamization in Java," in Levtzion 1979: 100–28.

—— 1981. *A History of Modern Indonesia, c. 1300 to the Present.* London, Macmillan.

Rijali, 1657. "Hikayat Tanah Hitu," ed. Z. J. Manusama. Ph.D. diss., Leiden University, 1977.

Riquel, Hernando 1573. "News from the Western Islands," 1 July 1573, in Blair and Robertson 1903–09 III: 230–49.

Robinson, M. 1986. *The Lead and Tin Coins of Pegu and Tenasserim.* Sale, M. Robinson.

Robinson, M., and L. A. Shaw 1980. *The Coins and Banknotes of Burma.* Manchester, M. Robinson and L. Shaw.

Rockhill, W. W. 1915. "Notes on the Relations and Trade of China with the Eastern Archipelago and the Coasts of the Indian Ocean during the Fourteenth Century, Part II," *T'oung Pao* 16: 61–159, 236–70, 374–92, 435–67, 604–26.

Rodgers-Siregar, Susan 1981. *Adat, Islam, and Christianity in a Batak Homeland.* Athens, Ohio University Center for International Studies.

Rojas, Pedro de 1586. Letter to Felipe II, 30 June 1586, in Blair and Robertson 1903–09 VI: 265–74.

Romano, Ruggiero 1978. "Between the Sixteenth and Seventeenth Centuries: The Economic Crisis of 1619–22," in Parker and Smith 1978: 165–225.

Ronkel, Ph. S. van 1919. "Een Maleische getuigenis over den weg des Islams in Sumatra." *BKI* 75: 363–78.

Rössler, Martin 1990. "Striving for Modesty: Fundamentals of the Religion and Social Organization of the Makassarese Patuntung." *BKI* 146: 289–324.

Rouffaer, G. P. 1904. *De voornaemste industrieën der inlandsche bevolking van Java en Madura.* The Hague, Nijhoff.

Rovere van Breugel, J. de 1787. "Beschrijving van Bantam en de Lampongs." *BKI* 5 (1858): 309–62.

Sá, Artur Basilio de (ed.) 1954–8. *Documentação para a história das missões do padroado portugues do Oriente: Insulindia.* 5 vols. Lisbon, Agencia Geral do Ultramar.

Saffet Bey 1912. "Bir Osmanli Filosunun Sumatra Seferi." *Tarihi Osmani Encumeni Mecmuasi* 10: 604–14; 11: 678–83.

Sakai, Robert K. 1968. "The Ryukyu (Liu-ch'iu) Islands as a Fief of Satsuma," in Fairbank 1968: 112–34.

Sakamaki, Shunzo 1964. "Ryukyu and Southeast Asia." *JAS* 23, iii: 383–89.

Salazar, Domingo de 1588. "Relation of the Philippine Islands," in Blair and Robertson 1903–09 VII: 29–51.

Salazar's Council 1581. "Bishop Salazar's Council Regarding Slaves," Manila, 16 October 1581, Blair and Robertson 1903–09 XXXIV: 325–31.

San Agustin, Gaspar de 1698. *Conquistas*, trans. in Schumacher 1979: 72–73.

San Antonio, Gabriel Quiroga de 1604. *Breve y verdadera relación de los successos del Reyno de Camboxa*, in A. Cabaton (ed.), *Brève et véridique relation des événements du Cambodge*. Paris, Ernest Leroux, 1914, pp. 1–83 (Spanish), 85–214 (French).

Sancta Maria, Fernandus de 1569. Letter from Goa, 26 December 1569, in *Exemplar Literarum ex Indiis*. Rome, 1571.

Sande, Francisco de 1576. "Relation of the Filipinas Islands," Manila, 7 June 1576, in Blair and Robertson 1903–09 IV: 21–97.

——— 1579. "Letter to Philip II," 29 July 1578, in Blair and Robertson 1903–09 IV: 125–35.

Sangermano, Vincentius 1818. *A Description of the Burmese Empire*, trans. William Tandy. Rome and Rangoon. Reprinted London, Susil Gupta, 1966.

Santo Ignacio, João de 1644. Letter from Macáo, 5 October 1644, in Jacobs 1988: 54–61.

Savary des Bruslons, Jacques 1723. *Dictionnaire universel de commerce*. 2 vols. Paris, Jacques Estienne.

Schärer, H. 1946. *Ngaju Religion: The Conception of God among a South Borneo People*, trans. R. Needham. The Hague, Nijhoff, 1963.

Schöffer, Ivo 1978. "Did Holland's Golden Age Coincide with a Period of Crisis?" in Parker and Smith 1978: 83–109.

Schofield, Roger 1983. "The Impact of Scarcity and Plenty on Population Change in England, 1541–1871." *Journal of Interdisciplinary History* 14, ii: 265–91.

Schouten, Joost 1636. "A Description of the Government, Might, Religion, Customes, Traffick, and Other Remarkable Affairs in the Kingdom of Siam," trans. R. Manley, in *A True Description of the Mighty Kingdoms of Japan and Siam*, by Francis Caron and Joost Schouten. London, Robert Boulter, 1671, pp. 121–52.

Schrieke, B. 1925. "The Shifts in Political and Economic Power in the Indonesian Archipelago in the Sixteenth and Seventeenth Century," in Schrieke 1955–57 I: 1–82.

——— 1942. "Ruler and Realm in Early Java," in *Indonesian Sociological Studies: Selected Writings of B. Schrieke*. 2 vols. The Hague and Bandung, Van Hoeve. Schrieke 1955–57 II: 1–267.

Schumacher, John 1968. "The Depth of Christianization in Early Seventeenth Century Philippines." *Philippine Studies* 16, iii: 535–39.

——— 1979. *Readings in Philippine Church History*. Quezon City, Ateneo de Manila University.

——— 1984. "Syncretism in Philippine Catholicism: Its Historical Causes." *Philippine Studies* 32, iii: 251–72.

Schurhammer, Georg 1963. *Francis Xavier: His Life, His Times*, trans. J. Costelloe. Vol. II. Rome, Jesuit Historical Institute, 1977.

Schurhammer, Georgius, and Iosephus Wicki (eds.) 1944–45. *Epistolae S. Fransisci Xaverii aliaque eius scripta*. 2 vols. Rome, Monumenta Historica Soc. Iesu.

Scott, Edmund 1606. "An exact discourse of the Subtilties, Fashions, Pollicies, Religion, and Ceremonies of the East Indians, as well Chyneses as Javans, there abyding and dweling," in *The Voyage of Henry Middleton to the Moluccas*, ed. Sir William Foster. London, Hakluyt Society, 1943, pp. 81–176.

Scott, William H. 1982. *Cracks in the Parchment Curtain, and Other Essays in Philippine History*. Quezon City, New Day.

——— 1982A. "Sixteenth Century Tagalog Technology from the *Vocabulario de la Lengua Tagalo* of Pedro de San Buenaventura, O.F.M.," in *Gava': Studies in Austronesian Languages and Cultures*, ed. R. Carle et al. Berlin, Dietrich Reimer, pp. 15–33.

——— 1984. *Prehistoric Source Materials for the Study of Philippine History*. Quezon City, New Day.

Sejarah Goa. Ed. G. J. Wolhoff and Abdurrahim. Makassar, Jajasan Kebudayaan Sulawesi Selatan dan Tenggara, n.d.

Sejarah Kerajaan Tallo'. Sejarah Kerajaan Tallo' (Suatu Transkripsi Lontara'), ed. Abd. Rahim and Ridwan Borahima. Ujung Pandang, Lembaga Sejarah dan Anthropologi, 1975.

Sejarah Melayu 1612. Ed. R. O. Winstedt. *JMBRAS* 16, iii (1938): 42–226. [English trans. C. C. Brown in *JMBRAS* 25, ii–iii (1952).]

Shellabear, W. G. 1898. "An Account of Some of the Oldest Malay MSS. Now Extant." *JSBRAS* 31: 107–51.

Shway Yoe [pseud. J. G. Scott] 1882. *The Burman: His Life and Notions* 2nd ed. London, Macmillan, 1896.

Siegel, James 1969. *The Rope of God*. Berkeley, University of California Press.

Silver, Cornelis 1699. "Dagregister in forma van rapport," 2 May–17 December 1699, ARA VOC 1637, ff. 96–126 [kindly made available by Ruurdje Laarhoven].

Skeat, Walter 1900. *Malay Magic: Being an Introduction to the Folklore and Popular Religion of the Malay Peninsula*. London, Macmillan. Reprinted New York, Dover, 1967.

Skinner, C. 1963. *Sja'ir Perang Mengkasar (The Rhymed Chronicle of the Macassar War) by Entji' Amin*. The Hague, Nijhoff for KITLV.

Skinner, G. William 1957. *Chinese Society in Thailand: An Analytical History*. Ithaca, Cornell University Press.

——— (ed.) 1977. *The City in Late Imperial China*. Stanford, Stanford University Press.

Smith, G. 1974. "The Dutch East India Company in the Kingdom of Ayutthaya, 1604–1694." Ph.D. diss., Northern Illinois University.

Smith, Thomas C. 1988. *Native Sources of Japanese Industrialization, 1750–1920*. Berkeley, University of California Press.

Smithies, Michael 1989. "The Travels in France of the Siamese Ambassadors, 1686–7." *JSS* 77, ii: 59–70.

Snouck Hurgronje, C. 1888. "Een Mekkaansch gezantschap naar Atjeh in 1683." *BKI* 37: 545–54.

———— 1893. *The Achehnese*, trans. A. W. S. O'Sullivan. 2 vols. Leiden, Brill, 1906.

Sourij, Pieter 1642. "Daghregister off journael gehouden . . . in legatie aen de Coninginne van Atchin," ARA KA 10516, ff. 551–88.

SP. Calendar of State Papers, Colonial Series, East Indies, China, and Japan, ed. W. N. Sainsbury. 5 vols. London, Longman, 1862–1895.

Speelman, Cornelis 1670. "Notitie dienende voor eenen Korten Tijd en tot nader last van de Hooge Regering op Batavia voor den onderkoopman Jan van Oppijnen." 3 vols. Typescript copy at KITLV, Leiden.

———— 1670A. "De Handelsrelaties van het Makassaarse rijk volgens de Notitie van Cornelis Speelman uit 1670," ed. J. Noorduyn, in *Nederlands Historische Bronnen*. Amsterdam, Verloren, 1983 III: 96–121.

Spiro, Melford E. 1967. *Burmese Supernaturalism*. Expanded ed. Philadelphia, Institute for the Study of Human Issues, 1978.

Stavorinus, J. S. 1798. *Voyage to the East Indies*, trans. S. H. Wilcocke. 3 vols. London. Reprinted London, Dawsons, 1968.

Steensgaard, Niels 1973. *The Asian Trade Revolution of the Seventeenth Century: The East India Companies and the Decline of the Caravan Trade*. Chicago, University of Chicago Press.

Sternstein, Larry 1965. " 'Krung Kao': The Old Capital of Ayutthaya." *JSS* 17, i: 82–121.

Stöhr, W. and P. Zoetmulder 1968. *Les religions d'Indonesie*. Paris, Payot.

Subrahmanyam, Sanjay 1990. *The Political Economy of Commerce: Southern India 1500–1650*. Cambridge, CUP.

Suebsang Promboon 1971. "Sino-Siamese Tributary Relations, 1282–1853." Ph.D. diss., University of Michigan.

Swearer, Donald, and Sommai Premchit 1975. "The Relations between the Religious and Political Orders in Northern Thailand (14th–16th Centuries)," in *Religion and Legitimation of Power in Thailand, Laos, and Burma*, ed. Bardwell Smith. Chambersburg, Pa., Anima, 1975, pp. 20–33.

Sya'ir Bidasari. "The Epic of Bidasari," in *Malayan Literature*, ed. Chauncy Starkweather. London, Colonial, 1901, pp. 3–89 [bound with *Moorish Literature*].

Syamsuddin, Helius 1982. "The Coming of Islam and the Role of the Malays as Middlemen on Bima," in *Papers of the Dutch-Indonesian Historical Conference*, ed. G. J. Schutte and Heather Sutherland, Bureau of Indonesian Studies, pp. 292–300.

Syamsu'l-din as-Samatrani 1601. *Mir'at al-Mu'minin*. Summarized in Nieuwenhuyze 1945: 362–73.

Symes, Michael 1827. *An Account of an Embassy to the Kingdom of Ava in the Year 1795*. 2 vols. Edinburgh, Constable.

Tachard, Guy 1688. *A Relation of the Voyage to Siam, performed by Six Jesuits*. London, A. Churchill. Reprinted Bangkok, n.p., 1981.

Taillandier, P. 1711. Letter of 20 February 1711, in Querbeuf 1781 XI: 363–420.

Tambiah, S. J. 1970. *Buddhism and Spirit Cults in North-East Thailand*. Cambridge, CUP.

———— 1976. *World Conqueror and World Renouncer: A Study of Buddhism and Polity in Thailand against a Historical Background*. Cambridge, CUP.

Tashiro, Kazui 1987. "Exports of Gold and Silver during the Early Tokugawa Era, 1600–1750." Paper presented at Keio University Conference on monetary history.

Tavernier, J. B. 1692. *Les six voyages de Jean Baptiste Tavernier, ecuyer Baron d'Aubonne, en Turquie, en Perse, et aux Indes*. 2 vols. Paris, n.p.

———— 1692A. *Receuil de plusiers relations et traitez singuliers et curieux*. Paris, n.p.

Taylor, Keith 1993. "Nguyen Hoang and the Beginning of Viet Nam's Southward Expansion," in Reid 1993: 42–65.

Tching-mao 1717. Memorial to Emperor, in Mailla 1717: 11–12.

Teeuw, A. and D. K. Wyatt (eds.) 1970. *Hikayat Patani: The Story of Patani*. 2 vols. The Hague, KITLV.

TePaske, John J. 1983. "New World Silver, Castile and the Philippines, 1590–1800," in Richards 1983: 425–45.

Terpstra, H. 1938. *De factorij der Oostindische Compagnie te Patani*. The Hague, Nijhoff for KITLV.

Than Tun (ed.) 1983. *The Royal Orders of Burma, A.D. 1593–1885*. Part I: *A.D. 1598–1648*. Kyoto, Center for Southeast Asian Studies, Kyoto University.

———— 1985. *The Royal Orders of Burma, A.D. 1593–1885*. Part 2: *A.D. 1649–1750*. Kyoto, Kyoto University Center for Southeast Asian Studies.

Thao Boun Souk 1976. *Vientiane: note sur les monuments historiques*. Vientiane, n.p.

Thomaz, Luis Filipe 1966. *De Malaca a Pegu: viagens de um feitor Português, 1512–1515*. Lisboa, Instituto de Alta Cultura.

———— 1979. "Les Portugais dans les mers de l'Archipel au XVIe siècle." *Archipel* 18: 105–25.

———— 1988. "Malaka et ses communautés marchandes au tournant du 16e siècle," in Lombard and Aubin 1988: 31–48.

———— 1993. "The Malay Sultanate of Melaka," in Reid 1993: 69–90.

T'ien Ju-kang 1981. "Chêng Ho's Voyages and the Distribution of Pepper in China." *JRAS* 1981, ii: 186–97.

———— 1982. "Causes of Decline in China's Overseas Trade between the Fifteenth and Eighteenth Centuries." *Papers in Far Eastern History* 25: 31–44.

Tobing, Ph. O. L. 1961. *Hukum Pelajaran dan Perdagangan Amanna Gappa*. Makassar, Jajasan Kebudayaan Sulawesi Selatan dan Tenggara.

Trevor-Roper, H. R. 1959. "The General Crisis of the Seventeenth Century." *Past and Present* 16, reprinted in Aston 1965.

Trimingham, J. S. 1971. *The Sufi Orders in Islam*. Oxford, Clarendon.

True Report 1599. "A True Report of the gainefull, prosperous and speedy voiage to Iava in the East Indies, performed by a fleet of eight ships of Amsterdam." Reprinted in *De tweede schipvaart der Nederlanders naar Oost-Indië onder Jacob Cornelisz van Neck en Wybrant Warwijck, 1598–1600*, ed. J. Keuning. Vol. II. The Hague, Nijhoff for Linschoten-Vereeniging, 1940, pp. 27–41.

Turpin, M. 1771. *History of the Kingdom of Siam*, trans. B. Cartwright. Bangkok, Vajiranana National Library, 1908.

"Tweede Boeck" 1601. "Het Tweede Boeck, Journael oft Dagh-Register," in *De Tweede schipvaart der Nederlanders naar Oost-Indië onder Jacob Cornelisz van Neck en Wybrant Warwijck, 1598–1600*, ed. J. Keuning. Vol. III. The Hague, Nijhoff for Linschoten-Vereeniging, 1942, pp. 1–186.

Uchibori Motomitsu 1978. "The Leaving of This Transient World: A Study in Iban Eschatology and Mortuary Practice." Ph.D. diss., ANU.

Undang-undang Laut. "Undang-undang Laut," ed. Sir Richard Winstedt, pp. 28–50, in "The Maritime Laws of Malacca," *JMBRAS* 29, iii (1956): 22–59.

Undang-undang Melaka. The Laws of Melaka, ed. Liaw Yock Fang. The Hague, Nijhoff for KITLV, 1976.

United Nations Centre for Human Settlements 1987. *Global Report on Human Settlements*. Oxford, OUP.

Valentijn, François 1726. *Oud en Nieuw Oost-Indiën*, ed. S. Keijzer. 2nd ed. 3 vols. The Hague, H. C. Susan, 1858.

Varthema, Ludovico di 1510. *The Travels of Ludovico di Varthema in Egypt, Syria, Arabia Deserta and Arabia Felix, in Persia, Egypt and Ethiopia, A.D. 1503 to 1508*, trans. J. W. Jones. London, Hakluyt Society, 1863.

Velarde, Pedro Murillo 1749. *Historia de Philipinas*, trans. in Blair and Robertson 1903–09 XXXXIV: 27–119.

"Verhaal" 1622. "Verhaal van eenige oorlogen in Indië." *Kroniek van het Historisch Genootschap te Utrecht* 27 (1871): 497–658.

Verhoeff, Pieter 1611. *De Reis van de vloot van Pieter Willemsz Verhoff naar Azië, 1607–1612*, ed. M. E. van Opstall. Vol. I. The Hague, Nijhoff for Linschoten-Vereeniging, 1972.

"Vertoog" 1622. "Vertoog . . . . des Koninkrijk Siam." *Kroniek van het Historisch Genootschap te Utrecht* 27 (1871): 255.

Veth, P. J. 1873. *Atchin en zijne betrekking tot Nederland*. Leiden, G. Kolff.

——— 1877. "Geographische aanteekeningen omtrent de Oostkust van Atjeh." *T. Aard. G.* 2: 233–46.

Vickers, Adrian 1989. *Bali: A Paradise Created*. Ringwood, N.S.W., Penguin Australia.

Vickery, Michael 1991. *The Travels of Mendes Pinto*, book review. *Asian Studies Review* 14, iii: 251–53.

Vieira, Francisco 1558. Letter from Ternate, 13 February 1558, in Jacobs (ed.) 1974: 230–40.

Villiers, John 1981. "Trade and Society in the Banda Islands in the Sixteenth Century," *MAS* 15, iv: 723–50.

Viraphol, Sarasin 1977. *Tribute and Profit: Sino-Siamese Trade, 1652–1853*. Cambridge, Harvard University Press.

Vlamingh van Outshoorn, A. de 1644. "Volcht 't verhaal wegens mijn bevindingh en verrichten in Atchien." ARA KA 1059 bis, ff. 542–52.

Vliet, Jeremias van 1636. "Description of the Kingdom of Siam," trans. L. F. van Ravenswaay. *JSS* 7, i (1910): 1–105.

——— 1640. *The Short History of the Kings of Siam*, trans. Leonard Andaya. Bangkok, Siam Society, 1975.

Volkman, Toby 1985. *Feasts of Honor: Ritual and Change in the Toraja Highlands*. Urbana, University of Illinois Press.

Voorhoeve, P. 1955. *Twee Maleise geschriften van Nuruddin ar-Raniri.* Leiden, Brill.

Wade, Geoffrey 1991. "The Ming Shi-Lu as a Source for Southeast Asian History." Paper presented at the Twelfth Conference of the International Association of Historians of Asia, Hong Kong.

Wake, C. H. H. 1979. "The Changing Pattern of Europe's Pepper and Spice Imports, ca 1400–1700." *JFEH* 8: 361–403.

——— 1986. "The Volume of European Spice Imports at the Beginning and End of the Fifteenth Century." *JEEH* 15: 621–35.

Wakeman, Frederic 1985. *The Great Enterprise: The Manchu Reconstruction of Imperial Order in Seventeenth-Century China.* Berkeley, University of California Press.

Wallerstein, Immanuel 1980. *The Modern World-System.* Vol. II: *Mercantilism and the Consolidation of the European World-Economy.* New York, Academic.

Wang Gungwu 1964. "The Opening of Relations between China and Malacca, 1403–1405," in Wang 1981: 81–96.

——— 1968. "The First Three Rulers of Malacca" [*JMBRAS* 41]. Reprinted in Wang 1981: 97–107.

——— 1970. "China and Southeast Asia, 1402–1424." Reprinted in Wang 1981: 58–96.

——— 1981. *Community and Nation: Essays on Southeast Asia and the Chinese.* Singapore, Heinemann for ASAA.

Wap, Dr. 1862. *Het gezantschap van den Sultan van Achin Ao 1602.* Rotterdam, H. Nijgh.

Warwijck, Wybrandt van 1604. "Historische Verhael vande Reyse gedaen inde Oost-Indien met 15 Schepen voor Reeckeningh vande vereenichde Gheoctroyeerde Oost-Indische Compagnie," in *Begin ende Voortgangh* 1646.

Weber, Max 1951. *The Religion of China: Confucianism and Taoism,* trans. Hans Gerth. Glencoe, Free Press.

Welch, David J., and Judith McNeill 1989. "Archeological Investigations of Patani History." *JSEAS* 20, i: 27–41.

Wenk, Klaus 1965. *Thailandische Miniaturmalereien.* Wiesbaden, Franz Steiner.

Wheatley, Paul 1959. "Geographical Notes on Some Commodities Involved in Sung Maritime Trade." *JMBRAS* 32: ii.

Whitmore, John 1970. "The Development of Le Government in Fifteenth Century Vietnam." Ph.D. diss., Cornell University.

——— 1983. "Vietnam and the Monetary Flow of Eastern Asia, Thirteenth to Eighteenth Centuries," in Richards 1983: 363–93.

——— 1985. *Vietnam, Ho Quy Ly, and the Ming (1371–1421).* New Haven, Yale University Council on Southeast Asia Studies.

Wicks, R. S. 1983. "A Survey of Native Southeast Asian Coinage, circa 450–1850: Documentation and Typology." Ph.D. diss., Cornell University.

Wijeyewardene, G. 1985. "Great City on the River Ping: Some Anthropological and Historical Perspectives on Chiengmai." *Political Science Review* (Chiengmai University) 6: 86–112.

—— (ed.) 1986. *The Laws of King Mangrai (Mangrayathammasart)*. Canberra, ANU Department of Anthropology.

Willemsz, Pieter 1642. "Atchins dachregister," 26 September–27 November 1642, ARA KA 1051 bis [VOC 1143] ff. 499–527.

Willoughby 1636. Letter from Banten to East India Company, 31 January 1636, in IOL E/3/15, f. 153.

Wills, John E. 1974. *Pepper, Guns, and Parleys: The Dutch East India Company and China, 1622–1681*. Cambridge, Harvard University Press.

Winkel 1882. "Les relations de la Hollande avec le Cambodge et la Cochinchine au XVIIe siècle," *Excursions et reconnaissances* 4, xii: 492–574.

Winstedt, R. O. 1961. *A History of Classical Malay Literature*. 2nd ed. Reprinted Kuala Lumpur, OUP, 1969.

Wisseman, Jan 1983. "Raja and Rama: The Classical State in Early Java," in *Centers, Symbols, and Hierarchies: Essays on the Classical States of Southeast Asia*, ed. Lorraine Gesick. New Haven, Yale University Council on Southeast Asian Studies, pp. 9–44.

Wolters, O. W. 1970. *The Fall of Srivijaya in Malay History*. Ithaca, Cornell University Press.

Wood, W. A. R. 1924. *A History of Siam*. London. Reprinted Bangkok, Chalermnit Bookshop, 1959.

Woodard, David 1796. *The Narrative of Captain David Woodard and Four Seamen*. London, J. Johnson, 1805. Reprinted London, Dawsons of Pall Mall, 1969.

Wusthoff, Gerrit 1642. "Journael van de reyse naer der Lauwen-Landt door Gerrit Wuysthoff, 20 Juli 1641 tot 24 October 1642," in Muller 1917: 149–215.

—— 1669. "Vremde geschiedenissen in de Koninckrijcken van Cambodia en Louwen-Lant, in Oost-Indien, zedert den Iare 1635, tot den Iare 1644, aldaer voor-gevallen," in Muller 1917: 1–57.

Wyatt, David K. 1982. *Thailand: A Short History*. New Haven, Yale University Press.

—— 1986. "Family Politics in Seventeenth- and Eighteenth-Century Siam." *Papers from a Conference on Thai Studies in Honor of William J. Gedney*, ed. R. J. Bickner, T. J. Hudak, and P. Peyasantiwong. Ann Arbor, Papers on South and Southeast Asia, pp. 257–65.

Xavier, Francis 1546. "Declaración," composed in Ternate, September 1546, in Schurhammer and Wicki 1944–45 I: 355–67.

—— 1548. Letter to Rome from Cochin, 20 January 1548, in Schurhammer and Wicki 1944–45 I: 375–96.

Yamamura, Kozo, and Tetsuo Kamiki 1983. "Silver Mines and Sung Coins: A Monetary History of Mediaeval and Modern Japan in International Perspective," in Richards 1983: 329–62.

Yule, Henry 1886. *Hobson-Jobson: A Glossary of Colloquial Anglo-Indian Words and Phrases*. New ed. Ed. William Crooke 1903. Reprinted New Delhi, Manoharlal, 1979.

Zhang Xie 1617. *Dong xi yang kau* [A study of the eastern and western oceans]. New ed. Beijing, 1981 [translated for me by Mo Yi Mei].

Zhenshe Shiji Wenu Xuan [Selections on the relics concerning Zheng He] 1985. Beijing.

Zhongyang Qixiang Ju Qixiang Kexue Yanjiu Yuan [Central Metereological Agency, Centre for Research in Metereological Science] 1981. *Zhongguo jin wubai nian hanlao fenbutu ji* [Yearly charts of dryness/wetness in China for the last five-hundred-year period]. Beijing.

Zwier van Haren, Onno 1769. *Agon, Sulthan van Bantam. treurspel in vyf bedryven.* New ed. Ed. G. C. de Waard. Zwolle, Tjeenk Willink, 1968.

Glossary

alun-alun (Javanese)   Public square to north of Javanese palace
amok (Malay)   Frenzied attack
anito (Tagalog)   Spirit
batik (Javanese)   Wax-resist process of cloth dyeing
berhala (Sanskrit/Malay)   Idol
berkat (Arabic/Malay)   Spiritual blessing
carreira da India (Portuguese)   Annual fleet from Goa to Lisbon
cash (Anglo-Indian)   Copper or lead-tin alloy coin of low denomination, especially Chinese; from Portuguese *caixes*, evidently picked up in South India, Sumatra, or Melaka from ultimately Sanskrit root, see *picis*
dalem (Javanese/Malay)   Palace
dar ul-Islam (Arabic)   "Abode of Islam," that part of the world under Muslim sovereignty and law
dirham (Arabic/Aceh)   Small gold coin; see *mas*
dusun (Malay)   Hill-garden, orchard
estado da India (Portuguese)   Portuguese state enterprise in Asia
picis (Javanese/Malay)   Vulgar coin of lead, lead-tin, or copper, with hole in centre to facilitate stringing; see *cash*
imam (Arabic/Malay)   Leader in Islamic prayer
jihad (Arabic)   Holy war
jong (Javanese/Malay)   Junk; large trading vessel
jurubatu (Malay)   Boatswain; in charge of anchor and leadline
kadi (Arabic/Malay)   Judge in Islamic law
kafir (Arabic/Malay)   Infidel; unbeliever
kampung (Malay)   Urban compound
kejawen (Javanese)   Javanese belief and practice

kiwi (Malay)   Travelling merchant

kota (Malay)   Fort; citadel

kris (Malay/Javanese)   Dagger

laung-zat (Burmese)   Irrawaddy river boat

malim (Malay)   Pilot

nakhoda (Malay)   Shipowner or owner's representative on the ship; super-cargo

nakhon (Thai)   City; state

nao (Portuguese)   Large freight-carrying ship

orangkaya (Malay)   Aristocrat, generally with wealth from trade

paseban (Javanese)   Courtyard in front of a palace or in a noble's compound

petak (Malay)   Partition, notably of a ship's hold

prahu (Malay)   Sailing vessel

salat (Arabic)   Islamic prescribed prayer

sangha (pali)   The brotherhood of monks in Hinayana Buddhism

sarung (Malay)   Sarong; wrap-around lower garment

shahada (Arabic)   Islamic confession of faith ("There is no God but God, and Muhammad is his Prophet")

shari'a (Arabic/Malay)   Islamic law code

syahbandar (Malay)   Harbourmaster

tukang (Malay)   Craftsman; or, on a ship, deck officer

ulama (Arabic/Malay)   Islamic scholars (plural in Arabic, but here used also for singular)

undang-undang (Malay)   (Collection of) laws

VOC (Dutch)   Dutch East India Company (Vereenigde Oost-Indische Compagnie)

wali (Arabic)   Representative (of God), saint; especially the "nine wali" to whom the conversion of Java is traditionally attributed

Measures and Coins

In the seventeenth century a number of silver coins, led by the reliable Spanish real, became fixed in their silver content. Before this development there was no such standardization of value. Asian measures were particularly varied between time and place. Although I have attempted for comparative purposes to give measures an approximate equivalent in the metric system or in weight of silver, these should be understood as no more than generalizations covering a great deal of variation on the ground.

bahar (Malay) Measure of weight (3 pikul), varying much from place to place, but here taken as 180 kg for pepper, and 272 kg for cloves

cruzado Portuguese coin taken as equivalent to a Spanish real, i e , 0.0255 kg silver

écu French equivalent of Spanish real

guilder Dutch silver coin; about 0.01 kg silver

kati (Malay) Weight; one hundredth of a pikul; 0.6 kg

kin Japanese weight; 0.567 kg

koyan (Malay) Measure of bulk; 3.5 cubic metres

kyat Burmese silver weight of roughly a tikal; 0.0163 kg silver

mas (Malay) Small gold coin, in Aceh worth a quarter or fifth of a Spanish real; in Makassar worth about four-fifths

pikul (Malay) Weight a man can carry; two sacks; taken as 60 kg for pepper

pond (Dutch) 0.494 kg

pound (English) 0.453 kg

quan Vietnamese weight of silver (Chinese *tsien*)

quintal (Portuguese) 50 kg

real (Spanish) *Peso de ocho* or piece of eight; 0.0255 kg silver *rijksdaalder*   Dutch equivalent of Spanish real; 2.5 guilders

tahil (Javanese-Malay) or *tael*   weight for precious metals, being one six-teenth of a *kati*, and conventionally the weight in silver equivalent to a string of 600 (or 1000) cash. The Indonesian equivalent of Chinese *tsien* and Vietnamese *quan*. About 0.04 kg

tikal (Anglo-Indian)   weight of silver

viss (Burmese)   Burmese weight of 100 kyat, taken as 2.4 kg

Index